A

DEBATE ON SLAVERY:

HELD IN

THE CITY OF CINCINNATI,

ON THE FIRST, SECOND, THIRD, AND SIXTH DAYS

OF OCTOBER, 1845,

UPON THE QUESTION:

IS SLAVE-HOLDING IN ITSELF SINFUL, AND THE RELATION
BETWEEN MASTER AND SLAVE, A SINFUL RELATION?

AFFIRMATIVE: REV. J. BLANCHARD,
Pastor of the Sixth Presbyterian Church, Cincinnati.

NEGATIVE: N. L. RICE, D.D.,
Pastor of the Central Presbyterian Church, Cincinnati.

NEGRO UNIVERSITIES PRESS
NEW YORK

Originally published in 1846
by Wm. H. Moore & Co.

Reprinted 1969 by
Negro Universities Press
A DIVISION OF GREENWOOD PUBLISHING CORP.
NEW YORK

SBN 8371-1178-1

ADVERTISEMENT.

The Publishers commend this work to public attention as a learned, spirited, and thorough discussion of the great moral question—whether the relation of slavery, divested of all circumstances not necessarily connected with it, is sinful. The debate grew out of the proceedings of the last meeting of the (O. S.) General Assembly of the Presbyterian church, in regard to slavery, in which Dr. Rice was a conspicuous actor, and the author of a series of resolutions, touching this subject, which were passed by that body. He was soon after invited to a debate, by some gentlemen of this city, and Mr. Blanchard was chosen as his opponent. Their respective friends regarded these gentlemen as their most able advocates, and each party, confident of success, relied on the skill and logical power hitherto exhibited by them, on similar occasions. The discussion was held in the Tabernacle, the largest room in the city, and was listened to by a crowded audience of great respectability, during the whole of the twenty-four hours it occupied. It was conducted on both sides with constant reference to publication, and everything pertinent to the subject was urged in as concise a manner as the mode of debate would admit. Two reporters of eminence, A. J. Stansberry, Esq., of Washington city, and Edward P. Cranch, Esq., of Cincinnati, were employed. The report was written out by them, revised by the parties, and is here given with a complete index prefixed. In short, nothing that could, in their judgment, increase the value of the book, has been withheld by either authors or publishers.

There is no subject at this moment receiving a greater share of the attention of christendom than this—none certainly involving more important consequences to our civil and ecclesiastical institutions. It employed the energies of the first minds of Great Britain for nearly half a century. We are at length called on as individuals, as States, and as a Nation, to examine the arguments, and to renounce, or defend and ameliorate the system, as we shall or shall not find it consistent with justice and truth. Diversity of opinion concerning it has already divided several of our largest and most influential churches, threatens others, and is influencing in a greater or less degree the political affairs of every State in the Union. Is not then a calm, truth-seeking, exhausting discussion of this question, a thing which should be welcomed by every lover of truth, of the State and the church? Such being the topic and character of the discussion, the publishers, with confidence, anticipate a large sale for this volume.

Cincinnati, Dec., 1845.

INDEX.

~~~~~~

MR. BLANCHARD'S SPEECHES.

PERSONS AND PAPERS QUOTED OR ALLUDED TO BY MR. BLANCHARD.

Aristotle, 21... Apelles, 42... Assembly Gen. of Free Church of Scotland, 224..."American Board," 458...Abbe Greguine, 236... Rev. R. N. Anderson, 164 .... Dr. Bailey, 15...Dr. Bullard, of St. Louis, 167....Dr. Beecher, 274....Robt. J. Breckenridge, 363.... Wm. L. Breckenridge, 115...C. M. Clay, 270, 397...Judge Catron, 54....Judge Crenshaw, 45....Dr. Cunningham, 222, 419...Dr. A. Clarke, 456...Dr. Coke, 390....Clarkson, 275, 297....Dulany, 22, 23....Rev. Jas. Duncan, 42, 203....Dr. Duncomb, 42....Edwards Pres't. Giesler, 231....Gregory the Great, Pope, 231....Heyrick Elizabeth, 238...T. Kellogg, Prest. Knox College, 165...Dr. Junkin, 182, 228...Professor Miller, 364....Maimonides, 412....Montesquieu, 364....Moore Thomas, 49....Charles Hammond, 49.... Charles James Fox, 15....Ignatius, 15, 230....McGuffey, W. H. 182...Rev. S. Steele, 165....Prof. Thornwell, J. H. 181....United Brethren in Christ, 390....United Associate Synod, 223....John

MR. RICE'S SPEECHES.

DEBATE.

Wednesday, 2 o'clock, P. M.

Gentlemen Moderators, Gentlemen and Ladies, Fellow Citizens:

The question which we are to-day met to discuss, to my own mind, borrows a melancholy interest from the slave-coffles which, in increasing numbers, are passing from the upper to the lower slave-country at this time. Three days since, sixty-four men chained together and separated from their wives and daughters, passed by our city on their way to the South.

While we are debating and you are listening, anxious to know the truth on this important practical question, the slave-pens of a sister city, Louisville, are increasing their number and enlarging their dimensions, to receive slaves brought in from the upper country to send to the lower states for sale. This infernal traffic has been stimulated by the late movements in Lexington against the property and person of Cassius M. Clay; and by the kidnapping of white men on the borders of the State of Ohio, and a practical refusal of bail; by which they now lie in prison in a sister State.

That human beings should be now suffering such inhuman usage in our midst, gives, in my mind, a painful interest to this debate; and must, I think, produce a tender and melancholy sentiment in the breast of all who hear it, independent of the points in dispute.

The question, however, must be considered and decided upon general principles, independent of, though it cannot be separated from, contemporaneous events. It ought therefore to be set forth with great distinctness, to enable us to apprehend clearly and fully the bearings of the argument. It is this. "*Is slave-holding in itself sinful, and the relation between master and slave a sinful relation?*"

To explain and set this question distinctly before you, I observe that, so far as I know, all well informed persons, believers in Christianity, hold, that there are two classes of human practices, as it respects church-discipline—one class, right, the other wrong: practices which ought, and practices which ought not to be received by the church into fellowship. We hold communion with persons engaged in the various vocations of life. If a man is a farmer and tills the soil, we commune with him. If he is a blacksmith, we commune with him. If he is engaged in trade, and conducts his business honestly and uprightly, we commune with him—because those vocations are good and right. But there are on the other hand, practices, such as smuggling, swindling, gambling, selling lottery tickets, &c., with which we hold no fellowship, but which ought to be met and questioned at the threshold of the church. Now the naked question before us to-day, and for the three following days, is, to which class of human practices does the holding of human beings as property belong? Ought the church to object to it?—is it wrong, or is it right?

Again, there are two classes of human relations; right relations, and wrong. Marriage, the Eden relation of life, we hold to be a right relation. It is the central source of light and warmth, intelligence and affection, to every branch and department of human affairs. It is a right institution—because it is God-appointed. It is universally recognized as right, and its solemnization every where marked by feasts and rejoicings. Over against this is another relation—the relation of false marriage or concubinage. This is a wrong relation. It is forbidden by scripture, and justifies its condemnation by the common sense of mankind, by the evils which it brings in its train. So there are right and wrong business relations. The relation of partners in a legitimate trade is a just and useful relation—founded on a right principle, that of the mutual dependence of men.

> " God builds on wants and on defects of mind,
> The glory, peace and virtue of mankind."

But there is also a false relation in business—such as that between smugglers, or that of the anti-social conspiracy, formed by men who are banded together to burn our cities, and, by general disorganization, to bring down society to their own level.

I will not detain you by speciffying other human relations. The point before us is; Is the relation between the master and his slave, just or unjust? Is it a holy or a sinful relation?

Since this debate was announced, fears have been expresssed by certain public prints that no real issue will be made by the disputants, but that the whole question will be made to turn upon extreme cases:—for there are extreme cases, even in morals. But such fears may safely be dismissed. For by a glance at the printed pamphlet which I hold in my hand, and which has been issued by my respected friend, since this discussion was proposed,—and, being an argument on one side of the question, has thus become a part of the debate,—you will see that the gentleman opposed to me has no disposition to skulk behind extreme cases. He, as Kentuckians are wont to do, will come square up to the point in discussion, whether *slave-holding*—American slave-holding—or slave-holding in every nation, is sinful or not! From the free quotations, which. in this pamphlet, he makes from the actual slave code of the country, you will see that we have not invited you to a feast of moral principles to serve you with the scraps;—to consume your time and our strength, haggling supposed cases of slave-holding; and amusing you with tricks of logic and special pleading—the mere gim-cracks of argument.

The question is whether slave-holding, *as practiced* by Americans, Englishmen, Romans or Greeks;—whether SLAVE-HOLDING! is sinful; and the relation which it creates and which exists between master and slave is a sinful relation?

Gentlemen; every man wishes there may be a pure Christianity. When Ethan Allen's daughter was dying, she asked her father whether she should believe what he had taught her, or believe her mother? Though a skeptic himself, he bade her believe her mother; and whether we are professors of religion or not, we all wish there may be on earth, one holy and unspotted shrine—a pure religion where the heart may worship while the mind approves.

Now, the question is, whether Humanity can look to Christianity and find protection? Whether the oppressed can flee to the sanctuary of the Gospel of Christ and find a refuge there—or whether religion affords no protection to human rights? In other words, whether the religion we profess is a humane or an inhuman religion?

The number of persons now held as slaves under nominally Christian governments is not quite seven millions. This is exclusive of the serfs of Europe who have legal existence and *some* rights. And as long as a human creature has *one* human right legally made secure, he is not, he cannot be, a *slave*. These seven millions of human beings —these slaves, touching whom we are met to hold colloquy, are in the United States and in Texas: the South American States, and in French, Spanish, Danish, Swedish and Dutch colonies of the West Indies.

Our Southern States and the Brazils together, contain 5,000,000, more than five sevenths of all the slaves in Christendom. Now, these seven millions of human beings are citizens of no country. They are neither Americans, French, Danish, Dutch, Spaniards, or Swedes; neither are they found in families. I know that in the skirts of the system, *i. e.* in the slave-raising States, there exists a something *called* families; but in the staple-growing plantations, for the supply of which slave-holding exists; and which are the market to which it tends; they are not in families; but they are illegitimate in their birth and in their death.— Their children are born out of lawful wedlock, and, dying, they can make no wills. Nor can their children receive what is willed to them. It is common for them to have no patronymics, but, like dogs and horses, to be called by single names.

Their condition is legally one and the same, with slight modifications, in all the countries where they are found; and it has remained the same from age to age. It is a condition clearly and well defined. They are held by individuals, as individual property, for individual uses. They are all held by one and the same property tenure, and ruled by the same property power—that is, (and there can be no worse word,) *they are slaves!*

Now, gentlemen, we are met upon the question, whether the holding of men and women, under this relation and in this condition, is a right or a wrong practice; whether the relation subsisting between the owner and the owned is right or wrong.

I propose here to advance certain considerations to show the vast personal interest which every one has in the subject under debate.

In the first place, it concerns seven millions of human creatures, born to all the hopes and fears to which we ourselves are born. It is precisely that class in whom Jesus Christ, the Son of God, did, while on earth, and does now, (for his disposition is unchanged,) take the deepest interest. For surely the lowest and most oppressed conditions of mankind received his most tender regards. For Christians, therefore, no question can be raised more fit to occupy their attention than this. But it equally concerns all others.

Every person, present and absent, has a personal and deep stake in the decision of this question. For all wish a pure Christianity; and all see that when they have convinced the people of the United States that there is no protection in Christianity for human rights, they will have taught them that we have an inhuman religion.

If we have no protection for our rights and liberties in the Gospel of Christ, then we have *no* protection for them except party politics, and all can see, nay, have already seen, what such protection must come to.

In 1776, there was no sentiment so popular, North, South, East, and West, as that "*God hath created all men free and equal.*" This sentiment, at the beginning of our national history, was taken in charge by political parties who vied with each other in its praises. Now, leading statesmen and public prints deny its truth, and ridicule it as a "rhetorical flourish."

The fact is, this fundamental idea of the American Declaration, has been running down for the last fifty years.— The last citadel of human rights is Christianity. If there is no protection, no refuge there, for the principles on which liberty is based, there is none *anywhere.* As a nation, as individuals, we have no protection. But we have all a *pecuniary* interest in this question. It was well remarked by Joshua Leavitt, the able and experienced editor of a weekly and daily paper, that the United States free population sustain the relation of conquered subjects to our 250,000 slave-holders, the same relation that a conquered people do to their conquerers. That, in short, the free States are governed for the benefit of the slave-holders. The truth of this is clearly set forth in a late article of Dr. Bailey's, in the Morning Herald, of this city.

Speaking of the slave-holders' demands, he says:

"We must allow these men a representation for their slaves; we must be called upon to stand guard over their runaway slaves; we are expected to aid them in keeping down their discontented slaves; we must expend forty millions of the Nation's treasure in breaking up a haunt in Florida for fugitive slaves; we must tolerate a monopoly of offices under the General Government by Southern men, because they have slaves ; we must sully the reputation and hazard the peace of the Union, in demands for compensation for shipwrecked slaves ; we must suffer the national legislation to be so shaped as, without any regard to the interests of freemen, to enhance the value of the labor of slaves ; we must violate all the compromises of the Constitution, and hazard the chances of a most wasteful, most disgraceful war with Mexico, for the sake of enlarging the area for slaves :"— and I will venture to add to this delineation ;   We must pay from the nations' revenue hundreds of thousands every year to carry the mail for slave-holders' accommodation.   We must behold the District of Columbia, the seat of our national government, become a national slave-mart—the chief slave-mart of Christendom—and our national jails. made national slave-pens, built and kept up at the national expense —so that every citizen at his anvil or loom—every man that labors in his shop or on the soil, stoops at his toil beneath the double load of personal labor and national disgrace : so that every person who pays a tax, or casts a vote, or serves in the army or navy, or buys a yard of ribbon, or consumes any other dutiable article, or writes or receives a letter ; every one in short who has a body to feed and clothe, or a soul to suffer disgrace ; every American who has either property or character, or the hope of either, is directly and personally concerned with American slavery . for every such person is taxed for its support.

Again.   The rapid increase of the slave population makes the slave question a matter of personal concern to all.

In 1790 there were in the United States 697,697 slaves : at the last census there were 2,483,436.   At the present time the number is above, 3,000,000 ; or one sixth part of the whole population of the United States.   Moreover, while the free population increases 1 per cent., the slave population increases 3 per cent.—the circumstances being equal, and exclusive of emigration.   It is obvious from this fact, that slavery is fast out-growing its bands.   The slaves are the majority in two of the States already.   These facts speak so

eloquently that they need not be enforced by argument. If
you hold your homes dear, you must consider, and ere long
you will consider this question of slavery.

To us who live upon " the land lying between Pennsylvania on the East, Mississippi River on the West, and the
Lakes on the North ; *i. e.* in the territory north west of the Ohio
River," no question can be more interesting than this now
in debate.   By the ordinance of 1787, July 13th, sixth article—" *There shall be neither slavery nor involuntary servitude* in the said territory otherwise than for crimes, where-
of the party shall have been duly convicted."   No soil on
earth was ever so committed and pledged to liberty as this.
In the language of Webster ; this ordinance " lies lower than
the local constitution " itself.   Now the question is, whether
the churches within this territory shall receive into fellowship as not sinful, a practice, which the States themselves
have barred out as a crime ?

If slave-holding be not sinful, then that is no sin in
the church which the State, in self protection, has agreed to
treat as a crime.   Can we debate out from under us the
foundation of our social fabric?   The ordinance of 1787 is
the very root of all the institutions of Ohio, Indiana, and Illinois, from which they derive all their sap and vigor.   To destroy it would be to destroy the titles of the people to their
houses and farms.   They hold their property by force of the
territorial rights acquired under the ordinance of 1787.   And
if my brother succeeds in convincing the people that the car-
dinal principle of that ordinance is an error, he will achieve
a ruin more dreadful than if he should strike out the under-
pinning of our houses and let them tumble to the earth.   It
would be a small evil to throw down our dwellings, compared
to the terrible calamity which must result from destroying
the first principle and vital source of all the laws by which
our houses and our persons are protected.

Fellow citizens, we must bear in mind that we are not
met to discuss the slavery of the negro, but the slavery of
man.   The practical question we have before us is, whether

slave-holding is sinful. Not whether American slave-holding alone is sinful. If we establish the doctrine that it is not sinful to hold *slaves*, then we shall commit no sin, if, at some future period, one portion of us shall drive the daughters of the other portion into the kitchen, and their sons into the field. We are discussing our own right to freedom, and the right of others to enslave us and our posterity. If any one thinks that the question now before us applies only to the African race, let him be reminded that white slaves have been no rarity in the history of mankind. Thousands of our English ancestors have been sold into slavery. Mr. Pitt, quoting Henry's History of Great Britain, has this passage, " Great numbers were exported like cattle, and were to be seen exposed for sale in the Roman market."

Before the Congress of European Sovereigns at Vienna and Aix-la-Chapelle, there were 49,000 white slaves in the Barbary States alone. Moreover, those who prove slavery to be sinless, prove it from the Bible—and the argument, if it proves anything, justifies the slavery of white people as well as black. For the bond-men of the Scriptures, from which they draw their arguments, were colored like their masters. The Bible knows nothing of determining men's rights by the hue of their skin. (A voice.—Good.)

No, Gentlemen : No, fellow citizens ! When he proves from the Bible that slave-holding is not sinful, he has justified the men who, at some future day shall hold my child, and the children of other poor men, in slavery. If any one still supposes that white children cannot be enslaved, let him look at the case of Mary Elmore in Philadelphia, the child of Irish parents, who was taken when eight years old, and sworn to by eight men as the property of the man who seized her, and would have been dragged into hopeless slavery but for the interposition of God in raising up friends who proved her free-born.

Read also the case of Sally Muller, lately freed from slavery in New-Orleans:—a German girl, who was held and treated

as a slave for twenty-five years, and was at last accidentally
discovered by a woman who was an acquaintance of her
parents, and was thus providentially restored to liberty. Many of you knew of the case of a woman upwards of 50 years
of age, who landed in our city several years ago, from the
South, on her way to Frederick County, Maryland, where
she obtained documents under the county seal, proving herself free. She was a white woman. Her father was a
Spaniard and her mother a German. There was no trace
of African blood in her veins—yet she had been held as a
slave in the Southern States for forty years, and all her children were in slavery. And if whites are thus enslaved under laws professing to enslave only the colored race, what
would be done could my brother establish, as sinless, the
slavery of *man* irrespective of color.

As we determine this question, as a nation, so it is the
appointment of God to determine it for us and our children.
As we measure unto others, so will it be meted unto us.

I propose now to consider, somewhat at length, the hinge-
point of this whole discussion, viz :—*slave-holding and the
slavery relation.*

And, Fellow Citizens, if you find the discussion somewhat dry, I must beg you will pardon me in advance: For
there has been so much misapprehension, (I will not say
intentional misrepresentation,) that some pains and patience
are requisite, to strip the subject of false glosses and set the
actual verities, slavery and slave-holding, distinctly before us.

It is not my intention to invent a definition of slavery
from which to reason, but to bring you to the *thing itself,*
the living fact,—the actual reality as it exists. In a late
published discussion of this subject, by two eminent Baptist
ministers, my soul was pained to observe that the whole
truth respecting slavery was compromitted, and the whole
subject itself confused and darkened, by the admission of Dr.
Paley's definition of slavery as the basis of their argument.
No moral philosopher's definition is fit to be used in the

discussion of practical questions, without first ascertaining whether it represents the thing defined—the living fact as it is.

Dr. Paley's definition of slavery—"an obligation to labor for the master without the contract or consent of the slave," is most obviously and fatally erroneous. For, in morals, as in mathematics, "it is essential to a perfect definition that it distinguish the thing defined from every thing else"—which Paley's definition by no means does. It makes slavery, nothing but forced labor, or labor without "contract or consent." Such is the labor required of paupers, of convicts, of the sheriff's posse, of impressed men in national peril, and even of children during minority. These all labor without their "contract or consent." And to give a definition of slavery which includes all these, is scarcely short of absurd. It is certainly erroneous. If slavery is only forced labor, then the paupers who labor in the poor-house are slaves. But the pauper asks for bread, and society asks for a consideration in the shape of labor, which is a just demanb. We set beggars to work, because idleness is a crime. Is that slavery? The person of a pauper is as sacred as yours or mine—and he is no more a slave. The State does not compel him to be a pauper. But if he comes to the community and demands bread, the community has a right to require his labor without his "contract or consent." So in case of the other kinds of labor named above. Neither the sheriff, the press-gang, the prison-warden, nor even the parent, wait for "contract and consent" when they require labor. And as Paley's definition includes all these, it is obviously false. For that which does not distinguish a thing from other different things, is surely no definition of it. No wonder that, with such a definition, Dr. Wayland should concede slave-holding to be not sinful.

But there is a still stronger objection to Paley's definition. It leaves out the whole relation between the owner and his slave, and defines only one of the incidents of slavery, to wit: the compulsory labor of the slave. Slaves are slaves,

work or no work. Mark how the very terms of the definition show its absurdity. He says—"slavery is an obligation
to work for the master without the contract or consent of the
slave." The very terms show that the master is a master,
and the slave a slave, before the "forced labor" begins.
Now that which makes the master a master, and the slave a
slave; THAT is slavery—that is the property-holding power—
the ownership of mankind. He who owns a slave, owns *a
man*. He who sells him, sells *a man*. He sells not only his
flesh and blood, but he sells his good qualities. If he has a
good disposition or any good quality or superior talent, the
auctioneer is sure to tell of it while he is under the hammer,
and this enhances the price. Yes, he sells the *soul of the
man*. If a man owns a plough and a horse, these will not
furrow his field. He wants an intellect to guide the plough
and direct the horse, and for this purpose he buys a slave.
In buying him, he knows that he is buying the soul of the
man. Dr. Paley's definition goes no farther than to give
the master a right to the services of the slave. It puts one
incident of slavery for slavery *itself*, and makes one right
of the owner to be the whole of ownership—one spoke in
this wheel of torture, the whole infernal machine.

To illustrate the absurdity of this definition, suppose a
slaveholder, robber, and murderer, on trial, and Dr. Wayland employed in their defence. He stands up to address
the Court; solemnly adjusts his wig and gown, takes a
volume of Paley, or some other learned doctor, from beneath his arm, and reads the following definitions: "I define slavery to be an obligation to labor for the benefit of the
master without the contract or consent of the servant."—
(Paley, B. 3. C. 2.) "Robbery, I define to be an obligation
to relinquish property to the plunderer without the contract
or consent of the plundered;" "and I define murder to be an
obligation to yield up life to the murderer, without the contract or consent of the victim." Where, I ask, is the difference
in the merit of these three definitions? and what but a smile
of compassionate contempt would such definitions excite, in

any court of justice where grave practical questions, like the one we are now discussing, were being tried?

Let us turn now from these pigeon-hole definitions, to those who have described slavery as a simple reality—a living fact. In introducing the following quotations, I have two objects in view: 1. to show that slavery and slave-holding are the same all the world over; and 2. to show what slavery is—to show that those who speak of different kinds of slavery—who suppose that one kind of slavery existed in the times of Moses, and another in our own times, are in error; I wish to show that there is but one kind of slavery—the property holding of men. My brother will tell you that, in Roman slavery, the master had the life of the slave in his power. This is a small item in the condition of a *slave*, and it was rather a custom than a law. It did not exist after the time of Antoninus Pius, in the second century. It was abolished by the Cornelian law; and was no part of the civil law of which Justinian was the founder and father, and which is never spoken of in the courts as dating back of the code of Justinian, A. D. 527. The Roman civil law first hardened slavery into a regular slave code, and the point I make, is, that nowhere on earth, has legal slavery been any thing else but what it is to-day among us. It may differ slightly in its incidents, in different ages; but it is by no means certain that Roman masters were worse than American. Corrupt Christians are not necessarily merciful men. But however kind or Christian the master, the slave is property, and follows the laws of property. This condition is a legal identity the world over, and the tie which binds him to it the same.

So was it among the ancient Greeks. Aristotle says, "with Barbarians the family consists of male and female slaves, but to the Greeks belongs dominion over the Barbarians, because the former have the understanding requisite to rule: the latter, the body only to obey." He calls the slave a "living instrument in the hands of the master: as the instrument is an inanimate slave." That is *slavery!* I trust we shall become familiar with this ground idea. For in defining a slave of his own days, Aristotle has exactly depicted the slavery of the present. The "Barbarians," thus declared by this leading and most influential mind of antiquity to be slaves by nature, included all the ancestors of the present American people, viz : the ancient Germans, Danes, Anglo-Saxons, Britons, Picts and Scots. And the *principle* of the Greek slave code was precisely the same with that of American slavery, viz: *the property-holding of men.* The slaves were "living instruments" in the hands of their masters.

These "Barbarians" however, in spite of the opinion of Aristotle, show themselves as capable as Greeks of holding slaves. I quote from Gibbon. "The Goth, the Burgundian, or the Frank who returned from a successful expedition, dragged after him a long train of sheep, oxen, and human captives. The youths of an elegant form were set apart for domestic service. The useful mechanics and servants employed their skill for the use or profit of their masters." That is, *they were property,* subject to the incidents of property.

Perhaps the Romans were the first who rigidly legalized and defined slavery. And as the Apostles planted churches under Roman law, and as American slavery, after European, has taken its ground idea and leading feature from the Roman civil code, it is necessary to enlarge a little upon Roman slavery.

"From the time of Augustus to Justinian," says a careful modern writer (Prof. Edwards), "we may allow three slaves to one freeman: we shall thus have a free population in Italy of 6,944,000 : and of slaves 20,832,000. Total, 27,-766,000."

The state and condition of these slaves is thus laid down by Dulany, a legal authority of Maryland :—

"By the (Roman) civil law, slaves were esteemed merely as the chattels of their masters : they had no name but what the master was pleased to give them for convenience. They were not capable of personal injuries cognizable by the law.

They could take neither by purchase nor descent, could have no heirs, could make no will. The fruits of their labor and industry belonged to their masters. They could not plead nor be impleaded, and were utterly excluded from all civil concerns. They were incapable of marriage, not being entitled to the considerations thereof. The laws of adultery did not (among themselves) affect them. They might be sold, transferred, mortgaged, pawned. *Partus sequitur ventrem*, was the rule indiscriminately applied to slaves and cattle. And this too, was not only the civil law, but the law of nations. *Nostri servi sunt qui ex nostris ancillis nascuntur;* and so was their incapacity of marriage on the principle above explained."—1. *Harris and McHenry,* 561.

This statement, easily verified by reference to the Roman code itself, shows clearly the following facts :—

That Roman slavery was a practical and deliberate placing of human beings in the legal and social condition of the brute creation. Nothing can be added to the provisions of this code to herd human beings with brutes. It is not possible to *make* them brutes, because they are men—but what human skill, armed with power, can do, is here done to dishumanize and imbrute human beings.

The Roman slave code, as you all see, was a complete repeal of all God's laws regulating human society. In obeying God, it was neccessary to violate the slave-code : and he who obeyed the slave-code trampled upon God's law. Is slave-holding sinful?

See how perfectly the American and Roman slave systems coincide ;—I read from the same authority who is contrasting English villeinage with slavery :—

"Villeins were capable of marriage because capable of the civil rights annexed to it by the laws of England, and the invariable principle of these laws being, that the issue should follow the state and condition of the father. If a villein took a free woman to wife, their issue were villeins. If a free man took a neif to wife, their issue were free. *Slaves* were incapable of marriage by the civil law, because incapable of the civil rights annexed to it. And the rule of that law was that the issue a female slave, should follow the state and condition of the mother."—1. *Harris and McHenry*, p. 560.

The serfdom, of Europe, was the lowest condition of human beings in civil society. Yet how infinitely below the serf of Europe is the slave! Yet this is Roman, English and American law. There is a case reported in Maryland, (Harris and McHenry,) where a testator died, and, by his will, freed his slaves and bequeathed them property. The question in court was, as they were slaves at the time of his death, could they take under the will? It was decided they could not, and the property bequeathed to them escheated to the State. This establishes the point that the Roman code and the American code are identical and the slave-condition the same.

I request you to bear in mind just where this discussion pauses. I will continue from this point.   [*Time expired.*

————

[MR. RICE'S FIRST SPEECH.]

By the correspondence which has been read in your hearing, you have learned the origin of this debate. It did not originate with me. I had no desire whatever to engage in a public discussion of the claims of abolitionism; yet should the discussion of this agitating question be properly conducted, much good, I doubt not, will result. Multitudes of well meaning and intelligent persons who as yet have formed no definite opinion, need and desire information on the subject; and surely it is not the true interest of any to believe that which is false, especially on a subject of so much practical importance. True, we are often told, especially by political editors, that public discussions of moral and religious subjects, convince no one; and yet none are more clamorous than they in favor of political discussions. By what process of reasoning they reach the conclusion that the truth is gainer by the discussion of political questions, but not of those of a moral and religious character, I leave them to determine.

I am happy to meet Mr. Blanchard on the present occasion, not as an *individual*, but as the chosen *representative* of the abolitionists of this city, selected by *ten* of their most respectable men. We have the right to conclude, that now full justice will be done to their cause; that if the claims of abolitionism can be sustained, it will now be done. I rejoice that the debate, as published, will be circulated both in the slave-holding and in the free States—that now at length the abolitionists will have the opportunity of spreading their strongest arguments before the slave-holders, as well as before the public generally.

It is important that the audience keep distinctly before their minds the question we have met to discuss, to wit: Is slave-holding in itself sinful, and the relation between master and slave a sinful relation? I was truly surprised to hear the gentleman speak *forty minutes* without reaching the question, and *twenty* more without defining what he means by *slave-holding!* I had expected to hear from a gentleman so long accustomed to discuss this subject, at least something in the way of argument, during the first hour, but it is passed, and the definition is not completed!

I am perfectly aware of the prejudices I must encounter in the minds of some of the audience, from the fact that I stand opposed, in this discussion, to those who claim to be *par excellence* the friends of liberty, and particularly of the slave. To remove such prejudices from the minds of the candid, I will state precisely the ground I intend to occupy; and, if I mistake not, before this debate shall close, it will be considered at least a debateable question, whether the abolitionists are entitled to be considered the best friends of the slave.

1. The question between us and the abolitionists, is not *whether it is right to force a free man, charged with no crime, into slavery.* The gentleman has indeed presented the subject in this light. He has told you, that I am about

to justify those who, at a future day, may enslave our children. Such, however, I need scarcely say, is not the fact. In the slave-holding, as well as in the free States, it is admitted and maintained, that to reduce a free man into a state of slavery, is a crime of the first magnitude. Far from defending the African slave trade, we abhor and denounce it as piracy. We, therefore, maintain, that American slavery ought never to have existed. But the slave-holding States have *inherited* this evil; and the important and difficult question now arises—*how shall the evil be removed?* The present owners of slaves did not reduce them to their present condition. They found them in a state of slavery; and the question to be solved is—how far are individuals bound, under existing circumstances, to restore them to freedom? For example, it would be very wicked in me, whether by force or fraud, to reduce a rich man to poverty, but how far I am bound to enrich a man reduced to poverty by others, is a very different question.

2. The question before us is not whether the particular laws by which slavery has been regulated in the countries where it has existed, are just and righteous. What has the present discussion to do with Aristotle's description of slavery, which the gentleman has given us? Or what has it to do with the laws by which in the Roman empire slavery was regulated? Does the gentleman really expect me, in proving that slave-holding is not in itself sinful, to defend the slave laws of Rome? It is impossible not to see, that those laws have nothing to do with the question he stands pledged to discuss. Still he entertains us with Aristotle's definition of slavery, and with Gibbon's account of slavery in the Roman empire. Many of those laws, it is readily admitted, were unjust and cruel in a high degree. But by the same kind of logic it would be easy to prove, that the *conjugal* and *parental* relations are in themselves sinful. *I do not place the relation of master and slave on an equal footing with those relations; but I do maintain that the gentleman has no right to use an argument against the*

former, that would bear with equal force against the latter.
The Roman laws gave the father power over the life of his
child, and the husband power to degrade and tyrannize over
his wife; and the same is true of almost all pagan countries.
But shall we denounce the conjugal and parental relations
as in themselves sinful, because they were regulated by bad
laws? Those relations, we contend, are lawful and right;
but the particular laws by which in many countries they are
regulated, are unjust. So the fact that many of the laws of
Rome concerning slavery were cruel, does not prove, that
the relation is in itself sinful. The gentleman's argument
proves too much, and, therefore, according to an admitted
principle of logic, proves nothing.

Many of the laws by which in our country slavery is regulated are defective, and ought to be amended; or unjust,
and ought to be repealed. But are those laws essential to
the relation between master and slave? They are not; for
different laws have existed in different countries, whilst the
relation itself has remained the same. Moreover, the laws
in the same country or State have been materially different
at different times. In Kentucky, for example, they have
been gradually changed and improved; but the relation between master and slave yet exists. They may be still further modified without affecting it. Indeed it is perfectly
clear to the most superficial thinker, that the relation between master and slave is not identical with the particular
laws regulating it. The laws may be most unjust, and yet
the relation may not be in itself sinful.

3. The question is not whether masters may treat their
servants cruelly, either by failing to give them abundant food
and raiment, by inflicting cruel chastisement, by separating
husbands and wives, parents and children, or by neglecting
to give them religious instructions. A master, a father, or
a husband, may be cruel. There is no relation in human
society, that may not be abused by wicked men. But is the
master *obliged* to treat his slaves cruelly? Must he of
necessity starve them, or abuse them? Is he compelled,

because he is a master, to separate husbands and wives? or to neglect their religious instruction, and leave their minds in pagan darkness? No—he may treat them with all kindness, providing abundant food and raiment; he may sacredly regard the marriage relation amongst them; he may have them carefully instructed in the truths of the glorious gospel; and yet he may sustain to them the relation of *master.*

But the gentleman commenced his speech by telling us what a melancholy interest was thrown around this discussion by the fact, that a slave-gang recently passed near this city. Why not say, a melancholy interest is thrown around the marriage relation, because not a great while ago a man in Cincinnati murdered his wife and three children in a few moments? Were I to employ my time in searching for them, I could furnish thousands of examples of inhuman cruelty in connection with the conjugal and parental relations, in the free States, as well as elsewhere. Will the gentleman denounce these relations because they are abused? because wicked men take advantage of them to tyrannize over the weak? True, cruelty is often found in connection with slavery; but it is equally true that many slave-holders treat their slaves with uniform kindness, as rational, accountable, immortal beings. We are not discussing the question whether cruelty of any kind is right.

4. The question before us is not whether it is sinful to speculate in human beings. The slave-trader is looked upon by decent men in the slave-holding States with disgust. None but a monster could inflict anguish upon unoffending men for the sake of accumulating wealth. But since Mr. B. feels so deeply on account of the multiplication of slave-gangs in Kentucky, it may be well for him to know, that this is one of the sad effects of the doctrine and practice of the abolitionists. They have sought to make the slaves discontented in their condition; they have succeeded in decoying many from their masters, and running them to Canada. Consequently masters, for fear of losing their slaves, sell them to the hard-hearted trader; and they are marched

to the South. Thus they rivet the chains on the poor slave, and aggravate every evil attending his condition. Such is human nature, that men provoked by such a course of conduct as that of the abolitionists, will, in many instances, resort to greater severity; and upon those who thus provoke men, rests in no small degree the responsibility of increasing the sufferings of the slaves.

5. The question before us, is not whether it is right for a man to treat his slaves as mere *chattels personal*, not as sentient beings. The Scriptures condemn cruelty not only toward man, but toward irrational animals. "A righteous man regardeth the life of his beast." A man ought to be excluded from the church, who would treat his horse inhumanly. Even the civil law would punish him for such cruelty. Yet it is not à sin to own a horse.

Christianity prescribes the duties of both masters and servants. The servant is required to render obedience to his master with all fidelity "as unto Christ;" and the master is required to treat his slaves with all kindness, even as rational, accountable, immortal beings. Cruelty toward slaves, therefore, would prove the master destitute of piety, and would be a just ground for his exclusion from the privileges of the church. On this subject the law of the Presbyterian church is clear and explicit. Sessions and Presbyteries were enjoined by the General Assembly of 1818, to prevent all cruelty in the treatment of servants; and to subject those chargeable with it to the discipline of the church. Let the abolitionists prove, that any member of our church has been guilty of cruelty toward his slaves, and I pledge my word, he will be disciplined. Let it be tried, and if it be ascertained, that the Presbyterian church will not exclude men from her pale, who are guilty of such conduct, then I will denounce her.

6. The question is not whether a great amount of sin is in fact committed in connection with slave-holding. This is admitted. Wicked men will act out their wickedness in every relation in life. Wicked husbands in ten thousand instances

treat their wives most cruelly; and ungodly parents inflict great suffering on their children. No wonder, then, that in this relation a great amount of sin is committed. But the question is not how much men can sin in this relation, but whether the relation is in itself sinful, whether a man is to be denounced as a heinous sinner, simply because he is a master. Abolitionists dwell upon, and magnify the sins of men committed in this relation; but the relation may, and in multitudes of instances does exist without the oppression and cruelty of which they speak. Consequently the sin is not in the relation itself.

7. Nor is the question before us, whether slavery is an evil, a very great evil, which should be removed as speedily as it can be done by the operation of correct principles. This I cheerfully admit. But there are many evils and great evils in connection with human society, which cannot be immediately removed. Whilst, therefore, I admit that slavery is an evil, I utterly protest against upturning the very foundation of society in order to abolish it. Shall we do evil that good may come? Nay—shall we in the mad attempt to remove immediately one evil introduce others a hundred-fold greater? The question, I repeat, is not whether slavery is an evil, but whether we are to denounce and excommunicate every individual who is so unfortunate as to be connected with it.

8. The question before us does not relate to the duty or the policy of Kentucky or any other State concerning slavery. There is a broad distinction to be made between the duty of a State as a body politic, and the duty of individuals residing in the State. I might maintain, that it is the duty of the State of Kentucky immediately to adopt a plan of gradual emancipation, and yet contend, with perfect consistency, that so long as slavery is continued by the civil government, individuals may own slaves without sinning. The duty of the State is one thing; the duty of individuals quite another. Moreover, I might maintain what I firmly believe to be true—that slavery is a commercial evil in Kentucky, and

that her true policy would be to rid herself of it as soon as possible—without at all admitting, that every individual who sustains the relation of master, is a heinous sinner.

9. In a word, we are not met to discuss the merits of any *system of slavery,* Roman, Spanish, English, or American. It is common now-a-days to declaim against " the system of American slavery." I confess myself unable to understand precisely what is meant by this phrase. It is not at all clear to my mind, that there is any such thing as a system of American slavery. Slavery exists in several of these United States, regulated by different laws in the several States; but what is meant by the *system,* I do not know. I hope the gentleman, if he is disposed to employ the phrase, will clearly define it. But whatever it may mean, we have nothing whatever to do with it. The question before us relates exclusively to individuals sustaining the relation of masters and slaves.

What, then, have we to do with Mr. Leavit's assertion that the free States have been governed for the benefit of the slave-holding States? Or what concern have we with Dr. Bailey's estimate of the taxes growing out of slavery? If we had undertaken to discuss the political bearings of slavery, these things might have been introduced with propriety; but why have they been lugged into a discussion of the moral and religious character of the relation between master and slave? The question stated by the challengers to this discussion, and the question the gentleman stands pledged to debate, is—whether slave-holding is in itself sinful, and the relation between master and slave a sinful relation. This question and this only will I discuss. It presents fairly the great question at issue between us and the abolitionists. It is stated by Rev. Thomas E. Thomas, a prominent abolitionist, in the following language: " That question, now in process of investigation among the American churches, is this, and no other: Are the professed Christians in our respective connections, who hold their fellow-men as slaves, thereby guilty of a sin which demands the cognizance of the church; and after due admonition, the application of discipline?"—*Review of Junkin, p.* 17.

Such precisely is the question. And here let us inquire, what is meant by slave-holding? The gentleman told us, that in Wayland and Fuller's discussion, the truth was compromised by adopting Paley's definition of slavery, viz: "An obligation on the part of the slave to labor for the master without consent or contract." To this definition Mr. Blanchard objects,—because, as he asserts, it does not distinguish slavery from other things. Paupers, for example, he told us, are obliged to labor; so that according to Paley's definition paupers are slaves. This objection is wholly unfounded. Paupers are not *forced* to apply to the public for assistance. When they voluntarily do so, it is the right of the institution to which they apply, to say on what terms they will grant the aid which is asked. The pauper acts voluntarily in asking aid, and he acts voluntarily in agreeing to comply with the conditions on which it is granted. He is not a slave, according to Paley's definition.

The sheriff's posse, the gentleman told us, must also be slaves according to Paley, because the law compels them to serve at the call of the officer. This objection is no less futile, than the one just noticed. By becoming members of an organized society, each individual agrees to abide by the laws, and to lend his aid to enforce their observance; in consideration of which he enjoys the protection of the laws and the advantages of society.

But the gentleman tells us, that the master owns the *man,* not only the body but the *soul,* and that he sells the soul? What use, let me ask, does the master make, or what use can he make of the slave, but to claim his labor—his services? If there is anything necessarily included in slave-holding, except the claim of one man to the services of another, will Mr. B. please inform us what it is? He has studied this subject for years with intense interest; and therefore he is just the man to tell us what else there is in the relation between master and slave.

By slave-holding, then, I understand the claim of the master to the services of the slave, with the corresponding obligation on the part of the master to treat the slave kindly, and to provide him with abundant food and raiment during life, and with religious instruction. Are there any circumstances which can justify such a claim? Or is the claim in itself sinful, and the relation founded on it a sinful relation? Mr. Blanchard affirms: I deny.

Let it be distinctly understood, that if slaveholding is in itself sinful; it is sinful under all possible circumstances, and must be instantly abandoned without regard to consequences. Blasphemy, for example, is in itself sinful; and therefore it cannot be justified by any possible circumstances. The gentleman informed us, that in two of the southern States the slaves constitute a majority of the population. Now if slaveholding is in itself sinful, and if the doctrine that all men are born free and equal, is to be carried out without regard to circumstances, those States are bound forthwith to liberate all their slaves, and grant them the right to vote and to fill any office within the gift of the people. Then a colored man might be the next governor; and colored men might constitute their Legislature, and set on the bench as judges in their courts. Thus the entire administration of the government in those States would be placed in the hands of degraded men, wholly ignorant of the principles of law and government. Will the gentleman go for this? Would he be willing to place himself under such a government? Will he contend, that those two States are bound immediately to place their slaves on an equality with their masters? He must contend for this, or abandon the principles of abolitionism.

In denying that slave-holding is in itself sinful, I do not defend slavery as an institution that ought to be perpetuated. I am not a pro-slavery man. I am opposed to slavery; I deplore the evils connected with it. Most sincerely do I desire its removal from our land, so soon as it can be effected with safety to the parties involved in it. Most heartily do I desire to see every slave free; not *nominally* free, as are the

colored people of Ohio, but truly free, as are many now in
Liberia, who were once slaves. I go for gradual emancipation, and for colonization; but I will not agree to denounce
and excommunicate every individual, who under existing circumstances, is a slave-holder. I maintain, that circumstances
have existed, and do now exist, which justify the relation for
the time being.

I oppose abolitionism, not because it tends to abolish slavery, and improve the condition of the slave, but because, as
I firmly believe, it tends to perpetuate slavery, and to aggravate all its evils. That such is its tendency, that such have
been its effects, I think I can prove to every unprejudiced
mind.

If the doctrine for which I contend, were held only by
slave-holders, or by men residing in slave-holding communities, I might be led strongly to suspect, that by early prejudices my judgment had been unduly biased; but when I remember, that it has been held, and is now held by the great body
of the wisest and best men; that every commentator, critic
and theologian of any note, however opposed to slavery,
interprets the Scriptures on this subject just as I do; I
cannot hesitate as to whether my views are correct. Sustained by such names, I go forward fearlessly in their defence.

I agree with the gentleman in regarding the subject before us as one of incalculable importance. It is important
to the church of Christ. For if the doctrine of abolitionists is true, we must refuse to hold Christian fellowship with
slave holders. The church in the free States must be separated from the church in the slave-holding States, as the
Jews and Samaritans of old. Already has the work of division commenced. The Methodist and Baptist churches
are divided; and other churches are likely to meet a similar fate. The importance of this subject is greatly enhanc-
ed by its bearings upon our civil Union. Already is it bitterly denounced by leading abolitionists; and if their doctrine prevail, the day is at hand when the northern and
southern States will form two distinct and hostile govern-

ments. Surely, then, the subject demands of every Christian, patriot and philanthropist a candid and careful investigation.

In this discussion I have nothing to prove. Mr. Blanchard has undertaken to prove that slave-holding is in itself sinful. It is my business to meet his arguments, and to show that they do not establish his proposition. Yet I intend, from time to time, to present arguments which, as I think, prove conclusively that the doctrine of abolitionism is untrue.

Having now presented before the audience the question for discussion, divested of the mass of extraneous matter so constantly thrown around it, I proceed to reply to that part of Mr. Blanchard's speech which has not yet been noticed.

He says, truly, that we all desire, or should desire, a *pure Christianity*. But whether abolitionism is pure Christianity, is at least a debateable question. To my mind it is clear that it is not Christianity at all. The question is not, as the gentleman says, whether humanity can appeal to Christianity for protection; whether we have a human or an inhuman religion. If this is the question, why discuss it?— Does it require a public debate to prove to the people of Cincinnati that we have a humane religion? No; the question is not whether the condition of the slaves ought to be improved, but whether the doctrine and the practice of abolitionists tends to improve it.

But the gentleman tells us that the slaves have no families; that their children are born out of wedlock, and are illegitimate, because the civil law does not recognize their marriage. This, however, is not true. The marriage of slaves is as valid in the view of God's law as that of their masters. Marriage is a Bible institution. Will the gentleman point us to the portion of Scripture which makes recognition of marriage by the civil law necessary to its validity? Or will he refer us to the portion of Scripture which prescribes any particular ceremony as essential to its validity?

By way of exciting our sympathies, he told us that the

slaves have no *patronymics*, but, like dogs and horses, are called Sally, and Bill, and Tom, &c.   Will the gentleman inform us what was Abraham's *sirname?*   Or what were the *patronymics* of Isaac and Jacob?   He can find multitudes of slaves named Abraham, and Isaac, and Jacob.   Indeed, he will find amongst them the names of all the twelve Patriarchs.   And, verily, he may even find amongst them George Washingtons!   I presume they are not suffering for lack of names.   I heard of one who, on having her child baptized, desired to give it a Scripture name; so she called it Beelzebub.   So far as I am informed, masters are not in the habit of interfering with their names.

The gentleman is under the impression that the fundamental principles of our government have been for some time running down.   But if those principles were so well understood fifty years ago, how happened it that slavery was permitted to exist in our country?   It is certain, that the principles of which he speaks, were not better understood then than now; for when the Constitution of the United States was adopted, it would have been much easier to exclude slavery from this country, than to abolish it at the present day.

I do not remember that the gentleman offered one argument to prove slave-holding in itself sinful, unless he intended his appeal to the Constitutions of Ohio, Indiana, and Illinois, to be so considered!   These three States, it is true, adopted Constitutions prohibiting the existence of slavery, but whether they did so on the ground that slave-holding is necessarily sinful, or for other reasons, I am not informed.— At any rate, they are not the rule of our faith, or of our morals.

I will now proceed to offer some arguments, as time may permit, proving that slave-holding is not in itself sinful.

1. My first argument is founded upon the admitted fact, that the great principles of morality are written upon the human heart, and, when presented, do commend themselves to the understandings and the consciences of all men, unless

we except the most degraded. But the doctrine, that slave-holding is in itself sinful—is a heinous and scandalous sin, has not thus commended itself to the great mass, even of the wise and good. Therefore it is not true. That the great principles of the moral law are written upon the hearts of men, and do, especially when distinctly presented, commend themselves to the understandings and consciences of men, is a Scripture truth, which, I think, the gentleman will not call in question. Would it be possible for even the basest of men deliberately and conscientiously to maintain, that falsehood, theft, robbery, murder, perjury, blasphemy, and the like, are not in themselves sinful? What would be thought of a man professing to be a minister of the gospel, who would gravely and earnestly contend, that the commission of such crimes is, in many circumstances, justifiable, and, therefore, ought not to be made a bar to Christian fellowship; and that the Apostles of Jesus Christ did receive such men into the churches organized by them.— Yet it is a fact which Mr. Blanchard will not deny, that the great body of wise and good men, in ancient and in modern times, including all the commentators, critics, and theologians of any note, have believed, that the Apostles of Christ did receive slave-holders into their churches, and that slave-holding is not in itself sinful! How shall we account for this singular fact?

That the force of this argument may be seen, mark the fact, that according to the teaching of abolitionists, slave-holding is a crime of the first magnitude. The gentleman himself, in a speech in the Detroit Convention, pronounced it one of the greatest abominations of paganism. I have here a pamphlet entitled "THE BROTHERHOOD OF THIEVES," in which the writer prefers against the churches and the clergymen in these United States, charges in the following language:

"I said, at your meeting, among other things, that the American church and clergy, as a body were thieves, adulterers, man-stealers, pirates, and murderers; that the Methodist Episcopal Church was more corrupt and profligate than any house of ill-fame in the city of New York; that the Southern ministers of that body were desirous of perpetuating slavery, for the purpose of supplying themselves with concubines from among its hapless victims; and that many of our clergymen were guilty of enormities that would disgrace an Algerine pirate!!"

This sweeping charge is made, not only against slaveholders, but against the Christian church, and the ministers of every denomination in our country, on the ground that they all directly or indirectly uphold slavery. If, then, we are to believe this author, there can be no greater iniquity than slave-holding. Stephen S. Foster is the author. I have no personal knowledge of him, but certain it is, he is an abolitionist of the first water. I have another pamphlet, of which James Duncan is the author, published originally at Vevay, Ia., republished in 1840, *by the Cincinnati Anti-Slavery Society.* This work is, of course, excellent authority. I read on page 39: "The crime of slave-holding may, by a very short process of reasoning, be shown to be much more aggravating than a common act of murder."— Again, on page 42: "Therefore, slave-holding involves both masters and slaves in the most aggravated degrees of adultery; and not only so, but it entails it upon all succeeding generations." * * * "The sins forbidden in the eighth commandment are theft, robbery, man-stealing, and knowingly receiving any thing that is stolen. That slave-holding implies all these kinds of thefts, will appear by analyzing the crime of theft, to discover wherein its principal point of criminality lies." Again, on page 45: "Considering, then, the true nature of slave-holding, as it deprives a man of all his natural rights during life, and taking into view the dignity of human nature, or high rank of man in the scale of created existence, compared with the most noble of the brute creation, it may be safely concluded that the crime of slave-holding is a degree of theft as much more aggravating than horse-stealing, as a man is better than a horse."

I might read much more of the same character; for the author attempts to prove that slave-holding is a gross violation of every commandment in the decalogue! If these representations are true, slave-holding is one of the most abominable crimes a man can commit, and consequently one of the grossest violations of the fundamental principles of morality. Yet such men as Matthew Henry, Dr. Scott, Dr. Doddridge, Dr. McKnight, Dr. Chalmers, and many others, teach us that God did permit the Jews to hold slaves, and that the Apostles did admit slave-holders into their churches as faithful brethren, and, of course, that slave-holding is not in itself sinful. Now, one of two things is true, viz: either the abolitionists are in most serious error on this subject, or the great body of the wisest and best men, with the Bible in their hands, have been blind to the fundamental principles of morality, and most profoundly stupid and degraded. I cheerfully leave this audience to judge which is most probable. Indeed, it would be as difficult to account for the peculiar illumination of modern abolitionists, as for the astonishing stupidity of men so universally esteemed eminently wise and good.

2. My second argument is this: There never was, and never can be, a man, or a class of men, heretical on one fundamental point of faith, or of morals, and yet sound on all the other doctrines of the Bible, and on all other important principles of morality. The rejection of one fundamental doctrine of the gospel, leads necessarily to the rejection of others; and the disposition of mind leading to the rejection of one, would lead to the rejection of others, as equally offensive to the carnal mind. So the rejection of a fundamental principle of morality evinces a destitution of moral integrity, which would certainly lead to the disregard of other principles, and the commission of other crimes.— The truth now stated is too obvious to be disputed. You might as well assert that a man may have vision so clear as distinctly to see every pillar in this house, except the one just before him; but that he cannot see it! Every one sees

at once, that the clearness of sight, which would enable him to see the other pillars, would equally enable him to see this.

Now, it is an acknowledged fact, that the ministers and churches in the slave-holding States, are as sound in the faith on all other points, except the one in question, as the abolitionists themselves. It is not, and cannot be denied, that, with the single exception of slave-holding, they are as pure in their moral character, possess as expansive benevolence, and abound as much in good works, as any abolitionist on earth. Yet these people, sound in faith, pure in morals, and of enlarged benevolence, if abolitionism be true, ought to be executed by the common hangman, or confined for life in the penitentiary; for they are guilty of stealing, kidnapping, murder, adultery, &c., in their worst forms! Who can believe contradictions so glaring? Yet we must believe them, or pronounce abolitionism false, glaringly false.

Having presented these two arguments, which to me appear unanswerable, I will offer no more at the present time. When Mr. Blanchard shall have completed his definition of slave-holding, and offered some arguments in favor of his affirmative proposition, I shall be prepared to present some others. The question before us is not to be decided by appeals to sympathy, but by scriptural argument. Yet if the gentleman is determined to rely on such appeals, I hope to be able to present a sufficient number of instances of cruelty in connection with the parental and conjugal relations, to demonstrate the utter fallacy of all such logic. Or if from it the conclusion be drawn, that slave-holding is in itself sinful; the conclusion that these relations are sinful, will follow, of course. To this result the audience, especially the younger portion, I presume, will be slow to come.— They must come to it, however, or pronounce all the gentleman's arguments from the cruelty of wicked men, destitute of weight.

We profess to be the friends of the slave ; and we are prepared to prove, that those who adopt substantially our views, have done and are doing incalculably more to improve their condition, than the abolitionists ; that wherever slavery has been abolished, it has been effected, not by the principles of modern abolitionism, but by the principles we advocate. We take the Bible of God as our guide; and to its plain teachings we confidently appeal. The question is not, as already remarked, whether the oppressed shall find in Christianity an asylum ; but shall we condemn those whom God has not condemned? Shall we denounce and excommunicate persons of such character as were admitted to fellowship by the inspired Apostles of Christ? Shall we preach the gospel to slaves, and thus secure to them happiness here and glory hereafter ; or shall we run a few of them to Canada, where their condition, instead of being improved, is made worse, and where they will rarely, if ever, hear the sound of the gospel? If I believed the doctrine so zealously propagated by the gentleman and his abolitionist brethren, tended to abolish slavery, and improve the condition of the slave, I should be slow to oppose it. But most fully am I convinced, that its tendency is precisely the reverse ; and, therefore, as the friend of the slaves I oppose it. [*Time expired.*

Wednesday, P. M., 4 1-2 o'clock.

[MR. BLANCHARD'S SECOND SPEECH.]

Gentlemen Moderators and respected Fellow-Citizens :

There are some things which have fallen from my brother which require a brief passing notice before I resume the thread of my remarks. He has quoted two authorities. With regard to the first, Mr. Foster, it is proper that I should say he is doubtless a sincere and well-meaning man, and he is as ardently opposed to the anti-slavery men with whom I act, as he is to slavery itself. His feelings have been exasperated, and some have said, his reason shaken. He has often been imprisoned in the jails of the Eastern

States. Whether his reason is affected or not, persecution sometimes " maketh a wise man mad," and friend Foster has had a good deal of it. I will also quote authority; (and I promise not to go to the jails or mad houses for it.) As to Rev. James Duncan, whom he has quoted, he was the father of Dr. DUNCAN our late representative in Congress and he wrote his book in Kentucky, and published it at Vevay, Indiana, in 1824, eight years previous to the first modern anti-slavery society; after preaching as a pastor at Warsaw, in Kentucky. I cordially recommend to all to read it as the production of an able and profound mind. Dr. Duncan, in conversation respecting his deceased father, declared to me that he held all the sentiments of the book on the subject of slavery.

My brother is not pleased with my making slow progress in this debate. I confess I can scarcely hope to please him. I fear that he will find my course of argument more and more in his way the farther we proceed. As he has told you some half dozen times, I have not yet got through the preliminaries. Some one reproached the Grecian painter, Apelles, it is said, because he worked so slowly. He replied in Greek; "True, I paint IN a long time, but I paint FOR a long time." He intended his work should stand.

One or two other things fell from my friend which I cannot stop to notice. I must here say, I wish we could each correct the other, as we go along. He has doubtless unintentionally misstated two of my propositions which were somewhat important. Now, if I happen to misstate him, I wish to be put right at the instant, for nothing is gained in discussion either by exaggerated or by false statements.

My friend condemns, he says, the holding of slaves for gain; and the buying and selling of them. He thinks he condemns these things as much as we do. If he acts up to these words I can show you that he is an abolitionist, in respect to southern slavery.

I read from a pamphlet, not of my afflicted friend Foster, but from the *Rev. James Smylie,* some time clerk of Amity Presbytery, Mississippi.

"If slavery be a sin, and if advertising and apprehending slaves with a view to restore them to their masters is a direct violation of the Divine law, and if the *buying, selling* and HOLDING SLAVES FOR THE SAKE OF GAIN is a heinous sin and scandal; then verily, *three-fourths of all* the Methodists, Episcopalians, Baptists, and Presbyterians in eleven States of the Union, are of the Devil. They hold, if they do not buy and sell slaves; and, with *few exceptions,* they hesitate not to apprehend and restore runaway slaves when in their power."—*Smylie's pamphlet,* 1837.

Here is the declaration of no mean authority—of the clerk of a southern presbytery—that three-fourths of all the Presbyterians, Episcopalians, and Methodists in eleven of the United States, *do hold slaves for gain.* Now if men have a right to "hold slaves for gain," they may surely buy and sell them for like reason. Yet Dr. Rice assures us that he condemns these things as strongly as do abolitionists. I turn him over to his southern brethren. He has said in round terms, in this atmosphere of abolitionism, (or what is fast becoming so,) that he condemned a practice in which three-fourths of all his southern brethren (who regard him as their champion, and who know that, in heart, he is so) are engaged.

His *skin argument,* which is, that if slavery were abolished we might have colored governors and judges, &c., I do not know whether I should answer formally. He told us he was in favor of giving colored people political privileges as fast as they should be fitted to exercise them by elevation of mind and character: his only objection stated, was that they wanted the requisite information, and qualifications for self-government. So, it seems, he has not so great a horror of colored voters and rulers after all, since it is certain that colored people must eventually get sufficient knowledge to take part in politics.

In reply, I simply state the doctrine of abolitionists on this subject of the political rights of colored people.

There are three sorts of human rights. Political, Social

and Natural. Voting is a political right. Abolitionists hold
that the right of suffrage is a commodity which the community have a right to dispose of with an eye to its preservation.
That it is therefore properly left to be governed by wise
and just political maxims, irrespective of color. The community has a right to protect itself. Foreigners, after coming to the United States, are not allowed to vote for one year,
and, in some States, for seven years after they arrive. Yet,
they are free from the instant they land on our shores.
Now, abolitionists do not say that the State governments are
sinful in not allowing unnaturalized foreigners to vote. The
whole subject of political rights lies out side of this discussion. So also does that of the domestic or social rights.
For example, a colored or white man might wish to marry
your daughter. But if you or she determines that the match
shall not take place, you do not rob him. or sin against his
rights. Voting and marrying, then, are not of this discussion. Abolitionists take their stand upon the New Testament doctrine of the natural equality of man. The one-
bloodism of human kind:—and upon those great principles
of human rights, drawn from the New Testament, and
announced in the American Declaration of Independence,
declaring that all men have natural and *inalienable* right to
to person, property and the pursuit of happiness. They
only carry out the admitted truth that *all* are equal.

My brother made a difficulty to see what the Roman and
Greek slave systems had to do with the question before us.
I answer that I adduce the Greek and Roman slavery, in or
der to show that they were identical with American slavery;
and also to show that those who justify Roman slavery
(which was the slavery of the Apostles' times) from the Bible, justify also our own slavery, auction-mart, plantation-dis-
cipline, and all, from the sacred word of God! For slavery
is, here and every where, one.

You will remember my brother told you he did not understand what is meant by "*a system of slavery.*" I adduced the Greek and Roman systems to show him what "a

system of slavery" is, and surely he should count it a charity in me. To show, also, that Burgundian and Gothic, Grecian and Roman slavery are all one and the same thing, viz: the *holding of men as property.* That the condition of the slave, in law, as I will show more fully hereafter, is his condition in fact. And that a man, who pretends to oppose the cruel laws of slavery, and yet justifies slave-holding, appears to be plainly talking without intelligence or reason.

To show that the slave's legal is his actual condition, I will refer in passing, to a case decided by Judge Crenshaw, 1 Stewarts' Rep. 320:

" A slave is in absolute bondage; he has no civil right, and can hold no property, except at the will and pleasure of his master. A slave is a rational being, endowed with under-standing like the rest of mankind, and whatever he lawfully acquires and gains possession of, by finding or otherwise, is the acquirement and possession of the master. And in 5 Cowen's Rep. 397, the Court held that a slave at common law could not contract matrimony, nor could the child of a slave take by descent or purchase."—*Wheeler's Law of Slavery, p.* 7.

This is a reported case. It is not statute law, which may or may not be executed. It is a common law decision. It is the *practice* of the law, and shows how the law handles slaves whenever it touches them or their interests.

My friend justifies slave-holding, yet tells us he is oppos-ed to the separation of man and wife! How absurd and irrational such a position is, the case cited shows.

I have already shown you that American slavery is iden-tical with that of all other ages and nations. Our whole system is condensed into one single paragraph:

" *Slaves shall be deemed, sold, taken, reputed, and adjudg-ed in law, to be chattels personal, in the hands of their owners and possessors, and their executors, administrators, and assigns, to all intents, constructions, and purposes whatsoever.*"—*2 Brev. Dig.* 229.

This is the definition of *actual* slavery. This **law of** South Carolina, with the consequent fact, that "*a slave can acquire nothing, can possess nothing, but which belongs to the master,*" is a re-enactment of the Roman English code. For this one property-holding principle contains, and includes in itself every principle and element of the slave code.

Not only is this one grand, all-pervading, and all-controlling principle of chattelism, taken literally from the Roman code, but also the minor enactments, such as the law by which the slave who is inhumanly treated, may be sold for the benefit of the master; and the statute giving the owner damages for the mal-treatment of his slaves, are copied from the same source. I will not dwell on the incidents of slavery; but beg you to mark, that this slave-holding is the slave-holding of American holders. It is the tenure by which all the owners, however kind or pious, Presbyterian, Methodist, Episcopalian, or Baptist, hold their human chattels. The noose of chattelism is around the neck of every slave, and brings back every fugitive to the most pious master, not as a *man*, but as an animal, a chattel, a thing!

Thus slave-holding is degrading men to the level of brutes as completely as the nature of the case will admit.

Will my friend tell us that the law which makes men property is only an incident of slavery, and not the thing itself Will he say that the law "*partus sequitur ventrem*" is o of those "cruel laws" which may be repealed and yet slavery exist, or a law which is "a mere dead letter?" Does not the slave's child follow the condition of its mother? Is not that *practice* as well as law? Is there a place in Kentucky, a county in Maryland, or town in Virginia where the child of a slave is not the slave of the man who owns its mother, let who will be the father? And what law of slavery can be more cruel than this? Yet to pretend to oppose this law as cruel, and still justify slave-holding as not sinful is—I had almost used a severe expression, and said, it is an insult to common sense. Gentlemen, I ask you all, who have minds to receive and understand truth, what law of slavery can be so cruel, as that which *makes* the man a *slave?* This *is* the cruelty of slavery, that it *is* SLAVERY. Away, then, forever, with such stuff as saying that you are opposed to the cruel laws of slavery, but not to slave-holding itself! Bear with me while I dwell on this point. As our friend regaled our senses with Mr. Foster's adultery cases, I will follow his example as far as severe justice to the cause of truth requires. It is the law "*partus sequitur ventrem*" that distinguishes slaves from men. You know that by the law of God the man is the head of the woman as Christ is head of the church, and the father also, of the house, and gives name to the child. But as slaves cannot marry,—as it never was designed that they should exist in families, they are put under the same law which applies to brute animals in the field, where, if progeny is found, the owner of the cow drives away and owns the calf! Does any one think these disgusting details are out of taste in this assembly? why then should christians be allowed to practice a law which is too shocking for me to describe?

God knows I did not make the law,—and I would not even name it, but with the hope of contributing something to bring it to an end.

But, as you see, this first principle of slavery utterly destroys, among slaves, God's law of paternity. The "Our Father," which begins with the eternal Father of all, and connects by heads of families the whole chain of intelligent being to its source, is annihilated. Slave-children, stript of parentage and subject to masters, cannot feel the sweet and awful force of the words, "Our Father which art in Heaven." For the great principle of paternity is swept from the slave code, and so far as possible from slave hearts.

See yon southern Tamar, as she goes weeping from the couch of her master, to which she has been first dragged, and then thrust away, in that after-hate which in mean minds sated lust generates towards its victims. Behold her, as she goes weeping from the house, to the plantation of her rav-

isher, or, it may be, sold to the far South at the instance of
a jealous mistress, going along weeping and bearing all the
weaknesses and woes of maternity alone—the weaknesses of
mother-hood *alone!* yes! alone; amid the evening scourgings, the brief and broken slumbers—the morning shell-blow,
and wasting toil, and drivers' blasphemies, and hurried
meals of insufficient food, and all the paraphernalia of that
hell on earth, a southern cotton plantation : and tell me, what
one evil has been perpetrated upon the person of that wretched young woman which is not provided for and sanctioned
by the law of slavery—which is not of the essence of the
slave-holding power? You know, and there are plenty of
living instances to show, that adultery is no crime when
perpetrated upon a slave. Why? Because the principle
of slavery is the *cattle principle*. The slave code, here, and
every where, formerly and now, and ever, places female
slaves precisely in the condition of female cattle on a common. It was never contemplated that they should have husbands, and their children, fathers. Oh listen, when I shall
sit down, and weep for sorrow while you listen, to a minister of the gospel, justifying slavery itself as no sin, yet
turning round and telling us that he is opposed to the cruel
laws of slavery?

Another circumstance showing the unique and terrible
nature of slavery, is, that amid the world's revolutions and
modifications it alone remains the same. While civil government has been advancing; while the ancient despotisms
have softened into regular monarchies; the monarchies into
aristocracies; and hoary and haughty aristocracies have
thence again melted into democracy;—while war itself has
put off half its ferocity; and even the deliberate murderer's
right to life is vindicated against capital punishment; slavery is the same. It exists to-day, in Kentucky, precisely as
it did on the Roman Campagna eighteen hundred years
ago. The only remedy for it, is destruction. The dire
principle on which it rests, the property-holding of men,
admits of no amelioration. Civilization has not humanized

ıt; letters have not liberalized it; nor has Christianity reconciled it with the gospel of Christ. Like the carnal mind, of which it is the offspring, it "is enmity against God, for it is not in subjection to the law of God, neither indeed can be." It has remained, and, until destroyed, must remain forever unmitigated and immitigable. And for this plain reason: being no part of civil society, but pure crime, it does not improve with civil society. It is the same dark and damning curse now, that it was eighteen centuries ago. Why? Not only because, like all crime, it is by nature incapable of improvement, but also because it is so bad a thing that it makes every one grow worse, who is connected with it. "Oh!" said the late Charles Hammond, of this city, upon his death-bed; "Oh! slavery is not the thing it was when I first knew it in Virginia. Then the slaves were treated like servants—called in to family worship, and considered members of the family. But men have grown sordid now; and God knows where things will end." I saw large tears steal down his cheek, deep-furrowed with emotion, as he uttered these monitory truths.

Ah! gentlemen and fellow citizens, that which is so bad that it makes all those sinners who partake of it, is itself a sin—evil only evil; uniformly and forever evil. The very poetry of the Irish bard becomes sober prose in the lips of a slave :—

> " One fatal remembrance, one sorrow that throws
> Its bleak shade alike o'er all joys and all woes,
> To which life nothing darker nor brighter can bring,
> For which joy has no balm, and affliction no sting."

I have simply to repeat, that while for eighteen hundred years every relation and department of civil society has been revolutionized and regenerated, slavery has remained the same. It has steadily held the same deadly antagonism to God and man. Nothing can be added to it—nothing taken from it which will change its nature. And the only human sentiment which it leaves free to the breast of its victims, is despair.

What is still worse, while slavery remains absolutely the same, relatively it is perpetually growing worse. By a principle which is plain and obvious, just in that proportion in which the light of liberty increases, the darkness of adjacent slavery grows more dense. For as civilization advances, it creates new wants and luxuries, and the burdens of society grow more numerous. And, as slavery is a condition of things which gives all the benefits of society to one class of the people, and lays all its burdens upon another, the increase of the slave's miseries keeps pace with the increase of the conveniences and comforts of the free. And thus, as the light increases in the Goshen of our Liberty, the darkness in the Egypt of our Slavery becomes more and more terribly "a darkness which may be felt."

[*Time expired.*

[MR. RICE'S SECOND SPEECH.]

I propose, in the present speech, to follow the gentleman, step by step, and reply to what he has now offered in support of his proposition. Mr. Foster, he says, is as much opposed to his views, as to slavery itself.

Mr. BLANCHARD. I said to the *party*, not to the *views.*

Mr. RICE. Mr. Foster is opposed to Mr. Blanchard's *party*, not to his *views*. So, then, Mr. Foster's views, after all, are the views of the abolitionists, just as I had supposed! Still the gentleman would escape the odium justly attaching to Foster's views, by representing him *insane!* Whether he is insane or not, I pretend not to know; but I have rarely seen an essay in which a writer has presented more clearly, or presented in a stronger light his views, than Foster has done in this. I have little doubt, that he was about as sane as any man who holds the ultra abolition doctrine can be.

But I was pleased to hear the gentleman give to Duncan's pamphlet, published by the Cincinnati Anti-slavery Society, an unqualified recommendation; for Foster has not, I believe, advanced one sentiment more *ultra*, than those contained in Duncan's pamphlet. Duncan, as we have seen, pronounces slave-holding a greater crime than murder, or theft, or adultery. Nay, he undertakes to prove it to be an aggravated violation of every commandment in the Decalogue! He does not stop at this. He contends, that it is not only the right, but the duty of the slave, to escape from his master; that it is his right and his duty to gain his liberty, if need be, by insurrection and bloodshed! He even asserts, that every man who should be killed in attempting to suppress a slave insurrection, would be punished in hell forever!!! Lest the audience should think, that I am slandering Mr. Blanchard, and the Cincinnati Abolition Society, by charging them with endorsing statements so abhorrent, I will read one or two extracts from the pamphlet. On page 109 the author says—"It appears self-evident that they are not only in duty bound to embrace the first favorable opportunity to escape from their tyrants, but it would be criminal to neglect it, so that no jury could decide such a case against the slave without contracting great guilt and incurring damnation." Again—"Should a slave State, in imminent danger of being overcome by an insurrection of the slaves, call upon a neighboring State for assistance, in either men, money, arms, ammunition, or provisions, for the purpose of suppressing the slaves, no part of that assistance could be granted without contracting blood guiltiness, nor without calling down the judgments of God upon the nation; and all such as might fall, when fighting in defence of a cause, that could not have even the color of justice, might be expected to spend an eternity in chains and darkness, with no better company than that of slave-holders." Again —"No slave State could have any legal claim on the Federal government for assistance to suppress an insurrection of the slaves; because slavery is directly contrary to the Federal Constitution," &c.

Such are the sentiments advanced in this pamphlet, published in 1840, by the Cincinnati Abolition Society, and recommended without qualification by Mr. Blanchard! Can we wonder, that the people of the slave-holding States have lost all confidence in the abolitionists; they hold their principles and their conduct in utter abhorrence? And is this the "pure Christianity," for which the gentleman and his associates so zealously plead? Are we to be told, that pure Christianity not only requires slaves to run from their masters, but sanctions slave insurrections and murders, and dooms to eternal punishment the man who would raise his hand to quell them? Yet, this is the doctrine advocated by the gentleman and his co-adjutors! This is the doctrine of modern abolitionism; and this doctrine I oppose, and ever will oppose. It is a slander on the gospel of Christ and its glorious Author to say, that it is sanctioned by him.

By the way, the gentleman was mistaken in supposing that I was displeased with his speech. I stated the fact, that he spoke *forty* minutes without reaching the question, and *twenty more* without defining it. Such speeches, if it were my object simply to gain a victory, would delight me. I must expose his entire failure to advance any argument in support of his proposition; but I shall not be displeased with him for his failure.

Concerning Mr. Smylie's book, I can only say, I have not had the opportunity to read it, and, therefore, can express no opinion concerning it. If the gentleman has correctly represented him, I decidedly differ from him; and so, I am persuaded, will the great majority of southern Presbyterians.

Whether Cincinnati is rapidly adopting the doctrine of the abolitionists, as the gentleman asserts, is, I think, at least very doubtful; but if the doctrines of Mr. Duncan's pamphlet, endorsed by the Cincinnati Abolition Society, be orthodox abolitionism, I am confident that few men can be found in this city, who are abolitionists, or likely to become such.

In reply to my inquiry, whether the gentleman would carry out his doctrines, so as to make the slaves *free and equal* in the two States where they constitute a majority of the population, he says, there are three classes of rights, political, social, and natural, that the abolitionists, whilst they contend for the two last, do not propose to have the liberated slaves enjoy the right to *vote* or *fill the civil offices.* Their *political* rights they leave it to the wisdom of politicians to grant or withhold as they think proper! But did he not, in his first speech, quote the Declaration of Independence, that "all men are born free and equal," as setting forth the doctrine for which he contends? Certainly he did. But now when pressed with the practical results of his principles, he says, he does not mean exactly to make the slaves *free and equal.* He does not contend that they shall have the right to vote for the laws under which they are to live, and by which only any of their rights can be secured. No—they must be governed by laws made for them by their betters, and be taxed without their consent! Surely the principles of the Declaration of Independence are "running down" with the gentleman himself! And if, for the good of society, he can consent to make so great a difference between the colored and the white population, if he can consent to deprive the former of their *political* rights; why not go a little further, if the good of society requires it? Why stop precisely at this point? Will he please point us to the principle in the moral law, which permits us to deprive the colored people of certain important political rights, but teaches that we shall not deprive them of certain other rights? Or will he show us, according to correct principles of morality, precisely how far we may go, and where sin commences? You may, he says, deprive them of the right to vote and to have a voice in making laws by which they are to be governed, because the good of society requires it; but you can go no further without sin. Now let him turn us to the law for this singular principle of morality. Truly the gentleman finds it difficult to get along with his moral principles.

He justifies his appeal to Roman slavery by asserting, that when we justify Roman slavery by the Bible, we justify American slavery. Are we discussing the question, whether *Roman slavery* is right or wrong? We are not. There were many things in Roman slavery, that were most unjust

and cruel.   The question before us relates simply to the relation of master and slave.   "Is slaveholding in itself sinful,
and the relation between master and slave a sinful relation?"
Such is the question proposed for the discussion by the ten
challengers; and yet the gentleman refuses to discuss it,
amuses us with Roman slavery and American slavery, and
seeks to excite our sympathies by reciting the cruelties inflicted on slaves by wicked men.   Let him prove, if he can,
that these cruelties are essential to the existence of the relation.   Let him prove, that any humane or even decent man
is guilty of inflicting them upon his slaves.   Let him, if he
can, point to the church session that refuses to discipline
members for such conduct; and we will see the matter attended to.

But these are the arguments by which abolitionism seeks
to sustain its claims.   Its advocates are untiring in their
search for extreme cases of cruelty; and these are held up
as essential characteristics of slave-holding wherever it exists.   "Look at that weeping woman," exclaims the gentleman, "dragged," &c.   Well—let me appeal to your sympathies against the conjugal relation.   Look at that weeping
widow fastened upon the funeral pile of her dead husband,
with whose body she is to be consumed.   See the fire kin-
dled, and the smoke rising.   Hear her piteous wailings,
which the beating of drums and the shouts of the unfeeling
multitude cannot drown.   Her only crime is, that she is
the wife of the man who is dead.   O the cruelty of the
marriage relation!   Who will not condemn and detest it!
No—I am opposed to the burning of widows; but I cannot
condemn the marriage relation, though it is made the occasion of so much cruelty.   Yet my appeal to your sympathies is as sound an argument against the marriage relation,
as the gentleman's appeal to the cruelty of wicked men
against the relation of master and slave.   Neither proves
any thing.

The gentleman repeats the declaration, that slaves cannot
contract marriage, and that their children are illegitimate.

And I again call upon him to point to the part of Scripture which makes recognition of marriage by the civil law essential to its validity. Let him, if he can, show where the Bible prescribes any particular ceremony through which the parties must pass before they can be truly married. This he is certainly bound to do; for marriage is a Bible institution. I affirm, that the marriage of slaves is as valid in God's law, as that of their masters, and their children as legitimate. Will the gentleman pretend, that any master is bound to tear husband and wife apart, because he claims their services? The truth is, it is as wicked to separate husband and wife amongst slaves, as amongst free men; and if any professor of religion is chargeable with so doing, let him be excluded from the church of Christ; and let the church be purged of all such sinners.

Mr. Smylie, says the gentleman, tells us that two-thirds of all the professors of religion in the South, hold slaves *for the sake of gain.* I have not said, that those who are masters must have no regard to their own interests. Doubtless kind masters endeavor to make the advantage mutual. But, I condemned, and still condemn, *speculating* in human beings—traffic for the sake of gain, and of course without reference to the happiness of the slave. No Christian can consistently purchase a slave without having regard to his happiness as well as his own advantage. It may be true, that the laws permit great injustice and cruelty toward them. But, are we debating the question whether the laws of Georgia, or of any other State, are right? We are not. Will the gentleman assert, that any master is obliged to inflict upon his slaves the injustice and cruelty which the law permits? In many countries, the laws regulating marriage are most iniquitous; and even in Ohio, a man may treat his wife very cruelly, without being in danger of incurring the penalty of the civil law; but it does not follow, that the relation is in itself sinful.

Mr. Blanchard asserts, that slavery is really getting worse, and the condition of the slaves becoming more intolerable. This I utterly deny. It is a fact, that in Kentucky the laws regulating slavery have been much improved within a few years; and the uniform testimony of those who go and see for themselves, is that the condition of the slaves is' far better than it was several years ago. Dr. Drake, of Louisville, when recently on a tour through several of the southern States, made it his business to inquire particularly into the condition of the slaves; and his testimony is, that it has greatly improved, and is now improving. It is well known, that many of the planters in the South not only freely admit ministers of the gospel to preach to their slaves, but that they even pay them salaries to secure their services. Everywhere in the slave-holding States the gospel is working a change in public sentiment, modifying the laws, and greatly improving the condition of the slaves, just as it did, for example, in the State of New York. Time was, when the slave laws of that State were more oppressive and cruel, than they now are in any one of the southern States. But gradually, under the influence of the gospel, a happy change was effected; cruel laws were repealed; better laws were enacted; and finally slavery itself was abolished.

But, says the gentleman, the best masters hold their slaves by a *legal tenure;* and the law makes them mere property. And does not the husband hold his claim to his wife, according to his own doctrine, by a legal tenure? Did he not assert, that the slaves are not married validly, because the civil law does not recognize their marriage? But the civil laws by which the marriage relation is regulated, are in many countries most defective and unjust. The laws of India make the wife the slave of the husband; and, as already remarked, even in Ohio, a man may so treat his wife as to render her life a burden, without being in danger of the penalty of the law. Shall we then denounce the marriage relation as in itself sinful? I repeat, that I do not place the relation of master and slave upon an equality with that of husband and wife; but I do maintain, that the gentleman has no right to urge against the former, arguments which will equally sweep away the latter.

To say, that we are opposed to the cruelties often practiced toward slaves, and yet deny that the relation is in itself sinful, is *to insult the common sense of men.* So said Mr. Blanchard; or he *almost* said it. Well, I suppose his common sense is not like the common sense of other men. The common sense of such men as Drs. Chalmers, Cunningham, Spring, Tyler, and a multitude of the wisest and best men, has led them to make precisely the distinction between the *relation* and the cruelty of wicked men in the relation, which Mr. B. pronounces an insult to the common sense of men! I fear, his common sense is almost peculiar to himself; and certainly it is not safe to base a judgment concerning so grave a question upon the *peculiar common sense* of one man. He may pronounce the common sense of other men " *stuff;*" but this proves nothing.

He denounces particularly that law—*partus sequitur ventrem*—the child follows the condition of the mother, and tells us, that slavery places human beings among the *cattle.* Well, if such be necessarily its character, why debate the question at all? Is discussion necessary in order to induce intelligent men to detest it? The gentleman constantly keeps out of view the real question at issue, viz : whether the relation itself is sinful, and dilates upon the cruel conduct of wicked men. He, as a minister of the gospel, professes to take the Bible as his only guide in faith and morals. He, of course, believes, that nothing can be condemned as sinful, which is not contrary to the written word of God. And yet we have heard him, during one hour and a half, labor to prove his proposition, without quoting one passage of Scripture! Carefully avoiding to appeal to the rule of right, he attempts to carry his point by strong appeals to the sympathies of the audience. He tells us what Mr. Hammond said about the neglect of masters in Virginia to call their servants in to family worship. No doubt, there has been great and very culpable neglect of this duty, and I certainly cannot excuse or palliate it. But I rejoice to know, that for some time past, there has been a growing interest in the religious instruction of the slaves. Never was there so large an amount of money and labor expended in this interesting cause, as now. The Christians of the South are waking up to a sense of their obligation to have the gospel of Christ proclaimed to the slave, as well as to the master; and in this movement I do rejoice.

But since Mr. B. has appealed to the testimony of Mr. Hammond, I must also give you the testimony of a great and good man concerning the effect of the late abolitionist movement. Rev. Dr. Spring, of New York, says—"The late Dr. Griffin, one of the most devoted friends of the colored race in this land, said to me a few months before his death, '*I do not see that the efforts in favor of immediate emancipation, have effected any thing but to rivet the chains of the poor slave.*' Is not this," adds Dr. S., "a lamentable fact?" *Obliga. of World*, &c. p. 249. The dying testimony of such a man as Dr. Griffin, is surely worthy of grave consideration.

I suppose I ought not to be displeased with the gentleman for failing to offer arguments in support of his proposition. Yet I certainly desire, that he would do the best that can be done for his cause. I shall continue to present such arguments as I think conclusive from the word of God, the only infallible rule of faith and life. The question before us is, whether the relation of master and slave, divested of all that is not essential to it, is sinful; and this question only will I discuss. We have now passed through near three hours of the discussion;—and yet Mr. B., though a minister of the Gospel, engaged in the discussion of a great moral and religious question, has made no appeal to the law of God! Surely we could scarcely have anticipated such a course by a gentleman who has devoted so much time to the discussion of this subject.

But like the ancient painter, he is doing work, he tells us, for *posterity*. He expects his work to stand forever. The painter, however, though progressing slowly, was doubtless putting on colors of some kind, adapted to the completion of the picture. But what argument has the gentleman offered in proof of his proposition? He has told of Aristotle's definition of slavery, of the supposed weeping woman upon whom a gross outrage has been committed, of the slave-gangs, &c. &c.; but what argument has he offered? I have some hope, that my work will endure for a time; but nevertheless I choose to direct my arguments to the subject before us.

I have presented two distinct arguments, to neither of which he has attempted a reply, viz : 1. The great principles of morality do, when propounded, commend themselves to the understanding and the conscience of all men, unless we except the most degraded. The truth of this declaration will scarcely be called in question. But it is a fact that the principle for which Mr. B. is contending—that slave-holding is in itself a heinous and scandalous sin—has not thus commended itself to the great body even of the wise and good. Therefore it is not true. If it be, how shall we account for this singular fact? 2. It is a fact that the history of the world affords not an example of a man or body of men heretical on one fundamental doctrine of Christian faith or of Christian morality, but sound on all others. On the contrary, one fundamental error necessarily leads to others. But it is admitted, that the ministers of the gospel and the laymen of churches in the slave-holding States, are as sound on all points of doctrine, as pure on all points of morality, as benevolent in all respects, as the abolitionists themselves, with the single exception of the question of slavery! They can see all the other great principles of morality ; but the greatest of all violations of the moral law, i. e. that of slave-holding, they cannot perceive to be necessarily sinful at all! Believe it who can.

3. My third argument is this : It is admitted even by many abolitionists that there are in the slave-holding States true Christians and Christian churches—churches accepted of God, and often blessed with powerful revivals of religion. If we are to judge of their piety by Scriptural marks,

they are not deficient in evidence; and their fruits surely prove them genuine. Professor Stowe, of Lane Seminary, though he is an abolitionist, and though he bitterly denounced the General Assembly of the Presbyterian church for its action upon the subject of slavery, says—"I know individuals who are slave-holders, and particular churches which include slave-holders, whom, according to all the evidence I can gather, Christ does accept—and those individuals, and those particular churches, on my principles, I cannot reject, and I *will not.*" *Watchman of the Valley, Aug.* 14. In these churches masters and slaves worship God together; and their prayers are heard, and a rich blessing granted. Mr. Duncan and "the Cincinnati Abolition Society" assert, that the slave-holder is guilty of the violation, in an aggravated degree, of every commandment in the decalogue; but Professor Stowe acknowledges many of them as true Christians ! Now it is certain, that if they are as wicked as Duncan accuses them of being, their prayers are an abomination to God. So that either those professing Christians and those churches are wretched hypocrites, and their revivals perfectly spurious; or abolitionism is false. I leave the audience to determine which is true.   [*Time expired.*

Wednesday Evening, 7 o'clock, P. M.

[MR. BLANCHARD'S THIRD SPEECH.]

Gentlemen Moderators and Gentlemen and Ladies, Fellow Citizens:

There are some things which have fallen from my brother in his last remarks which demand a brief and respectful notice. You will recollect what I advanced showing that slaves are incapable of marriage by statute and by practice: that their children are illegitimate in law and in fact: incapable of taking by will, or by descent; and that they are held and regarded as illegitimate persons. I might have added that the great majority have not even the form of marriage, and when there is the form, (for there are southern clergymen who are willing to mitigate the horrors of slavery) some ministers add a clause in the marriage service which shows that they are not married. Rev. Mr. Smith, of Sumpter county, Ala., informed me that when he married slaves, instead of pronouncing the clause "until death you do part," that he added, "until death *or some other cause beyond your control.*" I might also have added that one Baptist association formally decided that a slave may lawfully have several wives:—That if a slave is sold off a plantation ten, twenty, or thirty miles or more, and takes another woman, it shall not in-injure his standing in the Baptist church. Now what did my friend say in reply? I confess I was pained to hear such remarks fall from such a gentleman. I was sorry, not particularly in reference to this debate, but for the sake of the public morals. He asked me to point to the place in the Bible where the recognition of the civil law was made necessary to the validity of marriage. Can it be that he means to teach that a man and a woman may meet in a private place and marry each other by the law of God; and they who do thus are married?

Gentlemen, if I am asked, to point to the text requiring the recognition of the civil law to marriage; I point to the whole Bible *practice* of marriage, from Samson downward. The Jews of all nations, were the most ceremonious observers of the outward forms of marriage. Samson had a marriage feast of seven days, at the house of the bride, and a solemn procession at the close, like that alluded to by Christ in the parable of the virgins. Such were some of the formal outward recognitions of eastern marriages. I never heard before; I hope I shall never again hear from Presbyterian lips; that the recognition of the civil law was not necessary to constitute marriage. Joseph meets Betsey, some where, at some time or other and marries her—and that is all, according to the principle of my brother's reply, which was requisite to make them one!

One or two other remarks of his require notice.

He tells us in his printed discourse, which, being issued since it was agreed upon, is a part of this debate; and he tells us, also, orally, *iterum iterum que;* that the church-courts will regulate and correct all the ills of slavery. If any thing is done amiss just go to a southern church-session —that immaculate umpire—and all will be healed, mended and remedied. Take slavery before a Presbyterian session and that will plaster it up, bleach it all white, and sweep away all its abuses by the magic of its wand.

Well:—the only thing I have to say in reply, is to give the testimony of Rev. James Smylie (who belongs, I believe, to the same ecclesiastical organization with brother Rice) who states over his own signature, not as a doctrine, but as a fact; that three-fourths of all the Presbyterians, in eleven States *"hold slaves for gain."* And these are the church-courts to which he sends us to reform the abuses of slavery! He sends us to elders who "hold slaves for gain" to redress the evils of slave-holding As an example of what might be expected of such courts, I will relate a fact which was a common story in the newspapers of the day several years ago, which was as follows: Richard, a sexton of a Presbyterian church (in Danville, I think) who was a colored man and member of the church, was sold by his brother in the same communion, away from his wife and four small children, into Jessamine county. There was no church action heard of on that account. Another case is that of the Rev. Dr. Stiles, then of Kentucky, now of Virginia, who was stated in the papers of the day, to have sold eight slaves, just before he left Kentucky, to attend the last triennial Assembly in Philadelphia. So far from disgracing him, that Assembly (with which I am connected, perhaps, until after its next meeting) appointed him one of three to administer the sacrament of the Lord's supper. Such are the men who compose the church-courts, to which my friend would send us to reform the abuses of slavery. Further, in 1818, the General Assembly adopted a rule, in reference to the subject, declaring it to be the duty of Christians to instruct their slaves, prepare them for emancipation, and labor for the destruction of slavery, throughout Christendom. (See Minutes of 1818.)

The Rev. J. D. Paxton, of Virginia, well known by his "letters from Palestine," which were published in this city, undertook to practice upon this injunction. He instructed his slaves, and finally set them free. This was before the date of abolitionism proper, which began in 1832, in a printing office in Boston, where a society was formed, consisting of twelve men. While that good man was thus conscientiously obeying the law of the church, he was slandered as a dangerous fanatic, and eventually driven from his church into a free State, for no offence whatever but what he had given in emancipating his slaves.

This was the only case I have heard of, where any attempt was made to obey the injunction of the Assembly of 1818. I must say, therefore, that it is not entirely fair for a gentleman as well informed on this subject as my friend, to say to this audience that the southern church-courts will forthwith, on application, redress all the abuses of slavery, when he must know that the church has never disciplined the first man for such offences.

Exception was taken to my affirmation, that slavery has not improved—that it was always the same in all ages, and countries of the world—in Rome, in Greece, in Gaul, in Britain, and in America:—and that *the property-holding of men* is a principle which is not susceptible of amelioration. My friend insists, on the contrary, that slavery has improved, and that what I advanced on that head is without proof. In reply, I have only to state, that in the speech of Hon. Joshua R. Giddings, in the House of Representatives, on the Florida war, there is an abundance of documentary proof, that the runaway negroes who had taken refuge in Florida, actually fought for the privilege of remaining slaves to Indian savages, rather than go back and be slaves to the whites. This is a perfect illustration of the point which I made, viz: that as civilization advances, the burdens of civil society increase, and the task of the slave grows heavier in proportion.

There are ten thousand comforts, conveniences and luxuries required in a civilized state of society, which were unknown to the barbarous period. The burdened class, therefore, becomes more oppressed. Hence, it was, that those Florida fugitives accounted slavery among the Indians, as liberty, in comparison with slavery to the whites.

I have to notice one thing more before I proceed. My friend has complained repeatedly of the course I have thought proper to take in this argument. I recollect, however, that my friend said, that though he felt it his duty to complain of my course, in order to expose the unfairness of it, yet he was rather pleased than angry with it: to give him the victory over me he could wish me to pursue no other, etc.

I wish to say simply, in reply, that my object in coming here is not to gain a victory over Dr. Rice. I desire no victory over him. I do not wish to deprive him of one sprig of the laurels which he may acquire in his crusade to establish the doctrine that slave-holding is not sin.

But I have come here, prepared to discuss this subject of slavery, so that it will *stay* discussed. I have attended to the subject and prepared myself as well as I am able. I should not have treated you with proper respect, had I not. I, for one, have not invited you here to regale you with feats of logical skill, with tricks of polemicism and syllogism. I have marked out a consecutive train of thought, bearing on the point in debate, and I now regret that I did not furnish him with a syllabus of my whole argument when we begun. I mean to linger upon the subject of slavery till I am convinced that we all perceive distinctly what slave-holding is. I will then go to the word of God, and with his help, ascertain whether it is right or wrong. This, as the affirmant in this debate, I suppose it is my right to do; and I hope, meantime, my brother will address himself to disprove my sentiments, and abstain from complaint, as if I was departing from the just and ordinary rules of debate.

My desire is, so to settle this question of the sinfulness of slavery, that your minds will be at rest upon it.

Now, their main grand position is, that slavery and slave-holding are not in themselves sinful, but that many laws, regulating slavery, are cruel and unjust:—that all the evil lies in these cruel laws.

Now, I wish to show that this ground of theirs is simply no ground:—rather it is a yielding of the whole ground. For slavery is *a thing created by these very laws.* And if the laws are admitted to be cruel and sinful, then slavery, the product of those laws, is likewise sinful. Slavery is not a natural relation. It is the creature of laws. Repeal the slave laws and you repeal slavery. Such is the late decision of the Hon. John McLean, of this city: so all the jurists. So Chief Justice Shaw, of Massachusetts, in the case of the slave child "Med": that slavery is against nature, the creation of positive law, so that if a slave goes beyond the slave code's jurisdiction, with the consent of his master, that fact frees him.

I therefore put it to every legal mind in the audience, whether the pretence of opposing the laws regulating slavery, while justifying slave-holding, can be anything but pretence. Repeal those laws and what becomes of slavery? It perishes with the laws which give it being and birth.

Yet my brother, who is here to defend slave-holding, as sinless, tells us he is opposed to the cruel laws regulating slavery. If he is, why not tell us *what laws* he opposes? If he is sincere, let him specify the iniquitous statutes, and utter an honest and open condemnation of them. But no—this is precisely what he will not do. He glides delicately over these laws, *siccis pedibus*—dry-shod. Does he condemn the laws which require sheriffs to put up and sell the slaves of deceased masters, for a division among heirs; or slaves of living masters, to satisfy a judgment: does he condemn those statutes, which sell men, women and children, to the highest bidder, irrespective of family ties? If so, let him say it, and let that go to Kentucky. Thus, let him pass through the whole slave code, put his finger upon each statute, and condemn it as sinful, and let that go to Kentucky; and see what thanks he will get for defending slave-ry, while he condemns its laws? No: this he will never do. He knows the Kentuckians are not to be imposed upon thus. And I rest the matter here in clear sun-light. Slavery being the creature of the laws; the laws being repealed, re-peals slavery. And admitting the cruelty of the laws, he admits the sinfulness of the thing itself, which is created by them. And for a man to say that he is opposed to the cruel slave laws, and not to slavery itself, is to utter the most palpa-ble solecism of which language is capable.

But, leaving my opponent, I wish to give you half an hour's argument on this very point, to show you that slavery in law is slavery in fact;—that every slave is held by the noose of the chattel statute; and therefore to pretend oppo-sition to the laws, while defending slave-holding, is simply absurd.

My first proposition (already adverted to) is, that the most cruel of all slave laws *is the law which makes men slaves.*

I put it to your plain understandings as men, whether it be not so; whether this view is, as he says, an idiosyncrasy in me, and that my common sense is uncommon? He declares slave-holding in itself to be sinless; but the laws regulating slavery, to be unjust and cruel. Now, of two States; let one adopt the South Carolina law, making human beings property. Take but this one law, and let it have free course and full application, so that when the stat-ute comes to your house, it makes you all property—hus-band, wife and child—so that whether you are permitted to remain together until morning, depends not upon your own wills, but upon the will of your master. Let this single statute be the sole slave law in that State.

Now, let another State adopt every slave law in the code, excepting this one. I ask you, to which of these States would you go to live? Would you go where the law just makes yourself, wife and children, property? or would you go where the laws forbid you to read, to take by will, etc., etc., etc., but do not make you property? Which would you choose as a place of residence? I aver that you would go where you would be a man, though persecuted and afflicted, rather than go where you are made a brute on sight. Now I am not under the necessity of stating the case so strongly as this. Instead of comparing the chattelizing statute with *all* the rest, take any *one* law which he calls cruel, and compare it with this; and if the law which *makes* the slave be equally cruel, slave-holding is sin. Say that in Indiana, laborers are forbidden to read and write; but in Illinois, they are simply made chattels; which law would be the most cruel? But Dr. Rice *admits* the cruelty of the law forbidding to read; and reason and nature proclaims the other more so. If, therefore, my brother is a fair-minded and Christian man, honestly opposed to those less cruel laws; if he values his consistency a straw, he will openly confess himself an abolitionist—that he hates slavery from his heart's core, and we will go out and lecture together against oppression. If he will not, I regret it, and that is all I can say.

I will speak farther in this behalf. For this moral citadel of slavery, this main idea of the sinlessness of slavery, with the sinfulness of its laws, meets us, in some form, at every turn and step of this argument.

He says, in his last General Assembly's Report, whose authorship he acknowledges, " The question between us and the abolitionists, is, not whether the laws by which, in the several States, slavery is regulated, are just and righteous. Many of them are sadly defective, and some of them are oppressive and unjust in a high degree."—*Rice's Lectures, p.* 12.

Observe here, the milk and sugar expression, "many" (of these dishumanizing statutes) "are sadly defective." Surely, this is handling slavery with silk gloves.

This idea, that the laws of slavery are sinful, but that slavery is not sinful, is the last strong-hold of the slaveholders. But, by the blessing of God, this rampart shall not cover their retreat. The covering is too narrow where-

with to wrap them, and the bed too short for their repose.
These very laws *are slavery in fact;* and unless his object
is to throw dust in your eyes, he cannot help acknowledging
it.   I prove it, thus:—The Legislatures of these States hold
their sessions annually or biennially, and these cruel laws,
which they make, are laws which *they mean to use.*   This
Mississippi code, which I have before me, shows how the
slave codes are made.   They consist of laws enacted from
time to time, by the several Legislatures.   Laws and parts
of laws have from time to time been repealed—showing
that the laws which do remain, are living laws, and not
dead ; that *they* are enforced upon the person of the slave.
And these laws are made to enforce the chattel principle,
which he says is not a wrong principle.   Now I contend
that it is sinful; because these cruel laws, made to regulate
slavery, are made necessary by the first law, which makes
man property; and are included in it.   If there be any legal
gentleman here, (and I see several,) he will tell you that any
grant of power by the Legislature always includes the means
and the power to enforce it.   For example—a law is passed
at Columbus, by the Legislature, incorporating an Orphan
Asylum, and authorizing trustees to hold the property.
The charter does not read thus:—We incorporate A, B, and
C, to establish an Orphan Asylum, and we hereby declare
that John Dix shall carry the hod, and Bill Dixon shall burn
the brick, and Jedediah Burch shall lay them.   But the first
law includes all the powers necessary to its proper execution.

Now my friend comes before that Presence in which we
all shall stand at judgment, and tells Him and us that he
honestly believes that slavery is not sinful, but that the laws
regulating it are cruel and unjust.   Now I aver that
because slavery includes these cruel laws and makes them
necessary, therefore it is, in itself, sinful and cruel.   Besides,
it strikes me as utterly absurd, to oppose the laws regulating
slavery, after conceding, as sinless, the right to hold slaves.
Why, after you have struck down my manhood, by making
me a slave, by a law which regards my wife and my babes

as cattle and swine; after you have stolen the fire of my being, you may freely trample on the cinders that are left. Give me back my humanity, or do what you will with the rest. I care not how much whipping, and lacerating, and burning you inflict; the more the better, since it will be the sooner over.

Gentlemen; you are not, you cannot, be insensible to this truth: nor could my brother be, were it not for the searing, petrifying influence of long familiarity with slavery.— Southern men may be, many, perhaps are, better than myself. But he must be seared and callous who does not see that the law which makes slavery, is more cruel than that which regulates it.

Let me tell you, fellow citizens, when they have cannonized slave-holding as sinless, and set it up in the church of God; when they have persuaded us that they have God's warrant for the property-holding of *man*, be he colored or white; for keeping him in slavery, because his ancestors were enslaved by others; seizing his infants for slaves as soon as born;—Oh! sirs, they well know that all the rest of slavery follows. They know that the property power, by fatal necessity, draws every other slave law after it! Does not the gentleman know that if the State of Indiana, or any other State, should enact and enforce a law making its laborers property, that all the other laws of slavery would follow of course? Aye; my friend knows, and God knows, that such is the quality of human nature, that when you have put a bridle in the mouth, and a saddle upon the back, of one man, and vaulted another into the saddle, with whip in hand, and spur on heel, and placed the reins fully within the gripe of the rider, it is but insulting misery to cry — "Pray, sir, don't use him as a horse." He is property.— You have made him property; and he will be used as property.

So the slave-holders understand this matter, and they ask no better champion than Dr. Rice. Go read his argument at the evening slave-quarter; at the cotton-gin; at the auction stand, in the Exchange Coffee House in New Orleans; and, wherever heard, it will be greeted by the slave-holder with triumph, and by his slaves with despair. "Give us God's permission to *own* men," say the holders, and we will take care of the rest.

Mark well, I beseech you, the inconsistency and absurdity of his position. He is opposed to the slavery-regulating laws, yet justifies as sinless the law which creates that very slavery, for regulating which, he condemns other laws as cruel: as if to regulate were worse than to create it. Now, as a matter of fact, all the other laws are made to carry out the chattel principle—the property-holding law. I read from the Mississippi code: "*When any sheriff, or other officer, shall serve an attachment upon slaves, horses, or other live stock,*" &c. The law goes on to give leave to provide food, and charge it upon the execution. Now, *ab uno disce omnes.* (holding up the statutes.) Every other slave statute is, like this, a mere carrying out of the property-holding power.

Sheriffs' advertisements, also, show that slaves are held in fact as property. I recollect that the daughter of a southern judge, from South Carolina, whom I met in Cherry street, Philadelphia, said that she had a young slave girl as a personal servant, whom, by stealth, she had taught to read.— She treated her kindly, and supposed her happy. Coming unexpectedly into the room one day, where the girl was, she was surprised to find her in tears. "What has happened," said she "that you are sobbing so?" The girl pointed with her finger, to a newspaper, which she had been reading, where slaves were advertised to be sold with some hogs.— "Why, mistress," said she, "they put us on a level with the swine." Now, is not the slavery of the statute the slavery of fact? This girl had suffered no cruel usage, yet was she not a chattel? How absurd is this pretence of condemning cruel slave laws, and justifying slavery, which is more cruel.

Again: That legal slavery is the actual slavery, is evident from the fact that the laws made to guard the owner's right of property in the slave, provide for their own execution, while those which seem to protect the slave, do not.

My argument is this:—Because slavery in law is slavery in fact, he who condemns the law, must, to be consistent, condemn the thing. Now the laws which guard and enforce the owner's right of property in slaves, provide means for their own execution, by rewarding prosecutors, informers, and slave-catchers. But there is no such provision to enforce the laws made to prevent cruelty to the slaves. Thus the Mississippi code gives to a Choctaw Indian fifteen dollars for catching a runaway, and fifteen dollars to the United States Indian Agent who brings him in.—*Alden & Van Hoesen, chap.* 92, *sect.* 38. The United States Agent is made the catch-pole, or devil's-paw, (pardon the expression,) of the State Legislature, and paid fifteen dollars for bringing home a fugitive negro, betrayed by an Indian. So there is a law, that if you allow a slave to set up type, you are fined ten dollars. And if the sheriff does not enforce this law, he is fined fifty dollars—one-half to the prosecutor, and the other to the county. Thus the laws which are made for the master, oil their own wheels.

Another law gives the patrol (and the patrol are all who are able to bear arms) six dollars each, for taking up negroes found abroad without a pass, and whipping them fifteen lashes.—*Alden & Van Hoesen, chap.* 83, *sec.* 3. But if the patrol turns angel, (I never can think of my friend's Hagar case without laughing,) and brings in an outlying slave, the law gives him thirty dollars.—*A. & V. H., chap.* 92, *sec.* 36.

But there is nothing to insure the enforcement of the law professing to be for the slave's protection. [Reads *Miss. code, Digest,* 755, *sec.* 44, which enacts that no cruel or *unusual* punishment shall be inflicted on the slave.] "*Unusual*" means, of course, that the punishment must transcend and outrage public opinion in the neighborhood. This law pays no informer, or prosecutor, or costs of suit, but stands on the statute book like a broken tea-cup, with the whole side towards the front of the shelf—for show, and not for use.

But without this, its vagueness would destroy it. It leaves the cruelty of slave-punishments to be determined by custom and use: a curious way to define *punishment*. And then, if any man is rich and bold enough to prosecute the master to conviction, the slave is taken from one master, and sold to another.

By this transaction his misery may or may not be abated. It may but take him, like the fox in the fable, from flies that are full, to deliver him to flies that are empty. He may get a better master, and he may a worse. It certainly takes the slave from a master to whose passions he is accustomed, and delivers him over to one with whose temper he is unacquainted; and "the price obtained for his sale shall be paid over to his master from whom he is taken." There is nothing reserved to pay the costs, or the prosecutor, or expenses of the suit. The protection of the slave is, therefore, left to the precarious and gratuitous sympathy of fallen human nature! This is the slave's actual condition. Is it sin to hold him in it?

But again. It is plain that slavery in law is slavery in fact, from the circumstance that *the penal code of slave States, which is designed for men, does not take effect on slaves.* A law of Mississippi declares, that the criminal code shall not be so construed as to extend to slaves. A similar law exists in Kentucky, passed in 1802. It is enacted that, "when punishment for any offence shall be confinement in the penitentiary, such punishment shall be considered as applicable to free persons only."

Thus the slave is so far completely imbruted as not even to be punished with men for his crimes. But, does he therefore escape punishment? By no means. There is another penal code, viz: that executed upon mischievous brutes, whose penalties are whipping, selling, and killing; and by this code is discipline dealt out to slaves! I do not say it is actually made *lawful* to kill slaves. Excepting fugitives who resist, or will not stop when hailed, it is unlawful. But I say that the slave is left under the penal code applicable to incorrigible brutes, whom men do whip, and sell, and kill. For slaves there is a *slave* law—a law suited to men who are advertised and sold with swine. This is degradation complete. Stript of even the privilege of being punished as men. They are not governed as if they were men: and, if the slave is a man, no thanks are due to slavery for it. So far as it can, it dishumanizes and imbrutes him. [*Time expired.*

[MR. RICE'S THIRD SPEECH.]

Gentlemen Moderators and Fellow Citizens:

I certainly do not desire, that any who hold views on this subject in accordance with mine, should give expression to their feelings of approbation. I will not, however, find fault with those who differ from me, for pursuing this course. Such manifestations may be necessary to supply the gentleman's lack of argument. He has now spoken two and a half hours for the purpose of proving, that slave-holding is in itself sinful; he and I agree that the Bible is the only rule by which any thing can be proved sinful; and yet during the two and a half hours he has made not one reference to that infallible rule ! Two and a half hours to prove by a certain rule the sinfulness of a relation, without one reference to the rule ! Surely the gentleman stands in need of the applause of his friends. Thus far he has been employed in telling us what slave-holding is. What a mystery it must be ! How incomprehensible ! Nor does it appear, that he has yet completed his description or definition of it. Perhaps he will occupy another half hour on this point. If it requires so long a time to tell what slave-holding is, how long will it require to prove it sinful ?

For the present, I will follow the gentleman in his erratic course. Slave-holding, if we are to believe him, is in itself a most abominable thing. The question very naturally arises—if it be such as he has described it, why debate the question before us at all? One would think, it is only necessary to state what it is, to cause every decent man to loathe it. Then why discuss it? Why not simply state what it is, and go home? One of two things is true: either the relation of master and slave is not in itself what the gentleman represents it, or his friends were guilty of great folly in challenging me to the discussion of it. If the people are so besotted as not to see at a glance its detestable character, there is no use in debating it.

The gentleman repeats the assertion, that the marriage relation cannot exist among slaves; and he tells of a Mr. S., who, in going through a marriage ceremony for them, after the words, "till separated by death," added, "or some other cause beyond your control." In most cases, he tells us, there is not even *the form* of marriage. How has he ascertained this fact? Admitting it true, does it follow that there is no valid marriage among slaves? Will the gentleman tell us what particular form of marriage was prescribed for the Jews? With what ceremonies were Isaac and Rebecca married? Where in the Scriptures is any particular formulary prescribed? and what officer is designated to solemnize marriage? Every one acquainted with the Bible, knows that no particular ceremonies are required, and no officer appointed to solemnize marriage.

But he appeals to the ceremonies at the marriage of Samson, who had a procession and a feast of seven days. Why not go to an earlier period, and inform us by what ceremonies the old patriarchs were married? I presume, he will not deny, that their marriages were valid. But if all the ceremonies connected with Samson's marriage, are essential to the validity of the relation, I fear that very few of us are validly married; for not many, it is presumed, had a procession and a feast of seven days. Mr. B. is quite scandalized that I should deny the necessity of any particular forms or ceremonies to the validity of marriage. I have called for the Bible law on the subject; and he has not yet produced it; and Paul says, "Where there is no law, there is no transgression." The gentleman's argument is, that because the laws of the slave-holding States do not recognize the marriage of slaves, their marriage is not valid, and their children are illegitimate. The truth of this proposition I deny; because the Bible (and marriage is a divine institution) nowhere makes the recognition of the civil law essential to marriage. I assert, that the marriage of slaves is, in God's law, as valid as that of their owners, and it is as truly a violation of that law to separate the former, as the latter. But all this is aside from the question, whether the relation between master and slave is in itself sinful.

The gentleman has twice spoken of my Lectures on Slavery as a *part of this debate,* and as a kind of forestalling of public sentiment. Those Lectures, when delivered, were designed for publication; and the propriety of publishing them became still more apparent, in consequence of the manner in which they were misrepresented and caricatured by certain editors of abolitionist papers in this city. I presume, it will scarcely be questioned, that I had the right to publish them. Moreover, their publication placed before Mr. B. my arguments, and afforded him a fair opportunity to be fully prepared to refute them. He ought not, therefore, to complain.

Mr. Smylie, he says, is competent to testify to the fact, that two-thirds of the professors of religion in the slave-holding States, hold slaves for the sake of gain. I am at a loss to know how any man can be competent to bear testimony concerning the *motives* of all those persons. Doubtless, there are many masters whose sole object is gain; but it is not true, that professing Christians generally *traffic in slaves for gain.* To say so, would be to slander the church of Christ.

He tells a story concerning a sexton of the Presbyterian church in Danville, Ky., who was sold by his master, a member of the church, away from his wife, into Jessamine county. The man's name was Richard. I have had some acquaintance in Danville; and I do not remember to have heard of this Richard, or of any such occurrence. By the way, Jessamine county is not very far from Danville. I should like to have some proof of the truth of this story. I do not believe it; but if such a thing has occurred, and if the session of the church knew it, and neglected to call the master to account, let them be held responsible. It is admitted, that in many churches the discipline is far too lax; and that many cases of improper conduct pass unnoticed, because not brought before the church sessions.

As to the story related by the gentleman concerning the Rev. J. C. Stiles, that on his way to the New-School General Assembly he sold *eight* slaves, and that so far from being disgraced by such conduct, he was appointed to administer the Lord's supper to that assembly, I will say—first, that the gentleman pays a very poor compliment to his general assembly—that body which possesses abundantly "the New-England spirit," which Professor Stowe says, we have driven from our church. Second, I know Mr. Stiles well enough to deny, that he ever sold slaves where they did not wish to live. It may be, that when he removed to Virginia, he sold some; but if he did, it was for the purpose of leaving them with their families; and they were sold to masters of their own choosing. So I believe.

A precisely similar publication concerning the Rev. S. K. Snead, went the rounds of the abolitionist prints, some years since; though Mr. Snead was then an anti-slavery man, if not an abolitionist. He was charged with the cruel treatment of certain slaves that fell into his hands. And a writer for a religious paper in Scotland, who professed to know what he asserted, published as a fact, that in the slave-holding States ministers could, and did, with credit to themselves, choose the Sabbath for inflicting punishment on their slaves, in order to save time; that they would leave their victims tied to the whipping-post, go to the house of God and preach, and administer the Lord's supper, then return and resume their fiendish work! A more outrageous slander never was published to the world. Such are the slanderous tales by which the claims of abolitionism are sought to be sustained.

The gentleman says, that the General Assembly of 1818 passed a law requiring the members of the churches under their care, to instruct their slaves and prepare them for freedom, as soon as prudence would permit their manumission; that Rev. J. D. Paxton, then of Virginia, in obedience to this order of the Assembly, instructed and finally liberated his slaves; and in consequence of this, he was abused and slandered, and was obliged to leave his church and go to a free State. The whole of this statement is untrue. In the first place, the General Assembly *passed no law of the kind.* That body *recommended* to their members to instruct their slaves with a view to their emancipation, so soon as providentially a door could be opened for their freedom; but they passed no *law.* In the next place, it is not true, that Mr. Paxton was slandered, abused, and compelled to leave his church because he instructed and liberated his slaves. He had some difficulty with his church, in consequence of some discourses on the subject of slavery, the precise character of which I do not recollect; and in consequence of difficulties growing out of those discourses, he left his church and removed to Kentucky. The gentleman says this was the only instance in which the *law* of the church was complied with. Now, the fact is notorious, that it is common for Presbyterians to give religious instruction to their slaves, and to emancipate them, and that no one objects to it.

But instead of the appeal to the word of God, which we had a right to expect from a minister of the gospel, discussing a great moral question, we are entertained by stories such as these, the only tendency of which is, by slandering and aggravating slave-holders, to rivet the chains upon the slaves, and, to aggravate all the evils of their condition! As if men were to be induced to free their slaves by being pelted with rotten eggs! If he is resolved to pursue such a course, it is to be hoped that he will, at least, *prove* the facts he asserts. I pledge myself to prove every fact I may have occasion to state, should he call any one of them in question.

Mr. Giddings, he says, produced documentary evidence, that the fugitive slaves in Florida preferred being slaves to the Indians to returning to their white masters. Thus he would prove that the condition of the slaves is growing worse. We should like to see this documentary evidence. I shall believe the assertion when I see it; not before. I protest against the attempt to prove facts by documentary evidence, which Mr. B. cannot produce; especially since it is the uniform testimony of all who have taken the pains to inform themselves, that the condition of the slaves has been greatly improved throughout the slave States within a few years, and that it is still being improved. One of the most humane laws relative to slavery was passed by the Kentucky Legislature, I think, not more than four or five years ago, viz. : that which takes a slave from a cruel master, and places him in better hands. Any individual, knowing that a master treats his slave cruelly, or fails to supply him with sufficient food and raiment, can bring suit against the master, who, if the charges be proved, is obliged to pay all the costs of the suit. Nor would any reproach attach to a person instituting suit in such a case. On the contrary, no man can treat his slaves cruelly in Kentucky, without being scorned by decent men. There are cruel masters, doubtless, in all the slave States; and so there are everywhere men who treat their wives and children cruelly. By the way, I wonder if this Mr. Giddings is the gentleman who, for improper conduct, was expelled from Congress.

The gentleman tells us, that, as civilization advances, the labors of the slaves are more oppressive. This is news to me. I had supposed that the useful discoveries of the present age, were labor-saving machines. I did not know, that they tended only to increase the burdens of the laboring classes.

My friend does not like my speaking of his lack of arguments in support of his proposition. I should really be glad to hear him mention *any one argument* he has adduced to prove slave-holding in itself sinful. In what single instance has he appealed to any rule acknowledged by us as authoritative, to prove this proposition?

But he contends that the relation between master and slave is the creature of law; and he calls on me to say what laws I consider cruel. I am prepared to do so, so soon as he will tell us *what laws are essential to the relation.* He has mentioned a number of oppressive laws, such as place slaves, as he thinks, on a level with brutes. Now will he have the goodness to tell us which of those laws are essential to the relation of master and slave? For we are discussing simply the morality of the relation in itself considered. Does he not know, that there are, and ever have been, cruel laws regulating other relations which in themselves are not sinful? Why does he distinguish between the relations and the particular laws in all other cases, except the one in hand?

He has appealed strongly to the sympathies of the audience, by telling of the girl who was found weeping bitterly, because she saw slaves advertised in connection with swine. Wonder if she would not have wept as bitterly, had she read the following passage of Scripture, in which Abraham's pious servant gives to Laban an account of his master's wealth: "And the Lord hath blessed my master greatly, and he is become great; and he hath given him flocks, and herds, and silver, and gold, *and men-servants, and maid-servants, and camels and asses.*"—*Gen.* xxiv. 35. Men-servants and maid-servants are found precisely in a similar connection in the first chapter of Job. If you say, these are *hired* servants, you prove that the patriarch placed even these amongst brutes! The best plan for the abolitionists would be to denounce the Bible at once, and declare in favor of infidelity!

But let me also appeal to your sympathies. Go to Hindostan, and see the wife made the degraded slave of the husband. She dares not sit in her husband's presence, but must rise and stand. She is considered as a creature without a *soul;* and the law forbids her to read the sacred books. Behold her fastened on the funeral pile of her deceased husband, to be con-

sumed with his dead body! All these cruelties grow out of her
relation to her husband, as that relation is established and recognized by the law. Shall I stand up here, and assert, that all
the oppression and cruelty practiced upon wives in Hindostan or elsewhere, are part and parcel of the conjugal relation,
and that therefore it is in itself sinful? I might say so with
as much truth and propriety, as my friend can assert, that all
the oppressive laws by which slavery is regulated, and all the
cruel treatment of slaves, are part and parcel of the relation
between master and slave, and that therefore it is in itself sinful. This mode of reasoning is perfectly absurd, and is never
admitted in regard to any other relation. I ask the gentleman
whether masters are *obliged* to treat their slaves as badly as
the law permits? Is there a law in Mississippi or in any State,
requiring the master to deny the slave sufficient food and
raiment, or to separate husband and wife? But you say the
law *permits* cruelty. So I say, the law *permits* the husband
to maltreat his wife. Does it follow, that every husband is
chargeable with all the cruelty towards his wife, which the
law permits? It must be so upon the principle on which the
gentleman argues, viz.: that the slave-holder is chargeable
with all the cruelty, which the law permits him to exercise
toward his slaves. Every one is obliged to see the absurdity
of this principle. Hundreds and thousands of masters, guided
by God's law, avoid all such cruelty, and treat their slaves
with uniform kindness. Of course, if Mr. B.'s logic is worth
any thing, they are not slaves. Will he please to inform us
whether cruel treatment is essential to the relation of master
and slave? If it is not, why do we hear so much from him
on this subject? If cruelty is not essential to the relation,
then the relation may exist without it. Then why does he so
constantly harp upon the cruelties practiced by wicked men,
as if they were of the essence of the relation? But if he
asserts, that such cruelties are essential to the relation of master and slave; I reply, that the members of the Presbyterian
church are forbidden by the law of the church to treat their
servants cruelly; and therefore they, not being guilty, are not

slave-holders. So that his argument fails, if we take it either way. If cruelty is not essential to the relation, his declamation about cruelty proves nothing against it; if it is, our members are not slave-holders, and therefore are not exposed to his denunciations. Let the gentleman, then, denounce the cruelty practiced by wicked men, and let the relation alone; or let him admit, that those masters who are not cruel, are not slave-holders.

But, says Mr. B., (by way of exciting your sympathies,) when you make a man a slave, you have treated him as cruelly as possible. The law which makes him a slave, is of all laws the most cruel. The question before us, is not whether it is sinful to reduce a free man to a state of slavery. The question is concerning the duty of masters to a class of people, unrighteously enslaved by others. How far are they bound to manumit them at once without regard to circumstances? Can they be immediately liberated, consistently with their own good, or with the safety of society? This is the question. And let it be remarked, that, although those who enslaved the Africans, were by no means guiltless, yet there is no slave in America, who would not greatly prefer being a slave here, to being placed in the condition in which his fathers were, and in which he would have been in Africa. The slaves, therefore, have been more benefitted than injured by their removal to this country; and the question now arises—how far are masters bound, without regard to circumstances, immediately to give them their liberty?

Suppose all the slave-holding States were disposed, immediately, to abolish slavery; would the condition of the slaves be thereby improved? It is, in my opinion, a very debateable question. In very many instances, those who have been liberated amongst the whites, have turned out badly. Often, their condition is found to be worse than that of the slaves. They are thrown upon their own resources, without property, and without habits of industry and economy; and they know not how to provide for themselves. Suppose the whole slave population thus turned loose, what would be the result? On this subject the General Assembly, of the Presbyterian church, in 1818, said—

"As our country has inflicted a most grievous injury on the unhappy Africans, by bringing them into slavery, we cannot, indeed, urge that we should add a second injury to the first, by emancipating them in such a manner as that they will be likely to destroy themselves or others."

But all these things are entirely aside from the question before us. We are not discussing the duty of States, in reference to slavery, but the duty of *individuals*, whilst the system of slavery, as it is called, continues. Is it a sin for any individual, under any circumstances, to buy and hold a slave? Suppose, for example, I buy a slave from a cruel master, at his own earnest request, will you denounce me as a heinous sinner, and exclude me from the church? What injury have I inflicted on the slave? I did not reduce him to his present condition. My only sin in the case, is, that I have *improved his condition*. Is this a crime for which a man is to be excluded from the church as a robber and a man-stealer? Such cases are numerous. A slave, owned by a cruel master, who is about to separate him from his family, earnestly implores a Christian to buy him, and allow him to serve him, that he may live with his family. The Christian has not *five hundred* dollars to give him as a present; but he can purchase him, and take his services for his money. Thus, though he cannot put him into a condition so pleasant as he would desire, he does actually very much improve it.

To illustrate the principle, a poor man comes to you to beg assistance. You give him according to your ability, thus to some extent improving his condition. Are you chargeable with crime because you did not give him a fortune?

But, suppose a master to refuse to separate husbands and wives, provide abundant food and raiment, and carefully instruct his slaves in the doctrines and truths of Christianity; are they still slaves? Certainly, the relation of master and slave may exist without cruelty. The law, making men slaves, says the gentleman, is cruel. Admit it. You cannot, however, charge any *individual* with making such laws. But since the law exists, and the slaves have been brought into their present condition, how far may we, for the public good, continue to hold them in that condition? This question has been pressed upon Mr. B., and he has given no satisfactory answer. He says, we may deprive them of the right to *vote*. We may make laws for them. But by what rule of morals, I ask, does he stop there? Does the Bible furnish any such principle? If we may so far consult our safety, and the public good, as to prevent them from *voting*, why may we not, if the public safety require it, go further?

It is my purpose to keep distinctly before the audience the real question at issue. 1. It is not whether it is right to reduce free men to a state of slavery; but what is our duty to a class of men who were made slaves before we were born. How far may we consult our safety and the public good in our treatment of them? 2. It is not whether the laws of the slave-holding States, or of any one of them, are just. Let the gentleman prove, that cruel laws are essential to the relation between master and slave; and I will give up the question. 3. The question is not whether it is right for masters to treat their slaves as *things*, as *chattels*, or oppress them in any way. There is no controversy on this point. But do all masters, in fact, so treat their slaves? We deny that they do. 4. The question is not whether slavery is an *evil*. This is admitted; but all evils do not imply sin in those connected with them; nor can we at once free society from all existing evils. 5. The question, I repeat, is not concerning the *true policy of the several States.* Admit it to be the true policy and the duty of the State of Kentucky, at once to emancipate all her slaves; the question arises, how far are individuals responsible for existing laws? Every citizen of the State is responsible so far, and only so far, as his influence and his vote go to improve such laws. But what is the duty of *individuals* so long as the system continues? This is the question. 6. We are not discussing the question whether *the system of American slavery,* as it is called, is right or wrong. Distinction, says the venerable Dr. Chalmers, ought to be made between a *system* and individuals unwillingly involved in it.

7. The real question is, whether the relation between master and slave, divested of every thing not essential to it, is sinful? I have defined slave-holding to be the claim of one man to the services of another, with the corresponding obligation to provide him comfortable food and raiment, and suitable religious instruction; and I have called on the gentleman to show what there is in it beyond this claim to services. What have I omitted in this definition? Is the relation, upon which this claim is based, in itself sinful? If it is, as already remarked, it must be at once abandoned, without regard to circumstances; gradual emancipation is out of the question. I repeat what I have before said, that if the tendency of abolitionism, were to liberate the slaves and improve their condition, I would be the last to oppose it. But my clear conviction is, that its tendency and its effects are to rivet the chains upon them, and to aggravate every evil attending their condition.

I have now presented three distinct arguments against the doctrine of abolitionism—that slave-holding is in itself sinful; and Mr. B. has made no attempt to reply to either of them. I wish to keep them before the audience. They are the following:

1. The great principles of the moral law are written upon the hearts of men, so that, when presented, they do commend themselves to the consciences and the understandings of all, if we except the most degraded and depraved; but the doctrine that slave-holding is in itself sinful, has not so commended itself, even to the great body of wise and good men, to whose minds it has been presented; therefore it is not true. Does any man, for a moment, doubt whether it is sinful to lie, to steal, or to murder? None. But abolitionists assert, that slave-holding is one of the grossest, and most aggrava-

ted violations of the moral law, of which men can be guilty; nay, that to be a slave-holder, is to be guilty of murder, adultery, and indeed to violate every commandment in the decalogue. Now, it is a fact, that the great body of wise and good men, commentators, critics and theologians, have declared their conviction that it is not in itself sinful. Now, one or two things is true : Either the great principles of the moral law do not commend themselves to the understandings and consciences of men ; or abolitionism, which never has so commended itself, is false.

2. My second argument was this: it is an admitted truth, that you never find an individual, or a society, corrupt and heretical on one fundamental point in morals, or in Christian faith, and sound in all others. He who is rotten on one fundamental principle of the moral law, is a corrupt man, and will prove it by disregard of others. The same principle holds good in regard to the doctrines of Christianity. But it is an admitted fact, that the ministers and churches in the slave-holding States, are as sound in the faith, and as pure in morals on all other points, as any abolitionist. Now, if this principle be true, it follows, that those ministers and churches are a most remarkable class of hypocrites, or abolitionism is false. I assert, that the history of the world does not furnish an example to conflict with the principle I have stated. It is, therefore, clear, that abolitionism is false.

3. My third argument was: that there are Christian ministers and Christian churches, who are involved in slave-holding, but who, nevertheless, are owned and blessed of God. I was truly pleased to hear the gentleman admit, that there may be, and probably are, Christian slave-holders even better than himself. Prof. Stowe, as before stated, though an abolitionist, declares that he has evidence that there are slave-holding Christians and churches, whom Christ has accepted. Moreover, it is a fact, that many of the most efficient ministers in the free States were converted, if converted at all, in revivals in those slave-holding churches, and in answer to the prayers of those slave-holding Christians. Now, one of three

things is true, viz: God hears the prayers and blesses the labors of the most abominable criminals; or those revivals are all spurious, and the converts are hypocrites; or aboli-tionism is false.

The gentleman is at liberty to take either of the three posi-tions. I hope, he will take one or another of them decidedly. As yet he has made no attempt to reply to this argument. I regret that he has not. I am prepared to present other arguments; but my purpose was to occupy my appropriate position as respondent, and follow him. Since, however, I cannot do this, I will proceed to offer my

4th argument, founded upon what has been termed *the golden rule.* "Therefore all things whatsoever ye would that men should do to you, do you even so to them." *Matt.* vii. 12. This law, it is contended, proves slave-hold-ing in itself sinful; and indeed it is the great argument of abolitionists. What is the meaning of it? It does not mean, that we must do for others every thing which they may suppose, we ought to do; but it does require us to do for others what we would reasonably expect and desire them to do for us, if the case were reversed, and we were in their condition. I acknowledge, that this rule requires us to im-prove the condition of every fellow-being, just so far as we can, consistently with other paramount duties. Let us, then, apply the rule, as thus interpreted, to the subject in hand.— There, for example, is a slave belonging to a cruel master, who is about to separate him from his family. The case has already been presented. He earnestly begs you to pur chase him, and allow him to serve you, because thereby you will do him a great favor, and greatly improve his condition. The price demanded is five hundred or six hundred dollars. You do not wish to purchase a slave; and you have not that amount of money to give him as a present. But you can purchase him, and take his services for your money. This he begs you to do. With much trouble, it may be, you raise the amount of money demanded. The slave is purchased. He thanks God for his improved condition, and blesses the man who saved him from being torn from those he loves. Now enter your charge against the purchaser. Will you say, he has reduced a free man to slavery? No— he was already a slave. Will you say, he has made his condition more intolerable than it was? No—he has greatly improved it; *and this is his sin, if he have sinned at all!* But will you say, that, having conferred one favor, a very great favor, upon this slave, who had no special claims upon him, he is now bound to confer a second and greater favor, by emancipating him? O but, say the abolitionists, if you *enslave* a man, you do him a great wrong. I deny that the purchaser *enslaved* him. He was a slave before. Now let the gentleman place himself for a moment in the condition of such a slave, and tell us what he would desire to have done for him. He has already let us know, that he loves his family; and, doubtless, much as he loves liberty, he loves them more. I know what I would wish a man to do for me, were I in such a situation. I would desire him to purchase me, and allow me to serve him; and I would esteem him a benefactor indeed. Then am I not bound by the golden rule to purchase him? So far is that rule from forbidding slave-holding under all circumstances, that under circumstances such as I have supposed, and such as often occur, it makes even the most benevolent men holders of slaves. Yet according to the doctrine of abolitionists, slave-holders are the greatest criminals, and deserve to be executed by the common hangman !

Take another case. Suppose, as it not unfrequently happens, a man has fallen heir to some fifty or more slaves, of different ages. He desires now to do the very best for them. What must he do? Abolitionists say, he must forthwith liberate them. But there are difficulties in the way. Some are old and helpless; others are women and children who are incapable of supporting themselves. Shall he turn them all loose to provide for themselves? But the law, even in Kentucky, says, he must first give bond and security, in an amount sufficient to secure the State against their becoming

a public expense. Is it the duty of a man to give such
security for the support of a large number of slaves of different ages? With me, as a minister of the gospel, it is a
fixed rule never to become security for others, nor to ask
others to become securities for me. Without departing from
this rule, I could not liberate slaves whom I might inherit.
But suppose, as it not unfrequently happens, that a man
possesses little property except the inherited slaves; who
will be willing to become his security for such an amount
as the civil law requires? Would it be his duty to ask
any one to run such a risk ?

Some years since, when this subject was under discussion
in the Synod of Kentucky, an elder rose in his place, and
stated, that he owned, I think, about one hundred slaves, the
most if not all of whom he had inherited. Some of them
were far advanced in life, and could not provide for themselves ; others were women and children whom no one would
feed and cloth for their labor. He said, he had no desire to
hold them as slaves, but wished to do the very best for them.
If he should manumit them all, what would become of the
aged, and of the women and children? Besides, it was a serious matter to give bond and security for the support of so
many of different ages and character. He could not remove
them out of the State; for they were inter-married with the
slaves of others ; and as to giving them wages, he said, taking
them all together *they were eating him up.* With anxious feelings he asked the brethren who urged immediate emancipation, what he ought to do. And now I ask the gentleman
to tell us what *the golden rule* required him to do. Will he
enlighten us on this subject ? Was it his duty to turn them
out to take care of themselves? Then what would become
of the aged and infirm, and of the women and children?
Was it his duty to separate husbands and wives, parents and
children, and remove them to Ohio? But even in Ohio, this
land of liberty, of which the gentleman has spoken so eloquently, your laws require, that when a colored person proposes to reside in any county in the State, he shall, within

twenty days after coming into the county, obtain two free-holders as securities for his support and good conduct.

Or take the case of a man owning slaves in the more southern States, the laws of which forbid him to manumit his slaves, unless he will remove them out of the State; what is the duty of such a man·? A case precisely in point has recently occurred. A gentleman, I think, in Boston, fell heir to a plantation and a number of slaves in the South. He wrote to the person who had the management of the business, that he would not own the slaves. But he was informed, that he could not liberate them, unless he should remove them out of the State. After much perplexity in regard to his duty in the matter, he concluded to go and live with them, and do for them the best he could. Did he violate the letter or the spirit of the golden rule?

Wednesday Evening, 9 o'clock.

[MR. BLANCHARD'S FOURTH SPEECH.]

Gentlemen Moderators, and Gentlemen and Ladies, Fellow Citizens:

I will employ my half hour, first, in briefly adverting to some things which my friend has said in his last speech, and then proceeding with my argument. I wish to answer, categorically and briefly, some questions which he propounded: and I will here state the reason why I do not prolong my replies to his remarks, in order that I may not seem to treat his arguments with disrespect. My plan is this:— Where I have an argument in my brief which meets what he advances, I do not reply to that point as I go along, but wait until it assumes its proper place in my course of remark. For instance, I have a distinct argument on the "golden rule," which I have prepared with some care. I have, also, others upon different points touched upon by my brother; and I hope that in the three days before us, we shall have time to learn a variety of things, if we possess our souls in patience.

He asks me to show him a man, orthodox in all points of faith but one, and heterodox in that. I answer, that the Scribes and Pharisees were orthodox while they "sat in Moses' seat;" and our Savior himself bade the people hear them, and to "do what they said." But they were heterodox in the one point of rejecting the Lord Jesus Christ, their Messiah. Him they rejected because he was poor, obscure and unpopular. And I fear that some reject that same Lord in the person of the despised, stricken slave, and for a like reason.

He asked, also, concerning the civil rights of negroes, how far we may go in curtailing the rights of man before the sin begins? I answer as I did before, governments may, for just reasons, withhold civil rights without sin. He told you, and truly, that I spoke of the right of voting as a commodity which the community has a right to dispose of, with an eye on its own preservation. This, I believe, is not only true, but commonly believed. I ask, is the Irishman a slave, after landing in this country, and before he obtains his right to vote? I think, if you were to tell the Irishman or honest German that he was a slave, because not yet naturalized, he would be apt to show you a large pair of hands. Is there any similarity whatever between the unnaturalized foreigner's condition and that of a slave? The fact that my brother is in perplexity on this point, shows how slavery blinds and blunts the minds of good men, even on the subject of human rights. "How far may we go in restricting human liberty without necessarily sinning?" I answer: We may go till we come to "*certain inalienable rights; among which are life, liberty, and the pursuit of happiness.*"— *That* is "how" far we may go in curtailing men's rights without sin. He inquires, with all simplicity, "if we control civil, why not natural rights also?" Why not, as lawfully, go a step farther, and make the man a slave? If you may, for good reasons take away his vote, why not his services also? Because "God hath created all men free and equal, and hath endowed them with certain INALIENA- BLE rights!"—rights which they may not lay down— which no man, or body of men, called a Legislature, can take away without sin! This is WHY we may not make men slaves! This was the very point on which this country and Great Britain were at issue in the American Revolution. It was not the actual oppression suffered, but the principle in- volved, which caused the war. The Americans declared that men had some rights which the Legislature might not touch; while Parliament held that its power over the sub- ject's rights was limited only by its own discretion: and, with his present principles, my friend would have been found in that struggle shouldering, cheek by jowl, in goodly fellowship with Lord North, or the later Castlereagh.

The "good of society," then, may, for just reasons, pro- ceed in restricting men's rights, till it arrives at rights which are inalienable: and then, "hands off!" Property may go for taxes till you touch the means of life, if just necessity require. But you must not take out of the man himself, the right to acquire and own property. You may justly gov- ern and restrain men's bodies, but not mutilate their minds.

> "But for the soul! O, tremble and beware!
> To lay rude hands upon God's mysteries there!"

My friend told you that I said one thing which was incor- rect. Gentlemen, for the honor of Christianity, and the Christian ministry, I wish to avoid any thing like contra- diction with my brother; and I shall strive, so far as possi- ble, to do so. I had stated that the General Assembly, of 1818, adopted a law requiring its members to educate their slaves, and prepare them for emancipation. He replies, that the Assembly passed no such law, but only adopted a sim- ple recommendation. Now, I read from my friend's printed lectures; remarking, first, that though I was reared in the Congregational church, yet I have been Presbyterian long enough to know that the word "enjoin" carries the force of a law in the Presbyterian church.   My respected friend must, also, know it.   I now quote the act of the General Assembly, from " Rice's Lectures," page 17 :

" The law of the Presbyterian church, on this subject, is clear and explicit.   In 1818, the General Assembly gave the following injunction to all church sessions and presbyteries under their care.

'We *enjoin* it on all church sessions and presbyteries, to discountenance, and, as far as possible, prevent, all cruelty to slaves; especially, the cruelty of separating husband and wife, ect"

Certainly, the word enjoin, carries the force of law to Presbyterian ears; and I was correct in calling the Act of 1818 a "*law of the church.*"

The words of the Assembly are, " We enjoin," etc.   But, that you may not suppose that I rest on church technicalities, I read from the Act of the General Assembly itself, quoted in "*Rice's Lectures,*" same page:—" The manifest violation or disregard of the injunction here given, in its true spirit and intention, ought to be considered as just ground for the discipline and censure, of the Church."   Yet he tells us that this Act of 1818 is not a "*law,*" but an *exhortation.*   Surely, my friend must have forgotten, in the multitude of his engagements, what he printed a month ago!

My friend cautions me, with some little parade, against what he thinks the fault of abolitionists, viz: the making of assertions against slavery, without proof.   I have read my proofs, where proofs were required.   Yet all that I have said, or can say, is not a blister, to the bloody inflictions of slavery; inflictions, the merciless reality of which, I pledge myself to establish, if necessary: and you may remember, and see if I redeem my pledge.

Mr. Rice read to you, from a Scotch paper, " The Witness," what he calls a false and abusive statement, respecting slave-holders' cruelty, to the effect that ministers might whip slave women cruelly before preaching on the Sabbath, without disgrace.   I suppose that story was taken from the

statement of Rev. James Nourse, of Mifflin county, Pennsylvania, a brother whom I know, and who declares, in
substance, that upon a visit to a brother minister, he found,
tied to the post in front of his house, a woman, with her
neck and shoulders bare, whom the brother minister was
about to flog. Mr. Nourse plead with the brother minister
not to whip her; but he did not defer the chastisement, even
for the sake of his visiter, but proceeded to the infliction,
in his presence. He applied the raw-hide with such force
that the welts rose upon her back, under every lash.

Now, if ministers, under the restraints of reputation, and
in the presence of visiters, when offending children commonly escape, can inflict such scourgings upon women,—if
these things are done in the green tree, what may be done
in the dry?—out of sight, in the garret, or cellar, and when
no visiters are present?

My friend said, also, with an apparent candor which
touched my heart, that if I could show that these cruelties,
such as the practice of forbidding slaves to read, and the
separation of families, were not mere adjuncts, but integral
parts of slavery, he would go with me, for immediate abolition. If he will stand by that pledge, I do not despair
that we may yet hold abolition meetings together. For
you all can see, that if, for example, the sheriff were not
allowed to sell slaves on execution without regarding family
ties, the property-holding power would soon be abraded and
wasted away : or if administrators were not permitted to sell
separately at auction the slaves of an intestate ; the same results. If men were compelled to sell six or eight horses in a
bunch whenever they sell one, is it not plain that it would
lower and nearly destroy the property value of horses ?
But I have prepared an argument expressly on that point:
and I trust in God that he will give me strength to present
it in its place.

I now resume the course of my argument. I was showing that slavery in law, is slavery in fact, that the slave's actual condition is that of property. And the next proof which

I bring, is the fact that *the State pays for the slaves which it hangs.* See the Kentucky law of 1798. "When courts within this commonwealth shall determine that any slave shall suffer death according to law," &c. The auditor is to issue his warrant for the value of said slave, and the State treasurer is to pay the same to the owner on the clerk's presentation of the sheriff's certificate of the slave's sentence and execution!

This shows that the property law is a law "stronger than death;" that it outlives the slave, and is executed after he is in eternity!

My last argument, showing that slaves are actual property, is, that the reported cases in the books, are full of instances, showing that practical slavery is what theoretical, legal slavery is, viz: the human species made property. In the Supreme Court of Tennessee, in 1834, there came up for judgment the following case, to wit:

Frederick, a slave of Col. Patton, of the North Carolina line, with his master's consent, *enlisted and fought through the war of the American revolution.* Now, if ever there was an instance where the Shylock's bond of human flesh might have been relaxed—where the *laws* of slavery might have been mitigated in practice—it ought to have been in the case of this veteran slave soldier. Gentlemen and fellow-citizens, I beg you will mark the illustration of the slave-condition which this case affords. On the 8th of August, 1821, as Frederick's name was found in the muster roll, a warrant was issued to Frederick, giving him the soldier's bounty of one thousand acres of land. The question before the Court was, whether that thousand acres of land belonged to Frederick, or to his master? Remember, now, that this is not a statute which I am reading, but an adjudged case. JUDGE CATRON's decision is in these words: "Frederick, the slave of Col. Patton, earned this warrant by his services in the Continental line. What is earned by the slave belongs to the master by the common law, the civil law, and the recognized rules of property in the slave-holding States of this Union." This decision is a triple legal cord, binding Frederick to the condition of a brute ! *The land went not to Frederick, but to the heirs of Col. Patton.*

Aye, gentlemen, seven years' fighting for his country's liberties, could not, and did not, entitle Frederick to be considered a man. Nor could service during the war of the Revolution entitle him to soil enough in the country which his courage had helped to save, to bury his broken heart in. When this war-worn veteran returns home, amid a nation's shouts for liberty, and finds that, in the midst of those whom his toil, and sufferings, and dangers have made free, *he is still a slave !*

> " O shall we scoff at Europe's kings,
>   While freedom's fire is dim with us ;
> And round our country's altar clings
>   The damning shade of slavery's curse ?
> Go ! Let us ask of Constantine
>   To loose his hold on Poland's throat,
> Or beg the Lord of Mammouhd's line
>   To spare the struggling Suliote.
> Will not the scorching answer come,
>   From turban'd Turk and fiery Russ ;
> ' Go ! Loose your fetter'd slaves at home—
>   Then turn and ask the like of us ? ' "

Oh ! Sirs, " I tremble for my country when I remember that God is just! and that his justice will not sleep forever."

Gentlemen and fellow-citizens, I have done with this branch of my argument. I will simply recapitulate the points which I have sought to establish. First—that slaves are not only theoretically, but actually, in a property condition. The chattelizing statute—the frequent Legislatures adding to and repealing parts of the slave code—the laws made for enforcing and regulating this chattelship—sheriffs and administrators advertizing slaves with cattle, swine, and other property—the laws licensing auctioneers, and declaring slaves to be merchandize—the fact that the laws to protect the master's property-right in slaves, provide carefully for their own execution by paying prosecutors, informers, &c., while no such provision is made to execute laws which pretend to protect the lives or limbs of slaves—the fact that slaves convicted of crimes are not punished by the human penal code, but according to the punishment of brutes—that slaves are by law forbidden all weapons of defence, even to possessing a club—that slaves criminally executed are paid for by the State—and that slaves fighting for their country through the American Revolution cannot gain a title to a foot of soldier's bounty land, nor even to the ragged regimentals which they have worn out in the service—all these facts show, if aught can show, that the American slaves are actual as well as legal property. And when professed ministers of Christ vindicate the holding of slaves in this condition, and then tell the public that they are opposed to holding slaves as "mere" property, they discredit either their heads, or their hearts, or both. They must be, as I humbly conceive, either unfeeling men, or men wedded to error.

I now take up a second branch of my argument. My friend has said that "in Kentucky the slave has the same protection that the child has." — *Rice's Lectures, p.* **17.** And you have observed how he is constantly struggling to put in the slavery-relation among the holy domestic and home-bred relations of our race, such as marriage and parentage ; I must be excused for saying that there is nothing which I have so prayed for, as for patience—while listening to sentiments like these from my brother's mouth. Marriage is a relation God-given, and Heaven-derived ;—instituted in Eden ; and, thanks to the most merciful God, not taken away from our race at their fall. I have remembered the sweet assemblage of holy sanctities which belong to the marriage hour. When the young man first trembles to find her leaning upon him, who shall thenceforth lean upon him throughout after life : when both bow in the consummation of that union which each hopes will be perfected in heaven by a union of both in Christ. And when I heard him tell me that I have no better relation to my wife than the slaveholder to the miserable object of his avarice or his lust, I have

wept! and inly prayed to God for such strength of body
and powers of mind, as will enable me to show this monstrous doctrine in its true light. I wish to show that the
slavery relation is piratical and contraband ; that it has no
more business among the sacred relations of the family than
the Devil had in Eden. To class it among them is a sentiment alien from God and man, and unworthy of human
lips. My whole argument thus far has been on the naked
question:—What is this relation of master and slave ;—and
how it stands related to the gospel of Christ, which is the
" kingdom of heaven " on earth? I shall go steadily forward ; and if my friend, as he says, cannot find enough to
answer me as we go along, let him sing anthems, and wait.
[Applause.] I am here to show that this relation of master
and slave is not a natural relation. That it has no foundation in natural law. I stand with the pious John Wesley,
and exclaim, " I strike at the root of this complicated villai-
ny. I absolutely deny all slave-holding to be consistent with
any degree of natural equity."—*Thoughts on Slavery.*

And it falls directly in my course to examine at length
the proposition of my opponent that in Kentucky slaves are
protected as children are. What does my brother mean
when he says that *"In Kentucky the slave has the same protection that a child has?"* Upon what principle is he opposed to slavery, if he believes the relation in itself not sinful, and that the slaves have the same protection that children have? And what becomes of him if I show that he
has deliberately made a statement so grave and momentous,
without any authority whatever, and that his whole pamphlet is made up of such statements?

My brother knows that, in Kentucky, the slave child has
no legal parents to protect it. Slaves have no legal marriage:
that the slave has no family; that his wife is the property
of another man; that his children are sold, at the master's
will, to the cotton-field and sugar-plantation of the South.—
What does he mean? Is parental protection nothing? Almost
every free child in Kentucky is connected more or less with

property; and " money," says Solomon," is a defence." (I have quoted one Scripture, at all events.) [A laugh.] But slaves can have no legal connection with any property whatever. Is the protection of property nothing? Further: the slave child has no legal father, mother, uncle, aunt, or grand-parent, brother, sister, or cousin; whilst the free child has some or all of them. Are all these nothing? Will Dr. Rice say that some slaves have families, and that in the eye of God they are married? What protection does the law of Kentucky give them in that relation? That is the point. For he says, " *In Kentucky, the slave has the same protection that the child has.*"—*Lectures,* p. 17.

I wish you to put down a pin at this place, for I am going to show, that this declaration, thus deliberately uttered, and afterward printed by him, that, " in Kentucky the slave has the same protection that the child has," is made totally without all authority, and is as perfectly opposed to the truth as any proposition which can be put into human language.

[*Time expired.*

———

Wednesday Evening, 9 1-2 o'clock.

[MR. RICE'S FOURTH SPEECH.]

Gentlemen Moderators, and Fellow-Citizens:

I will not charge the gentleman with intentional departure from the truth; yet I am constrained to expose two very gross misstatements in his last speech. I have long since learned that abolitionism cannot sustain itself, except by weapons of this kind. It does not march up to the question, and rely upon sound argument and established facts. The gentleman stated, that the General Assembly of 1818 passed a law requiring slave-holders in their communion to prepare their slaves for freedom, and then to manumit them.

Mr. BLANCHARD here explained. I did not say so, but said, "with a view to set them free."

Mr. RICE. The explanation does not remove the difficulty.

The Assembly, he says, passed a law requiring the members of these churches to prepare their slaves for freedom, with a view to their liberation. I denied that any such *law* was passed. Mr. B. produced my Lectures on Slavery, and told you, he would quote "Dr. Rice" against himself; but he took care not to read the quotation. I beg leave to supply his "lack of service." The language of the Assembly is as follows:

" We enjoin it on all church sessions and presbyteries under the care of this Assembly, to discountenance, and as far as possible, to prevent all cruelty, of whatever kind, in the treatment of slaves: especially the cruelty of separating husband and wife, parents and children; and that which consists in selling slaves to those who will either themselves deprive these unhappy people of the blessings of the gospel, or will transport them to places where the gospel is not proclaimed, or where it is forbidden to slaves to attend upon its institutions."

It is true, the Assembly enjoined something; but what is it? That body enjoined it upon sessions and presbyteries to prevent all cruelty in the treatment of slaves by the members of their churches; but where is the injunction to prepare them for freedom? This was *recommended,* not *enjoined.* Yet the gentleman turned to the very page on which this quotation was found. I hope, for his own sake, he had not read it. I expose this matter that you may see how carelessly he makes bold assertions. The *injunction* of which he spoke is not here; as he would have proved, had he read the quotation which he commenced reading. Why did he stop so suddenly?

But, he has also misrepresented my statement, that the slave in Kentucky has the same protection which the child has. I spoke, as the connection will show, only of protection from cruel treatment. If a father can be proved to have treated his child cruelly, he is liable to suffer the penalty of the law; and if a master can be proved guilty of cruel treatment of his slave, he is likewise liable to prosecution before the civil tribunal. So that the slave has the same protection from cruelty from his master, which the child has from cruelty from his father. If the gentleman so glaringly misrepresents what is before his eyes, or what he has just heard, how can we rely on his statement of facts?

My second argument against abolitionism was founded on the fact, that individuals or associations, are never found to be heretical on one fundamental principle of morality, or one fundamental doctrine of Christianity, and sound on all others. I called on Mr. B. to produce an exception to the statement. He gives as such an exception *the Pharisees* in our Savior's time! They, he tells us, were orthodox on all points but one, viz: the rejection of the promised Messiah! Never before did I hear a minister of the gospel assert, that the Pharisees were orthodox on all points but one. Did not the Savior charge them with tithing mint, anise, and cummin, and neglecting " the weightier matters of the law, justice, judgment and mercy?" Did he not compare them to "whited sepulchres," and charge them with cleansing " the outside of the cup and platter," whilst they left the inside in its filth? Did they not wholly err in regard to the nature and design of the ceremonial law, relying upon the strict observance of its ceremonies for justification and salvation? Nay—in rejecting Jesus Christ as an impostor, did they not necessarily reject every distinguishing doctrine of his gospel? Being ignorant or God's righteousness, they went about to establish their own righteousness. The gentleman knows they were in gross error concerning almost every fundamental doctrine of revelation; and yet he produces them to prove, that men may be heretical on one fundamental principle of morals or doctrine of the gospel, and yet orthodox on all others! These are the men who are compared with the Christians of the slave-holding States, who are admitted to be sound on all points of doctrine and morals, unless they err concerning the sin of slave-holding! Verily, the gentleman needs the applause of his friends to enforce such arguments!

I have called on Mr. B. to inform us by what principle

of morality he, whilst admitting the right of the slaves to be equal with their masters, proposes to deprive them of the right to *vote*—to aid in making the laws under which they live; and, if he may go so far, why not go farther? In reply he asks, are the German emigrants *slaves* before they are permitted to vote? And then he tells us of "inalienable rights," viz: "life, liberty, and the pursuit of happiness"— Does he not know that the Declaration of Independence, which he so freely quotes, was drawn up in view of, and because of, the fact, that the British Government insisted on taxing us without our consent? Was it not on this account that those noble spirits of the Revolution sunk their tea into the ocean? Did not the authors of the Declaration of Independence regard it as one of their "inalienable rights" to aid in making the laws by which they were to be governed? Yet the gentleman intimates that we may prevent the colored people from voting, may make laws for them, and impose taxes on them, without infringing their "inalienable rights!" If this be true, of what worth is the Declaration of Independence? He quotes that noble instrument as declaring that " all men are born free and equal " How can he carry out this doctrine, and yet allow one class of men to impose laws and taxes upon another, without allowing them a voice? Is there one kind of freedom, of "inalienable rights," for the blacks, and another for the whites? After all the gentleman's declamation about the Declaration of Independence, and " the one-bloodism of the New Testament," he admits that he is not unwilling to deprive the African race of the right to vote and hold civil offices; thus, " for the public good," abandoning his own principles!

Mr. B made another statement concerning the cruelty of Christian slave-holders, which is about as correct as those already exposed. I refer to the story, he said, was related by Rev. Jas. Nourse, of Mifflin county, Pa. I have no personal acquaintance with Mr. Nourse; but I have just been informed by a gentleman in the house, who was a member

of Mr. N.'s church, that he heard him deny having said that
he witnessed any such cruelty.

Mr. Blanchard.—Please to name him.

Mr Rice.—Mr. James Lindsay, now a member of the
Central Presbyterian Church, of this city.

But admitting this story to be literally true, does it afford
any ground for the charge, that Christians are *commonly*
guilty of such conduct? Such a charge would be an
outrageous slander on the ministers of Jesus Christ. Yet
these isolated cases are constantly paraded by abolitionists as
characteristic of slave-holding amongst professing Christians
generally. Thus are the church of Christ and his ministers
traduced and slandered by the pretended friends of human
rights! I cannot say, of course, that Mr. B. does not believe those improbable tales, for he seems to have a wonderful facility for believing whatever favors his views on this
subject.

He promises to prove that laws forbidding slaves to read
are essential to the existence of slavery. Then he will
prove more than he wishes; for, it so happens, that in Kentucky there are no such laws. He will prove, therefore,
that, in Kentucky, there is no slavery; for the laws of that
State, according to his logic, lack one essential ingredient of
slavery. And in Virginia, whatever may be the letter of
the law, slaves are, in many instances, taught to read. Possibly we may, as the gentleman suggests, yet lecture together; for he is likely to prove Kentucky a free State! Let
him only maintain the position, that a law forbidding slaves
to read, is essential to the existence of the relation between
master and slave, and I will, at once, prove that there is no
slavery in Kentucky!

But the State makes the slave *property*, even after he is
dead, says Mr. B.; and hence, he infers the sinfulness of
the relation between master and slave. Is the master responsible for all the laws of the State? Would not Mr. B.
rebel, if he were held responsible for all the legislation of
the State of Ohio? Yet where is the difference? Why is

not he as justly responsible for the laws of Ohio, as the slave-holder for the laws of his State? Abolitionism can sustain itself only by charging upon individuals all the injustice of the State, and holding them responsible for all that the State permits. All the bad laws of Louisiana, he contends, are part and parcel of the relation, and are essential to it; and the relation is sinful, because the laws are oppressive. Yet when I prove that some of those laws do not exist in Kentucky, he insists that the relation, to which they are essential, still exists! We cannot but see that there is no candor in such reasoning.

We are now about to close a discussion of *six hours* on the question: "Is slave-holding in itself sinful, and the relation between master and slave a sinful relation?" And although this question can be determined only by an appeal to the Bible, the gentleman in the affirmative has not quoted even a solitary passage from that book, if, perhaps, we except that in which the wise man says, *money is power.*— The argument, I presume, would be this: money is power; therefore, slave-holding is in itself sinful! How conclusive! It is truly marvellous that he has not thought it worth while to quote one passage from the only rule which he and I acknowledge as infallible, by way of proving his proposition!

As I have nothing to reply to, it may be interesting to the audience to hear a brief recapitulation of the gentleman's arguments. He began with the melancholy interest he felt because of the slave gang which passed near Cincinnati, a few days since. 2. He spoke of the condition of the slaves on the plantations in the South. 3. He complained of their lack of *patronymics*, that they are called Jim, Polly, &c., seeming to forget, that in this respect they were not more degraded, than Abraham, Isaac and Jacob. 4. He told us, that Mr. Leavit said, the free States are made to support slavery; and Dr. Bailey calculated the taxes imposed upon the free States on account of slavery. 5. He told us how dear liberty is to Ohio, and dilated upon the constitutions of Ohio, Illinois and Indiana. 6. He declaimed against the sin of reducing free men to a state of slavery, concerning which, by the way, there is no difference of opinion. 7. He told us of Sally Muller and some other girl, who, being free, were kidnapped and held in slavery. 8. He gave us Aristotle's definition of slavery together with a dissertation on Roman slavery. 9. He quoted from Delaney a legal definition of slavery. 10. He asserted and repeated, that amongst slaves the marriage relation cannot exist, and their children are illegitimate. This assertion he finds it very difficult to prove. 11. He declares the slaves not validly married, because the civil law does not recognize their marriage. But when pressed to prove by the word of God, that the recognition of the civil law is necessary to the validity of marriage, he could give no better proof, than the fact that Samson, at his marriage, had a procession and a seven day's feast! 12. He read from the law books some of the laws by which in the southern States slavery is regulated. His argument was this: All the unjust and oppressive laws concerning slavery are essential to the existence of the relation; therefore, since there are bad laws, the relation itself is sinful! But I proved that in Kentucky, for example, several of those laws do not exist; therefore, if they are essential to the relation between master and slave, Kentucky is a free State! 13. He told us of the girl who wept because slaves were found in connection with swine. Therefore, it would seem, the relation is in itself sinful. 14. He asserted that the condition of the slaves, so far from being improved, is growing worse—an assertion contradicted by all who know any thing on the subject. 15. He told us how Richard the sexton of the Danville church, was sold away from his wife—a fact which requires proof. 16. He told us of Mr. Stiles selling slaves, and of Mr. Paxton being obliged to leave his church, because he obeyed a law, which never had an existence!

This is an outline of what we have heard in proof of the sinfulness of the relation between master and slave! Such are the arguments by which it is proved (by the Bible, of course!) that slave-holding is in itself sinful, and the relation

between master and slave a sinful relation! So much for
a debate of *six hours!*

But I must now resume the train of thought, I was pursuing, when I closed my last speech. A man living in
Mississippi, or some one of the southern States, inherits fifty
or five hundred slaves. The laws forbid him to manumit
them, unless he will remove them from the State. What is
he to do? He finds serious, and even insuperable difficulties in his way. They are inter-married with the slaves of
other men; and it would not be right to put asunder what
God has joined together, even for the sake of liberty. But
suppose this difficulty removed, and the slaves brought to
Ohio; he is required to find two freeholders in the county
where each of them is to reside, who will go security for
their support and good conduct. Is it so very easy a matter
to get such security? What, I ask, is the duty of such a
man, viewed in the light of the golden rule?

A case in point, as I remarked in the close of my last
speech, recently occurred. A gentleman in Boston became
heir to a plantation, and a number of slaves, in the South.
He wrote to those who had the business in charge, to set the
slaves at liberty. They informed him, that this could not
be done, unless he would remove them out of the State.
After much perplexity, he determined to go and live with
them, and endeavor to do his duty as a Christian master.
This case is related by Rev. Dr. Cunningham, of Scotland,
who says, the gentleman is now living with his slaves, and
fully discharging the duty of a Christian. But if the doctrine of abolitionism is true, that man is a heinous and scandalous sinner, little better than a murderer, and ought to be
excluded from the church! True, he is doing the best for
his slaves that the law allows; but if slave-holding is in
itself sinful, he is living in sin, and must be condemned!

Take another case. A man has purchased 500 slaves.
He afterwards becomes pious, and desires to act towards
them in accordance with the golden rule. What can he
do? He cannot separate husbands and wives; and if he

could, difficulties meet him on his arrival in Ohio. Will
you denounce that man, because he continues to be a slave-
holder, though contrary to his wish? Suppose him, sacredly, to regard the marriage relation, provide for them abundant food and raiment, and conscientiously to instruct them
in the religion of Christ; is he a sinner?

Do you say, let him pay them wages? But it depends
very much on circumstances, whether their support, the care
taken of them in sickness and old age, will not be as much
as their wages would amount to. Dr. Cunningham states,
that in Scotland many persons labor twenty hours out of the
twenty-four, and yet cannot obtain a support. Circumstances must determine the amount of wages which a conscientious man would give.

It is in vain that we call upon abolitionists to tell us what
is the duty of men, under existing circumstances. The
truth is, there are insuperable difficulties in the way of those
who would liberate the slaves. Admit, if you please, that
Mississippi is bound, as a State, to liberate all her slaves
without delay. Still the question returns: what is the
duty of *individuals* living in Mississippi, so long as she refuses to do this?

You may appeal to the sympathies of men, talk of weeping women, and all that; but the question still returns,
what are men to do under existing circumstances? Gladly
would they place the slaves in a better condition ; but difficulties press upon them on every side. Yet abolitionism
denounces them as upholding the vilest system of oppression, and seeks to exclude them from the church of Christ.

In all the cases I have presented, the relation continues;
but the cruelty against which the gentleman declaims, is not
found. Let him, if he can, point out one passage or one
principle in the Bible, by which, under such circumstances,
it is proved sinful. Such an argument would be worth
more than all his declamation. Why does he hesitate to
come to the source of all light, and from it establish his
proposition?

5. I now offer my fifth general argument against the doctrine of my opponent, that slave-holding is in itself sinful, viz: this doctrine leads its advocates to pursue a course of conduct widely different from that pursued by the inspired Apostles—a course of conduct deeply injurious to society, and especially to the slaves, whose happiness they professedly seek. They do not go, for example, into Kentucky, and calmly and kindly reason on this subject, with the slave-holders, who are supposed to be living in sin, out of that Book, which both parties acknowledge to be the only infallible rule of right. They remain at a distance, publish books, pamphlets and papers, like that of Duncan, in which slave-holders receive indiscriminate denunciation and indiscriminate slander. They get up meetings, make speeches, tell anecdotes of cruelty, and work themselves up into great excitement. The slave-holder is slandered and denounced; but he is not kindly reasoned with. These zealous reformers venture not amongst the benighted people whom they would reform.

Did the Apostles of Christ assail sin in this way ? Did Paul remain at Jerusalem, and write abusive letters against the Pagans? Far from it. Like a man and a Christian, he went and stood in the midst of Mars Hill, and said to the superstitious multitudes—" Ye men of Athens, I perceive that in all things ye are too superstitious; for as I passed by and beheld your devotions, I found an altar with this inscription—*To the unknown God*," etc. If a neighbor of yours were acting very improperly, you would not expect to reform him by abusing him to another neighbor. The Apostles did not collect at Jerusalem, and form a society against Paganism. They went amongst them and reasoned with them, face to face.   [*Time expired.*

Thursday, Oct. 2, 1845.

[MR. BLANCHARD'S FIFTH SPEECH.]

Gentlemen Moderators, and Gentlemen and Ladies, Fellow-Citizens:

At the close of last evening's debate, my brother Rice seemed still to complain, that I had not, as holding the affirmative in this discussion, taken the question directly to the words of Scripture. I must reply again to his difficulty, as I have done before: First—I advance no sentiments in this place which I do not hold myself ready to prove from the Word of God. All the principles upon which my arguments have been based, are written out in full in the sacred Scriptures. I rest my opposition to slavery upon the one-bloodism of the New Testament. All men are equal, because they are of one equal blood. Secondly—I reply, that I have not come directly to the words of Scripture as yet, (though I am certainly disposed to accommodate my brother,) because I supposed the interests of truth to require the course I take, so far at least as the value of this argument is concerned. And I confess it seems to me a novel thing in forensic argument for the negative to become the affirmative, and assume to dictate the line of discussion. I supposed that my brother would not give his time to complaining, but reply, or prove his own sentiments, if he has any. As he seemed at a loss for work to do, I playfully suggested to him to occupy his spare time in the singing of anthems, until I came to the argument from the words of the Old Testament. It is not my purpose to consume this discussion in verbal criticisms and logical hair-splitting; quoting and re-quoting about a dozen lexicons, and as many commentaries, from the beginning of this debate to the end. But I would not have you suppose me anxious to decline such a discussion at the proper time. I am determined that my friend shall have an opportunity to display all his learning and skill, and treat us to the sense of DOULOS and *Ebedh*, in the Hebrew and Greek lexicons, and in the commentators, as long, at least, as you will be disposed to listen. But let us possess our souls in patience!

My friend asks me for the evidence of the truth of Mr. Giddings' statement, that the slaves to the Seminole Indians preferred Indian slavery to slavery among the whites. I reply. The evidence of it is found in every shilling of the 40,000,000 of dollars paid by the people of the United States for the destruction of a few Seminole Indians for the breaking up of the haunts of runaway negroes who had taken refuge among them; and who lived with them as their slaves. The whole object of the war was to bring back those runaway negroes, who had taken refuge in the Indian country to escape slavery to their white owners in the southern States.

There is a large class of topics introduced by my friend, at different times, which I have purposely omitted to notice, but which I have not forgotten. Generally, when the objection is not a very large one, it is economy to wait and put several together—enough to make a mouthful—before undertaking to reply.

For example, he asserts, and repeats the assertion, that abolitionists have aggravated the condition of the slaves, and have rivetted their chains. Then, in another part of his argument, he stated that slavery is so much improved of late years, that he would lead one to suppose they were virtually free, and almost ready to be actually so. I shall briefly sum up all he said on these points: first giving you a key of judgment by which you may always tell whether a man is uttering truth or error. If a man is defending truth, all the parts of his argument will commonly be consistent with each other. But if he is teaching error, one part of his argument will be sure to break its head against another.

Because, as was said by Mr. Webster, in the trial of the Knapps, "every truth in the universe is consistent with every other truth." Let a man speak at length, and if he is defending error, you will see one part of his argument evermore running against the other, and breaking it in pieces.

In illustration of this truth, I will read several of my friend's propositions in the present debate. In the first place, he said, "there never was so much money and time spent in the South, as at present, for the instruction and education of the slaves." In another part of his argument, he said that slavery was greatly "improved" of late years. In another part, that abolitionism had, within a few years, broken up all the schools for slaves, and had rivetted the chains closer upon their unhappy limbs, and was driving them in coffles to the South. In another part, he said that, in Virginia, the laws were disregarded, and the slaves were still taught to read. I might pursue this farther. But I do not wish to be or to seem unkind. I deplore his error. He probably thinks that I am in error. We can honestly hold these opinions of each other, and you are empannelled as an impartial jury, to try the question between us, who is right?

I will, however, just read a paragraph or two, bearing upon the question whether abolitionists have broken up schools in the South: or, whether our agitation of the subject of slavery has produced all the evils attributed to it. I have here a recent pamphlet by Rev. Hugh S. Fullerton, a respectable minister of Chillicothe presbytery, belonging to the same General Assembly with Mr. Rice; which says:—

"The Assembly declare that the severity of the slave laws, and the sensitiveness of the slave-holders is mainly attributable to abolitionists. And yet it is a fact, that has been shown times without number, that the most of these laws are from fifty to one hundred and fifty years old. And that this sensitiveness has existed ever since slavery has existed. Rev. Dr. Hill, of Virginia, in the last N. S. Assembly, brought the same charges against abolitionists. And yet, before he finished his speech, he said,—That when he was a boy, but twelve years old, he was obliged to take his father's slaves to the woods, when he would teach them to read. This, I am told, is not less than sixty years ago

More than fifty years have passed since Rev. Dr. Wilson, (late President of the Ohio University,) established a Sabbath school, in a little village in South Carolina. He was compelled, by threats of violence, to withdraw his school from the village. About thirty years ago, Rev. Dr. Bishop, (late President of Miami University,) was more than once presented to the grand jury, for opening a Sabbath school for slaves, in Lexington, Ky. And now the blame of these severe laws, and this exquisite sensitiveness, is laid at the door of abolitionists."—*Pam. p.* 15.

This is giving to abolitionism, a power of retrospective action, more than fifty years before it was born. I request special notice, that Dr. Bishop, not unknown in this region, was more than thirty years ago presented to a Lexington grand jury, for teaching slaves in Sabbath school. Yet, we are told, vauntingly, that Kentucky has no statute opposed to the education of slaves! Grant that teaching slaves is not expressly, and in terms, prohibited; yet, the laws make their condition such as to render their not being instructed, a moral certainty. I will just read what my friend says :— " *There is no law against teaching slaves to read, in Kentucky.*" Yet, he says, also, that abolitionism broke up all the schools in Kentucky. What is this but a confession by Dr. Rice, that slavery, and its friends, out of spite toward abolitionism, broke up the schools for slaves in Kentucky, *against* law? This is worse for him than if there were a *law* against teaching slaves. I will, moreover, prove shortly, that slavery and the instruction of the slaves, cannot co-exist. That enlightened slaves will not remain slaves; *i. e.* that ignorance is of slavery itself. Thus, I will bring forward the very points which he calls for, in due time. But, I respectfully suggest to my friend, that he had better answer the arguments which I do adduce, while they are fresh, instead of calling for those which I do not adduce. It seems to my brother, that if I were to bring any other arguments but just the ones which I present, he could get along better.

And now, gentlemen moderators, and respected fellow-citizens, though it is unpleasant to dwell upon the subject of cruelty to slaves, I must briefly advert to one fact. Last night I adduced a statement by the Rev. James Nourse, of Mifflin county, Pa., a gentleman with whom I am acquainted, who said that a minister had, on a visit to a ministerial brother, found that he had tied up to his gate-post a female slave, for the purpose of flogging her;—that he plead with him not to whip her, but that he did lash her severely. As an offset against this statement, which is in a printed volume, compiled by a committee, who published a book of statistics of slavery, my brother receives the chance testimony of a Mr. Lindsley, a member of his church, now in this house, who says the fact was not so. I refer to this matter, not to controvert Mr. Lindsley's statement. I cannot find in my heart to comment severely on him. Seeing his pastor, whom he loves, embarked in this unfortunate undertaking, he naturally wished to throw him a plank. Yet, I must say, that for my own part, I am not influenced by testimony coming in this way: mere oral testimony, struck out by debate— a side whisper thrown in to rebut a printed document, long spread out before the country, and never answered or disputed. I know Mr. Nourse, and I do not think it probable he would make two contradictory statements of the same fact.

Moreover, as to the cruelties of slavery, I may be compelled—though I was not, by nature, designed for a surgeon or butcher, or to look on pain unmoved—to consider the lacerations and scourging of slaves at length. I hate this topic of the cruelties of slavery; yet, after what has been said, I must devote a few minutes to its consideration, which I shall do in a short speech.

There are three circumstances, which, when you see, you will feel the force of; which show that the slave is liable to worse cruelties than the brute. I wish this proposition to be distinctly understood. I say not, that the slave is worse treated than the brute—that is not my proposition. My friend is not happy in quoting my remarks. and, therefore. I am, perhaps, over-particular. I say there are three circum-cumstances, each of which goes to show that the slave is *liable* to many cruelties to which the brute is not, and to worse cruelties than brutes are. First—the slave is of a race superior to brutes. He is a man, with soul and body, and made in the image of his God. "After his own like-ness created HE *him*." He belongs to an order of beings as high above animals as that platform on which his God hath placed him, "*a little lower than the angels*," is above the bottom of the stye! Now, *because* he is so superior to brutes, he is capable of provoking his master worse than brutes, and thus is exposed to greater cruelty. That is the point which I make. I have seen a man smite his fist against a post, which had hurt him, though, being an inani-mate object, he will not punish a post much. But a very irri-table man will do that. The same man will beat an ox worse than he will a post, because an intelligent creature. And he will beat a horse still worse, for a similar reason: the horse provokes him worse. And if we travel on, up through the immense vacuum, between the brute and the human race, and remember that when a man undertakes to make intelli-gence property, he has *got his match*, you see, at once, that a man can provoke another man a thousand times worse than a brute can; and if he is in the power of his hand, as the brute is, then comes that horrid, haggling cruelty, undiscribea-ble for its savage excess, which man practices upon man alone.

The "New Orleans Picayune," of Tuesday, June 10, 1845, contains a late example of this monstrous inhumani-ty; and the New Orleans Tropic states that the Attorney General, who was consulted, gave his opinion, that there is no law by which the owner of Auguste, or the jailer, could be punished, for their merciless brutality.   m

The case, here detailed at length, is this: A young slave boy, named Auguste, was sent by his owner to the jail of the first municipality, and, so flogged, for a succession of days, that he was one mass of putridity. He was discov-ered by his falling down, when attempting to crawl home;

was placed by humane persons on a window-shutter, face downward, and carried to the hospital; where some of the first physicians examined him, and pronounced that there was little hope of his life. This is not from an abolition publication, but from the New Orleans Picayune, of June 10th, ult.

Remember, that this inhumanity was perpetrated at the police jail, of the first municipality, where it is customary for slaves to be sent to be whipped, and where the lash is applied according to the direction of masters, or the flogger loses his fee.

Remember, too, that the Attorney General has given his opinion, that there is no law in Louisiana by which this outrage could be punished! It is true, that some citizens, disgusted at the shocking enormity, interposed and remonstrated. And, I thank the living God, that not all men are yet brutes, who are involved in this brutal system; that, even in New Orleans, some sentiment of humanity still remains.

I adduce this instance to show that such is slavery—that cruelty is of its essence; not to show that slave-holders are monsters, and not men. They are *men* like ourselves in their condition; men whose race God made upright; but they have sought out many inventions; and one of the most infernal and unaccountable of them all, is, that man should make human beings property.

And now, what signifies the pretence that abolitionists slander slavery by tales of cruelty.

Tell me not that such revolting inhumanities are incredible; that masters are kind and gentle, etc., etc. Human nature is a streaked thing; and the heart of man is hard and soft, in streaks. The same person may be gentle and kind to his equals, but a savage monster to his slaves. And when the owner of a slave is provoked, and the law puts it in his power; as there is no animal which can provoke like man, so none were ever known so to maul, and mutilate, and haggle the victims of their rage.

But as to the possibility of such diabolical cruelties actually existing, or whether they are only mere false reports and stories of abolitionists, I have an authority, which, I know, my brother will be glad to hear quoted, viz: his own synod of Kentucky. I will quote from a document prepared by some men whose names stand high with him, no others than his own father-in-law, Mr. *Burch*, Nathan H. Hall, of Lexington, President Young, of Danville, Breckenridge, of Louisville, and others—-all Kentuckians, and most of them slave-holders. This committee of the Synod of Kentucky, in a published address on slavery, which they were appointed to prepare, say:

" Cruelty may be carried to any extent, provided life be spared. Mangling, imprisonment, starvation, every species of torture may be inflicted upon him, and he has no redress. But not content with thus laying the body of the slave defenceless at the foot of the master, our system proceeds still further, and strips him, in a great measure, of *all protection against the inhumanity of every other white man who may choose to maltreat him.*"

["In Kentucky the slave has the same protection that the child has."]—*Lectures on Slavery, by N. L. Rice, p.* 17.

Synod add: "In describing such a condition, we may well adopt the language of Sacred Writ—'Judgment is turned away backward, and justice standeth afar off; for truth is fallen in the streets, and equity cannot enter. And the Lord saw it, and it displeased Him that there was no judgment.'

"Such is the ESSENTIAL character of our slavery."

Address of Synod of Ky. p. 6.

Again: as to the infliction of barbarous cruelties, synod say:

"There are now, in our whole land, two millions of human beings exposed, defenceless to every insult and every injury short of maiming or death, which their fellow-men may choose to inflict. They suffer all that can be inflicted by wanton caprice, by grasping avarice, by brutal lust, by malignant spite, and by insane anger. Their happiness is the sport of every whim and the prey of every passion that may occasionally, or habitually infest the master's bosom. *If we*

*could calculate the amount of wo endured by ill-treated
slaves,* it would overwhelm every compassionate heart; it
would move even the obdurate to sympathy." [Synod seem
to think that my brother himself must feel for their intolerable sufferings; but they proceed.]

" There is also a vast sum of suffering *inflicted upon the
slave by humane masters,* as a punishment for that idleness
and misconduct which slavery naturally produces. The
ordinary motives to exertion in man are withdrawn from the
slave. Some unnatural stimulus must then be substituted,
and the whip presents itself as the readiest and most efficient.
But the application of the whip to produce industry is like
the application of the galvanic fluid to produce muscular
exertion."—*Synod's Address, p.* 13.

My friend, he tells us, is exceedingly anxious to get this
discussion into the Bible. Let him now take up his Bible,
and tell us where, in the Old or New Testament, he finds a
system like this; and show that Christ approved of it. This
is the Synod of Kentucky's plain description of *slavery*—
not of its cruel laws and adjuncts—but slavery itself; a system to the carrying on of which, the Synod show that cruel
punishment is as necessary, as a whip is in driving a wagon.

I shall now quote an author, as respectable as any I have
adduced, still further to show the actual sufferings of slaves
under this system; I mean the Rev. David Rice; whose
memory is justly honored as one of the first pioneers of
civilization and religion in the wilds of Kentucky. He
was one of the framers of her constitution, and went to sleep
with his fathers, respected and beloved by all. Nor do I
think the worse of him for being, collaterally, one of my
brother's ancestors; but I commend his doctrines to the notice
of his posterity.

In his speech in the convention to form the constitution
of Kentucky, 1790, Dr. Rice says:

" The master may, *and often does, inflict upon him* (the
slave) *all the punishment the human body is capable of
bearing!*"

And, as I have shown, the one circumstance, that slaves are capable of provoking their masters as much worse than brutes, as they are superior to them, shows fully the reason *why* they are often subjected to inhuman barbarities which brutes never suffer.

My second proposition on the subject of cruelties is, That there are a multitude of crimes and offences, which slaves can commit, and for which they are punished, which brutes cannot commit.

Slaves may upbraid, insult, and reproach their owners; but I never heard of but one brute's rebuking his master. A special power and permission was given to an ass to reprove Balaam. A horse will not commonly be whipped for petty larceny. An ox cannot have his leg broken for insolence. There is thus a large class of offences which slaves can commit, which render them liable to more and greater cruelty than brutes. On this point I have only farther to quote Dr. David Rice, in the convention which formed the Kentucky constitution.

" He [the slave] is a rational creature, reduced by legislation to the *state of a brute,* and thereby deprived of every privilege of humanity." [The very teachings of the abolitionists of the present day, rife and rampant in the convention which formed the Kentucky constitution.]

" The brute, (adds Dr. R.,) may steal or rob to supply his hunger; but the slave, though in the most starving condition, *dare not do either, on penalty of death, or some severe punishment.*"

Compare this bold language of the progenitor, with the talk which you now hear from this his descendant. But enough on the point, *that slaves are punished for a multitude of crimes and offences for which brutes are not;* and their condition, therefore, in this respect, worse than that of animals.

3. My third and last point, showing that the slave's condition is, in some respects, worse than that of brute animals, is this:—*That the owner of a brute is not goaded to cruelty*

by the guilt of ownership.   Oh! an upbraiding conscience often makes a man a ruffian! There is nothing so cruel as the criminal in heart, conscious of guilt; yet unwilling to make reparation. And this is precisely the condition of the slave-holder, with the spectacle of his crushed and stricken slaves perpetually before him, whom he has reduced to, or holds upon, the dead level of the brute, in whose state they are, according to Dr. Rice, and the slave code. As the wretched creatures move to and fro across the kitchen, before his eyes, slinking to their unpaid tasks, that conscience, which was placed in the bosom for wise and just purposes—Oh! that conscience, gnawing evermore at his heart-strings, drives him to his cups; and in the triple intoxication of liquor, remorse, and rage, he wreaks his savage vengeance on the slave, because he has first deprived him of being a man.

I have now shown you three distinct grounds on which slaves are liable to more and worse cruelties than brutes. And it has struck me, how patiently the justifiers of slavery, who are scandalized at the cruel stories of abolitionists, will listen while I am proving general propositions, a thousand times worse for slavery than particular inhuman acts. No one winces under this. But if I state a fact—an instance of barbarity, that has actually occurred, the cry is raised, that slave-holders are slandered; and shoals of testimony, from wincing auditors, is got up to disprove it. Yet it is necessary, not only to prove general principles of cruelty against slavery, but to illustrate and impress them by particular facts which they cause; lying, like all general principles, at the root of individual cases.

I now give you the testimony of the Rev. Francis Hawley, pastor of a Baptist church in Wallingford, Connecticut—taken from a work called "Slavery as it is," which contains the testimony of one thousand witnesses, most of them from slave States, on the subject of slavery. It was compiled with the greatest care, and every precaution taken to secure correct testimony. Where unknown persons sent testimony to the committee who made the book, such persons were required to refer to some persons mutually known, that the committee might, by correspondence, ascertain the credibility of the witness.

I now read the testimony of Rev. Francis Hawley, one of these witnesses, who has resided fourteen years in North and South Carolina. The Baptist State Convention [N. C.] a few years since, made him their general agent to visit the churches in their bounds. He says:

"I will now give a few facts, showing the workings of the system. Some years since, a Presbyterian minister moved from North Carolina to Georgia. He had a negro man of an uncommon mind. For some cause, I know not what, this minister whipped him most unmercifully. He next nearly drowned him. He then put him in the fence. This is done by lifting up the corner of a worm fence, and then putting the feet through—the rails serve as stocks. He kept him there some time—how long I was not informed—but the poor slave died in a few days. And, if I was rightly informed, nothing was done about it either in Church or State. After some time, he moved back to North Carolina, and is now a member of —— presbytery. I have heard him preach, and have been in the pulpit with him. May God forgive me!"

"In R— county, North Carolina, lived a Mr. B., who had the name of being a cruel master. Three or four winters since, his slaves were engaged in clearing a piece of new land. He had a negro girl about fourteen years old, whom he had severely whipped a few days before, for not performing her task. She again failed. The hands left the field for home. She went with them a part of the way, and fell behind. But the negroes thought she would soon be along. The evening passed away, and she did not come. They finally concluded that she had gone back to the new ground to lie by the log-heaps that were on fire. But they were mistaken She had sat down at the foot of a large pine. She was thinly clad—the night was cold and rainy.

In the morning the poor girl was found: but she was speechless, and died in a short time."

" While travelling as agent for the North Carolina Baptist State Convention, I attended a three days meeting in Gates county. Friday, the first day, passed off. Saturday morning came, and the pastor of the church who lived a few miles off did not make his appearance. The day passed off, and no news from the pastor. On Sabbath morning, he came hobbling along, having but little use of one foot. He soon explained; said he had a hired negro man, who, on Saturday morning, gave him *a little slack jaw.* Not having a stick at hand, he fell upon him with his fist and foot, and, in kicking him, he injured his foot so seriously that he could not attend meeting on Saturday."

." I was present and saw Rev. J— W—, of Mecklenburg county hire out four slaves to work in the gold mines in Burke county. The Rev. H. M—, of Orange county, sold for nine hundred dollars a negro man to a speculator, on Monday of a camp-meeting.

" Runaway slaves are frequently hunted with guns and dogs. I was once out on such an excursion with my rifle and two dogs. I trust the Lord has forgiven me this heinous wickedness! Yours, for the oppressed,

" Colebrook, Conn. March 18, 1839.   FRANCIS HAWLEY."

The above are not selected for any speciality of cruelty, though sufficiently horrid. They fall indefinitely short of a mass of facts which might be taken from the book, in point of savageness and suffering. They are simply ordinary household specimens of slave-holding society.

I pause here to remind you that my brother told us, that if the abolitionists would go down south, and prosecute the church members who are guilty of cruel treatment to slaves, they would be turned out of the church. You here see what ministers and members compose the courts to try such offenders.

And now, why have I read these things? to show that

slave-holders are are not men?   No: but to show that they are men, under cogent temptations to be cruel men.

I will here anticipate the answer of my brother to one point. He will tell you, perhaps, that great cruelties are practiced also in the free States, and upon white men.   He says, that if I venture to appeal to your sympathies against the slave relation, on account of these inhumanities, he "hoped "—yes, that was his word—he "*hoped*" he should be able to find a thousand instances of husbands treating their wives cruelly, so as to satisfy you that according to my reasoning marriage is wrong in itself.   The best I can say is, that I "*hope*" he did not mean what he said ; but that his expression was a *lapsus linguæ;* and that he does not serious'y " hope" to find domestic cruelties to cover slavery with. I reply, that, when my friend saw the graves in Cincinnati, of the wife and children who had been murdered by the husband, he saw an instance of *punished* cruelty.   There is all the difference in the world between *punished* and *un-punished* cruelty. Punished cruelty shows a healthy condition of society: while, if a man can strip and flog my daughter, and go unquestioned for it, it shows—what is just the fact in slave-holding society—that every person in like condition is liable to the like outrage, without redress.   And this proves cruelty inherent in slavery.

Now let him show, if he can, the elder, or the minister, or the member, who has been dealt with by his church for such acts of barbarity, in any slave State, in this age and country, or any other.   Or let him find among all the reported cases, one instance where a master has suffered capitally for murdering his slave. It will then be time to compare cruelties to slaves with the punished cruelties gathered up in the free States.   High legal authorities assure me that there never was one such case.

I have now done with the subject of cruelties to slaves. These brutalities offend the public nostril, and to exhibit them, is against my inclination and my taste. Would to God there were no necessity for such developements.   I should be thankful if the occasion which has made them necessary, were forever removed.

I am told I have yet ten minutes. I wish here to direct your minds farther, to the statement made by my brother, that in Kentucky, the slave has the same protection that the child has.

Dr. Rice has told you that I misrepresented and perverted his meaning, last night. I acknowledge that a defective impression would have been left, if I had no more to say than I then said; but I was drawn off by the introduction of the subject of cruelties; the abolitionists having been repeatedly arraigned, as slanderers of the *South*.

I now wish to present exactly what *Dr. Rice* affirms concerning the protection enjoyed by Kentucky slaves. I read the whole paragraph from his pamphlet, p. 17.

" If, then, it be true, as Dr. Beecher and the Editor of the Watchman would have the people believe, that the system of slavery cannot be sustained, unless the master have unlimited control over his slaves, it must soon be, abolished, and the abolitionists need give themselves little farther trouble. *In Kentucky the slave has the same protection that a child has.*"

Protection from what? I ask. Why, from the cruel disposition of the master; for, says Dr. Rice, " if it be true that slavery cannot be sustained unless the MASTER have unlimited control over the slave," the "*protection*," whch Dr. Rice declares that the slave has, is "*from this unlimited control.*" If he does not mean this, let him explain his meaning. (A pause.) Now I desire to show that this proposition is as entirely without authority and sanction, in truth, as any other proposition in human speech. My argument will be but just entered on when I sit down. If, in Kentucky, there is no more protection for the child than for the slave, there is many a Kentucky Rachel will soon be weeping for her once free children, " refusing to be comforted because they are not." For such fate, every one knows, awaits the slave, and the slave, he says, is protected like the child. My brother means (he can mean nothing else, having quoted in the same connection, the Kentucky slave code) that the slave has the same protection from *bodily injuries* as the child of free parents. I will quote Dr. David Rice on the subject of the power of the master to inflict bodily injuries on the slave. He says:

" The slave is a rational creature, reduced by the power of legislation, to the state of a brute, and thereby deprived of every privilege of humanity, that he may minister to the ease, luxury, lust, pride or avarice of another, no better than himself."

" The law leaves the chastity of a female slave entirely in the power of her master. If a master attempts their chastity they dare neither resist nor complain."

Is this the protection which Kentucky extends to her domestic relations? Is this the protection of a free child in Kentucky?

Let us now see what protection the Kentucky slave has in his earnings. I still quote David Rice:

" All the slave receives, is the bare means of subsistence, and that is not bestowed until he has earned it; and then, not in proportion to his labor, nor out of regard to him, but for selfish purposes."—*David Rice.*

Is that the protection Kentucky law gives to Kentucky children in their earnings? If so, may God send Kentucky children a speedy deliverance! Rather, may He send Kentucky a ministry who will explain the gospel to be what it is, a defence of human rights; and especially the rights of the laboring poor.

I have now but one minute left, which I will use in giving notice that I will compare the condition of an orphan child in Kentucky, without mother, father, uncles or aunts, or any other natural protector,—with that of the slave, in respect to protection from cruelty. And surely in such a case, the slave must have an equal protection with the child, if anywhere. But before I have fully done with this statement of my opponent, you will see that it is a most unhappy *declaration* for him that made it. [*Time expired.*

[MR. RICE'S FIFTH SPEECH.]

Gentlemen Moderators and Fellow-Citizens:

No one, I presume, could learn from the speech of one hour, to which we have just listened, what is the subject under discussion. Those who heard, if not otherwise informed, would be likely to conclude, that I had undertaken to prove, that all the cruelties permitted by the laws of the slave-holding States, or practiced by wicked men, are right; and that Mr. B. was laboring to prove those cruelties sinful! If it was the purpose of the gentleman and his ten challengers to discuss that subject, why did they not propose the following question: *Is it right to beat, abuse, and kill slaves?* Why propose one subject for discussion, and then insist on discussing one radically different? I do not intend to charge the gentlemen who invited this debate, with practicing deception; but certain it is, that their representative is spending his time on quite another theme. He might, with as much propriety, discuss the religious character of the grand Turk! What is the question before us? "*Is slave-holding in itself sinful, and the relation between master and slave a sinful relation?*" Is every master a heinous and scandalous sinner, however kindly he may treat his slaves, and however conscientiously he may afford them religious instruction? Is a man to be condemned as a sinner, simply because he is a slave-holder? Have we heard one word from the gentleman on this subject? He has occupied the time in declaiming concerning the cruel treatment of slaves which we, and indeed all decent men condemn as severely as he. Why has he spent an hour in denouncing what even the vilest men will not defend? Is this community so degraded? Has public sentiment indeed become so corrupt, that all this denunciation is necessary to induce the people to detest inhuman cruelty? Verily the gentleman pays you a poor compliment.

I am resolved to keep the question under discussion dis-

tinctly before the audience. We are discussing simply the
relation between master and slave. Is it in itself sinful?
Must every man sustaining this relation forthwith dissolve it
without regard to circumstances, or expose himself to just
condemnation as a heinous sinner? For let it not be forgotten, that if the relation is in itself sinful, it must be immediately abandoned without regard to circumstances or consequences. But if there are circumstances which justify it,
for the time being, circumstances must determine whether
in any given case it is sinful. Then it would not be proper
to revolutionize society and tear up its very foundations in the
attempt to abolish it.

I am fully pursuaded, the gentleman will not discuss the
question before us. Mark the prediction: *he will not do it.*
Nevertheless, I will follow him in his remarks for a time.
He says, he finds his principles justified by " *the one-bloodism*" of the New Testament. Are we to understand him as
saying, that under all circumstances he would insist on carrying out in practice his doctrine that all men are born free
and equal? Would he have every young woman in England claim to be in all respects equal to Victoria? Does it
follow from the fact that all are born equal, that all are to be
reduced to the same condition in life? Would he denounce
Queen Victoria, simply because she is Queen of England?
Is every king or emperor of Europe a heinous sinner, simply because he exercises arbitrary power? If not, where
is the stopping point? How far may circumstances and the
good of society justify restricting the privileges or liberties of
individuals?

I claim no right to dictate to Mr. B. what course he
shall pursue in his argument; but I have the right, and it
is my duty to expose his departure from the question before
us, and his failure to adduce even the shadow of evidence
of the truth of the proposition he affirms. I cannot, indeed,
spend my time in singing psalms, as he suggests; but if he
will furnish me with a few of the select songs sung by
some of the colored fraternity during the late abolition con-

vention in this city, I shall be glad to *read* them for the edification of the audience. Perhaps Mr. Clark, the celebrated abolitionist singer, can furnish some of them. Shall I hope to obtain a few of them?

Mr. B. has told us truly, that when men contend for the truth, their arguments will be consistent with each other. It does not follow, however, that *his version* of them will be so. Whilst I deny that my arguments are inconsistent with each other, I feel it to be my duty to apply his principles to his own statements; which, if not inconsistent with each other, are contrary to truth. In one of his speeches last evening, he made a statement which, in at least four particulars, turns out to be incorrect. He told us that the General Assembly of the Presbyterian church, of 1818, passed a law making it obligatory on all the slave-holding members in the churches under their care to instruct their slaves, and prepare them for emancipation; that Rev. J. D. Paxton, then of Virginia, obeyed the law of the church, instructing and emancipating his slaves; that he was in consequence of pursuing this course, denounced as an abolitionist, and obliged to leave his church, and go to a free State; and that no other individual had pursued a similar course. Now, in the first place, the General Assembly passed no such law. They *recommended* instruction with reference to emancipation. In the second place, Mr. Paxton was not the only individual who instructed and liberated his slaves. It is notorious, that many others have done the same thing. In the third place, it is not true that he was obliged to leave his church because he instructed and liberated his slaves. He had some difficulty with his church, in consequence of some discourses on the subject of slavery, the precise character of which I do not know. In the fourth place, he did not go to a free State, but removed to Kentucky, and took the pastoral charge of the Presbyterian church in Danville—one of the largest and most respectable churches in the State. Moreover, he is now pastor of a church near Shelbyville, in the same State; and no minister in the State enjoys more fully the confidence of the churches, than he. So much for the gentleman's facts.

But what was my inconsistency? Why, I said that the abolition excitement had riveted the chains on the slave, and aggravated every evil connected with his condition; and I said again, that, recently, the condition of the slaves has been much improved; that there never was so much done to afford them religious instruction, as at this time. — This is all true, and all consistent. Abolitionism had its day; and the excitement it produced, extended through the length and breadth of the land. It put it in the power of demagogues and designing men to break up the Sabbath schools in which the colored people were instructed, and to counteract, to a considerable extent, all efforts made by Christians to improve their condition. In Kentucky, where there was a strong disposition amongst the people to adopt a plan of gradual emancipation, candidates for the Legislature, however favorable to such an object, were unwilling to avow their sentiments, lest the opposing party, by branding them with abolitionism, might defeat their election. Such was the state of things, that any effort to improve the condition of the slave population, seemed almost hopeless.

But, thank God, a reaction has, to some extent, taken place. Christians have resumed their labors for the benefit of the slaves. Prejudices have given way; and, in despite of abolitionism, the work of religious instruction is going forward. Southern and Western Christians are doing something better than running slaves to Canada—an employment peculiar to abolitionists. Recently, a public meeting was held in Charleston, South Carolina, for the purpose of maturing plans for extending religious instruction more generally to the slaves. One of the leading men in that Convention was Rev. C. C. Jones, who, though a man of no ordinary talents, and of extensive learning, has devoted himself, for more than twelve years, to the religious instruction of the negroes, and whose labors have been greatly blessed in the conversion of many of them. The Convention was also attended by prominent political gentlemen, who lent all their influence to carry forward the benevolent enterprize. They have published, and circulated extensively, the report of their proceedings. In some of the letters addressed to the meeting, I was pleased to see statements of the number of slaves in the different churches who could *read.* So far as I know, there has never been manifested so deep an interest in the religious instruction of the slaves. This interest extends through the West and South. Masters are found in the South, who erect churches on their own plantations, and pay from $500 to $800 to ministers of the gospel to preach statedly to them. Abolitionism has, indeed, done much to retard and hinder this good work; and its influence is still felt; but I rejoice to know, that the Christians in the slaveholding States manifest so fixed a determination to give to the slaves the word of life.

Dr. Bishop, we are told, had difficulty in instructing slaves in Kentucky *thirty years* ago; and hence it is inferred, that the destruction of the Sabbath schools, a few years since, was not caused by abolitionism. Many and great changes have taken place in Kentucky in thirty years. Public sentiment has been gradually elevated and purified by the gospel; and, in process of time, there was a disposition on the part of Christians to see the slaves more generally taught the glorious truths of divine revelation. To this there was no opposition of sufficient strength to prevent them. But the abolition excitement arose, and put it in the power of every demagogue to get up so much opposition, that in a little time, every school, I believe, was closed. Thus were the efforts of good men, to improve the condition of the slaves, effectually hindered by the ill-judged course of abolitionists. By the way, some of the best laws of Kentucky, relative to the slaves, have been very recently passed. At the time to which I have reference, it is true, there was no law against teaching the slaves to read; but prejudice once excited, was as strong as law; and that prejudice was excited by abolitionists. Even in Cincinnati, scenes were enacted in connection with this excitement, and cruelties were practiced upon the colored population, which every respectable citizen must condemn and denounce. Is it, then, surprising that, in Kentucky, the Sabbath schools were broken up?

But the gentleman dwells on the cruelty of wicked men toward the slaves, as if he were resolved to make the impression, that I have engaged to defend it, and he, in great benevolence, is laboring to convince you that it is sinful.— Surely, he regards the audience as very stupid, if he expects to convince them that all this declamation is to the point. I have been engaged in several debates, in which I thought my opponent pursued a singular course; but I must confess, the gentleman excells them all! [A laugh.]

I have seen the book to which he refers as authority for the statement, that Rev. Mr. Nourse said he saw a minister publicly whipping a negro woman; and it is not true that Mr. N. says he saw any such thing. He is made to say, that the Rev. Mr. —— told him that he saw Rev. Mr. —— do this thing. The amount of it is this: Rev. Mr. Nourse told Rev. Mr. Somebody, the Rev. Mr. Somebody saw Rev. Mr. Nobody do this cruel thing. I am done!—[a laugh.]— But, says the gentleman, these are *printed* documents. Unfortunately, however, the fact that a story is *printed*, is no evidence of its truth at this day. I have no confidence in this second handed and third-handed testimony against the character of ministers of the gospel. They are no better than Romish traditions. Men print all sorts of things now-a-days. For example; let me read an extract from the *Edinburg Witness*, a Scotch paper, professedly religious, the author of which professes to write what he knows. I have already referred to it.

"What shall we think," says the writer, "of the state of society, where a *minister of the gospel*, with credit to himself, avails himself of the Sabbath for inflicting special punishment, as *is usual*, that field-labor may not be interrupted, and being engaged in flogging a poor negro, when the hour of worship comes, leaves his victim fastened to the post, goes to the house of prayer, conducts the worship, dispenses the communion, comes back, and, with unabated zeal, goes on with his barbarous work?"

Of such conduct, this writer says, ministers of the gospel can be guilty "with credit to themselves," and it "is usual." I pronounce the whole statement one of the grossest slanders ever invented by the father of lies. I defy all abolitionists to produce the slightest evidence of its truth. Such are the potent arguments by which abolitionists seek to abolish slavery! Can we wonder that the people of the slaveholding States, thus slandered and outraged, have lost all confidence in the abolitionists, and utterly refuse to hear them?

But the gentleman has brought forward the testimony of a Mr. Hawley, who brings serious charges against a certain minister, and against a Presbyterian elder. I place no confidence in such testimony. If he saw the things concerning which he testifies, he knew what was his duty as a Christian. Why did he not inform the Session and the Presbytery of the facts? Then had they refused to subject the offenders to the discipline of the church, he might, with propriety, have denounced them. Mr. H. gives no *names.* I desire to know the names of the men. Then if the charges are false, they may vindicate themselves; and if true, let them bear the reproach. Give us evidence that we have in our church such wretches, and I will prosecute them even to the highest court of the church. The gentleman shall not be troubled with the prosecution. But now suppose all these disgusting details of cruelty, to which we have been treated, be true to the letter, does it follow that the relation of master and slave is in itself sinful?—that where no such cruelty is practiced, it is yet sinful?

But a little colored boy in New Orleans, we are told, was cruelly beaten, and there was no law to protect him. Admit the story to be true, I do not undertake to defend the laws of Louisiana. Are we discussing the question whether those laws are right or wrong? There is no State whose laws are what they should be on all subjects. Those of Kentucky are not by any means perfect. Yet the gentleman ought not, in his denunciation, to forget that even the law of Moses permitted the master to enforce obedience by chastisement.—*Exod.* xxi: 20, 21. "And if a man smite his servant, or his maid, with a rod, and he die under his hand; he shall surely be punished. Notwithstanding, if he continue a day or two, he shall not be punished: *for he is his money.*" Will the gentleman say, this law related not to slaves, but to *hired servants?* This will not mend the matter; for it will prove, that even hired servants might be severely chastised. The truth is clear, that the master was allowed to enforce obedience by chastisement, whilst all the protection possible was extended to the slave. Will Mr. B. denounce the Bible, and be governed by nature's light? If so, we may hope, that he will not be so inconsistent as to abandon the Declaration of Independence, and permit the negroes to be deprived of the right to vote in making the laws by which they are to be governed. Just now he seems pressed by the principles of abolitionism.

He has read what the Synod of Kentucky said against what is called *the system of slavery.* Am I here to defend any system of slavery? Does the question before us relate to the system of American slavery? When I deny that slaveholding is in itself sinful, do I thereby defend all the laws by which in any of the States it may be regulated? Or do I approve the cruelty of wicked men? I agree with the Synod of Kentucky, that there is much evil connected with slavery. I believe that the State of Kentucky would do wisely to get rid of it. I do desire that it should everywhere come to an end.

But Mr. B. has referred to my venerated kinsman, Rev. David Rice, to prove that in Kentucky the slave has not the same protection from the cruelty of his master, which a child has from the cruel treatment of his father. It is true, that David Rice was an eminently wise and good man—one whose memory is dear to many an aged disciple in Kentucky.

He said, slavery degrades human beings.   Admit it; but is
every slave-holder obliged thus to tread down his slaves, as
much as the civil laws permit?   Or is a slave-holder who
does no such thing, still chargeable with heinous and scandalous sin?   But as to the protection afforded the slaves in
Kentucky, does the pamphlet of Rev. David Rice treat of
their *present* condition ?   It was written when he was a young
man, before the constitution was adopted.   He lived to an
advanced age, and has been a number of years in his grave.
His pamphlet, therefore, can give no information concerning
the state of things now.   He spoke of slavery as it existed,
not particularly in Kentucky, but in New York, and in other
States.   As to his anti-slavery views, it is proper to remark,
that he was a member of the convention by which the con-
titution of the State was formed.   Standing in that position,
he plead that slavery should be excluded by the constitution,
and that Kentucky should be a free State.   Would to God
that convention had listened to him and adopted his views.
My native State would have been greatly the gainer thereby.
So the majority of the people, I presume, now believe.   With
my present views I would take the same ground, if placed in
similar circumstances, which he took.   But his wise counsels
were not heeded; and slavery was admitted.   Our discussion relates exclusively to the duty of *individuals* living in
those States where the evil has been admitted.   David Rice,
having failed to exclude slavery from the State, preached the
gospel ever afterwards both to master and slave, just as did
Paul and the other apostles of Christ.   Never did he treat
masters as criminals, simply because they were masters.
He opposed the system, as it is called, but very properly distinguished between the duty of the State and the duty of
individuals living in the State, after slavery was admitted.   I
choose to pursue the same course.   It is wrong, then, to quote
that venerable man as teaching doctrines different from those
I am defending.   But abolitionism sustains itself by misrepresentations of this kind.

Whilst on the subject of cruelties, I remember, that very

recently a black man was murdered in the streets of Indianapolis, for no crime whatever. Had such a thing happened
in a slave-holding State, we should not soon have heard the
last of it. It would have stood prominent in abolition books,
tracts and papers. But it happened in a free State; and
therefore, we hear little concerning it. The gentleman has
not had occasion to speak of it! Why are such things so
lightly passed over, when they occur in a free State, and so
bitterly denounced when they occur in the slave-holding
States ? Let impartial justice be done.

But, as we have had so many facts stated, showing the
cruelty of slave-holders, it may be proper for me also to
state a few. Some years since, as I am credibly informed,
a citizen of Danville, Ky., sold a negro woman from her husband to a slave-trader. It was soon known in the town ;
and such was the excitement that he was constrained to follow the slave-holder, and re-purchase the woman at considerable loss. He could scarcely have lived there, if he had
not done so. Not a great many years ago, a prominent citizen of Lexington came near being mobbed, because he had
cruelly chastised a negro woman. And Dr. Drake, of Louisville, whilst travelling through Alabama, not long since, met
a sheriff and his posse returning from the penitentiary where
they had safely lodged a man who owned a plantation and a
number of slaves. He had been convicted of the murder
of one of his slaves, chiefly on circumstantial evidence derived through his slaves, and was sentenced for *ten years*,
if my memory serves me. Such facts show the real state
of feeling in the slave-holding States.

It is, perhaps, true, as the gentlemen says, that a white
man is rarely executed for the murder of a negro; and I
may add, they are not very frequently executed for the murder of white men. The laws, it is admitted, are not strictly
executed. His non-resistant brethren of New England, however, are for abolishing all capital punishment. Yet, our
western abolitionists maintain that slave insurrections are
right, and that it would be a damning sin to suppress one of

them! May we not hope they will catch the pacific spirit of some of their eastern brethren?

I must here say a few words in regard to the protection the slaves enjoy, from cruel treatment, in Kentucky. I did not say, as the gentleman seems to understand me, that the slave has all the *advantages* of a child, but simply that he is, by law, protected from cruelty on the part of the master. My remarks on this subject were made in view of the following article in the *Watchman of the Valley*.

"*Nothing wrong in the relation itself.*—Dr. Edward Beecher, at the late meeting of the Massachusetts Abolition society, adduced the following law case: a man was tried in North Carolina, for shooting his own female slave. Judge Ruffin decided, that, according to slave law, the act could not be pronounced criminal, *because the master must have unlimited control over the body of his slaves*, OR THE SYSTEM CANNOT STAND. In regard to this decision, the judge confessed, that he felt its harshness, and that every person in his retirement must *repudiate it;* but in the actual state of things *it must be so: there is no remedy.*"

"According to the decision, then, of a southern judge, extorted from him by the inexorable necessity of his legal logic, in opposition to his humane feelings, the *relation* of slavery, as constituted *by law*, is, *in itself*, cruel, authorizing the unlimited control of the master over the body of his slave, *life not excepted.* Why? Because without such control, the system could not stand; *i. e.* the relation could not exist, as it is now legally constituted. No sin in such a relation? Then there is no sin, a Carolina jurist being judge, for doing whatever is necessary (be it stripes, torture, or death,) to preserve this sinless, lawful relation!"

Dr. E. Beecher, and the editor, were agreed that the relation of master and slave could not continue, unless the master had the right to kill his slave! Now let us look at the law of Kentucky, on this subject, passed in 1830—long since Dr. Bishop had his difficulty. You see, this law affords evidence conclusive, that the condition of the slaves has improved, the gentleman's assertion to the contrary notwithstanding. The law is as follows :

" If any owner of a slave shall treat such slave cruelly and inhumanly, so as in the opinion of the jury to endanger the life or limb of such slave, or shall not supply his slave with sufficient food and raiment, it shall and may be lawful for any person acquainted with the fact or facts, to state and set forth in a petition to the Circuit Court, the facts, or any of them aforesaid, of which the defendent hath been guilty, and pray that such slave or slaves may be taken from the possession of the owner, and sold for the benefit of such owner, agreeably to the 7th article of the Constitution."

According to this law, you perceive, if a jury of twelve disinterested men can be convinced, that a master treats his slave cruelly, or fails to supply him with sufficient food and raiment, the slave is sold into better hands ; and the master pays the costs of the suit. Has the child more protection against the cruel treatment of a father ? May not a father chastise his child very severely without being exposed to the penalty of the civil law ? I do not undertake to defend the slave laws of Kentucky, but only to make good the statement called in question by the gentleman.

I have now paid due attention to all the gentleman has offered. He says, I ought rather to answer the arguments he offers, than complain that he does not present others. The question under discussion is this : " Is slave-holding in itself sinful, and the relation between master and slave a sinful relation?" If he will mention *one* argument he has offered on this point, I will immediately reply to it. He and I agree that the Scriptures are the only infallible rule of faith and practice, and that nothing can be condemned as sinful, unless it can be shown to be contrary to that rule. If I were debating with an infidel, I might take different ground ; but, as a minister of the gospel, he is bound to abide by the decision of the law which he holds to be inspired of God. Has he adduced one solitary passage of Scripture to prove that slave-holding is in itself sinful? What single text has he quoted? Not one.   Then what have I to answer?

His great argument, if argument it can be called, is this: Wicked masters treat their slaves cruelly; therefore the relation between master and slave is a sinful relation. By an argument precisely similar, as I have repeatedly stated, I can prove the conjugal relation in itself sinful. Many husbands treat their wives cruelly ; therefore it is a sin to enter into the marriage relation.   But he charges me with placing the relation between master and slave upon an equality with that of husband and wife.   I do no such thing ; but I maintain, that he has no right to urge against the relation of master and slave, an argument which, if sound, will sweep away every other relation.   His argument proves too much, and, therefore, proves nothing.   He cannot consistently urge it, unless he is prepared to go the whole length with Robert Dale Owen, and sweep away entirely the marriage relation. In every other relation men distinguish between the relation itself and the particular laws by which it may be regulated, and the conduct of wicked men in the relation.   Why does the gentleman so constantly insist upon an entire departure from an admitted principle, when he comes to reason concerning the relation between master and slave?

In Hindostan the wife is in law and in fact more degraded, than any slave on a southern plantation.   Whilst compelled to yield to her lord implicit obedience, she is not permitted to enjoy the poor consolations of the Hindoo religion. She is believed to have no soul ; is degraded to the condition of a brute ; and when her husband dies, she is burned upon his funeral pile.   No slave is so degraded in the eyes of his master, unless he be an atheist.   Shall we, then, argue, that, since in Hindostan the wife is the degraded slave of the husband ; therefore, the relation is sinful ?   Nay, not only in Hindostan, but over a large portion of the globe, the wife is thus degraded.   Still the conclusion does not follow, that the relation is sinful, because regulated by unjust and cruel laws.

This argument bears with equal force upon the *parental*

relation. Hindoo mothers expose their infants on the banks
of the Ganges. Infanticide has been common in the islands
of the South seas. The ancient Roman laws gave the father
power over the life of his children. Shall we conclude,
that, because the laws by which in different countries this
relation has been regulated, are unjust and cruel, and because
unfeeling parents have treated their children cruelly, therefore the parental relation is sinful? Were I to reason thus,
my logic would be quite as conclusive as that urged by Mr.
Blanchard. His logic is indeed very sweeping. It stops
not with destroying the relation of master and slave, but carries before it all the relations of life. It strikes at the foundations of civil government. For it is a fact, that the dark-
est pages of this world's history, are those which record the
oppression, the tyranny, and the cruelty which have been
practiced in the name and under the sanction of civil law.
Nero practised all his cruelties by virtue of his office as a
civil ruler; and all the forms of tyranny on earth, are but
organized governments. Shall we say, what an abominable
thing is civil government! how detestable the relation between ruler and subject! What crimes against God are
committed under its sanction! How fearfully the innocent
are made to suffer under its strong arm! Down with all
civil government! The relation between ruler and subject
is a sinful relation; therefore, wash your hands of it at once!
To such results does this gentleman's principles of reasoning
infallibly tend. His brethren, the abolitionists of the East,
at least many of them, have carried out these principles, and
do in fact denounce all civil government as in itself sinful,
and every individual engaged in its administration, as a
heinous sinner, because men have been oppressed and deprived of their rights by its operation! The gentleman's
logic proves far more than he would be willing to admit. It
begins with destroying the relation of master and slave, and
ends with sweeping away the relations of husband and wife,
parent and child, ruler and subject! All are swept away by

one fell swoop. What glorious liberty men will enjoy, when these principles shall have been carried out!

Such arguments, every intelligent hearer must at once perceive, prove nothing; are absolutely worthless. The question before us is not whether bad laws may be enacted to regulate a certain relation; or whether in that relation wicked men may be guilty of cruelty; *but whether the relation itself obliges those who sustain it to act in this way.* If Mr. B. can prove, that every master, or any master, is obliged to treat his slaves cruelly, I will forthwith yield the question. If he cannot, then circumstances must determine whether, in any given case, the master is guilty of sin.

The gentleman told you truly, that when a man is contending for the truth, his arguments will be consistent one with another. I am happy to be able, now, to apply his principle to himself, that you may see the very awkward predicament in which he has placed himself. He has occupied his time, partly in relating isolated cases of cruelty, practiced by wicked masters, several of which have been proved untrue, and none of which have any applicability to the question under discussion; and partly in telling you what slave-holding is. How has he defined or described slave-holding? By enumerating the worst laws of ancient Greece and Rome, and of some of the southern States, and asserting that these laws are the thing itself. He insists that those laws are essential to the existence of slavery—that the relation cannot exist without them. Let him only *prove* this, and I give up the question. If the relation of master and slave cannot exist without cruel laws and inhuman treatment, away with it. Let us, then, inquire whether these things are essential to the existence of the relation.

But, first, mark how differently the gentleman reasons concerning this relation and others. He insists that all the bad laws which are made to regulate the relation of master and slave, are essential to its existence; but when I refer to the cruel laws by which other relations have been regulated, he at once distinguishes between the bad laws and the relation.

1

When I ask, in view of the degrading laws, by which, over
so large a portion of the earth, the marriage relation has
been regulated, whether it is in itself sinful, he finds no
difficulty in admitting that the laws are wrong, and the relation right. Although he makes the recognition of marriage,
by the civil law, essential to its validity, yet he does not
condemn the relation because the laws are bad.

And when he is pointed to the bad laws by which the
relation of parent and child has often been regulated, does
he contend that those laws are essential to the relation? By
no means. The civil law recognizes the relation and regulates it; and he finds no difficulty in discriminating between
the relation, as recognized by law, and the particular laws
for for its regulation.

But the gentleman may tell you, that these relations are
right, because instituted by God; whereas the relation of
master and slave is wholly the creature of law, and consequently all the cruel laws are part and parcel of the thing
itself. I reply, that organized civil government—the relation between ruler and subject—is not properly a *natural*
relation, but is established by men. Will it be pretended,
that all the oppressive laws, and all the tyranny connected
with civil government, are essential to the relation between
ruler and ruled? Civil government, we know, is, in a sense,
of divine appointment; and the relations belonging to it are
right. Mr. B. finds no difficulty in distinguishing between
the relation of governor and governed, and the ten thousand
bad laws by which men have sought to regulate this relation.
The truth is, that in regard to all relations, whether natural
or constituted by the organization of human society, there is
a broad distinction to be made between each relation, and
the laws enacted for its regulation. Why, then, I ask, must
the relation of master and slave be confounded and identified
with all the particular laws enacted for its regulation? Are
we, for the special accomodation of abolitionism, to reason
about this relation as we do about no other? Does it require
special advantages in order to sustain its claims?

Let it be kept in mind, that if anything which is essential to the relation of master and slave, be taken from it, the relation itself ceases to exist. Now it is a fact, that according to the slave laws of Rome the master had unlimited power over the life of the slave. This, Mr. B. says, was rather a *custom* than a *law*. I will read the law on this point, as quoted by the *Biblical Repository*, from the Justinian Code. This is a New-England publication; it comes from a region where, it is said, the spirit of freedom prevails. I read in vol. 6. p. **419**. " All slaves are in the power of their masters, which power is derived from the law of nations; for it is equally observable among all nations. that masters have had the power of life and death over their slaves; and that whatsoever is acquired by the slave, is acquired for the master." Now Mr. B. contends, that all the slave laws are essential to the existence of slavery. Then if the power over the life of the slave be taken from the master, the relation must cease to exist; because one of its *essential features* has been destroyed. If, then, his principles are correct, Kentucky is actually a *free State;* for there the master has not power over the life of his slaves; and, therefore, an essential feature of the relation being wanting, the relation itself does not exist ! This argument applies with equal force to most, if not all, the other slave-holding States; for in no one of them, I believe, has the master any such power. Consequently, we reach the conclusion, that they are all free States !

Again. The law forbidding slaves to be taught to read, we have been told, is essential to the existence of slavery. But in Kentucky there is no such law; therefore Kentucky is a free State ! And it is a fact, that, years before New York abolished slavery, a law was passed for having the slaves instructed. Though, according to Mr. B.'s logic, slavery was abolished when that law was passed ! yet it is a fact, that the relation between master and slave existed there for a number of years after the law was passed. I might give other examples, were it necessary.

But the gentleman's argument also proves the Presbyterian Church to be an abolitionist church; for her law forbids all cruelty toward slaves, the separation of husbands and wives, &c., and calls upon masters to give them religious instruction. Yet Mr. B. and some of his friends have denounced our church as, "*par excellence*, the *slave church* of America!" The law is as follows:

"We enjoin it on all church sessions and presbyteries, under the care of this Assembly, to discountenance, and, as far as possible, to prevent all cruelty, of whatever kind, in the treatment of slaves; especially the cruelty of separating husband and wife, parents and children; and that which consists in selling slaves to those who will either themselves deprive these unhappy people of the blessings of the gospel, or who will transport them to places where the gospel is not proclaimed, or where it is forbidden to the slaves to attend upon its institutions. The manifest violation or disregard of the injunction here given, in its true spirit and intention, ought to be considered as just ground for the discipline and censures of the church. And if it shall ever happen that a Christian professor, in our communion, shall sell a slave who is also in communion and good standing with our church, contrary to his or her will or inclination, it ought immediately to claim the particular attention of the proper church judicature; and unless there be such peculiar circumstances attending the case as can but seldom happen, it ought to be followed, without delay, by a suspension of the offender from all the privileges of the church, till he repent, and make all the reparation in his power to the injured party."

Such is the law of our church, proclaimed in 1818, and never repealed, but reaffirmed substantially by the last. General Assembly. The gentleman has proved, at least to his own satisfaction, that the right to separate husband and wife is essential to the existence of slavery. Since, therefore, our church does not permit her members to do this thing, she ought to be regarded most decidedly as an aboli-

tionist church. Now one of two things is true, viz : all the
the cruel laws and all the cruelties practiced under those
laws upon the slaves, by wicked men, are essential to the
relation of master and slave; or they are not. If they are
not, the relation may exist without them, and all the gentleman's declamation concerning them, does not prove it in
itself sinful. If they are essential to it, as abolitionists affirm, then our church has no connection with slavery; because she has condemned a number of its essential ingredients.
So that either Mr. B. has spent his time in discoursing of
matters which do not bear on the subject in hand, and do not
prove slave-holding in itself sinful; or he has proved the Presbyterian church to have no connection whatever with slave-
holding. If the abuses of which we have spoken, are essential to the existence of slave-holding, Presbyterians cannot
hold slaves. If they are not, his argument falls to the ground,
as perfectly worthless; for his whole argument has been
based upon the assumption that they are essential to it.

Yet, with singular inconsistency, the gentleman denounces the Presbyterian church as *pro-slavery ;* although
she refuses to tolerate in her members a number of things
which he considers *essential to the existence of slavery !*
The relation still exists, when divested of all those abuses.
What, then, is slave-holding? It is the claim of a master to
the services of the slave, with the corresponding obligation to
treat him kindly, as a rational, accountable, immortal being.
Where has he offered even one argument to prove, that this
claim is, under all circumstances, sinful? His whole argument
has depended upon the circumstances which may, or may not
attend the existence of the relation. It is therefore, wide as
the poles from the question under discussion. He has not
yet touched that question.

Thursday, 4 o'clock, P. M.

[MR. BLANCHARD'S SIXTH SPEECH.]

*Gentlemen Moderators, and Gentlemen and Ladies, Fellow
Citizens:*

If I should say nothing in reply to the constant affirmations of my brother that I do not speak to the question, I
might seem to treat him with disrespect. It is not my wish
to do so. You will recollect that the subject of cruelty was
introduced three times by himself in accusations against abolitionists, saying that we have slandered slave-holders by at-
tributing to slavery cruelties which no not in fact exist. I
replied, showing there are three circumstances, which are
part and parcel of slavery; which three things make the
slave liable to more and greater cruelties than brutes are;—
that slavery is therefore essentially cruel and *therefore* SIN-
FUL, if cruelty is a sin. My friend seems now angry that I
spoke about cruelty at all, asking " what is that to the question?" So that I can take no course but he finds some fault
with me. It seems that whether I drink at the brook above
or below him, I still roil the water for him. Now I certainly wish to do all that fairness requires of me. Such has
been my endeavor from the first; and I am constrained to
fear my friend has some special motive for finding fault.

But his last complaint, with his remark in connection,
were somewhat ludicrous. He told you that I had not yet
spoken to, and would not debate the question at all. Speci-
fying certain topics which he put in my mouth, he declared
with solemn emphasis that he would not discuss such irrel-
evant matters but keep himself rigidly to the question.
Then in less than five minutes he said, " Now I will follow
the gentleman through his remarks." [a laugh.]

The proposition I lay down, and which I was attempting
to prove, is that the slave is without protection in Kentucky;
and that the statement of my friend, that in Kentucky slaves
have the same protection as children, is certainly without authority. Was not *that* debating the question? Most cer-

tainly: for surely, to deprive unoffending human beings
of protection is sin; and to hold them in such a situation that
they must be deprived of protection is sin also; because it is
a continuation of the sinful act—the first deprivation.   Surely, this is upon the question, *Is slave-holding a sin.* I am
proving that slave-holding is a sin upon the same principle,
and for the same reason that it would be a sin to hold your
head in an exhausted receiver, where you should be bereft
of air, which God made free for all; and because He made
the air free to all, holding you where you are deprived of it
is murder: so holding men in deprivation of protection by
civil government, is robbing them of the benefit of God's ordinance establishing human society, an ordinance given by
God to shelter all. The argument is not what I call direct;
but it is cogent and conclusive. You all see plainly enough
the bearing of my remarks upon the question. It is not
needful for me to hold a guide-board every moment to your
heads, crying, " This is to this point, and that goes to that."
I may safely, I think, leave something to your judgment, and
compliment you so far as to presume you capable of perceiv-
ing the bearing of an argument upon the question without
uttering a nota bene at the end of every paragraph.

I resume my argument. I said I would institute a comparison, between the protection enjoyed in Kentucky by the
most friendless orphan child, and that of a Kentucky slave.
If I show that the latter has literally *no* protection by the
civil law, then, I show you that slavery holds man in a condition bereft of what God intended for him, which is sinful,
and establish the affirmative of the question, by proving
slave-holding to be sin.

Take now a Kentucky orphan child, as bereft as bereav-
ment itself can make him—without guardian, mother, father,
uncle, or cousin.

I have here, copied out in full, the laws of Kentucky applicable to such persons.

If the orphan be a boy, he is bound out by the proper
officer, as a servant. There is, in Kentucky, a threefold dis-

tinction of persons rendering service—apprentice, servant, and slave. The "law of master and servant" regulates the lowest form of free labor; one grade below that of apprentice. For the master is not bound to teach the bound servant a trade, as he is bound to teach an apprentice. The servitude of a bound servant is, therefore, the lowest form of free labor known to the law. Now what is the protection secured to the bound servant? 1st. He cannot be bound for more than seven years. As he is supposed to be young when indented, this ordinarily makes him his own master at about twenty-one years of age. But slavery is perpetual in the person and posterity of the slave. Again, the master of the indented servant is bound to provide him with "wholesome and sufficient food, and clothing," as compared with that of the family (not with his peck of corn per week,) and, at the end of the indentures, to give him a "new coat, waistcoat, pantaloons, (or 'breeches,' as the law has it,) shoes, two pairs of stockings, two shirts, hat, and blanket."

Stat. Ky. 1798.

This is the protection which the law gives to the servant in his earnings. Again; the statute provides a punishment for "injurious demeanor" to the servant: and we find what "injurious demeanor," in a master towards a servant, is, by the adjudged cases. Thus in McGrath *vs.* Hernden, 4 Mun. Rep. 380: McGrath, the master, sued Hernden, the father of the bound boy who had runaway, for the service of his son. The father put in a plea that McGrath, "by whipping and cow-hiding, had driven the boy away." The Court allowed the plea and declared the boy free. The operation of such a principle as this would have freed before this time, two-thirds of all the slaves in the United States. If that runaway boy had been a slave, the laws would have rewarded the man who should take him up and deliver him to his master. The utmost which they would do to relieve him would be, to allow a neighbor to take up his case, if his master's cruelty went much beyond the slave-holding standard in the neighborhood, sell him to a second master, and *pay his whole price to the first.*   By this change, the slave may be worse off than before; for he is taken from a master with whose passions he is acquainted and sold to one of whose temper he is wholly ignorant.

The motive of this law, which my brother boasts of as a specimen of Kentucky clemency, does not seem to be to protect the slave; for if the end was justice to the slave, why not give him his liberty, which is equally his own with his life.   It seems to have been made, like the law forbidding cruelty to animals, to protect the sensibilities of the community, rather than from any sense of justice to the creature suffering.   The inhuman master is not punished by the sale of an obnoxious slave.   It may be a relief to him to be rid of the slave he hates.   Yet this is the sum of all the legal protection afforded to the slave in Kentucky; while the bound servant goes free if the master but cow-hide him. And what is most important of all, (and I beg your special attention to it,) by a statute of 1797, "the courts of every county shall, at all times, hear the complaints of apprentices and hired servants, and may determine such cases in a summary way."   The Bible gave the same protection to the Hebrew bond-servant.   All that he had to do was to walk to the judge sitting in the gate of the city, and he obtained summary justice.   The court may be sitting, engaged in some important case, when a rap is heard at the door.   The sheriff goes to the door and returns with the boy bleeding from his scourging, before the judge: who immediately arrests proceedings, hears his case, reads the statute, declares the boy free, and delivers him to some friend or guardian who will protect him.   But if he be a slave he cannot stand in judgment in a Kentucky court-house; he has no rights which that court-house represents.   If another does not chance to take up his case, there is no bar where he can plead this side the bar of God.   His own quivering lip, and wet eye, and frame, gashed and gory, must never speak before a tribunal of human justice.   Another must tell his tale, or it is untold : and for this plain reason, that in law he is not a man but a brute!

Yet my brother says that in Kentucky, this wretched, though innocent outlaw has the same protection with the child!

Let us now trace out the protection which slaves enjoy in Kentucky in its details. Suppose a master travelling in Kentucky, die suddenly, without heir or acquaintance, except one slave attending ; let us follow and see what protection the laws afford this slave. His master, buried by the coroner while he is away ; a stranger, in a strange land, he wanders to the next plantation where he is taken up and "found without a pass." The law begins its protection by laying ten "stripes on his bare back." If he happens to have a "gun," "club," or "any other weapon whatever, offensive or defensive," the arms are forfeit to the seizer, and the mercy of the law adds lashes, not exceeding 39, on his bare back. *Stat.* 1798, *sec.* 5. He offers to swear that the gun was his master's who is dead : and the law answers ; " No negro or mulatto shall be a witness except in pleas of the commonwealth against negroes or mulattoes, or in civil cases where negroes or mulattoes alone shall be parties." *Stat.* 1798, *sec.* 2.

These proceedings ended, a drunken ruffian seizes him to drag him to jail, and advertise for a master. The negro indignant at the assault, raises his arm and knocks his assailant down. He is forthwith taken to the next justice who reads the law as follows :

" If any negro, or mulatto, bond or free shall, at any time, lift his or her hand in opposition to any person not being a negro or mullatto, he or she so offending, shall for every such offence, *proved by the oath of the party* before a justice of the peace of the county where such offence shall be committed, shall receive thirty lashes on his or her bare back well laid on by order of such justice." *Stat. Ky.* 1798, *sec.* 13.

The ruffian assailant, if not too drunk, stands up and swears to the lifting of the hand, and the law administers its protection in the shape of thirty lashes more.

[I have purposely avoided supposing the slave to be a

young female, thus receiving Kentucky protection, but you will observe that the slave-code knows no distinction of mercy for sex. It is the lifting of "*his or her hand*," at "*any* time," against "any person," which constitutes the offence. And the stripes are laid upon "*his or her bare back.*"]

Sold, after imprisonment, to pay his jail-fees, to a master whom he hates and who hates him, the despairing creature refuses submission. He runs away and is killed in the pursuit, or resists his master and dies under "moderate correction," and the verdict is "*Justifiable Homicide!*"

Now I do not suppose that precisely such a concatenation of horrors is likely soon to happen, but I do affirm that there is statute for every step of the case supposed for illustration; and wherever there is any, the practice coincides with the law.

Now let *Dr. Rice* go *read* at the grave's head of this lonely victim of slave-law *protection* (? !), his most extraordinary assertion, that, "In Kentucky the slave has the same protection that a child has!" Would not a hollow murmur come back from the very grave and lips of the dead; "Forasmuch as your treading is upon the poor—ye have built houses of hewn stone but ye shall not dwell in them. For I know your manifold transgressions, and your mighty sins; they afflict the just: they take a bribe, and they turn aside the poor in the gate from their right."

I know that when I speak as I feel, and as every man ought to feel on this subject, my friend thinks I "appeal to your sympathies." Well, fellow citizens; God appeals to our sympathies, aye and to our feelings for our wives and children too, when he says—"Thou shalt not vex a stranger nor oppress him. If thou afflict them in any wise and they cry at all unto one, I will kill you with the sword, and *your wives shall be widows and your children fatherless.*"

My friend is anxious for the Bible—"the Bible,"—"only give us the Bible for the doctrines advanced." Well, let him well consider the sense and bearings upon slavery, of the texts against oppression just quoted: and if he wishes for other Scriptures they are at hand.

"Woe unto him that buildeth his house by unrighteousness, and his chambers by wrong, that useth his neighbor's service without wages, and giveth him not for his work."—*Jer.* xxii. 13.

"Thus saith the Lord, for three transgressions of Israel and for four I will not turn away the punishment thereof, because they sold the righteous for silver and the poor for a pair of shoes."—*Amos* ii. 6. "And they have given a boy for an harlot, and a girl for wine that they might drink."—*Joel* iii. 3.

"Therefore thus saith the Lord God: Ye have not hearkened unto me in proclaiming liberty every one to his brother, and every man to his neighbor: behold I proclaim a liberty to you, saith the Lord, to the sword, to the pestilence, and to the famine, and, I will make you to be removed into all the kingdoms of the earth."—*Jer.* xxxiv. 17. "Is not this the fast that I have chosen, to loose the bands of wickedness, to undo the heavy burdens, and to let the oppressed go free, and that ye break every yoke?"—*Isa.* lviii. 6.

"Open *thy* mouth for the dumb in the cause of all such as are appointed to destruction. Open thy mouth, judge righteously, and plead the cause of the poor and needy."—*Prov.* xxviii. 8, 9. And if there be another Scripture requisite to utter God's abhorrence of slavery, and our duty concerning it, it is this: "Remember them that are in bonds as bound with them."—*Heb.* xiii. 3.

When he shall have reconciled these stern and terrible denunciations of every element, principle and practice of slavery, with slavery itself, I shall doubtless be fully ready to enter with him upon the critical examination for which he seems to pant. Until which time, I must be excused for conducting the affirmative of this discussion, in that way, which, after prayer, and much reflection, I have prescribed to myself as wisest and best for the audience, for the book we are to make, and for the cause of truth.

Hitherto, in this debate, my main object has been to get slavery, in full shape, fairly before us. I now come to what I call the *direct argument*, proving that slave-holding is sinful. And the ground which I first assume is this: *Slave-holding is sinful, because treating it as sinful, has abolished it, and no other treatment ever did.* And, as error cannot remove seated evils, if I shall prove that the doctrine that "slave-holding is sin," has abolished slavery wherever it has been abolished, without blood, then I shall prove that the doctrine that slave-holding is sinful is true. In other words, as nothing but truth could produce such effects, therefore it is true that slave-holding is sinful.

I know that I propose to myself a grave task—to prove that wherever slavery has been abolished by Christianity, it has been done by the force of the doctrine, express or implied, that slave-holding is sin. I know that this is the very doctrine of abolitionism, and that Dr. Chalmers has pronounced it a dogma of comparatively recent date. I know, also, that my friend, Dr. Rice, asks triumphantly, in his late pamphlet: "Where did their [abolitionists'] principles ever abolish slavery?" And he answers—"Nowhere on the face of the earth."—*p.* 68.

Now, I propose to undertake what may seem the presumptuous task of proving, not only that our principles have abolished slavery somewhere on earth; but that nothing but the doctrine "that slave-holding is sin" has ever destroyed slavery anywhere, in any age, except where it has perished amid bloody revolutions. While, on the other hand, the tame assertion of Dr. Rice and his Assembly, that "there are evils connected with slavery," never yet converted a slave-holder, emancipated a slave, or did any other good. In short, I intend to show, by an argument which I shall only begin, before I sit down, That the teachings of abolitionists are truth as to the sinfulness of slave-holding: and that the doctrine of their opposers, on this point, is error. And I must beg my auditors to pardon me in advance, if the arguments I shall now bring forward shall seem a little dry and didactic.

I have before me the double object of making a speech which shall convince, and a book that shall be read. And when CHARLES JAMES FOX, one of the most eloquent of statesmen, and of men, heard a speech praised, he used to ask those who heard it, " Was it fit to print?" " Will it read well?" And if answered in the affirmative, he would reply, " then, depend upon it, it was not an effective speech." I hope, therefore, if my next speech seems dull, you will charitably attribute it to the fact, that I have a book to make.

Ignatius, the eminent Christian father, who died a martyr, at Rome, in the year of our Lord, 107—only seven years after the death of the Apostle John, whose disciple he was, while on his way to suffer martyrdom at Rome, wrote letters to the Christian churches; also a letter to Polycarp, of Smyrna, exhorting and instructing him how to manage matters and carry himself in his church. There is in this letter the following passage, which shows that the slaves of heathen masters, who joined the churches planted by Paul in Asia Minor, wished to have the church money applied to buy their freedom. This is the passage:

"Despise not slaves of either sex; yet let them not be puffed up, but serve more faithfully to the glory of God, that they may obtain a better liberty from God. *Let them not desire to be set at liberty at the charge of the church,* lest they be found slaves of lust."—*Miln. Cent.* II.

This desire of the Christian slaves to have their brethren in the church apply the church funds to buying them of their heathen masters, shows clearly that those brethren were not slave-holders; nor those Apostolic churches slave-holding churches. So far from this, the slaves were asking to have the church funds applied to buy them, which could not have happened in slave-holding churches: the idea of a church composed of slave-holders, non-slave-holders, and slaves, all working to pay one part of the members for ceasing to enslave another part, being absurd on the face of it.

[*Time expired.*

[MR. RICE'S SIXTH SPEECH.]

Gentlemen Moderators, and Fellow-Citizens:

I must really be permitted to say that my worthy friend, who is opposed to me in this debate, exceeds all the men I ever heard for the mis-statement of facts. I do not charge him, by any means, with doing this intentionally; but the mis-statements are oftentimes so very glaring, that they are, to me, perfectly unaccountable. For example: By way of apology for introducing the subject of the cruelty sometimes practiced in connection with slavery, he says that I myself first introduced that subject in the course of the present debate, no less than three times. Now, what was the fact? Those who heard him, must remember that, in the very first sentence of his first speech, (the opening speech of this debate,) he adverted to the passing of a slave gang near this city, and then dilated, at considerable length, on the cruelty of slavery. He knows that my remarks were made in reply to him: and yet he now says, that I first introduced the subject! If the gentleman is so very forgetful, how can we rely on his statements?

He charges me with inconsistency, because I had said, I would debate only the question before us, and immediately proceeded to reply to his speech. The truth is, I proceeded to prove, that he had not debated the question, and that, in the course of his argument, he had contradicted himself, and refuted his own statements. I am not discussing, nor will I discuss, *the system of American slavery;* nor have I alluded to it, save to expose his inconsistency, and his contradictory statements.

His argument, during the last half hour, amounts to just this: In Kentucky, the slave does not enjoy that degree of protection which ought to be extended to him; therefore, the relation of master and slave is, in itself, a sinful relation!— Q. E. D. Because the laws regulating slavery in Kentucky do not adequately protect the slave; *therefore,* all who hold slaves there, or anywhere, are scandalous sinners! According to the gentleman, every individual slave-holder is chargeable with all the defects of the laws of the State in which he happens to live! How would he like to be held personally responsible for all the defects in the laws of Ohio? Would he like such a rule, if applied to himself? I fancy not.— And yet he would hold every slave-holder in Kentucky responsible for the acts of the Kentucky Legislature. Who ever heard before of a man's being held responsible for all the laws of his State? This I understand to be his argument: certainly, then, it is not to the point; it bears not on the subject before us.

But the gentleman says, it is wrong to hold a slave, because the master holds that slave in a position where the laws do not, in fact, protect his rights. Now, in reply, I say that his argument proves too much: and he knows it is an established rule of logic, that an argument which proves too much, proves nothing. Apply his argument to the case of a man in Hindostan. The laws of India do not extend to *wives* that measure of protection to which they are entitled. The husband, in entering the marriage relation, places the woman in a position where the laws do not adequately protect her: therefore, the relation of husband and wife, in Hindostan, is, in itself, a sinful relation; and every man who has a wife, is a gross and scandalous sinner! The ancient Roman laws gave no protection to a child, but allowed the father to treat him most cruelly; therefore, it was gross sin for any one living in the Roman empire to be a parent! So, because the laws of France do not protect all the religious rights of the citizen, as we hold they ought to be protected, therefore it is sin to have a family in France! His argument, in plain English, amounts to this: It is a sin to place a human being in a position where the civil law does not protect him in all his civil and religious rights; therefore, except under a government absolutely perfect, it is a sin for a Christian man to have a wife or a child! Such an argument sweeps all before it. It would destroy all the relations of human society. But if he will use arguments such as these, I suppose I must follow him, and expose them. He tells us, however, that he is coming to the question in his next speech. Well, I have not heard him say anything since the commencement of the debate, which afforded me so much pleasure. [Laughter.]

What I did say about the legal protection of slaves in Kentucky, was this: that the slave had, in Kentucky, the same protection from cruel treatment by his master, which the child has from the cruelty of his father. In reply, he does not deny that the law provides for the protection of the slave from cruelty, but seems to think the law will not be executed—that no one will bring the case of a suffering slave before the proper tribunal. A child may suffer much from a cruel father, before he can secure the protection of the law; and so may a slave suffer from a cruel master. But, I believe, there is no county in Kentucky, where an oppressed slave, cruelly and abusively treated by his master, will not find some one to espouse his cause, and protect him in his rights.

From the speeches of the gentleman, the audience, unless otherwise informed, would suppose the question under debate, to be this—" are all the laws of Kentucky, in relation to slavery, just what they should be?" I have never said, they are. The Legislature might enact a law empowering every master to kill his slave at pleasure: and if they should, what then? Would it follow, that every man is a vile sinner who, holding a slave, does not kill him, but, on the contrary, treats him with all kindness? If the law gave the father power to kill his son, would that prove every man a cruel wretch, who is a father, but who, despising the cruel law, treats his child with all the affection of a father?

Moreover—the laws quoted by the gentleman, were passed in 1798; whereas, the law to which I have referred, was enacted in 1830. The laws concerning slavery, have greatly improved since '98.

Having thus answered this one argument, I am about

through with the gentleman's speech. To answer nothing, is one of the most difficult tasks I ever undertook; and in what the gentleman has been saying, there is, really, nothing to answer.

I must, however, notice a statement he made in relation to the Rev. J. C. Stiles, of Richmond, Va. He referred to a report or statement he had somewhere heard or seen, that Mr. Stiles had, on his way to the General Assembly, (New School,) sold eight slaves, and so disposed of them as to separate those bound to each other in the family relation : and that such was the state of moral feeling in that Assembly that he was not disgraced by this, in their estimation, but was actually appointed to administer the Lord's supper to that body.

Now, there is a gentleman here present, who is an Elder in Mr. Stiles' former church, who has acted as one of the attorneys of Mr. Stiles, in the settlement of his pecuniary business, and who assures me, there is not one word of truth in the assertion: so far from it, Mr. Stiles gave $700 (a most enormous price,) for a negro man, not worth half that sum, because he was the husband of a colored nurse in his family, and he wished to prevent the separation of husband and wife. See the misrepresentation! Instead of separating family relations by selling, he paid double price in purchasing, expressly to prevent it. This was like a christian: this was conduct worthy of a man, a christian, a christian minister, a friend of God and of his species. He paid his money freely to promote the happiness of his servants. No wonder that he was not disgraced by it. See, I pray you, how the gentleman's *facts* turn out; yet he says that he is careful to state nothing that is not true.

I shall try to avoid such an example : what I state here, I will prove, if called upon to do so. I will not gather up reports and anonymous statements out of newspapers, to wound the character and destroy the usefulness of ministers of Jesus Christ.

But the gentleman is at last, going to make a point: he is

going to pro e that wherever and whenever slavery has been
abolished, it has been abolished by the doctrine he advocates.
If he proves this, he will prove, I undertake to say, what no
man ever found out till now. The wisest men before him have
failed entirely to discover it. Dr. Chalmers, who ought to
be pretty well informed on a question like this, being one of
the ablest and most eminent men now in the Church of
Scotland, says that the doctrine and practice of the abolitionists is wholly new, and was totally unheard of till within a
few years past. Now, Dr. Chalmers is grossly ignorant of
the whole matter; or, he has wilfully asserted what is not
true; or, the gentleman is wrong. I might safely leave the
audience to decide which is most probable. Let us look at
the first evidence he adduces in support of his assertion. He
tells us somewhat boastfully, that he is now actually on the
question in debate! That, he has really got on the question
at last! I have heard of an Irishman who, wishing to leap
a fence, ran two hundred yards to get a start, and then sat
down to rest before he jumped. [Much laughter.] So my
worthy friend has been running for nine hours of this debate,
and then sat down to rest before he makes an argument! [A
laugh.] Well, he says he has reached it at last. Be it so: better late than never.

He quotes Ignatius, as his first proof that the doctrine of
abolitionists has abolished slavery. And what does Ignatius say? He exhorts Polycarp, not "to despise slaves of either sex." That is right—it is good doctrine. So I say.
What christian would despise a pious slave? And what
next? "Neither let them be puffed up: but rather let them
be more subject to the glory of God, that they may obtain
from him a better liberation. Let them not desire to be set free
at the public cost, that they be not slaves to their own lusts."
Aye: but why did he not exhort Polycarp to decoy them
from their masters, and run off? Perhaps he never thought
of this expedient. The slaves, says Mr. Blanchard, wanted
the church to purchase them from their masters. Now the
abolitionists of the modern times, seem wholly indisposed to

purchase slaves, and liberate them. They have discovered an easier plan! They are not so liberal with their money. Oh no—they run them off to Canada—a process which costs much less. Wonder how Ignatius failed to think of such an easy plan! Possibly, because Canada was farther from Polycarp than it is from the gentleman and his friends! He says, this extract proves, that the churches could not contain slave-holders, because the converted slaves begged them to buy them from their heathen masters. If they did, the churches did not think fit to do it. They seem to have thought with Paul, who said to slaves so situated, " Art thou called being a servant? care not for it."

So much for the gentleman's first proof that slave-holding is, in itself a sin, and that the doctrine of the abolitionists has set all the slaves free who ever got their freedom. If this is his best proof, alas for the balance! [A laugh.]

I have here an article on the subject of Roman slavery, in the *Biblical Repository,* published in New England—a region which is famous for its love of liberty—where what Rev. Dr. Stowe terms " the New England spirit," certainly prevails. The conductors of this periodical, I presume, will not be suspected by the gentleman, or any body else, of being what he calls " Pro-slavery men." I will in due time read a few extracts from it and place them by the side of his argument, when he shall have completed it.

And now I will take the liberty of reminding the audience, that I have adduced three several arguments against the gentleman's position that the relation of master and slave is in itself sinful, and he has not yet found time to answer one of them. We have been debating for nine hours, and he has not only not answered these arguments, but not yet noticed more than one of them in any way. Let me recapitulate.

My first argument was, that the great principles of morality are so obvious as to commend themselves to the conscience of all men, except the most hardened and degraded, yet the immorality of the relation in question has not been perceived by the wisest and best of men.

Will any man deny the first part of this position? Do not the first principles of morality commend themselves to the understanding and conscience? Does any man hold murder to be right? Will any man pretend that theft is not wrong? Now this very question of the morality of the relation between master and slave has been presented to the minds of many of the wisest and the best of men, and yet but few, very few of all who have examined it, adopt the views of the abolitionists of our day. Now all those men must have been extremely stupid, or modern abolitionism is without foundation. Have abolitionists alone eyes to see and hearts to feel what is right and wrong? How does the gentleman account for the fact? He says that slavery is the greatest abomination of heathenism. How then comes it that the wisest and the best men never saw it to be, in itself, a sin at all? He has not attempted an answer.

My second argument was this: There never has been found a class of men rotten on *one* fundamental point of doctrine, or of the moral law, and sound on all other points.

The gentleman did make a feeble effort to reply to this: and how? Why he told us, that the Pharisees among the Jews, in our Saviour's day, were heretical on only one single point; and what think you was that? Why, they rejected Jesus Christ as God's Messiah and the only Saviour of sinners! That was all. Only on this *one* point were they unsound! Just as if this "one point" did not substantially include the whole Christian faith? Sound on all points but one? And yet Christ says, they made void the law of God by their traditions; that they were whited sepulchres; that they neither entered into heaven themselves, nor would let others enter! Again, then, I call upon him to point me to any set of men since the world began, who were wholly unsound on any one great fundamental point of faith or of morals, and sound on all others. It is an admitted fact, that the churches in the slave-holding States are as sound in the faith, as pure in morals, as expansive in benevolence, and in all other matters as exemplary Christians as the best abolitionist that ever breathed. Let the gentleman answer this argument. I venture to say, it never will be answered.

My third argument was this: and I now press it, once more, on the gentleman's attention. It is a fact, admitted by Dr. Stowe, a leading abolitionist, and not denied by Mr. Blanchard himself, that there are true Christians and Christian churches in the slave-holding States; that they have been blessed with the same tokens of the divine favor, and have enjoyed the same glorious revivals of religion with those on this side the Ohio river. And it is a fact, that some of the most eminent, devoted, and successful ministers in the free States were converted, if they were converted at all, in the revivals with which those churches were blessed. The prayers of these slave-holders have been heard and abundantly answered in blessings on themselves and others. Now, then, according to the gentleman, God has heard and gloriously answered the prayers of cruel tyrants, robbers, man-stealers and murderers, men guilty of worse than highway robbery, and still living in all these abominations! Does God hear the prayers and bless the labors of robbers, and of man-stealers, who, whilst they pray, continue in their sins? Does he listen to their prayers, grant abundantly their largest requests, water their souls with the refreshing dews of his heavenly grace? The man whose eyes Jesus opened, reasoned very differently. He made the following declaration, which the Pharisees could answer only by excommunication: "Now we know that God heareth not sinners, but if any man be a worshipper of God and *doeth his will*, him he heareth."

It is admitted, that there are glorious religious revivals in the churches in the slave-holding States: this cannot be denied. How will the gentleman account for these remarkable facts? How would he answer the declaration of the man whose eyes Jesus Christ healed, that God does not hear the prayers of wicked men? The Pharisees could not answer him, but they could excommunicate him. What say our friends to the same appeal? Will they resort to the same reply? I hope the gentleman will answer.

My fourth argument against the doctrine of the abolitionists was this: and I shall press this, too, on my opponent's attention. Their doctrine leads them to a course of conduct the very opposite of that pursued by Christ and his apostles, in relation to all sin, particularly in relation to slavery. The apostles did not form societies and pass harsh resolutions denouncing heathenism, and all the other sins of men in their day. Had they thus attacked and reviled the heathen, perhaps even the unbelieving Jews would have been willing to join in the work. But the apostles do not seem to have believed that this was the way to convert men's souls, or to reform their lives. They went into the very midst of those whose practice they sought to reform. Paul went and stood in the midst of Mars' hill, and there preached that they ought not to think that God dwelt in temples, or was worshipped with men's hands, or was like to gold and silver, but that they should repent. They preached boldly, firmly, fearlessly, yet mildly and kindly. They were maligned, persecuted, imprisoned, stoned—yet still they went forward from heathen country to heathen country, converting sinners, founding churches, changing and reforming the whole face of human society.

Does the faith of the abolitionists lead them to a course like this? Does it lead them into Kentucky, to preach boldly to slave-holders, telling them to their face that they are living in sin, and exhorting them to repentance and newness of life? But if they did this, they would be persecuted? Ah, there's the rub. And were not the apostles persecuted? Had the abolition reformers met imprisonment and threatened death, as Paul did, yet loved and prayed for them, as did Stephen, there would have been some more probability of persuading them to change their course. But did you ever hear of men's being converted by denouncing them *at a safe distance*, as murderers, thieves and man-stealers? Who was ever persuaded to virtue by being called a villain and a cut-throat, by a man he never saw? Alas! if they hope, by staying at home, and hurling abroad papers and tracts, and pamphlets, and harangue, painting slave-holders in the blackest tints of hell, to persuade them to set free their slaves,— they hope in vain. Never, in this way, will they effect their conversion. Did they hold the faith of the apostles in this matter, would not their practice be the practice of the apostles? "Shew me thy faith without thy works," said James, the apostle, " and I will show thee my faith *by my works*." Did they ever hear of Paul's saying to Silas, in a distant province, do you preach faithfully out there, while I stay at home: be instant in season and out of season, quit you like men, reprove, exhort, rebuke with all faithfulness,—whilst at the same time he kept out of danger? But our zealous abolition brethren exhort ministers in slave-holding States, to preach abolitionism, which they regard as pure Christianity, and fear not the opposition of slave-holders, while they themselves dare not set a foot upon the soil—no, not a man of them! They bind on others heavy burdens and hard to be borne, but they themselves will not touch them with one of their fingers. [*Time expired.*

Thursday Evening, 7 o'clock.

[MR. BLANCHARD'S SEVENTH SPEECH.]

Gentlemen Moderators, and Gentlemen and Ladies, Fellow-Citizens:

Those who were here when the debate closed last night, will recollect that Mr. Rice restated three arguments, which he said, he had adduced to prove that slave-holding is not sinful. The first, to which I will reply briefly, is this:— "Slavery is not necessarily sinful, because revivals of religion occur in slave States and slave-holding churches: and abolitionists admit that there are genuine conversions in them."

The inference is, "that God would not thus bless sinners;

therefore, slave-holding is not sin." I think this is a *fair* statement of my friend's argument; and my answer is this: 1st. That there are thousands of poor people in the slave States who do not own slaves. There are only 31,000 slave-owners in Kentucky, and only some 250,000 in the United States. The vast majority of the Southern people are non-slave-holders. Hence, there may be revivals, and genuine conversions, in their churches; and there may, also, be spurious conversions; and the slave-holders may be the spurious ones. Because, if they do not come to God, "loving their neighbor as themselves," (and the spirit of slave-holding is the very opposite of equal love to our neighbor,) they come in disregard of this law. And, "he that turneth away his ear from hearing the law, even his prayer shall be abomination."—*Prov.* xxviii. 9. Slave-holders' hopes MAY BE false hopes.

Secondly: We may account for revivals in slave-holding churches, upon the principle that the wicked man, like Manasseh, son of Hezekiah, is often blessed in consequence of the prayers of the holy dead. We read, in the Scriptures, that God blessed the nation of the Jews after King David's death, "because of David, his servant;" and, for aught I know, it may be, that these churches are trading upon the unexpired consciences of their forefathers—the holy dead. There once was a "David" in Kentucky, whom the Lord loved as the patron of his poor. Dr. David Rice was an enlightened and holy man. He denounced slave-holding, and taught all the doctrines of abolitionism, and, honestly striving to apply them, he resisted *in limine* the entrance of slavery into the Constitution of his State. It is true, his practice afterwards, in tolerating slavery, was not consistent with his teaching, but he was a good man. May it not be, that the prayers of that "David" are answered to this day in the conversion of souls in Kentucky?

On either of the above named grounds, revivals in slave-holding churches may be accounted for consistently with the idea that slave-holding is sin.

But, in the third place, I by no means deny that slave-holders may be Christians. I do not lay down the doctrine that every man whom circumstances may have thrown into a wrong relation and practice, is, necessarily, not a Christian. I do not say that Abraham was not a child of God, while in concubinage with his serving woman. My brother admits that concubinage is bad, both as a relation and practice; but does that admission, if true, prove that Abraham was not "the friend of God?" Certainly not. It simply proves that, in dark ages, and pressing circumstances, good men may get into a monstrous bad thing, just because they know no better. God will judge such men according to their light, and not I. But I hold that the slavery relation is sinful, and the practice sin: not that all slave-holders are *ipso facto*, sinning with every breath they draw. The practice of my doctrine is not to denounce slave-holders, and give them over, but to require them to depart and come out from their sin. This is what abolitionists teach. That they should be warned affectionately; that they should be met at the very threshold of the church, as they are already met in many churches, South and North, and told, that when they enter the church, they must "*put away the evil of their doings;*" and that slave-holding is one of them.

I beg you will remember that we distinguish between the sinfulness of the relation of slavery, and the personal wickedness of those *who are* in this relation. Abraham was a good man, yet he was in a bad relation and practice, and one totally inconsistent with the original constitutions of God, as afterwards explained by Christ. Jacob was a good man, yet he was found in the same miserable condition. So may it be with slave-holders.

God forbid that I should lay a "flattering unction" to the heart of slave-holders, calculated to content them in their sins. But when I see the whole political press, backed by a venal clergy at the South, and their brethren like-minded at the North, engaged in belieing abolitionists, perverting their doctrines, and caricaturing their measures, and justifying slave-holding out of God's word ;—when I see the Rev. **Dr. W. S.** Plummer indirectly advocating the burning of aboli- tionists at the stake; " roasting them at their own fire ;" and the Rev. **R. N.** Anderson recommending the application of Lynch law to them ; and men and women of all classes, and occupations who draw their bread, by merchandizing, or public house-keeping, or coast-wise shipping, from the labor of the slaves—all joining in the cry that abolitionists are in- cendiaries, and slave-holders all gentlemen ;—I can well im- agine that good men at the South, who really desire to be rid of slavery, may be confounded by the hubbub, and not know what to do.

That there are such good men at the South I certainly know. I have by me three letters from a gentleman, a Methodist professor, whom I lately saw in this city; then and now a citizen of Mississippi, born and educated in the extreme South. He had brought four slaves from Mississippi, to emancipate them. While here, he chanced to hear a sermon in which the doctrine of the sinfulness of slave-holding was maintained, and he uttered the deepest expressions of grati- tude to God that he had lived to hear the truth declared against the sin and curse of his native State. He emancipated his four slaves, and is gone to prepare the way (there are some legal embarrassments) to free the rest. He is now in active correspondence with a friend in this city.

Yes, I bless God, that while the haters of abolition,—the worshippers of public sentiment and of mammon, the aris- tocratic, timid, profligate; the mercenary, and the slavish minds are leagued to bolster up slavery, and malign and run down its opposers ; there are good men in the slave States who will not be deaf to their warnings, nor slow to practice when they once see the truth. And the holy struggle now going on in the consciences of many such men, shows that God has heard our prayers. Alongside of this Mississippian; I will now place the Rev. Mr. Smith, of Sumpter county, Alabama, whom I fell in with a few years ago, while tra- veling up the Ohio river. He had one slave, a woman, with him. He said she was forty years old, and had had two or three husbands : that they had been sold away from her, and he did not now know (though she was *his* slave) whether she had a husband, or whether she could read. She could probably spell a little—finally, he was sure she could. These statements he made to President Kellogg, of Knox College, Illinois, Rev. S. Steele, of Ohio, and myself. And when I told him that his slave was free—that the Supreme Bench of Ohio had decided that if a man brought his slave to Ohio ; or suffered one to come with his free consent, it was equivalent to emancipation ; and that if he took her back he would be taking a free woman into slavery ; he became alarmed and went to the forecastle and told the men that he was likely to get into trouble with some abolitionists about his servant, and hoped they would aid him. He told me haughtily, that he " did not suffer interference with his domestic arrangements."

Before that, he had been so mild and soft that you would have thought he was born with lambs' milk in his mouth. So anxious was he to learn the truth. " We of the South," he would say, " have this difficulty, and that difficulty." " We of the South," wish to know our duty, &c. &c. (Yet this poor clerical creature was Ohio born, and educated in the North, but had sold his conscience for the lucre of the slave-system.) But the moment I told him the woman was free, and that he could not take her back into slavery without being, by the law of God and man, a kidnapper ; he was in a flame of anger and alarm. As soon as the boat touched at Parkersburg, or Wheeling, Va., I forget which, we saw him go ashore, with his slave woman marching after him, (though he had intended to go higher and land in Ohio,) to put her in safe keeping, in Virginia, as we supposed, while he attended the O. S. General Assembly at Philadelphia, to which he was going, as a Commissioner.

At the right hand of every fair-minded and honest slaveholder, stand such men as this preacher Smith. And they will as surely find themselves at the left hand of Christ, at the judgment day, as Christ's word is true, in which he has said, "Inasmuch as ye have not done it unto one of the least of these, ye have not done it unto me." He deliberately took this woman from freedom, to where she had been forty years a slave, without marriage, and, though in a minister's family, without learning to read the Bible.

Before resuming my course of remark, I briefly advert to one matter:—

If my friend, who is unfortunate in his understanding of my arguments, objects to any statement of mine, I wish he would disprove it. It is not pleasant to me to hear from him, "It is not so," "That is false," &c., and that I am the "most remarkable man for misstating facts, whom he ever heard." It would gratify us more if he would give a clear reason for denying the facts which I state, than to hear him speaking thus. In the instance, which I adduced to show the spirit of the church; of Dr. Stiles, selling eight slaves, just before he went to the General Assembly, where he was appointed to administer the communion;—if I was mistaken, it was simply a mistake, not a falsehood or untruth. I said simply, as the reporters' notes will show, that 'it was published in the papers as a fact.' I was particularly guarded in my statement. I saw the fact in the public prints, and have never seen it contradicted, or heard of its being a mistake, and I now believe it to be true. But my friend has got some lawyer, whose statement, given by Dr. Rice, shows that he is a slave-holder's agent, in this audience, to say that the printed account is wholly false, and "he never sold the slaves," &c. This informer admits that Dr. Stiles had slaves in Kentucky; that he is gone to Virginia; and does not tell where the slaves are. Yet, my statement goes for nothing, because an unseen slaveholder's agent in this house says it is not true!

I wish to say, once for all, that I do not reproach men by wholesale; but wish to err on the charitable side, if I err at all. Yet, I confess, I scarcely know what to believe from the lips of slave-holders and their apologists, speaking on

the subject of slavery. They seem to me to attach a different meaning to the words which they use about slavery from
what we do. For instance. An amiable and respectable
gentleman, when lately I was in St. Louis, made the following statement respecting the pastor of the First Presbyterian
church in that city. He said that a slave-holder, at the
point to die, requested this minister to administer on his estate, which included slaves. That the clergyman objected to
administer on slave-property, and was told by the dying man
that the object was to set them free. That the physician
was requested to stop, as a witness that the pastor had not suggested the emancipation; [and my informant praised the
foresight of the minister in providing a witness to prove that
he had not urged a dying man to free his slaves!] That the
pastor administered on the estate, and set the slaves free.

I, of course, rejoiced in their freedom: but I am since informed by two gentlemen, on their personal knowledge, that
those slaves were not freed at least for some years after the
letters of administration were taken out; that they have seen
the negroes coming to the pastor to know what they should
do; that one of them who worked on a boat used to come to
the minister with his earnings; that, in short, this minister
who, while laboring in this city, professed the strongest aversion to slavery, was then, and for aught I know, is renting
out those slaves, who, I was told in St. Louis, were set free.
I put these statements in with that respecting Dr. Stiles by
the slave-holder's agent, and leave them with the single remark that I scarcely know what to believe concerning slavery from the lips of its apologists and defenders.

I now take up the thread of my remarks from the point
where I laid it down in the close of my last speech.

I address myself gravely and directly to prove that slave-
holding and the slavery relation are sinful. I have said that
there are two classes of human practices and relations, and
I wish to show that slave-holding and slavery are among the
bad. That they do not belong in the class with marriage,
parentage, with merchandizing, farming, manufacturing and

all other good, wholesome and useful relations and ways of
men : but that they belong to those relations which are founded in error and enforced by sin, as concubinage, smuggling,
piracy, and the like.

I mean, in short, to show, what I confess seems to me sufficiently evident without proving, that slave-holding is a repeal
and violation of the whole kingdom of God on earth, which
the Apostle has concisely defined to be, " RIGHTEOUSNESS,
PEACE, and Joy in the Holy Ghost."

It is unrighteous as a relation, for it is not founded in natural equity, but in force. It is unrighteous as a practice, for
its principle is to take every thing from the slave, even the
possession of himself, thus excluding the possibility of giving him a just consideration. It is therefore simple, pure,
unmixed, unrighteousness, and wherever it exists the kingdom of God cannot come. For righteousness is the basis
of that kingdom.

Slave-holding is also the destruction of the second element, of the kingdom of God which is " PEACE. " for slavery is a state of war. " Ours, " says the Hon. Mr. Pickens of South Carolina, in his speech in Congress, " Ours is a
frank and bold system, which sustains itself by naked, undis-
guised force."   And it needed not this avowal to prove it.
For the slave code is bristling with the appliances of war ;
and the whole South is one vast camp, and every able-bodied
citizen a minute man, who, under the name of a patrol, is
even now doing a sort of military duty—being liable in an
hour to be summoned to immediate and bloody action. And
as to the third element of God's kingdom, I know, O Thou
Most High and Holy One, that the spirit of Slavery is not
" JOY IN THE HOLY GHOST."

Whoever, therefore, utters the " Lord's Prayer," that God's
kingdom may come on earth, as it is come in heaven, if he
prays intelligently,—prays for the immediate and total abolition of slavery. For marriage, parentage, equal neighborhood ; every principle and element, and regulation of that
state of society which constitutes the kingdom of God, is

repealed, and resisted, and shut out by slavery. It must therefore be destroyed, that the kingdom of God may come.

I have neither inclination nor occasion to traduce (as we are accused of doing) our neighbors of the South. If I know my own heart, I harbor no enmity toward slave-holders. Many features in their general character I admire. They are frank and open, and hospitable; far less addicted to tergiversation and quibbling, so far as I have experience, than those non-slave-holders who defend their slavery from the Word of God.

The revered Dr. Baxter—("*De mortuis nil nisi bonum,*") I know that he is dead, and am pained to speak aught of him but his praise. Yet this reverend doctor, and president of Union Theological Seminary in Virginia, was the first Presbyterian I have heard of, to broach the doctrine, that slavery is not sinful in itself. At the meeting of synod where he did it, an elder, who is a lawyer and Virginian, I think his name is Maxwell, started to his feet with astonishment, and declared he never could subscribe to such doctrine. "Why," said he, " we have always admitted slavery to be an evil, and have justified its toleration only on the ground of necessity; but to declare the thing itself consistent with the Bible, is both new and strange."

Ah! replied the doctor, the rise of abolitionism has changed the issue on this subject. If we admit that slavery is wrong in itself, we cannot resist their inference that immediate emancipation is a duty. On no other ground can we meet the abolitionists, than that slavery is not a moral evil or sin in itself.

Now I have always more patience with the ruffian appeal to brute force, than with this ecclesiastical truckling, and pitiful church-legerdemain. I would far rather hear a man confess the plain truth at once, and say, " we love money, and don't like to give up our property; and therefore we hold on to our slaves," than to hear a man get up and say, " he condemns the laws of slavery, but justifies the thing;" that he is " opposed to its parts, but likes it as a whole." He is opposed to its legs, its arms, its teeth, eyes, ears and head; but put them all together, and—slavery is not wrong!

For my own part, I prefer the Southern doctrine of force. It has, at least, the merit of candor and openness. God knows I would not traduce our Southern brethren, or set ourselves up as holier by nature than they. I know that though their depravity flows in one set of channels and ours in another, yet we are all depraved. Yet I feel that I could no more hold a slave, than I could other stolen goods. The slave was stolen. Either he was stolen from Africa, or his father was; and whether born in Africa or America, having done nothing to forfeit his liberty, he was born free, and was stolen the instant when he was made a slave. At best, I have but a thief's title to hold him, whether I bought him of another, or stole him for myself—a thief's title to one made in God's image, and, like Him, free!

But while I speak thus, I think a clear and careful distinction should be kept up between the sinfulness of slavery in itself, and the personal wickedness of slave-holders. The sinfulness of slavery is seen by bare inspection; while the slave-holder's is shown by his acts. "But why," says my friend, "do you propose to turn them out of the church, if you admit that they may be children of God?"

I answer: Simply and for no other reason than because they hold slaves. If he will faithfully perform his duty to the souls of his people, the minister of God is bound to tell them to quit their sins if they would be Christians. If he cannot do this he must either give up his charge or lose his soul. I by no means declare a man unconverted because I will not take him into the church. Peter was converted, yet if I had seen him cursing and denying Christ, he must have quit that practice and repented of it before I would have taken him into the church. "But it's no use to repel slave-holders," says one; "why not take them into the church and reclaim them by kindness?" Because the command of God is directly and positively against it: " *Thou shalt not suffer sin upon thy neighbor.*" A true spirit of kindness, too, forbids it. Paul commanded the church to deliver a certain one to Satan, not because he was a devil and hopeless, but "*for the destruction of the flesh, that his spirit might be saved.*"

It is perfectly consistent with brotherly kindness and charity to tell slave-holders, at the threshold of the church, "You will not be justified in entering this church till you get out of your sins— till you shake yourselves from what you know is evil." This is traducing nobody—slandering nobody—either South or North. It is simply disallowing the entrance of sin into the house of God, not slave-holding alone, but sin of any and every description; and thus by setting Christianity against the wrong practices of men, allow it to act, as the salt of the earth and the light of the world.

And I will here take leave to add, that all I have said in this debate has tended to this one point—the very question before us. Yet my brother has told you, I know not how many times, that I have uttered nothing on the question. My friend rises to address you—strikes the hour of the debate as regularly as a clock—crying: "So many hours of the debate gone, and nothing on the question yet." "Take notice, the gentleman has not done this; and the gentleman has not done that! ! "

Now I confess I have but one mouth, and that, perhaps, not a very fluent one. But I shall use it to the very best purpose I can, and do some things if not others. Now, Gentlemen Moderators and Fellow-Citizens, let me say, that, while we do hold slave-holding to be a sin, we do not take this ground, in the words put into our mouths by others, viz: " that it is sin under all circumstances." That phrase is deceptive. It is not true, taken one way, and yet it is true if understood another. I will illustrate.

James G. Birney went to Louisville, Kentucky, to receive his portion of an estate. He took his share of the slaves, and set them free: then went to the other heirs and told them that he would receive his whole portion of the estate in slaves, which he did; giving them all the money. He took his entire share in slaves, and set them all free. Now after he came in possession of these slaves, and before he had made out their free papers, he was not a slave-holder, but a redeemer, in the very act of redeeming men from slavery. It is a gross perversion of speech to call that slave-holding. Yet some delight to seek out such temporary transition instances, and use them to prove that " slave-holding is not a sin in all circumstances." It is sin wherever it is slave-holding. But suppose 50 rods of Kentucky soil intervene, and he must lead them over the line to free them. Is he a slave-holder while they walk that 50 rods? Surely not. The state is *in transitu;* and no man can call it slave-holding, unless he is quibbling, without feeling that he gives it a name which does not belong to it. The act is redemption, and the man, a redeemer of his species from bondage.

Yet it is from instances in the nature of this, they draw all their examples to prove that " slave-holding is not a sin under all circumstances." If you will keep this in mind, you will have no difficulty in understanding what we mean by the proposition, " Slave-holding is sin :" not the relation when in the article of death—but living, actual slave-holding; such as exists in ours and all other slave States.

And, respected fellow-citizens, I feel as if I could cheerfully lay down my life at the close of this hour, could I, on that condition, have the intellect and utterance of an angel, to transfer to the mind of this large assembly, the truth which presses and burns upon my own—the one great truth that God is to rule and shape the practical affairs and relations of men ; and that, consequently, where there is no every-day justice among men, there can be no religion. God wishes to control the great mass of daily and hourly doings of men. The question whether slave-holding is sin, therefore, does not turn on the hinges of extreme and supposititious cases of slavery—it is not to be decided by the one case to ninety-nine, but by the ninety-nine cases to one. It is a practical question. What we wish to know, is, whether the mass of slave-holders sin in holding slaves.

I have already said that the man who has set his face steadfastly to free his slaves, though still in the legal relation of a slave-holder, is not a slave-holder in the eye of law, or of reason: for the common law always allows a "reasonable time" for transacting business, and the relation expires from the time the first step in the business of emancipation is taken; and the matter is in a transition state, till completed. The individual emancipating is simply, and from the outset, a redeemer. But a slave-holder, is one who *holds slaves*, and uses them under the chattel statute.

And that there may be no mistake as to the persons meant, I remind you of Smylie's testimony, that " three-fourths of the Presbyterians, Episcopalians, Baptists, and Methodists, of the slave States are slave-holders for gain." Not three-fourths of the *people*, as he stated in his reply, but of the *Presbyterians, Methodists, Baptists,* and *Episcopalians* in eleven States. These are the slave-holders, whose slave-holding is meant.

Great events often hinge upon trivial circumstances; and I am persuaded that it is no vain fancy which gives me a premonition that this debate is to be one of those little pivot incidents upon which the mind of this city is turning from a wrong to a right state on the subject of our national sin of slave-holding. I know the people of this city better than you have known me. I know that a temporary prejudice has closed the minds of some to anti-slavery truth, and they in turn have helped to close the minds of many. But our people do not wish to remain in error, and the hour of darkness is fast passing away; and the day is near when every fair-minded person in Cincinnati shall be an abolitionist in understanding, as he is one already in heart. And though my labor here is almost done, and a few weeks closes my sojourn here forever; though in my short stay I shall not see the outward manifestation of this change of opinion, yet I am permitted to exult in the tokens of its coming, and I trust in God that the results of this debate may herald its approach.

Suppose we had met in Sparta, some centuries ago, and the question for discussion had been—"Is stealing sinful!" Suppose my friend were in the negative of that question, and I upon the affirmative. You are aware, that in Sparta stealing was not only allowed, but, in certain cases, held honorable. You recollect the story of a youth, the son of noble parents, who having stolen a young fox, concealed it under his toga, and suffered it to gnaw into his bowels rather than, by complaining of the pain, be detected in the theft. It was honorable to steal adroitly, but a disgrace to be detected. And this child was a true Spartan. He would rather die than be brought out in his theft. Sparta was a military republic; and the object of this regulation was to accustom their young men to dexterity in foraging in war. Now, in this state of popular opinion respecting this crime, suppose there were a number of Spartans who thought that stealing was sinful, and, living in a particular district, they had an anti-stealing society of their own. I submit, whether every argument which my friend brings against abolitionists, and the doctrine that slave-holding is sinful, would not, in Sparta, have applied with equal force and justice against those who were enforcing the law, "Thou shalt not steal?" Many of the people might be sound in every point but this one. And then, he might say to these: "Why do you not go down there, where stealing is believed in, and preach to them?" "Why," says I, "I believe I would rather take my own way. We build our church upon non-stealing principles, and so far as it is respected our principles will be felt." Still, you can see, we should be reproached by all those whose character or connections predisposed them to condemn us. Everything, in short, said against abolitionists, could have been said against a Spartan anti-stealing society. "What! Do you mean to say that stealing *in all* circumstances is sinful? You will turn many of the most liberal, amiable, and, in other respects, pious men of Sparta out of your church. How can our wars be carried on without foraging and plunder? What will you do with that lovely orphan girl who yesterday inherited a fortune which her father stole from still living heirs? Will you upturn society from its foundations, just to remove one practice which has evils connected with it?"

All this, and more, might be urged, but the answer to all such objections in favor of stealing, or slavery, is just this: that theft and oppression ought to exclude men from the church.

But look how the very principle of their objections proclaims their error, and proves our doctrine true, *that slaveholding is sin.* Their doctrine is, that slave-holding is not sinful in itself, and to prove it they bring up certain hard cases, as they suppose, where it would be cruel to condemn the slave-holder as sinning. But WHILE *they justify stealing or slave-holding in certain extreme and unusual cases, they tacitly confess, that in all ordinary cases, they are sin!* Else why not come square up to the point? Why slink and burrow in extreme or unusual cases—the nooks and corners of the slave-system? Why not meet it in the main, and say, "the thing is right, and I support it?"

No: they do not even pretend that out-and-out slave-holding can be justified. But to prove that slave-holding is not sinful, they commonly state cases where the owner (they say) has ceased to regard his slaves as property; and is waiting the first fair opportunity to set them free! That is, *they scrape up their vindication of the relation out of the very circumstances which show that it is perishing!* Thus they vindicate the relation from the charge of being sinful, as one would vindicate a man near you from the charge of being an ill neighbor, who should tell you that he could not be a bad neighbor, because he is in the consumption, and must soon die! "Slave-holding is not a sin under all circumstances," say they. "Very well; bring on your circumstances to justify it." They state them, and lo! every circumstance which they adduce, is tending *from* the relation, not *towards* it. Nay, their justifying circumstances are a consumption upon the slavery relation: they vindicate it by its diseases; and to prove its right to live in the church unmolested, they show it in circumstances where it only seems harmless, because struck with death. But, gentlemen, if ordinary cases would answer, extreme ones would not be adduced. Think of any honest relation, as marriage, being justified by extreme cases, and the very fag-endism of argument! Their mode of defending it is a full admission THAT SLAVE-HOLDING IS SIN.

But I prove *directly*, that slave-holding is sin, *because it annihilates marriage.*

Eminent jurists have decided this fact. Observation has decided it. We know it. " Slaves," says Dulany, "are incapable of marriage, because incapable of the civil considerations annexed to it." And because slave-holding prevents unions which God hath permitted; or, (if they were married before they were enslaved,) "puts asunder those whom God hath joined together," it is sin.

Several instances have occurred in the history of American slavery, illustrating the practical operation of the property principle upon the marriage tie. Instances, where a young girl has been tenderly reared to womanhood, educated, and knew not that she was a slave until after her marriage, when the heirs of her deceased master, who was also her father, came and claimed her as their property. And such instances are constantly liable to occur, wherever there are fathers of slave children who will not send to the negro-quarter, and sell their own offspring.

Now, bring this case home. Suppose one of the Elders of my brother's church, spending the evening in the bosom of his family, has just opened the Bible, and commenced the sweet solemnities of the hour of worship, when a rap calls him to the door, and a stranger takes him outside, and tells him that himself and wife are descended from persons held as slaves, and that they are property—the property, if you please, of the most amiable and pious man the Southern States ever held.

Nothing has touched this family yet, but simple slavery—the property-holding power. The husband returns to worship, but his lips refuse their office. He retires to his pillow, but sleep has fled from it. He groans inwardly as he turns upon his bed. "Oh, God, I have no wife! My wife is the property of another man!" "My children all the property of another!" That is precisely the truth respecting, not some few slaves, but of every slave-family on earth.

"Husband! my dear!" at last sobs the wife, "what on earth did the man want? Do tell me what has happened?" "Oh, nothing, only we are all slaves!" "Slaves!" cries his companion; "then may God regard us in mercy! But who owns us?" "Oh, an excellent good man, the Rev. Dr. ——; but if he dies tonight, we know not who will own us tomorrow! And what is worse still, our continuance together does not now depend on our own sacred rights, but upon his permission; and that permission again depends not only upon his disposition, but his debts. He may be compelled to sell us, or his creditors may take us. What we shall do, I know not. We are hopelessly undone."

This is the natural, necessary, and invariable operation of the pure slavery relation upon the family ties, when stripped of every law and circumstance of cruelty. And now will my friend, and he a minister of Jesus Christ, stand up before this audience, and tell you that slavery does not separate husband and wife; that this separation is no part of slavery; when he knows that the property-tenure always prevails over the marriage tie; that creditors' rights are saved without asking or caring about such a relation; that the slave who should plead it would only be an object of derision: when, in short, he knows there is none, and can be no marriage between slaves? If he does, in the face of all this, still assert that the separation of families is not justly chargeable upon slavery, but upon the chance cruelty of the master, all we can do farther, is to pray for him to Almighty God.

Gentlemen, pardon my earnestness. It is made an offence that I feel concerned at the destruction of an institution from which, as from a fountain, all the feelings of humanity flow—the institution of marriage. God has made one man to be the husband of one woman. My wife, by divine appointment, is one flesh with myself. But the slavery relation touches us, and God's law is made to give way before it. We are no longer "one flesh." The slave husband calls his wife to go with him, and the owner of the woman calls her at the same time to himself: which must she obey? You know, and my brother knows, she must forsake her husband and follow her owner. It is not that *they* may be separated, if the owner is cruel enough to do it; slavery has already separated them, and they are waiting to be driven apart. The marriage relation, that invisible tie of nature and of God, has given place to another invisible relation armed with power—the property relation. And the moment the husband and wife become property, they are separated as far from the holy state of wedlock, in which they lived before, as hell is separated from heaven. If, therefore, contravening, resisting, transgressing the law of God is sin, then IS SLAVE-HOLDING SIN. For it turns back the tide of holy affection in human hearts, sets Jehovah himself at defiance, and hurls back in his face all the merciful regulations which he has given to human society, by destroying the central law of them all—"*What God hath joined together, let not man put asunder.*"

My second *direct* argument in support of this proposition is: *Slave-holding is sin, because it is but a continuation of kidnapping:* in other words, *it is kidnapping stretched out.*

Kidnapping is the infliction of sinful violence upon unoffending men; and slave-holding is its perpetuation. The one is simply the other continued. Both are off one piece, spun from the same wool, and wove in the same loom. And

if kidnapping justly merits and receives the execrations of
the earth, slave-holding is fast coming in for its share.

I do not say that kidnappers are not commonly more hard-
hearted than slave-holders. I suppose, perhaps, they are.
Though John Newton was a missionary and a kidnapper,
and went to Africa, carrying Bibles and shackles for its people at the same time.

I read somewhile since, in his church of St. Mary, Wool-
noth, London, the epitaph which he wrote for his friends to
set up over his remains. On that marble slab he speaks of
himself as " *Once a servant of servants on the coast of Africa.*" He doubtless went there in blind benevolence from
the double motive of the gospel and gain. There is no evidence at all that he was a hardened reprobate while engaged in wholesale kidnapping. The only reason why that
business is now reprobated, is not that all who have followed
it were cruel monsters, but because it is intrinsically wicked.
As slave-holding is a mere continuity of the same thing, if
one is of the Devil, the other is also

Every one knows how the kidnapper acquires his title to
the slaves whom he fetches from Africa. He fires their villages at night; (or pays some petty chief whom he has made
drunk to do it.) Lies in ambush for wretched men and women who have never injured or owed him. Catches them.
Takes them from manhood and reduces them to slave-hood.
They cease to be moral agents. Their free wills are taken
out of them, and other wills substituted in the place; so that
if thereafter they will serve God in worship, they must ask
time to do so of a master, who may himself be an atheist.

Now what has the kidnapper done? He has set up the
propulsion of criminal force to move moral creatures, instead
of the free wills, which God gave them, and meant them to
obey.

On the kidnapper's return, another man stands at the wharf
and buys the kidnapper's title to the slave, for three hundred dollars. Of course he buys a kidnapper's title, for the
kidnapper has no other to sell. He buys the privilege of

continuing upon the person of the slave, the criminal violence which the kidnapper begun; and if one is sin, the
other is.

But one says, *"they inherit their slaves."* But how can heirs
lawfully inherit what their parents had no right to ? " Oh,
but my slaves did not come from Africa; they were born
slaves."

" Born slaves !" Did *God* make them slaves in the womb,
or from the womb? Or did some man take them and make
them slaves at their birth ? Your title to the parent was
nothing : your title to the child, if possible less. The enslaving of infant children is a horrid accumulation of guilt ;
for they can have done nothing to forfeit their rights. And
if the enslaving of grown persons is sin, which my friend,
even admits; how much more the enslaving of infancy ?
Smiling, speechless, helpless infancy, as lying upon the
mother's breast, it first opens its unconscious orbs upon a
world, dim with oppression and woe !

Thus slave-holding, whether of parent or infant, of the
African or American born, is simply a perpetual out-stretch-
ing of kidnapping. It is but a continuation of the sin of the
first man who first conceived the devilish possibility of yok-
ing men with brutes to the plough.

I now leave this point and make another. It is this :—
*Those who oppose us, concede that slave-holding is sin, by con-
ceding that slavery is an evil.* It is fair to prove that slave-
holding is sin by the concessions of its defenders ; for it is
not supposed that they would make admissions against themselves, if the truth did not compel them to it.

Now my brother has told you that he is cordially opposed to slavery, and wishes its abolition upon correct principles. Would to God he had told his General Assembly so ;
or that there had been in his report to that body, the 1000th
part of the abolitionism there is in his speeches here. Why
did he not there insert his opposition to slavery, or even hint
it in his remarks before that body ? Perhaps I can throw

some light on the question why he did not let his assembly
know how ardently he longed for the abolition of slavery.

There was a Professor *J. H. Thornwell*, in the last Old
School Assembly, which met last May in the first Presbyterian Church of this city. This Professor Thornwell was a
companion with my friend Dr. Rice, in the lead of their Assembly, and is the author of a book on the "*Errors of Popery*," which was gazetted at the doors of the Assembly during its sittings. Being from South Carolina, he is one of
those pious protestant divines who are bold and dexterous in
exposing the sins of Papists in withholding the Bible from
their poor laity, at the same time one of those southern ministers whom brother Rice lauds for giving *oral* instruction
without the Bible to their slaves; who thus cannot be said
even to

> " Atone for sins they are inclined to,"
> " By damning those they have no mind to ; "

seeing they practice the very sin for which they curse the
Papists.

This Professor Thornwell, I take to be "*Rev. J. H. Thornwell*," the supporter of certain resolutions which I will now
read. They were adopted at a public meeting in Lancaster-
ville, S. C.; and we are told by the *Southern Christian Herald* that the *Rev. J. H. Thornwell* and *Rev. Mr. Carlisle*
addressed the meeting in their support.

The resolutions are these :

1. " *Resolved*, That slavery, as it exists in the South, is no
evil, and is consistent with the principles of revealed religion;
and ALL *opposition* to it arises from a *misguided* and *fiendish fanaticism*, which we are bound to resist in the very
threshold."

2. " *Resolved*, That ALL interference with this subject, by
fanatics, is a violation of our civil and social rights—is
unchristian and inhuman, leading necessarily to anarchy
and bloodshed ; and that the instigators are *murderers* and
assassins."

So you see that Professor Thornwell puts brother Rice's

opposition to slavery, into the same box with mine, and denounces us both as "murderers and assassins." Well, I will cheerfully bear a part of brother Rice's reproach in this matter.

But you can now see that if Dr. Rice had uttered, in his Assembly, the anti-slavery sentiments which he has freely spoken here, that delightful harmony for which the unhappy Dr. Junkin was in an extacy of thanks, would have been broken up. *Professor Thornwell* declares slavery to be *no evil*. My brother Rice says it *is an evil;* and that he would have stood with David Rice to resist its admission into the Kentucky Constitution. He even says, (but I thought I per‑ ceived a slight twinge about his face when he said it,) that he is in favor of doing away slavery—*pret-ty tol-er-a-ble, con-sid-er-a-bly, speed-i-ly.* These were not his exact words, but as near as I can recollect, the sense.

At any rate, had I spoken the same words against slavery that he has here, slave-holders would not have forgiven me for it. But they will forgive Dr. Rice, for if I must tell you the secret—they know he utters against slavery, only what he is driven to, and that *he is not sincere.* His opposition to slavery is like that of our Dr. McGuffey, who was quite an abolitionist in his lectures, at the College Hall, in this city; but who is gone to a professorship in a slave-holding University, billing and cooing and shouldering with slave-holders, like pigeons of the same pen.

Yet, such men would have us believe them opposed to slavery, and feel hurt if we doubt their sincerity; when, per‑ haps, they never in their lives uttered one word in public against slavery, except when they were opposing the doctrine of some abolitionist, that slave-holding is a sin!

Yet, their admission is useful; for, conceding slavery to be an evil, they, in effect, grant, that slave-holding is sin. For "*love worketh no ill* [evil] *to his neighbor.*" But slavery, they admit, worketh evil to our neighbor: therefore it is contrary to that "love" which "*is the fulfilling of the law.*" Therefore it is "a transgression of the law;" and the transgression of the law is sin. Therefore, "SLAVE-HOLDING IS SINFUL."

I have yet one minute, but my voice is over-worked, and my strength exhausted. [*Time expired.*

[MR. RICE'S SEVENTH SPEECH.]

Gentlemen Moderators, and Fellow-Citizens:

I am truly gratified that my friend, after going through a debate of nine hours duration, has at last actually got to the question. I hope now, that we shall be favored by him, with something like argument, in every speech—that there will be something to answer. I am glad to hear him attempt to answer, at least, one out of three or four points made by myself.

And how does he reply to it? He admits that there are Christians, and Christian churches, in slave-holding States, and that there are even Christian slave-holders. And he does not deny, that real revivals of religion are enjoyed by the churches in the slave-holding States. The question, then, very naturally arises, *how is this to be accounted for?* How can he explain the fact, that God hears the prayers, revives the souls, and blesses abundantly the labors of those who, if the doctrine of abolitionists is true, are thieves, man-stealers, and, in a word, the vilest men on the face of the earth? It is certainly a hard task. Hard as it certainly is, however, he has undertaken it. He says, in the first place, that in those churches there are many who are not slave-holders, and that revivals are granted, and the souls of men converted, in answer to the prayers of such. But here arises a great difficulty. The whole of these non-slave-holding Christians do hold fellowship with slave-holders; thus conniving at, and virtually upholding robbery, kidnapping, man-stealing, and all the abominations which, he says, form part and parcel of slavery. Now, I do not think that such men are one whit better than the slave-holders themselves. Suppose I should tell you of a large company of *thieves*, having among them some who are not, themselves, actual thieves, though they live among, and countenance the rest who are; and suppose I should inform you, that these people have formed themselves into a church,—and that no sooner have they done so, than God hears their prayers, lifts on them the light of his countenance, sends down his Holy Spirit, and grants them to enjoy a most blessed and gracious revival of religion—they continuing to rob and steal as before. What would the gentleman think of me? Could he believe, that there were true Christians among them? And could he account for the singular fact that they have amongst them a revival of religion, by saying that God heard the prayers of those who did not themselves steal, but who only held fellowship with those who did steal, and connived at their sin, and encouraged them in it? Would such an answer satisfy himself? I think not. His first reply to my argument, therefore, is an utter failure.

But then he has another way of accounting for the puzzling fact I have presented to him. God, he says, blesses those thieves and kidnappers for the sake of " the *pious dead*," as he blessed many of the Jews long after David's decease, for the sake of the man after his own heart! Yes: God blesses these soul-drivers, thieves, man-stealers, kidnappers and murderers, for whom no perdition, according to some of our abolition friends, can furnish an adequate punishment, although they persevere in all their abominations, without reformation, or symptom of repentance ; and this he does in answer to the prayers of some good man or men, now dead, who, when alive, prayed for them !!! I do not think he has helped his cause much by this answer. The Bible furnishes no example to sustain him ; nor does it contain one intimation that " times of refreshing " from the Lord are granted to wicked men and corrupt churches, for the sake of the pious dead.

Ah, but holy David Rice taught, among slave-holders, all the doctrines of the abolitionists ! So says Mr. Blanchard

Now, I would give something to hear the gentleman read to us the true abolition doctrine from the writings of that good man. He was opposed, I know, to the introduction of slavery into Kentucky, and he was opposed to " the system of American slavery;" but I deny, and I challenge the gentleman to the proof, that David Rice ever held or taught that slave-holding is in itself sinful, and that every slave-holder is among the greatest of human sinners. I know that he lived and died among slave-holders, preaching to them the glorious gospel, that they held him in the highest veneration and affection, and that his name and memory are venerated by them to this hour. Never did he attempt to exclude men from the church simply because they were holders of slaves.

But Abraham, though a good man, lived in the sin of concubinage, and yet his prayers were heard. It is true, that there are some things in Abraham's life, which cannot be justified ; and it is true that he was a pious man. But let it be remembered that he lived in the twilight of gospel day, in the dawn of religious knowledge and gospel revelation. And let it also be remembered, that the sin of Abraham was by no means a sin of such heinous character as slave-holding, if the doctrine of abolitionism is true. I will read from the pamphlet of James Duncan, a work republished under the sanction of the *Cincinnati Abolition Society.*

" From what has been said of the real character of a slave-holder—how his authority over his slaves contravenes the authority of God's law relative to the slaves, and intercepts and prevents all relative duties between husbands and wives, parents and children, and turns the entire system of obedience due from the slaves, both to God and man, into a channel of honor and profit to himself,—it appears that SLAVE-HOLDER, considered as a term expressive of his station, office, and usurped authority, is a name of blasphemy ; and, like that of the Devil, ought not to be mentioned but with horror, and when imperious necessity requires it." Again, " In the whole volume of Divine providence, there is no one thing which shows the absolute necessity of a hell, more than the

practice of involuntary, unmerited, hereditary slavery."—
Duncan's Treatise on Slavery, pp. 118, 119.

There you hear what degree of sin they hold slave-holding to be; yet the fact that God hears the prayers of such
men, is attempted to be accounted for by the fact that he
heard the prayers of Abraham, "the friend of God!" They
tell you that nothing proves the necessity of a hell so conclusively as the fact that a slave-holder exists among men;
and yet the gentleman himself tells you, that some living in
this sin are good men, that God hears and answers their
prayers, and that there are genuine revivals of religion
among them! Why does he not come out, as Foster does,
and say that the whole American church are no better than
pirates and murderers?

But then he says that Dr. Plummer, and other ministers
of the gospel, keep the poor slave-holders (the poor pirates
and murderers) in the dark, and therefore it is no wonder
that they do not repent, and no wonder that they have revivals! Aye, but he passes by the fact, that the labors of
these very men, these blind guides, who keep the people in
the dark as to the sin of slave-holding, are owned and blessed
by the God of truth, and that multitudes of sinners are converted under their teachings. Does God bless the labors of
men who betray their trust by keeping sinners in the dark?
who even encourage what the gentleman and his friends call
robbing, kidnapping and stealing, by appeals to his word?
Such is the reply of Mr. Blanchard to one of the arguments
I have offered against his doctrine. I cheerfully leave the
audience to judge of its weight.

I have nothing to say about the case of Mr. Smith. I
know nothing of it, and therefore I can say nothing about it,
one way or the other. But from the gentleman's own account of the matter, he was interfering with the business of
others, and might have expected a stern rebuke.

My friend says he always laughs when he hears the Hagar
case alluded to. He laughs, I suppose, at the ignorance of
the angel, who directed Hagar to return to her mistress. The

angel was not living in this day of light—this nineteenth century! He had not the advantage of the discoveries of modern abolitionism in moral science, and in the exposition of God's word! The gentleman enjoys all these advantages. No wonder, then, that he should laugh at an angel that lived so many thousand years ago. He would not, I suppose, have given Hagar such advice had he lived under the laws of Ohio, and in the light of the nineteenth century!

I have recently read an account of a very zealous abolitionist who attempted forcibly to take away a colored woman from her master, in Boston; but the woman did not want to go, and she brought a suit against the quixotic gentleman for false imprisonment, laying the damages at the round sum of four thousand dollars! Not being able to obtain bail, he was conducted to prison. The silly woman, it seems, was not willing to be "kidnapped" by so benevolent a friend of the slave.

By way of excusing his slander on the character of Rev. Mr. Stiles, my opponent says, he read the account in a newspaper! It must have been true, of course! One cannot but remark the marvellous frequency with which accounts of this character, find their way into the abolition papers. The Psalmist gives as one of the characteristics of a good man, that he will not "take up a reproach against his neighbor." Yet, in making his threatened book, the gentleman is willing to stereotype such a report against a brother minister, although, as he acknowledges, he does not know it to be true! Is this right? Yet this is precisely the course the abolitionists are continually pursuing, and by such slanders it is, that they exasperate the South and West. But he says, it is anonymous testimony of some agent of a slave-holder! I informed the audience that the gentleman on whose authority I contradicted this anonymous newspaper statement, is an elder in Mr. Stiles' church, and intimately acquainted with all his business, having been engaged in the settlement of it. He says, that so far from selling eight slaves and separating families, he bought a slave at an extravagant price expressly to prevent the separation of husband and wife. I did not before mention his name. I will now give it to the gentleman : the elder in question is Mr. ALEXANDER, of Woodford county, Kentucky—a man of as high standing and as unimpeachable moral character as any man in the State. Again I ask, how would the gentleman like statements so injurious to be made concerning himself, on no better authority than a newspaper paragraph ? Would it not be well for him seriously to ponder that commandment, "Thou shalt not bear false witness against thy neighbour ?"

But another reason brought by the gentleman to show that slave-holding is always sinful, is that the kingdom of God is righteousness and peace and joy in the Holy Ghost; and slave-holding is the reverse, as he says, of all these; therefore it is essentially, and in itself sinful. Let him prove this. In proof he quotes Mr. Pickens, of South Carolina, who declared that every slave-holder in that State is a minute-man, ready to march at one hour's warning : and this does not look like peace. But is it not quite as peaceful as the doctrine of Mr. Duncan's pamphlet, endorsed by the Cincinnati Abolition Society, that the man deserves, and will suffer the pains of hell fire, who would aid in suppressing a slave insurrection, and prevent the slaves murdering their masters ? Yet Mr. Duncan was a minister of the gospel of peace, while Mr. Pickens is a politician, and man of the world. I submit the question whether abolitionism breathes the spirit of peace. The gentleman referred to Dr Baxter, a man beloved and venerated by all who know him, and told us that on a certain occasion he declared, in Synod or Presbytery, that slave-holding was not in itself a sin; and that one of his elders instantly rose to his feet and said that would never do: for we had always admitted it to be a sin; and the contrary doctrine was entirely new. I, of course, do not know anything of this matter, nor am I acquainted with the elder named. But in the first place, it is notoriously not true, that slave-holding has been generally admitted to be sinful in itself; and, in the second place—this I do know, that Dr. Baxter was a man of incorruptible integrity, who would defend what he believed to be truth, living and dying. Knowing the character of that eminent servant of God, I do not believe one word of the story told by the gentleman. But this is all aside from the question : I am not here to discuss personalities, or defend individual character, but to refute the arguments by which it is attempted to be proved, that slave-holding is in itself sinful.

The brother tells us, there is a broad distinction between the sin of slave-holding, in itself considered, and the sin of slave-holders who are guilty of it. There may be some ground for this distinction; but if slave-holding be such an enormity as he represents it,—the greatest abomination of paganism—a man professing godliness in this day of religious light, can hardly be guilty of it without being a most flagrant offender. Such a man could not therefore, be recognized as a Christian.

But mark the gentleman's admission : he says that he does *not hold slave-holding to be sin under all possible circumstances.* Is not this giving up the whole question? If slave-holding is a sin *in itself,* then it is sin always, under all circumstances. Blasphemy, for example, is a sin *per se,* a sin in itself; and is it not always sin ? It is a sin to blaspheme for one moment as truly as for a thousand years; and no possible circumstances can make it anything but a sin. And this is true of all other acts in themselves sinful.

I shall not say anything about being willing to die at the end of my speech, as the gentleman did, (provided my voice will hold out to the end of it;) and I must be pardoned for expressing a very strong doubt whether my good brother, if put to the test, would not shrink in the moment of trial. [A laugh.]

The gentleman's first argument, to prove slave-holding sinful, viz: that it makes marriage impossible, has been presented and answered before. I utterly deny the truth of the position. He has given quite a moving illustration, by supposing one of my elders, after spending a pleasant evening, and when about to retire, to have ascertained that he and his family are slaves. Truly this would be bad enough; but it proves nothing in favor of his proposition. He severely condemns the attempt to argue from *extreme cases*, though he evidently has no objection to this mode of argumentation, provided it favors his views. This supposition of an extreme case, is really the only proof he has presented, that slavery makes marriage impossible. He has told us, that a man defending the truth will always be consistent with himself. Surely, then, he should not have condemned a resort to extreme cases in argument, and then forthwith have relied upon just such cases.

The law of Constantine constrained the purchaser of a married slave to take the whole family: it expressly forbade the separation of husband and wife. Did this law destroy the relation of master and slave? It did not; the relation continued; yet the law prohibited the separation of married slaves. It is perfectly clear, then, that slavery may exist where the civil law forbids the separation of husband and wife; and, therefore, it is not true, that it necessarily destroys the marriage relation. Consequently, separation, where it does take place, is not chargeable on the relation of master and slave, but on the cruelty of a particular master.

The law of the Presbyterian Church in America forbids a church member to separate married slaves, and subjects the man who will dare to perpetrate the cruel act to excommunication. Will the gentleman, then, admit that ours is an abolition church? He will not; he denies it; consequently, he himself admits, that the relation between master and slave may exist unimpaired, even where masters are not permitted to separate married persons. Slavery, therefore, does not destroy the marriage relation. The brother, you perceive, is attempting to prove a certain relation sinful, from the wickedness of men in that relation, a course which if valid against slavery, is equally valid against the married relation, the parental relation, the civil relation—in a word, against every relation of man's social existence.

Mr. Blanchard's second argument is, that slave-holding is

only kidnapping continued, or drawn out; and therefore it is in itself sinful. The slaves were originally kidnapped in Africa; and therefore the present owners of them have only a kidnapper's title to them. This argument is founded upon a principle nowhere recognized as true, viz.: that a man can have no just title to any property, unless all who possessed it before him obtained it justly. What would be the consequence of carrying out this principle? Much of the land in these United States was obtained from the Indians by force or by fraud. Consequently, all the present owners of these lands are chargeable with holding them by unjust and unlawful titles, and must either give them up, or be expelled from the church. Will the gentleman take this ground? There are not a few now in New-England, living on princely fortunes gained by traffic in slaves. Will Mr. B. go to his New-England brethren, and denounce them as robbers, unless they will give up their ill-gotten wealth? If the abolitionists will carry out this doctrine, it will, doubtless, cause quite an uproar in "the land of steady habits." I question very much whether there are not some zealous abolitionists, who would not feel so pleasantly under its operation. They are said to hold on to the cash with a pretty tight grip; and however they may condemn the relation of master and slave, they would not be so ready to dissolve the relation between themselves and their fortunes. [A laugh.]

I was a little amused at the gentleman's pathetic appeal, in which he represented the *beautiful* little babe in the cradle, born free and equal with the children of the owner, yet stolen from the cradle and reduced to slavery. Yet, he has no great objection to depriving the liberated slaves of the right to vote—to have a voice in making the laws by which they are to be governed. He is willing to deprive them of their most valuable political rights, and leave them completely under the government of the white population; but he denounces the man who goes one step farther, for any reason whatever. By what law of morality he proceeds, I know not.

But he seems to forget, that God speaks of Abraham as having servants "born in his house," as well as servants "bought
with his money." *Gen.* xvii. Does the Bible, then, justify
kidnapping, stealing babies from the cradle ? Why does not
the gentleman act consistently, and denounce not only Abraham, the father of the fathful, but the Bible itself? It is impossible for him to be a consistent abolitionist, without rejecting and denouncing the Bible. Its tendency is to infidelity;
and already has it lead some of the most prominent of its
advocates into that dark region. Garrison and his coadjutors now bitterly denounce that blessed Book, and the church
of Christ.

But look at the absurdity of the charge, that slave-holding
is but kidnapping *continued.* A slave who is likely to be
separated from his family, comes and begs me, as a special
favor, to purchase him. To improve his condition, I buy
him, and because I hold him as a slave, I am denounced as
a man-stealer! Why? Have I deprived him of his liberty? No—he was before a slave. I have not reduced him
from a state of freedom into a state of bondage. That would
be kidnapping. But I purchase, at his own request, a right
to his labor, for the express purpose of placing him in a
better and a happier condition. Yet, our charitable friends,
wholly indisposed to give even a sixpence to redeem any human being, brand me for this as a robber, and a "kidnapper
of soul and body!"

Let me again revert to the case already mentioned, of a
Presbyterian elder in Kentucky, who became heir to a large
number of slaves, some old and nearly helpless, others, women and children, incapable of supporting themselves.
When the duty of immediate emancipation was urged, he
inquired of the brethren in Synod what they would have
him do. Was it his duty to turn them all out to provide for
themselves? Was it his duty to give bond and security that
they should never become a public expense? Was he bound
to separate husbands and wives, and remove his slaves to
Ohio? No man in Synod could give him advice of this

, kind. I have presented to the gentleman this plain case, and called upon him to say what the elder was bound to do. He is silent. Why will he not answer? *Because he cannot.* I have also presented the case of a gentleman in Boston, who fell heir to a plantation and slaves in the South ; and I have asked Mr. B. what was his duty? He is silent. Yet, according to his doctrine, those excellent men held their slaves by a "kidnapper's title," and were guilty of the sin of man-stealing! They both resolved to live amongst their slaves, and endeavor to do their duty to them. Will Mr. B. "shew us a better way?" Do you believe, they were guilty of the sin of kidnapping? Common sense decides unhesitatingly, that they were not. The law of God denounces no man, because he cannot perform impossibilities.

The gentleman's third argument is, that by admitting slavery to be an *evil,* I, of necessity, admit slave-holding to be in itself sinful. And here let me turn aside to notice his ardent wish, that I had said to the last General Assembly, what I have said here, concerning the evil of slavery. The duty of the Committee, of which I had the honor to be the chairman, was simply to report on the memorials presented to the Assembly. Of these petitions and memorials, (and their number was much smaller than the abolitionist prints have represented them,) none, so far as my memory serves me, asked the Assembly to decide whether American slavery is an evil or not. Some of them desired that body to devise means by which the condition of the slaves might be ameliorated, with a view to the ultimate removal of slavery. What was their reply? They said—" The apostles of Christ sought to ameliorate the condition of slaves, not by denouncing and ex-communicating their masters, but by teaching both masters and slaves the glorious doctrines of the gospel, and enjoining upon each the discharge of their relative duties. Thus only can the church of Christ, as such, now improve the condition of the slaves in our country." The apostles devised no other plan ; and the Assembly did not claim to be

wiser than they. And have those who have bitterly denounced the action of that body, shown themselves wiser? A
convention of Congregationalists and New School Presbyterian ministers met, not long since, in Detroit; and they
passed resolutions condemnatory of American slavery; but
what plan did they devise for the removal of it? None whatever. Yet some of them dealt out unmeasured condemnation to the General Assembly, because that body could not
do what the Convention did not attempt!

Another class of memorialists, the abolitionists, asked the
Assembly to make slave-holding a bar to christian fellowship, on the ground, that it is a heinous and scandalous sin.
They replied, that they could not do this, because the Apostles of Christ did not so act. They received slave-holders
into the church without requiring them to manumit their
slaves. For this decision, the Assembly was denounced as
" *pro-slavery.*"

I must here notice a very gross misrepresentation of the
action to the Assembly. Because that body expressed their
satisfaction at learning that increasing efforts are being made
in the slave-holding States, to have the gospel preached to
the slaves, they are charged with approving the withholding
of the word of God from the slaves, as the Pope withholds it
from his followers! Now the gentleman cannot help seeing
that this charge is not true. What was the action of the Assembly on this point? They said—"Every Christian and
philanthropist should certainly seek, by all peaceable and lawful means, the repeal of unjust and oppressive laws, and the
amendment of such as are defective, so as to protect the slaves
from cruel treatment by wicked men, *and secure to them the
right to receive religious instruction.*" Now, what laws are
those, the repeal of which the Assembly said, should be
sought? There never were laws in any of the slave-holding
States, which forbid slaves to receive *oral instruction.* The
laws referred to, therefore, were those which forbid their being
taught to read the Word of God. Yet that body is charged

with approving the withholding of the Scriptures from the slaves!

[*Mr. Blanchard* here explained, that he did not charge the Assembly with seeking to withhold the Bible from the slaves, but with approving the course of instruction pursued in the South, which embraced only *oral instruction.*]

Very well. I now, then, ask my brother, is it right, or wrong, to give to slaves oral instruction, touching the way of salvation? to preach to them the word of life? He admits that it is right: he cannot do otherwise. Yet, he blames me and the Assembly for approving and rejoicing in that which is right,—for rejoicing that the poor slaves are permitted, in any way, to be instructed in the gospel of Christ. The Assembly did not approve the withholding of the Bible from them. On the contrary, they urged the propriety of repealing those laws which forbid their being taught to read it. But they did rejoice, that they heard the gospel, by the faith of which, they may be saved. But I really begin to fear, our abolition friends will not let the Southern slaves have the gospel at all. The laws forbid their reading it, and the abolitionists will not go there to preach it to them, nor let us commend those who do. On the contrary, they teach principles which, if carried out, would banish every minister from the South. Then, what would be the condition of the slaves? What would be their prospects for eternity?

But he says I am for removing slavery ———— "pretty considerably soon." I admit that I have never preached, as have the Cincinnati Abolition Society, that every slave is bound to run away from his master, or that the slaves, in a body, are morally bound to get up an insurrection. No: I am not quite so much in haste to secure their liberty, as to " do evil that good may come." I am for removing the evil as soon as it can be done consistently with the safety of the parties concerned. But I hold, that there are other duties besides that of giving liberty to the slaves, which I am not at liberty to disregard.

I have never read the resolution which the gentleman

says Prof. Thornwell advocated, and therefore can express no opinion concerning it. All I can say, is, that if he does not hold slavery to be an evil, I differ from him on that point.

The doctrine of the American Colonization Society is that slavery *is* an evil: they propose one way to get rid of it: I shall be glad when I hear our abolition friends point out a better.

But if slavery is an evil, the gentleman argues that slave-holding must be in itself a sin. That remains to be proved. It may be admitted, that "the system of American slavery" is a great evil, the removal of which should be sought in all proper ways; and yet it may not be the duty of every slave-holder immediately to manumit his slaves. Some of those circumstances have been mentioned. Nay, circumstances may exist, in which a real injury would be done to the slaves by their liberation.

A despotic government is a great evil, and the Roman government was most oppressive and arbitrary in its treatment, especially of the Provinces. Does it follow, of course, that every officer who aided in administering that government, was an atrocious sinner? The Russian government is a depotism, and was most cruel and oppressive to the Poles: therefore, every officer, civil or military, and every private man in that country, who takes an oath of allegiance to the government, is a great sinner, and ought to be excommunicated! Such is the absurdity of the principle upon which the gentleman undertakes to prove slave-holding in itself sinful. It is most manifestly unsound. On the contrary, I maintain, that when by buying and holding a slave, I can materially improve his condition, the golden rule, which bids us do to others as we would that they should do to us, requires me to do it. And although I hold slavery to be a great evil, yet, in purchasing a slave, under such circumstances, I am committing no sin, but am doing what the law of God requires.

But the gentleman quoted the passage: "Love worketh

no ill to his neighbor." Very true: it does not. And do I do an injury to my neighbor in the case I have just stated? The tears of gratitude, on many a black cheek, tell a very different tale. What! because I cannot do him all the good I would, do I injure him by doing what good I can? If I am not able, without disregarding other paramount duties, to buy him and give him his liberty; or if circumstances are such, that manumission could not improve his condition; yet, if I greatly better his condition in that relation, and do this at his own earnest request, do I violate the law of love? —What profound absurdity! Yet this is the force of the gentleman's argument! I leave the audience to determine whether it proves slavery to be in itself sinful, and the relation of master and slave a sinful relation.

I have never pleaded that slavery ought to have existed, or that it ought to be continued. Never. All I insist on is, that the slave-holder should not be denounced as the worst of malefactors because he finds himself born in the midst of it. And especially, that he is not to be called a kidnapper who does for a supplicating slave the best that, under existing circumstances, he is able.

When I sat down, I was urging against the doctrine of the abolitionists the fact, that the course which their faith leads them to pursue, is very different from the course of the Apostles who lived in the midst of slavery in its worst forms. I stated, that the faith of our abolition friends does not lead them to go into the midst of a slave-holding community, and preach and remonstrate as the Apostles did, against prevailing sins. They stay at home and publish papers containing libels on christian ministers, such as that on Mr. Stiles; and they feel at liberty to spread such libels merely because they find them in a newspaper, (just as if newspapers never lied!) and they can abuse and denounce all slave-holders, and teach that the slaves ought to run from their masters, however kind they may be; that they would be justified in rising in a general insurrection and cutting the throats of their masters. But did Paul take this method of converting men from Paganism?

Did he thus seek to abolish Roman slavery? Never. I say, then, the fact that the *practice* of the abolitionists is in direct contrast to that of the Apostles, affords the strongest evidence that their doctrine is not the doctrine of the apostles. The man is even regarded as a good abolitionist, who denounces the whole Amercan Church *en masse*, as made of the vilest of malefactors! Is this the spirit of the Apostles?

By the way, the gentleman referred to the laws and customs of ancient Sparta, where theft was not regarded as a crime, but rather as a virtue, if the thief were not detected; and he asks, whether we ought not to preach in such a community the doctrine, that theft is in itself sinful? Ought we not to proclaim the command—*"Thou shalt not steal?"* Precisely so. The language of the law is clear and conclusive authority. And now all that I ask of him, is to produce a prohibition equally clear of slave-holding. Let him produce the law which says—"Thou shalt not hold slaves." I ask not for the precise words, but for a law which by fair inference forbids it; and so soon as it can be produced, I will yield the question. Till he can produce such a law, his reference to Sparta will not help his cause.

I repeat it, if the abolitionists held the principles of the Apostles of Christ, they would act as the Apostles acted. But mark the contrast. They remain at a distance, and denounce slave-holders; the Apostles went amongst them, and preached the gospel to masters and slaves. They seek to render the slaves dissatisfied, and to run them to Canada; the Apostles commanded them to be obedient to their masters, and to serve them with all fidelity. They justify slave insurrections. Point me to the passage in the epistles of Paul and Peter, which gave the slightest encouragement to slaves to form an insurrection against their masters. Yet slavery, far more intolerable than that which exists in our country, existed all around them. The fruits being different, the doctrine is different, else our Lord was mistaken, when he said, " The tree is known by its fruit."

My next argument against the doctrine of the gentleman, is this: (And it is, like the last, a practical argument.) The actual tendency of abolitionism is to perpetuate, not to abolish, slavery, and to aggravate all its evils; and especially, to take away a preached gospel both from master and slave.

The abolition papers abound in details of the most extreme cases of the cruel treatment of the slaves; and those cases, such as rarely ever occur, are held up as common occurrences, as characteristic of slavery. When the people of the slave States see this unfair course systematically followed, its necessary effect is to irritate them in a very high degree: for a good man, as the gentleman has said, may be made mad by injustice. Such a course of conduct kills all confidence in those who would, as they profess, turn their brethren from sin. The Southern slave-holders, seeing such gross misrepresentations of their character and conduct published to the world, regard abolitionists as base slanderers: and so believing, is it strange that their homilies have no manner of influence at the South, unless it be the very reverse of that which is professedly sought? It is vain for men who run off their slaves, and preach insurrection to those that remain, to attempt to influence the people of the slave-holding States. He who knows anything of human nature, must know that it is impossible.

But they take care not to preach their doctrines in person No, no. They say to their ministerial brethren, in the slave States, "Brethren, be faithful—lift up your voice like a trumpet—clear your skirts of the blood of the slave." Yes: and why will not you come over and help us do it? Ah, that is another affair. The brother said, he would be willing to die at the end of his speech, if he could but persuade all this audience to become abolitionists; but he is in free Ohio. I believe he has never gone over the river, to show how cheerfully he would lose his life in this good cause. [A laugh.] But they tell us, if they go into slave States, they will be persecuted! Suppose this true: what then? Did persecution stop the Apostles? Were not they persecuted? aye, and put to death, while testifying the truth?   n

But now, supposing all the ministers at the South should turn abolitionists, before tomorrow morning, what would be the result? We should see them come teeming over the Ohio, like squirrels, with the wind in their tails. In a few days not a minister would be left, and neither slave nor master would hear the gospel more!

Yet, if slavery is ever to be abolished in the slave-holding States, the gospel, it is admitted, must do it. All our old churches in the older free States were formed and organized by slave-holders, and in the midst of slave-holding. They admitted slave-holders, without hesitation, to membership in the church. The brother himself, I have little doubt, came out from such a church. All the churches began with just such doctrines as are now preached in the South and West. Yet, in many of the States, slavery has been abolished. Public sentiment was gradually moulded and elevated under the influence of the gospel, until the work was quietly effected. The gospel will abolish it in the residue, if abolished it ever shall be. And how? By its soul-elevating, and purifying principles and spirit, brought to bear directly on the slave-holder: not by denunciations and slanders, hurled at him through tracts and newspapers. He will awake at the still small voice of love; not at the thunders of excommunication. But if you take the gospel out of the Southern States, how are they ever to be delivered from the evil? This is the direct tendency of abolition: it kills the only influence that ever will induce Southern masters to liberate their slaves.   [*Time expired.*

Thursday Evening, 9 o'clock.

[MR. BLANCHARD'S EIGHTH SPEECH.]

Gentlemen Moderators, and Gentlemen and Ladies, Fellow-Citizens:

I am not certain that I shall be able to detain you for thirty minutes. I shall notice a few things which my brother has said, and then if I feel the pain in my head less, I shall proceed.

I should be more happy if my brother would waive the privilege, of seeming to accuse me of unwillingness to meet the question. As regularly as a clock, when he rises, he strikes the hour of the debate, and then tells you what I have *not* done, and what he fully believes that I will not do. Many of his arguments I have met. Yet, leaving these, he tells you I have " not answered his argument from the golden rule," etc. I have prepared an argument on that subject, which I will deliver at the proper time. He tells you, also, for the third or fourth time, what Dr. Cunningham and Dr. Chalmers have said concerning abolitionism. I have also an argument on the general subject of authorities, these included. It would not be necessary to notice these affirmations of his about myself, but for that they may lead some simple minds to suppose that I am not here, as a Christian man, to meet and reply to every point vital to this debate. He does not appear to be doing much himself, or to have any sentiments which he is anxious to prove, except concerning myself. For this, he told you, very logically and gravely, that I was " the most remarkable man for misrepresentation of facts, whom he had ever heard speak." I think my friend is in danger of falling into the sin of scoffing and railing.

He gave you, however, a reply to what I said upon his lauding those Southern Presbyterians, who, professing to teach slaves, withhold the Bible from them. He says he "does not praise their Bible-withholding, but he praises the oral instruction which they do give!" This is capital.

But why does he not treat the Papists in the same way? Do they not give much good *oral* instruction? Why not praise them for that, and blink at their withholding the Bible? The steward of the ship in which I came across the Atlantic, was a Roman Catholic, yet a faithful, conscientious man. He had his Douay Bible, which he read often. He had also some excellent tracts, which he kept carefully, and read. He prayed daily; and I would, after careful observation, sooner take his chance of heaven than that of many a slavery-defending protestant minister. So also, a nurse, on board, had been taught, in infancy, by her Papist mother, to pray—" *Our Father*," and "*now I lay me down to sleep*"— as my mother taught me. Why does my brother conduct a paper against Roman Catholics, and yet laud slave-holding Presbyterians, who teach religion upon the same plan? viz: giving some good oral instruction, yet withholding the Bible? He tells you that he condemns the Papists for the errors which they teach. And is it not a damning error in Presbyterians to withhold the Bible from those whom Christ has commanded to " search the Scriptures?"

I dislike to bring forward the derelictions of my brother; but there are some things which have fallen from him, which, if I pass unnoticed, I might be thought to countenance. I mean his sneers at the " colored fraternity," their " hymns," etc., etc. I spoke of the enslaving of smiling, helpless, unconscious " infancy," etc. My brother told you that I described a little babe smiling in its mother's arms, but that I " *did not say whether it was handsome;*" referring, I suppose, to its colored skin. Now, I suppose that every babe is handsome *to its mother* at least; and I must take leave to say, that such sneers at the complexion of colored people, do no credit to either the head or heart of a minister of Christ.

I am pained also, at my friend's apparent zeal to cast opprobrium on the Rev. James Duncan. I have told you that he was the father of Dr. Duncan, our late representative in congress, who, in conversation with me, declared his father's

sentiments on slavery to be his own. The Rev. James Duncan wrote and published his book on slavery, in 1824, eight
years before the first modern anti-slavery society. He had
just left a pastoral charge in Kentucky, some sixty miles
below Cincinnati, and crossed to Vevay, Ind., where he published his book, with a soul burning with the wrongs and
wretchedness endured by the slaves. His was an original
mind, of giant mould. He preached from log cabin to log
cabin, in the early western settlements; always poor, yet
learned, and studious, and laborious. He saw principles
with amazing clearness, and uttered them with corresponding strength. He died on one of these mission-tours,
preaching as he went, at a house where he put up for the
night, in the borders of Indiana. *"Requiescat in pace."* I
hope my brother will let his ashes rest. If he must have
something to find fault with, I will give him some of my
pamphlets.

Gentlemen Moderators—I will give a further brief reply
on the subject of marriage. My brother, with a pertinacity
as strange as it is illogical, insists, that slavery is not destructive of marriage. While he was speaking I could not
but ask myself what blinding cause oppressed him? and,
in what corner of his mind the source of his error lay? And
I confess, I know not how or by what fallacy he is kept
from seeing the truth, unless it be that slavery cannot travel
up to God, and make his judgments coincide with the deter-
minations of slavery. "God will not punish slaves for
'taking up' without marriage," (he seems to mean,) "and
therefore, in God's eye, they are married." But this is
monstrous reasoning. Are they married as by slavery?
that is the question. If not, (and he knows they are not,)
then by denying that slavery destroys marriage will be merciful. His argument gives to slavery the merit of God's
mercy. Slavery adjudges slaves unmarried, and incapable
of marriage. It holds the slave-pair in separation; ready
to be sold apart. He tells us, but they are vain words, that
the husband and wife are not separated in slavery, unless the

master chooses to part them. But if I come to own a man and his wife, are they not already separated so far as the nuptial tie bound them, and ready to be sold apart whenever I will to sell them? Suppose I sell the woman, and the purchaser goes to get her; has he anything to do but lead her off? Is there anything to be done to separate her from her husband? Obviously nothing. She ceased, by the theory of slavery, to be her husband's *wife*, when she became my *woman*. The property principle is stronger in law and practice than the marriage principle, and prevails over it. And brother Rice is here to maintain, that when I have fairly bought the woman, *she is mine.* Slave-holding is not sinful. He gives me God's permission to hold her: and they are separated by the naked fact that they are property.

True, God may not punish in hell the slave man and woman, who, being prohibited marriage, take up together, and are true to each other; but no thanks are due to slavery that he does not, for if he followed either its laws or its practice, he would declare the parents unmarried, and illegitimate their children. What candor, or sense, therefore, can there be in declaring that slaves may be and are married, in the open face of the fact that marriage has never existed among slaves from the times of Aristotle down. I read from the learned Dr. Robertson's History of Charles V., p. 13, *Note* 9:—

Of slaves, he says—" They were not originally permitted to marry. Male and female slaves were allowed and even encouraged to cohabit together. But this union was not considered as a marriage; it was called *contubernium*, not *nuptiae or matrimonium.*" And again:

" All the children of slaves were in the same condition of their parents, and became the property of the master. Slaves were so entirely the property of their masters, that they could sell them at pleasure. While domestic slavery continued, property in a slave was held in the same manner with that which a person had in any other moveable."

So was slavery in Greece: so was it in Rome: so is it to-day in Kentucky. What was slavery then is slavery now.

And if my friend can now rise up and tell you, against authorities such as Dr. Robertson,—against the authoritative declaration of all the slave-codes ever enacted,—against history itself, and against what you know to be the uniform practice, heretofore and now,—that marriage exists among slaves, and that slavery is free from the sin of marriage-breaking, I feel certain that few will believe him.

I am aware that my friend calculates on the adherence of friends from Kentucky, of whom there are many present. But I trust that here even he will find himself mistaken. There is a force in truth to leave impressions which the mind cannot shake off, and especially in the truth that it is sinful to make merchandize of men. It will follow them to their homes, and live and burn in their consciences, when the prejudices of the hour are, with the circumstances of this debate, passed away.

A money-loving, hardened man, in southern Pennsylvania, told me that when he put his hand to paper to sign a bill of sale for the transfer of a human being, his arm trembled and shook to his shoulder-blade. There is not a power, principle, or faculty included in the awful circle of humanity but shudders at the motions of this horrid property-power, as the trees of Eden trembled at the movements of Satan in the fall of man, You may go, Kentuckians, to your homes, but the truths to which you here listen, apart from any power of argument, by their own vital force, will abide with you as an omnipresent blaze, showing you everything about your negro-quarters in a light in which you never beheld them before, and making you one in understanding and heart with the promoters of liberty, and friends of the slave.—For the truth is God's, and God's unseen power is in it.

I met Theodore F. Leftwick, a tobacco merchant, of Liberty, Va., upon a steamboat; told him I was an abolitionist, and, knowing him for a southern man, asked him of his slaves. "Thank God, I have none," was his prompt and warm reply. Though opposed to what he understood to be abolitionism, and pitying me because an abolitionist, he said that he had

some twenty-five slaves, who, if sold, would have brought
an average of $500 each, when Joshua Leavitt was editing
the *N. Y. Evangelist;* that he was provoked with the paper, on account of the editor's denouncing slavery as a sin,
but continued to take it on his wife's account, "until," said
Leftwick, "I should be ashamed to tell you what harrowings
of conscience, and what horrid images followed me, even in
my sleep, till I resolved to free every slave I had. From
that hour, I have slept as sweet as a child, and if I had had
ten thousand slaves, I would have emancipated them every
morning since; though," he added, " I know, and my friends
will tell you, that I love money full as well as my neighbors."

Facts of this kind—and there are thousands, are their own
argument. They are the voice of nature in the first born
elements of man proclaiming war against the grinding tyranny
of personal slavery, with God and conscience on their side.
You may cloud the solemn truth that holding slaves is a sin
with prejudice, or darken it by reproach; or dazzle and
confound it with the ecclesiastical subtleties of trained polemicism, and wire-drawn argument; yet, there it stands,
bold, honest, open, and uncompromising; and its voice will
be heard, and obeyed, when the flimsy and carping objections
which may be heaped upon it are perished, passed away and
forgot.

In resuming, as I now do, the direct argument to prove that
slave-holding is sin, I wish to observe that one of my friend's
propositions, to wit: that the minds of men apprehend and
admit general principles in morals, is *generally*, though by
no means *universally* true. Even at the present day, when
truth is eclipsed and overborne by the practical corruptions
of society, it is yet true, with exceptions, that the soul con-
structed upon the model of God's law, will bear witness to
those moral principles which are the elements and substance
of that law. The exceptions are those minds which are bias-
sed by corruption or interest; those who cannot see right principles through a guinea. It is by reason of this principle that
slaveholders themselves testify that emancipation is a blessing

and slavery a curse. And I present, as my next direct argument the following :

That holding innocent men in slavery is a sin, is proved by the action of those slave State legislatures and grateful masters, *who have emancipated slaves for meritorious services.*

Every such emancipation (and these have been many) is proof that the legislature and the individual emancipator, know that slavery is an evil, and liberty a good.

Does it require argument to show that they know also that inflicting an evil upon unoffending persons, and withholding good which is their right is sin ? This is precisely what slave-holders are doing to their slaves—and their slave-holding is therefore sin.

They make liberty a reward for the most meritorious services, and slavery the punishment for certain kinds of crime ; what then is the moral character of depriving a man of that which is in itself a reward, and inflicting upon him what is in itself a curse ? If I hang an innocent man, I am myself a murderer; if I deprive an innocent man of his goods, I am a robber. What am I, if I deprive him of his liberty—a possession brighter than gold, and dearer than life ? A slave-holder ! I know it is said that, though liberty is of priceless value to them who have enjoyed and can appreciate it, it is less important to those who have always been slaves and know no other state. But it is *slaves* who are freed for meritorious services. Liberty is thus solemnly declared to be the highest boon which can be bestowed on slaves. He then who holds *slaves* in slavery, holds them in deprivation of what slave State legislatures have declared a blessing and a good to them ;—and he holds them thus bereft, without pretence of crime on their part. Slave-holders, therefore, by granting freedom as a *reward*, admit that every slave-holder is *punishing the innocent*—and punishing the innocent is sin.

But, they say: "We did not deprive the slaves of liberty but we found them so."

This is true of those who were adults, or were born before the slave-holders; but infants are not "found slaves" by their owners, but *made so*. But what is this plea of "finding them slaves?" My father, or father's father, enslaves men, and I take them and their descendants and retain them in slavery. I then admit that to enslave them in the first instance, was wrong, but adopt and prolong, and justify the crime! My father locks an innocent man in prison, and dying, wills me the key. I put the key in my pocket, and keep the man in prison. Where, I ask, is the difference between my father's sin and mine? Was not my father's act a sin? "Certainly," it is said, "when slavery began, it was a sin in the enslaver." But if you were in prison, and knew I had the key of your dungeon in my pocket, would you not justly hold me equally guilty with the man who put you there? And what is American slavery but keeping up, on the persons of innocent men, a punishment fit only for criminals?

But I argue further, that slave-holding is sin, because *it is going with a multitude to do evil.*

Slave-holding is not a solitary, but a social sin. It requires conspiracy and combination to perpetuate it.

Suppose, for illustration, one hundred men, cast upon an Island, find themselves its only occupants. They have no civil polity, no mail, none of the appliances of government, and no distinction of ruled and rulers, but are individuals in a state of nature. Suppose, now, one out of this hundred wishes to enslave ten or twenty of his fellows, it is plainly impossible for him to do so, because no one has the strength of ten, and without interference by the others, it is impossible for him to make them his slaves.

My own native State has even been in this state of nature in respect to slavery. A slave-holder who had pursued his fugitive to Vermont, brought him before one of the courts, proved that the runaway was his property, and asked for the necessary authority to take him home. The Judge declared the testimony insufficient to sustain his title. Per spiring with vexation, the slave-holder asked his honor "what evidence would be sufficient?" "Nothing," said Judge Harrington, "nothing short of a bill of sale from the Almighty will enable you to take that man from this Court as your property?" The man-holder was obliged to relinquish all hope of his victim. He had not power, personally, and unaided by the laws, to re-enslave his fugitive.

Thus, gentlemen, while men are in a state of nature, anterior to society, slavery cannot exist, and does not. Among the hundred Islanders, no one can enslave ten by his individual force. He must ally force with fraud, and bring cunning to the aid of cruelty. He must first mould and concentrate the individual force of the whole hundred into a government, and, by dexterous management, wield that for the enslavement of his ten. This is precisely what he does; and thus, under the name of government, and the sacred forms of law, he achieves an object which, had he attempted it by his own single strength, would have cost him his life, as a despicable and impotent tyrant, and pirate upon the persons and peace of other men. This is *"going with a multitude to do evil."* And this is slave-holding.

The slave-holder does not rest his claim to his fellow-man upon his own prowess or force; but feels about for some system of slave-legislation, which he may take advantage of to compel his slaves to bear his burdens—thus wielding the power of the whole hundred to enslave his ten. What then is holding slaves by law, but " going with a multitude to do evil?" Is not this precisely the case of the American slave-holder at this day?

But my brother tells you, over and again, that the question is not whether kidnapping and enslaving men is right; he therefore contends that such illustrations as that of one man using the power of an hundred to enslave ten, are not relevant. The question, he says, is whether holding these kidnapped persons and their descendants in slavery is sin; or, in his own words; whether, holding persons in slavery, who are already enslaved, be sinful? That is true enough:

and that is the very question I am discussing. But I am showing also that American slave-holding—taking free infants from God's hands and placing them in slavery is kidnapping and slavery too.

But to set the whole matter wholly beyond cavil; suppose those Island citizens all die, after ten had become slaves to one; that I am the son of that slave-holder, and I make that fact a pretext to hold in slavery the children of those ten persons whom my father enslaved? And that I take their infant offspring as fast as born and reckon and register them among my cattle and swine, as my property. Where then would be the least moral difference between my case and that of the present American slave-holders? Can any one fail to see that, if I am the robber and plunderer of my species, he is no less?

The whole United States' power is but the hand-vice into which the slave-holder screws his slave, and by which the slave "is held to service or labor," and the United States statute, a tether to bind the hands and feet of those whom the rapacity and violence of our ancestors have enslaved and placed in our power. Slave-holding, is therefore explicitly forbidden by God in the words: "Thou shalt not follow a multitude to do evil."   [*Time expired.*

[MR. RICE'S EIGHTH SPEECH.]

Gentlemen Moderators, and Fellow-Citizens:

In closing the discussion of this day, I confess that I have been disappointed, and so, I presume, have the audience. They were informed by the gentleman, that they would hear the *Bible argument* in favor of his views this evening: You have heard what sort of a Bible argument it has been.

[Mr. BLANCHARD, interposing.—I said I would come to the *direct* argument.]

Then the *direct* argument in favor of abolitionism is *not* a *Bible argument*, the gentleman himself being judge. [Great laughter.]

The gentleman is now through; we are closing a discussion of twelve hours; he agrees with me, that the Bible is the only rule of right and wrong; yet, in the whole of that time he has brought but one solitary passage to show that his doctrine is true! The direct argument, it is evident, is not a Bible argument. This he has virtually admitted, and I thank him for the concession. The truth is, no abolitionist relies upon the Bible for proof of the doctrine, that slave-holding is in itself sinful; and I am glad my friend has come to "the *direct* argument," and given us no Bible.

The gentleman is quite disturbed that I should so frequently tell the audience what he has *not* done. Well, I do not doubt that it is distressing: I hope he will be as comfortable as possible; but really I cannot help it. The fact is, that he has argued twelve hours, and has not only failed to support his doctrine by the Bible, but has scarcely touched one of the main arguments I have offered against it!

He has, indeed, placed before us in glowing colors, the cruelty which wicked men sometimes practice toward their slaves. And he asks whether there was anything about that slave coffle with which he opened his side of the debate, which I condemn? He knows that I condemn traffic in slaves as severely as he does; but does that prove the relation of master and slave to be in itself sinful? I condemn the burning of Hindoo widows, but I do not on that account condemn the marriage relation as sinful. Does my opponent condemn the conjugal relation, because wicked men take advantage of it to treat females cruelly, as he does the relation of master and slave for the same reason? The sufferings of the slave-gang are not caused by the *relation*, but by *the cruelty of slave-dealers.* Does the fact, that Nero was a monster of cruelty, prove that the relation of ruler and ruled is sinful? Will my brother on this account denounce civil government? Yet the principle on which he reasons, requires that he should; for the cases, as to the principle involved, are the same.

But he asks, why I do not praise the Papists for the truth

they teach, as I approve the conduct of southern Christians in having the gospel preached to their slaves? I do give them due credit for every word of truth they teach; but this does not hinder me from exposing their errors, where they err. But he charges the General Assembly with sanctioning the withholding of the Scriptures from the slaves. The truth of this charge I denied, and disproved. Now what did the Assembly say on this subject in their report? Did they not say, that every Christian and philanthropist should use all proper means to have the laws repealed, which forbid the slaves being taught to read the word of God? Where in that Report does the Assembly sanction the giving to them *merely* oral instruction in Christian doctrine? Nowhere. On the contrary, it exhorts masters to give them the Bible. And in the very face of these facts, my opponent charges the Assembly with sanctioning the withholding of the Bible from the slaves! Has he not strangely misrepresented that body?

I uttered no sneer, as the gentleman charges, against my colored brethren;—far, very far from it: I was, indeed, amused at his eloquent description of the *beautiful* babe stolen by the hard-hearted master from the cradle; and because I was amused at him, he would make the impression that I was sneering at colored persons!

My friend is disturbed by my quotations from Duncan's pamphlet, republished by the Cincinnati Abolition Society, and he says, he does not approve of *every comma,* and *every semicolon,* in Mr. Duncan's pamphlet. Perhaps he does not; but I did not quote either commas or semicolons, but the abhorrent sentiments, that the term SLAVE-HOLDER, like the word DEVIL, is a name to be uttered only with abhorrence; that nothing proves so clearly the necessity of a hell, as the fact that there are slave-holders in the world; that servile insurrections are justifiable, and the man who would raise his arm to suppress them, will be eternally punished in hell! Will he attempt to escape the odium justly connected with these abominable principles, which run through the entire work, by saying, that he does not approve every comma and semi-colon in it!!! Are these sentiments commas and semicolons? But Mr. Duncan has deceased; and he thinks, therefore, I ought not thus to comment on his sentiments. He could state facts injurious to the reputation of the venerable Dr. Baxter, without producing one particle of proof of their truth; but it is quite improper for me to say a word about Mr. Duncan's published sentiments! Ah, it is one thing for *your* ox to gore *mine;* quite another for *my* ox to gore *yours.*

But the gentleman is kind enough to offer me some of his publications, if I will only spare Mr. Duncan's. I am obliged to him; but I prefer Mr. Duncan's pamphlet, for the plain and important reason, that it has been endorsed by the *Cincinnati Abolition Society,*—an honor which, so far as I know, has not been conferred on any one of his. This pamphlet is now no longer Mr. Duncan's; it is the Cincinnati Abolition Society's work, and contains their sentiments—sentiments which every enlightened Christian and patriot must abhor, as adapted to excite servile insurrection, and deluge our land in blood. But the gentleman objects only to some of its *commas* and semicolons!!!

My opponent once more reiterates the assertion, that slave-holding destroys the marriage relation. Marriage is a divinely constituted relation, the validity of which depends simply upon the authority of God. Has he proved that slavery annuls it? What would have been the proper course for him to pursue in proving it? It would have been, first, to show, from the Bible, what marriage is, what is essential to the relation; and then show how slave-holding abolishes this. But did he take this course? Not at all. There was no reference to the Bible in his whole argument. I might meet his assertion by a simple denial; but neither assertions nor denials will settle the point.

But I have proved that Constantine passed laws forbidding husbands and wives, parents and children, among slaves, to be separated. Will the gentleman assert that these laws abolished slavery?—that it no longer existed in the Roman

Empire? This he will not pretend, for he admits that it existed for several centuries after they were passed. He must, therefore, admit that slavery may exist, that it has existed, without destroying the marriage relation. Under the laws to which I have referred, and which I have quoted, husbands and wives could not be separated. They remained together till death. Precisely such laws might exist, and I will add, ought to exist, in Kentucky, and other slave-holding States.

The gentleman proves, by two arguments, that slave-holding destroys the marriage relation. The first is, that the outward formalities of marriage, sanctioned by the Bible, are not observed. I have called upon him to state what formalities or ceremonies are sanctioned by the Bible. His only reply is, that Samson had a procession and a feast of seven days! Well, does the Bible teach that the procession and feast were essential to the validity of the marriage? I hope not; for if so, very few of us, I fear, are lawfully married. For myself, when I was married, I really had not time to enjoy a seven-days feast. [A laugh.] I was certainly not aware that the Scriptures required any particular ceremonies as necessary to marriage; and it would save the gentleman's time and his voice, (for he complains of hoarseness,) if he would point us to the Scripture which requires ceremonies of any kind. He says he has proved it; but I presume he only means, that he has *asserted* it.

His second argument is, that the civil law does not recognize the marriage of slaves. Suppose it does not, I have asked him to show us where the Scriptures make recognition of marriage by the civil law necessary to its validity, and I have asked in vain. But, as I have proved, the laws passed by Constantine did recognize the marriage of slaves, and did forbid the separation of husbands and wives. Still Mr. B. asserts, that slavery necessarily dissolves the relation, or rather makes it impossible!

My friend seems to think, he is pouring out truths which will burn most awfully in the consciences of the Kentuckians who happen to be present; and he tells of us a man in Adams county, who trembled *clear up to the shoulder*, whenever he signed a bill of sale of a slave. [A laugh.] Well, he ought to have trembled, if he was selling them against their will, or into a worse condition. And there was a slave-holder in Virginia, who took Mr. Leavitt's paper, and he could not sleep, because he "*kept saying*," that slave-bolding is a sin, (not because he proved it;) but when he had liberated twenty-four slaves, he slept soundly. So he *keeps saying* that slave-holding is an abominable sin; and he expects thus terribly to burn the consciences of Kentuckians. [A laugh.] But one fact the gentleman stated about that man, struck me as very singular, viz: when Mr. Blanchard told him, that he was an Abolitionist, he said—"*then I pity you!*" And yet the man had himself been made an abolitionist by Mr. Leavitt's paper? Why did he, then, pity Mr. B.? Did he pity him because he was so much more *enlightened* than most men? Do abolitionists thus pity abolitionists? This is certainly a very curious story!

But legislatures have sometimes liberated slaves; and this fact is brought forward to prove slave-holding in itself sinful. It proves, I admit, that they considered slavery an evil, and freedom a very desirable blessing. But does it prove, that when I buy a slave at his own request, so as to improve his condition, I have done a very wicked thing? Surely the premises and the conclusion are as far as the poles apart. Yet, this is the gentleman's "*direct* argument"—or more properly, his *direct* assertion."

Or, does the fact referred to, prove, that the immediate emancipation of all the slaves of the slave-holding States, amongst the white population, would be a blessing to them? Liberty is, indeed, a blessing; but it is a blessing which all men are not prepared to improve. It is more than doubtful, whether, should a constitution, such as that of the U. States, be adopted to-morrow in Mexico, the condition of the people would be any the better for it. And why? Because they are

not prepared to live under a government so free as ours.
Nor is it at all clear, that the inhabitants of Russia or of
South America would be happier or more prosperous under
a government administered upon the principles of our government.   Admit that a constitution so free as ours is the
best in the world, does it follow, that every man who fills an
office in a more despotic government is a heinous sinner?
Whether the immediate emancipation of the slaves, with
their present character, habits, and circumstances, would
prove a blessing to them, is, to say the least, a debateable
question.

The gentleman, whether by way of illustration or as an
argument I know not, imagines a hundred men cast on a
desolate island, and ninety of them combined to reduce ten
of their number to a state of slavery.   Such conduct would
indeed be most reprehensible; but does this supposed case
present the principle we are met to discuss?   If it was his
intention to discuss the question, *whether it is right to reduce
by force free men to a state of slavery*, why did he not say so?
Why did not the challengers state this as the question for
discussion?   Had they done so, I would not have thought
of accepting their challenge, for a single moment.   But the
question, I must once more remind him, is, *whether slave-
holding is in itself sinful;* and I will further remind him,
that the wisest and best men, even in his own New-England,
assert openly that it is not.   If the matter is so perfectly obvious as his supposition makes it, how happens it, that those
good and eminent men answer it in one way, and my brother
in another?   The question, as I have repeatedly remarked,
is not whether it is right to enslave free men ; but since the
Africans have already been enslaved, without my agency,
and before I was born, how far I am bound immediately to
set them free, and how far I can do it consistently with other
paramount duties ?   What is the duty of men who own a
large number of slaves in the southern States, where the laws
forbid emancipation ?   What is the duty of the man who
purchased slaves at their own request, in order to improve

their condition, and promote their happiness? Why cannot the gentleman be induced to meet the cases I have repeatedly presented, and dispose of them?

[Mr. BLANCHARD. I will.]

He promises fairly; but why has he not done it? I venture the assertion, that he never will fairly meet and dispose of them. I do not say, he will not *try*.

He repeats the assertion, that slave-holding is kidnapping; I have listened for the proof, but I have not heard it. This is the capital defect in his argument.

One of the arguments I have urged against abolitionism, is, that its tendency is to perpetuate slavery, and to aggravate all its evils. I remarked, that if all the ministers of the slave-holding States should suddenly become abolitionists, if they should imbibe the spirit of the abolitionists on this side of the Ohio river, they would all forthwith abandon their fields of labor, and seek the free States. And what, let me ask, would be the consequences? Would such a course abolish slavery? Would it not have the opposite tendency? It would take from the masters the gospel, the only influence likely to dispose them to emancipate their slaves. The abolitionists remind me of one of your steam-doctors, who, to effect an immediate cure of a disease, kills the patient by one tremendous dose. They have succeeded, it is true, in running off a few slaves to Canada—a course which, without benefiting them, seriously injures those left behind. By aggravating masters, and making them suspicious of their slaves, it makes them less inclined than before to treat them kindly, or to grant them their liberty. Believing such to be the tendency and the effect of abolitionism, I must oppose it. How different the course pursued by the apostles of Christ. Far from advising slaves to leave their masters, and from industriously collecting and publishing all manner of stories injurious to the character of slaveholders, they went amongst masters and slaves, proclaiming to each "the unsearchable riches of Christ," and exhorting each to the faithful discharge of their relative duties.

But what is worse still, the tendency of abolitionism is to take the gospel from the slaves also, and leave them without the consolations of religion,—the hopes of eternal life. Only let its doctrines prevail, and Rev. C. C. Jones and other ministers who are engaged in preaching to them the word of life, must cease their labors, and retire to the free States. Then what will become of the *souls* of the slaves? Will they become the freedmen of Christ? Paul, the apostle, said to slaves—"Art thou called being a servant, care not for it." His great concern was, that the soul—the immortal part—should enjoy the liberty wherewith Christ would make it free—that the slaves might enjoy eternal liberty and happiness in heaven. But the great concern of abolitionists seems to be for their *bodies*—their freedom from the yoke of man, not from bondage to sin and Satan. In the day of judgment, multitudes of the slaves will stand on the right hand of the Judge, clothed in garments of spotless white. And to whom, under God, will they ascribe their salvation? To those very ministers who are the objects of the vituperation and reproaches of abolitionists. And for whom, in that day, will those pious slaves thank God? Will they thank him for the labors of those men who stood at a distance, and abused their masters, because they did not set them at liberty; or of those who, more concerned for the salvation of their souls, than for their bodily freedom, went and preached to them the glorious gospel? I leave the audience to answer the question. And now, in view of the tendency and effects of abolitionism, compared with the views I am defending, let me ask the candid and unprejudiced, which doctrine is true—theirs or ours?

The gentleman may attempt to refute the arguments I have offered; but I doubt it. Certain I am, that the attempt, if made, will prove unsuccessful. I confess, I have been disappointed by the course he has thought proper to pursue; and so, I doubt not, have the great majority of the audience. I did suppose, that what he calls his "direct argument" would be a *Bible argument;* but I have heard nothing adduced from the inspired volume.

To-morrow I purpose to enter more directly on the Bible argument, whether my opponent does so or not. I shall go to the infallible rule. I will measure strength with the gentleman on scripture ground, which after all, is the true ground. Let us leave the slave gang, and the cruelties of slave-dealing, and the oppressions and wrongs perpetrated by wicked men, and go "to the law and to the testimony." Let him shew from the Bible, that the Patriarchs did not hold slaves: let him prove from that authority, that there were no slaves in the apostolic churches; that the Apostles excluded slave-holders from the church of God. Let him prove these things, and we will give up the question. After debating twelve hours, this has not been done. Nothing bearing on the question we are discussing, has been adduced either from the Old Testament or from the New. Half the debate, if not more, is over; his "*direct* argument" is nearly completed, and no Bible argument has yet been heard from the gentleman. This is truly singular, if it be true, as he believes and asserts, that I am in darkness, and he in the pure light of the gospel. Has it ever yet been found, that men who love darkness, insist on going to the light? And that men who love the light, are reluctant to come to it? The gentleman thinks that we are in darkness; his bowels of compassion yearn over us; and he pours out his prayers in our behalf. And yet, though we cease not to urge him to come to the Word of God, we cannot induce him to approach it!! When I came here this evening, I brought my Bible with me. I expected to need it; but I have had no use for it in replying to him; nor, judging from his past course, am I likely to have.   [*Time expired.*

Friday, 2 o'clock, P. M., Oct. 3, 1845.

[MR. BLANCHARD'S NINTH SPEECH.]

Gentlemen Moderators, and Gentlemen and Ladies, Fellow-Citizens:

I regret more than you will, though you will regret it, that I have to beg the indulgence of the audience, for an over-worked voice, and frame somewhat enfeebled by present illness, and enfeebled health.

I left my bed after 12 o'clock, to-day, for the first time, having been all the while under the influence of medicine. But with great patience on your part, and prudence on mine, I hope, with God's help, to set my arguments before you with sufficient clearness, so that you may not regret the time and attention you have given here.

I wish, while the audience is coming in, to reply briefly to one point which has been so repeatedly urged by my brother ;—I mean his argument from *authority.* The Scotch divines, Dr. Cunningham, and Dr. Chalmers, have been frequently mentioned, as having declared themselves against modern abolitionism : and because they, who have been long and worthily trusted as orthodox divines, have condemned our views, it is presumed that we are in error. He relies upon the fact, also, that Dr. Chalmers said that the doctrine of modern abolitionists, that slave-holding is a sin, is a new doctrine. I shall say somewhat respecting this, after I have replied to both these points with distinctness and care.

1. I must ask you to remember, first, that these Scotch divines labored under two difficulties in coming to right conclusions as to the duty of American Christians, respecting slave-holding. First, that, in Scotland, church-censures inflict certain civil disabilities which do not follow church-discipline here. Till a year ago last May, the sheriff, under the State authority, was as frequently called upon to enforce the decrees of Presbytery, as the Presbytery officers them-

selves, as may be seen by the Presbyterian Minutes. Another difficulty under which the Scotch divines labored, in judging of our duty, is, that the civil law interfered with the church discipline, in the British Empire. The English law of libel is such, that if a churchman, who is a drunkard, &c., is accused of it, he may bring his action for libel, and the truth could not be pleaded in defence. As long, therefore, as the plaintiff has money, and respectability enough to sustain his suit, if you have accused a member of the established church of drunkenness, he can amerce you in damages, though there is no doubt of the truth of your charges.

This danger from the law of libel, with other like causes, embarrasses and weakens the discipline of the European churches : and this leads Scotch divines to think it more difficult for American churches to discipline slave-holders than it actually is.

But when I shall read the opinions of the Scotch divines, they will be found to agree in principle with abolitionists, though, in practice, they differ.

I will now read Dr. Cunningham on another subject, where human rights are concerned—I mean his opinion as to the right and propriety of the people to form " *voluntary churches,*" such as our American churches, of all denominations ; as the "Central Presbyterian Church," of which my brother Rice is pastor ; and as, excepting perhaps the Romish church, we have none but voluntary churches in America, it may, perhaps, be interesting to know that Dr. Cunningham, my friend's, oft-quoted authority, holds all such churches to be little better than infidel establishments. Nor is it strange that otherwise sound and clear men, who have been raised in an established or State church, a church regulated by the civil statute and ruled by a house of commons and ministry about as pious as our house of representatives, should have crude and defective notions of the duty of keeping the church communion pure from practical corruptions ; especially when these corruptions consist in an invasion of human rights, of

which the structure of the government which they live under
is a practical contempt.

I now read Dr. Cunningham's opinion of "*voluntary
churches*," from his very abusive reply to Dr. Wardlaw,
an eminent Congregationalist minister of Edinburgh, in the
"*Church of Scotland Magazine*," August, 1835.

"As Dr. Wardlaw has, on a variety of occasions, manifested a want of simplicity and godly sincerity ; and as he has
displayed considerable dexterity in quibbling and shuffling
to evade a difficulty and get out of a scrape, I must take the
liberty of warning the public that if he shall be bold enough
to attempt to prove the truth of his calumny, it will not be
enough for him to show that the friends of the church (of
which Dr. Cunningham was then a member) have often
alledged against the VOLUNTARIES that they were associated
infidels in the promotion of a common object; that from this
circumstance we have deduced inferences and derived pre-
sumptions unfavorable to *voluntary views*, or that they have
described *voluntary principles and measures* as having an
infidel character and tendency.   These allegations, it is admitted have been very fully and very largely made, and,
what is more, *they have been established*, and no friend of
the church need be ashamed or afraid of being charged with
having made them."—[*See article in Church of Scotland
Magazine, August*, 1835, *by* Rev. W. CUNNINGHAM, *Edinburgh.*]

Dr. Cunningham then, in 1835, thinks that he and his
friends have " established " that " voluntary churches," " principles " and " measures," (Dr. Rice and the Central Presbyterian Church of this city of course included ;—for that was
lately formed by a " voluntary "colony, upon " voluntary principles,") " are of infidel character and tendency." Yet this
same Dr. Cunningham is Dr. Rice's oft-quoted authority in
this debate, which is upon the sin or innocence of withholding this *voluntary principle* from slaves.   When my friend
will settle this charge of infidelity made against his church
and himself, grounded on their voluntary action, by his fa-

vorite Dr. Cunningham, it will be time to quote his opinion as worth something on the subject of slavery. I consider him a good authority in neither.

So much has been made of Scotch authority in this debate concerning American slavery, it may be desirable that I should show you the opinion of those Scotch ministers who have not breathed from infancy the corrupt atmosphere of a State Church. I read from "An address on negro slavery to the Christian Churches in the United States of America, by the United Associate Synod" of Scotland. This Synod includes the greater part of the Presbyterian churches in Scotland, which were out of the pale of the Establishment, previous to the great division of May, 1843; and the formation of the "Free church of Scotland." It has 22 Presbyteries, and 350 Congregations. Following is their unanimous action on the subject of American slavery transmitted in the pamphlet address which I hold:

I. " Resolved, That we hold as 'one of those things that are most surely believed among us,' that the treating of human beings as property, without an express permission of him who is the supreme proprietor, is utterly repugnant to the principles both of reason and revelation—equally inconsistent with the law of justice and of love—an outrage on human nature, and an insult to its author."

V. "Resolved, That in proportion to the esteem and affection with which we regard the christians and the christian churches of the United States of America, are the astonishment and grief with which *we have heard*, that among the members, and even among the office-bearers of some of the churches, are to be found PROPRIETORS of, and even dealers in slaves—that not only individuals but some ecclesiastical bodies, have engaged in a shocking, but happily hopeless attempt to reconcile *these monstrous practices* with the law of God and the Gospel of Jesus Christ."

Thus, the free unhampered Christianity of Scotland sees no moral difference between being " THE PROPRIETOR of slaves " and " slave-dealing." It styles both " *monstrous* practices."

And, now, though the Cunningham and Chalmers party, which cast off the State tether and became a " FREE *Church of Scotland* " only two years ago last May, are not, for reasons obvious and already given, the safest and soundest authorities in questions of human rights; especially, since but few years are passed since Dr. Chalmers went up to London, (where not one of the established churches were open to him,) to lecture in favor of State church establishments, and against the " Voluntary principle." I will read the action of the Cunningham and Chalmers Assembly on the subject of American slavery. I read from the " *Glasgow Examiner*," of June 7th, 1845, extracts from the Report on American slavery read by Dr. Candlish, and adopted by the General Assembly of the Free Church of Scotland," last May.

" There is no question here as to the heinous sin involved in the institution of American slavery, nor can there be any terms too strong to be employed in pointing out the national guilt which attaches to the continuance of that accursed system, and the national judgments which, under the government of a righteous God, may be expected to mark the Divine displeasure against it. Neither can there be any doubt as to the duty incumbent on American christians *to exert themselves to the utmost in every competent way for having it abolished.*"

Farther on, the Assembly say—" All must agree in holding, that whatever rights, the civil law of the land may give a master over his slaves as ' chattels, personal,' it cannot but be a sin of the deepest dye, in him to REGARD or *treat* them as such: *and whosoever commits that* SIN IN ANY SENSE, or deals otherwise with his fellow man, whatever power the law may give him over them, OUGHT TO BE HELD DISQUALIFIED FOR CHRISTIAN COMMUNION."

This is the doctrine of Dr. Rice's authority. Dr. Cunningham after the adoption of this report, arose and expressed his " entire concurrence" in its sentiments.

Thus, this same Cunningham, my friend's favorite authority, holds, that to "*regard*" or "treat" men as property, is a sin which disqualifies for christian communion; and that American Christians are bound to "exert themselves to their utmost, in all proper ways, to have slavery abolished!" Yet, Dr. Rice is here to prove that "slave-holding is not sinful, nor the relation between master and slave a sinful relation:" and as to zeal for the abolition of slavery, his report in his last General Assembly speaks for itself. You can all see that whatever inconsistencies Dr. Cunningham has broached since he was here collecting money for his church from slave-holding churches, Dr. Rice is at least as far from him, as he is from me, on this subject; but it is not my business to reconcile him with his Scotch authorities. The abolitionists hold no stronger doctrine than is here fully avowed by the Free Church Assembly of last May, (1845,) and endorsed by Cunningham himself, to wit: that "*regarding men as property is a sin of the deepest dye, and which ought to disqualify for Christian communion;*" and Christians are bound "*to exert their utmost for the abolition of slavery.*"

I know that my friend seeks to avoid the force of this quotation, by making a vain and unmeaning distinction between "holding men as slaves and holding them as property;" as though men could hold slaves any other way than as property. This distinction might blind persons farther off; but if there be twenty slave-holders from Kentucky, I am willing to refer the question to them, whether they do not hold and regard their slaves as property, and whether they do not understand Dr. Rice as justifying their practice from the word of God? Whether, in short, the doctrine of the Free Church of Scotland, just read, is not as unacceptable to professing slave-holders in the South, as anything which abolitionists have ever taught? The fact is, that they ridicule the idea of a man holding slaves and not regarding them as property.

Since this subject has been up, a slave-holder present said to a friend of mine, that he knew of no slave-holders who would thank a man for putting in such a wretched plea, in defence of slavery, as that slave-holders do not regard their negroes as property. "We hold our slaves because we want them; and we use them as property because they are our property, and we wish to make what money we honestly can." Small thanks will Dr. Rice get for such a vindication of slave-holding, from his slave-holding brethren, unless they take the will for the deed—knowing that, whatever he says, he *means* to support their cause.

I will now read another testimony that American slave-holders "*regard men as property*," and so are declared worthy of excommunication by my friend's Scotch authorities. I will first read the testimony proving that professing slave-holders do actually hold their slaves as property, and because they desire to have their services, and when I have read it I will tell you who is the author.

"The Jews were expressly permitted to *buy* men; and that which I buy with my money, belongs to me for all the purposes to which it may be lawfully applied. A man may not use his horse as he may a piece of timber; nor may he use his slave as if he were a horse. But if I buy a horse, he is mine; and I may use his services lawfully. *If I buy a man, he is mine, so far as his services are concerned!*"—*Rice's Lectures, p.* 26.

This is [the testimony: and the author *sits at that table!* [Pointing to Dr. Rice.]

Now, it is true, that he adds, in immediate connection with the above quotation, "and I am bound to treat him as a man." Yes: but as a "man" who "*is mine;*" whose services I may command on the ground that he is mine. If this is not "regarding men as property," then that idea cannot be put in human speech. But the doctrine of the Free Scotch Assembly, and Dr. Cunningham, is, that "regarding men as property is a sin of the deepest dye," and which disqualifies for church membership. Thus, the very authorities which Dr. Rice quotes as on his side, *would turn him out of the church*, if he would practice the doctrines of his pamphlet; and they would be consistent with their own, for, says Dr. Rice, " *If I buy a* MAN, *he is mine!* "

Now, when we consider that Dr. Cunningham wrote what my friend quotes under most unpropitious circumstances;— that he was born and reared amidst the corruptions of a state church, and a "by authority" religion;—that he is now preaching in a tolerated and taxed church, when not lecturing his classes; (for dissenting chapels are licensed in England as grog-shops are here.) Environed by such darkening circumstances, hampered in his ideas of church discipline by the law of libel, and holding men and measures to be of infidel character because they form voluntary churches, like Dr. Rice's, we may perhaps excuse him for not being exactly clear on the subject of slavery.

Yet in the midst of their distant island location—blinded, too, by the misrepresentations of our slavery-ridden assemblies and high church courts, and tainted leading men, who tell them that American slaves are not held as property;—this Scotch church declares, that the man who regards man as property ought to be turned out of the church. I have done with the Scotch divines.

Gentlemen and fellow-citizens: I will here state at large, for your satisfaction, and that it may appear in the book, why I have not, at my brother's urgent request, so vehemently repeated, taken this discussion at once into Bible criticism.

I have an argument of three hours' length of the kind he calls for, which I have prepared with labor and care;—an hour and a half on the Old Testament, and an hour and a half upon the New. But I would not present that class of arguments at the beginning of this debate; because I consider that, the strongest part of my argument, and I wished to present the weakest first. Because all my arguments are Bible arguments, every principle which I advocate being found in the word of God. Because, moreover, I felt it my duty to God to manage this debate as wisely as I could for the truth; and I therefore did not wish to take a solemn practical question at first into Greek and Hebrew lexicons, grammars, critics, and commentators, one half of whose ideas are baked stiff in the oven of German hermeneutics. Before letting in what light may be had from these sources, (and a just use of them yields much.) I have thought proper to argue the question of slavery, for a time, as it is, a solemn matter of fact, and upon the broad principle of common equity and common sense.

And the event has proved the wisdom and necessity of my course. You have seen that the real point of dispute is, whether slave-holding be this or that. 'Prove,' he says, 'that slavery includes these cruelties—the prohibition to read —the complete power of the master, etc., etc., and I will be an abolitionist.' Here has been his main labor—to deny that certain things belong necessarily to slavery. Was not my long discussion to show what slavery is, therefore, necessary? Besides, one well prepared argument upon the Scriptures is enough; and I take no advantage in putting it off to the last. He has the closing speech at every session, and the benefit, if there be any, of a last impression. I am willing he should. He will, therefore, have full opportunity of presenting what he may have to say upon the teachings of Scripture.

I have said that I felt bound to conduct this debate wisely for the cause of truth, and I am not unacquainted with the course commonly taken by the defenders of slavery. Shunning all clear ideas of slavery, they are accustomed to dip the people at once into the Mosaic institution, and haggle their minds with "doulos," and "ebedh," and "kaunah," etc., etc. It was thus that Dr. Junkin, in the synodical debate in the first Presbyterian church in this city, last fall, Junkinized the minds of the people for two whole days; and when he had done, I do not believe that the heads of his auditors contained two substantial ideas on the topics which he handled.

Now I determined not to let my brother take this course. I resolved, before giving him an opportunity to display his learning, to give you a chance to judge of his candor and sense. I desired that the public should know; I myself wished to know, to what class of minds my brother belongs. This is a legitimate object sought in a proper way. He is active, unwearied in the propagation of his opinions, and it is material that we know what weight we ought to attach to them, as coming from him.

I have, within these few years past, met a class of men, whom the late ecclesiastical agitations in this country and in Europe have thrown up into notice—of whom, I think, it may justly be said, that the world were better if the species were extinct: having few original ideas of their own, they are great gatherers and retailers of the ideas of others; men of fourth or fifth rate minds, who, being of narrow intellect, and stimulated by a large ambition, seek, by sectarian services, to wind their way up to the top of some old ecclesiastical organization, founded by the piety of a former age, to reign amid the moral owls and bats that peer and chicker amid the twilight of its tower.

When slavery is the subject, I have never known a man of this class willing to meet and discuss it, as it actually exists, upon the ordinary and well-known principles of right and wrong. Instead of this, they dive into the dusky regions of antiquity, like rats into cellars, and, guided to despotism by an instinct as precise as that which guides that animal to cheese, they pick up all the instances of restriction upon human liberty which belonged to dark and despotic ages, and twist them into a snake-coil of argument to bind down American Christianity to the toleration of slavery in an age of liberty and light. Slaves themselves, in heart, to authority, as are all caterers to despotism, they are great for lexicons, and profound in commentators; classes of writers, who, from the number of topics which they treat, must necessarily take the most they write upon trust from other men; and they never scruple to weigh the opinion of " Doctor This," and " Doctor That," against the clearest elements of equity, and the plainest principles of justice!

I do not say that brother Rice belongs to this class of minds. I would not bring a railing accusation against Satan, much less against my brother. But I wished, for the cause of righteousness, that the public should know, and to know myself, whether he was or was not of this sort and grade of men; and I knew that if he was, if I took him out of the beaten track of pro-slavery argument he would be utterly at loss what to do. Whether this has been true of him, thus far, I do not say. The book which we make will show. I have now done with this matter. If he twits me hereafter with being unable to argue with him, he shall have what benefit that course will bring him. I shall go straight forward with my work.

I wish now to reply to the remark quoted from Dr. Chalmers, *that the doctrine of abolitionists is a dogma of recent date;* and to show, if I am able, that the truth, that *slave-holding is sin,* has been struggling with the mind and conscience of the church ever since the time of Christ and the apostles. I have cited to you the fact, that Ignatius wrote to Polycarp, in the year 107, not to appropriate the church money for buying those slaves of heathen masters, who were converted to Christianity from heathenism. The reason of Ignatius's advice is obvious, viz: that if the church bought the freedom of all the slaves who entered it from heathenism, it might tempt the servile population to spurious conversions, as they would join the church for the sake of gaining their freedom. But the fact proves this, that the churches founded by the apostles were far from being slaveholding churches, that the slaves who joined them were importuning the members to club the church money and buy their freedom.

No proof is needed to show that the owners of these slaves were not church-members. The idea of a whole church giving the money of the whole, to buy the bodies of one part of its members called slaves, from another part called masters, is too absurd for even slaves to ask.

I now resume my argument, (which was suspended at this point several meetings since,) to prove, that, whenever slavery has been abolished without blood, the doctrine *that slave-holding is sin* has abolished it; that therefore Dr. Chalmers is mistaken; and as this doctrine yields the fruits of truth, by destroying slavery, it is therefore true that slave-holding is sin.

I must now take you through a little history, and but a little; as the notices of slavery in early church history are not extensive. We find in Giesler, that, about A. D. 316, Constantine ratified the manumissions of the church, and empowered those thus emancipated to take property by will.

These two items of history do not show that the Christian church in the years 107 and 316, understood the doctrine of abolition precisely as now taught. But the first shows that the churches of the Apostles were non-slaveholding churches, and the second, that, in the day of Constantine, the church was forcing emancipation upon the State. For Constantine ratified church manumissions to make himself popular with the Christian party. Whereas, at this time churches and ministers in the South, take the lead of the State in vindicating the principle of slavery. Leaving the age of Constantine and coming down through a period of 300 years, we find what doctrines and sentiments prevailed in the church respecting slavery, that is, upon what *theory* their *practice* of church-manumission was based. I read from *Robertson's Charles V.*, p. 24, *Note* 20.

"When Pope Gregory the Great, who flourished toward the end of the sixth century, granted liberty to some of his slaves, he gives this reason for it:—

" ' *Cum Redemptor noster, totius conditor naturae, ad hoc propitiatus, humanam carnem voluerit assumere, ut divinitatis suae gratia, dirempto (quo tenebamur captivi) vinculo, pristinae nos restitueret libertati; salubriter agitur, si homines, quos ab initio liberos natura protulit, et jus gentium jugo substituit sertutis, in ea, qua nati fuerant, manumittendis beneficio, libertati reddantur.'* "

Which I thus translate :—'Since our Redeemer, the builder of all nature, set apart for this, has voluntarily assumed human flesh, that, by favor of his divinity, (the chain by which we were bound being broken,) he might restore us to our pristine liberty ; it is a wholesome act, (salubriter agitur,) if men, produced by nature free at first, but subjected to the yoke of slavery, by the law of nations, may be restored, by act of the emancipator, to that liberty in which they were born.'

This document bases the duty of freeing slaves upon the atonement itself, the center and sum of all Christian doctrine ; and practically, and almost in terms, declares that Christians ought to free their slaves, because Christ came to free them: and it distinctly declares the great doctrine from which the duty of immediate abolition flows, that " *men are born free !*"

Now considering that this man was a Pope, a human head of the church, and like other human heads, probably borne along by the body ; it is fair to suppose he rather *represented* than *led* the anti-slavery opinion of the church in his day ; in short that he was pressed to what he did by the truth which prevailed among the membership. It surely would be a rare occurrence—one which has never yet happened, to see a single Pope setting himself *against* the opinions of both church and world. I say therefore, that this act of emancipation by Pope Gregory the Great, based on abolition principles, not obscurely expressed, shows that the gospel of Christ was a battering-ram before which slavery instantly gave way wherever it came, and that the sentiment that slave-holding is sin, Dr. Chalmers to the contrary notwithstanding, is as old as the church of Christ. I do not say or suppose that this gospel duty of manumission, at that day was perfectly practiced, or that those Christians were abolitionists in the exact modern sense. But I aver that slavery was abolished by the sentiment, then in the church, that slave-holding is sin, and by nothing else.

From Gregory's time (6th century) to that of Louis X., A. D. 1315, the deeds of manumission clearly recognize the abolition doctrine that slave-holding is sin.

"A greater part of the charters of manumission previous to the reign of Louis X.," says Robertson, (*note* 20 *to page* 24,) "were granted, '*Pro amore Dei; pro remedio animæ; pro mercede animæ, et pro timore omnipotentis Dei:*'" that is—"for the love of God," "for the remedy of the soul," "for the consideration of the soul," and "for the fear of the omnipotent God," etc. Now, the distance between freeing slaves for the soul's salvation, and freeing them to escape its damnation, is not so great but quickened consciences would soon travel it. Certainly, these deeds of manumission, every time one was issued or read in Church, (and great numbers are on record,) must inevitably and instantly have forced the inference upon the minds of Christians, that slave-holding was against "the fear of God, and the salvation of the soul." And they show most clearly that the operative principle which impelled to emancipation was the truth, which is now stated, in simple language, viz: "that *holding slaves is sin.*"

"These deeds, freeing slaves for the "fear of God," etc., run down to the time of Philip the Long, and Louis X., A. D. 1315, and 1318, when, we read in Robertson, "the enfranchisement of slaves became more frequent." These two monarchs then issued ordinances, declaring, that, "*as all men were by nature free born,* and as their kingdom was called the Kingdom of Franks, they determined that it should be so in reality as well as in name; therefore they *appointed* that enfranchisements should be granted throughout the whole kingdom, upon just and reasonable conditions. *These edicts were carried into* IMMEDIATE EXECUTION *within the royal domain.* And servitude was gradually abolished in almost every province of the kingdom."

Thus, the self-interest of the world completed, what, in the Church, the fear of God began. The sentiment among Christians, that slave-holding was contrary to religion, first produced emancipations, and proved them beneficial; and the ordinance of these two monarchs with the example of *immediate emancipation* on the royal estates, completed the overthrow of slavery in what is now France.

The abolition of slavery in Britain followed soon after, the particulars of which, says Robertson, "*are found in the charter granted Habitatoribus Montis Britonis*, A. D. 1376."

Before this time, children were sold into Ireland, at a regular market in Liverpool: and Henry, as quoted by Pitt, says, that "great multitudes were shipped from the British coast, and were to be seen exposed, like cattle, for sale in the Romish market." This charter of British abolition, in 1376, is an immediate abolition charter. "1. The right of disposing of their [slaves'] persons by sale or grant was relinquished. 2. Power was given them of conveying their effects by will, or any other legal deed. 3. Their services and taxes to their liege lord are precisely ascertained. 4. And they are allowed the privilege of marrying, according to their inclination." That is, they ceased to be instruments in the hands of their masters, and became men under a government of law.

A system of villeinage, however, continued in England near two hundred years after this, to the times of Henry VIII.; which, though not slavery, was yet grinding oppression. Villeinage, therefore, like slavery, was abolished by the conviction of its sinfulness. I read the interesting and instructive account of its abolition from *Cooper's Justinian*, *p.* 414: *notes.*

"Sir Thomas Smith, who was secretary of state to Edward VI., and then to Elizabeth, observes that he never knew any villeins *in gross* in his time; and that villeins appendant to manors (villeins regardant) were but very few in number; that *since England had received the Christian religion, men began to be affected in their consciences at holding their brethren in servitude.*" (Dr. Rice's religion teaches that slave-holding is not sinful.) "And that upon this scruple, in process of time, the holy fathers, monks, and friars so burthened the minds of those whom they confessed, that temporal men were glad to manumit all their villeins. But," he adds, "*the holy fathers themselves did not manumit their own slaves, and the bishops behaved like the other ecclesiastics.* But, at last, some bishops enfranchised their villeins for money, and others on account of popular outcry: and at length the monasteries falling into lay hands were the occasion that almost all the villeins in the kingdom were manumitted."

The same things which were enacted in England, at the abolition of villeinage, are, in principle, now being enacted in this country. The religious teachers of the day instructed the people in Christianity, and made them see that slaveholding and villeinage were inconsistent with it. But the priests, trusting in the reverence of the people for their religious character, would not submit to a practical application of their own principles, till compelled to it by a public sentiment, the reflection of their own teachings, rising from the people. "And the bishops behaved like the other ecclesiastics." A year or more since, a man from this city travelling down the Ohio, said the boat took on board the *Right Reverend Bishop Polk*, of the Protestant Episcopal Church, and brother, I believe, of our worthy President of the United States, with his sixty slaves, whom he was taking to his plantation. "A few miles below," said my informant, "a swine-merchant came a-board, with a large drove of hogs." And in legal and social condition, the slave-gang of this "Holy Bishop" were precisely on an equal footing with that herd of swine; and both sustained the same property relation to their masters.

As to the question, whether any teachers of religion, at the present day, are driven by public opinion to act against slavery, it is most humiliating to reflect on what would be the course of our General Assemblies, and General Conferences, on the subject of slavery, if no petitions had gone, or should hereafter go up from the people to them on that subject. The monks, friars, and bishops of England freed their bondmen under the same pressure that has, in our day, procured the reading of anti-slavery notices, viz: "*popular outcry.*" But the main-spring, which kept the whole of the machinery of emancipation in movement was the conviction, seated in the conscience of the nation, that slave-holding was sinful.

I now call your attention to the abolition of slavery in the British West Indies.

Opposition to West Indian Slavery, was formally commenced by Granville Sharpe, in the year 1772, and the first fruit of his labors was the decision obtained in that year, by the English Bench, that slaves became free by setting foot upon English soil. This was the celebrated case of the negro Somersett. Peckard, Benezet, Gregoire, and others, had already written against the enslavement of the Africans, which, till now, was pursued as a lawful christian calling. In 1785, Dr. Peckard, vice-chancellor of Cambridge University, gave to the Senior Bachelors, as a subject for a Latin dissertation, the question, "*Is it right to make slaves of others against their will?*" Thomas Clarkson obtained the prize upon this thesis, and the investigation of his subject so wrought upon his mind, that he devoted his life to the destruction of slavery. A committee was soon organized, of which Granville Sharpe was chairman, which for a time labored alike against slavery and the slave trade. But they afterwards thought it would be wiser to drop direct opposition to slavery, and oppose the slave-trade alone, as the most obnoxious of the two, and easiest suppressed. They were induced to this course by two considerations,—the great strength and endless ramifications of the slavery interest in England; and the idea that the slave-trade, once abolished, slavery would speedily die, as a stream when its fountain is stopped. That was a great error. When the Abbe Gregoire heard of it, he wrote to the British abolitionists: "*In your late change of policy, I hear the groans, and see the falling tears of coming millions.*" This prophecy has been verified.

The slave-trade was abolished in England, under the

Grenville administration, in 1807 ; from which time the British philanthropists took up opposition to slavery itself. But they labored for years under the incubus notion of gradual emancipation. They had not yet learned the truth of the proverb—"*Give the sinner to-day, and he and the devil will take care of to-morrow.*"

I may as well stop here to say, there is nothing, there can be nothing but immediateism in morals. You have no right to tell a man he is sinning, and that it is his duty to repent next week. The only command which God ever gave to men involved in wrong practices, is in the present tense— "*Cease to do Evil;*" and whoever holds another language grants indulgence to sin. But while this is the only correct theory of reformation ; in practice, the law always allows "*a reasonable* time" for change. If slave-holders were now preparing to emancipate their slaves in six weeks or two months, and would actually do so, would not that be "immediate emancipation ?" The slavery ceases when the emancipation is honestly and effectually begun.

My first public lecture against slavery, was delivered while I was a student. It was in the little town of Haddonfield, New Jersey ; where I met, after the mob, a thing of course at that day, a New Jersey farmer and explained to him our doctrine of "Immediate Abolition" I urged that slave-holding is sin—because slavery repeals and resists the laws by which God has regulated human society : that it is a repeal of the marriage relation. That it is not the taking apart a man and his wife that makes the separation. The Atlantic ocean has rolled between me and my wife, but I thanked God that I had a wife then. It is not distance which parts man and wife in the slave system, but slavery. They could remain married while an ocean is between them, but they cannot be married while they are slaves.

I showed him that slavery forbids the required promises of parents to instruct their children to read the Word of God, and thus virtually forbids infant baptism itself. That by the law of several States, it is a punishable crime in parents to teach their children to read the name of God.

When the old man (for he was a parent himself) began to see that my doctrine was truth, one present said: "Oh ! but it will never do to free them all at once ! " The farmer replied, " I don't see any particular danger of that; but we all say the thing must be brought to an end; and though a man has his knife on the grindstone and another at the crank, it never begins to sharpen till he begins to turn. If we are ever to get rid of slavery, I think its time to begin to turn."

But I return to the British abolitionists. Their teaching of gradual emancipation not being founded in truth, influenced conscience little or none, and produced *no* emancipation. But about the year 1824, a change occurred in their teaching, and a corresponding change in their tone. They still taught the same principle, that slave-holding is sin, but they varied their application of it, and demanded immediate repentance. A pamphlet issued from the press this year, written by Elizabeth Heyrick, of Leicester, entitled " *Immediate not Gradual Abolition*," which expressed, and perhaps helped to mould the anti-slavery movement into the form, and possibly gave it the name, of " *immediate abolition*."

The result of this agitation you all know. On the 31st day of July, 1834, at midnight, 800,000 human beings knelt down slaves, when the clock began to strike twelve, (if brother Rice had been there, he would have struck the hour of the debate,) [a laugh] and when the clock ceased striking, arose up men.

There is no doubt upon what principles the British emancipation was brought about; that it was the principle that slave-holding is sin, and immediate abolition a duty. Principles urged and carried forward by abolitionists, almost all of whom are still living, as Clarkson, Sturge, Buxton, Thompson, Scoble, Scales, and their coadjutors, with whose minds and hearts modern abolitionism may almost be said to have originated, and from whose operations, perhaps, derived its name.

I will read the record of the event, which took place in the West Indies, at midnight, August 1, 1834, from Kimball & Thome's "*Emancipation in the West Indies*," p. 144:

"The Wesleyans kept 'watch-night' in all their chapels on the night of the 31st July. One of the Wesleyan missionaries gave us an account of the watch-meeting at the chapel in St. Johns. The spacious house was filled with the candidates for liberty. All was animation and eagerness. A mighty chorus of voices swelled the song of expectation and joy, and as they united in prayer, the voice of the leader was drowned in the universal acclamations of thanksgiving and praise, and blessing, and honor, and glory to God, who had come down for their deliverance. In such exercises, the evening was spent, until the hour of twelve approached. The missionary then proposed, that when the clock on the Cathedral should begin to strike, the whole congregation should fall upon their knees, and receive the boon of freedom in silence. Accordingly, as the loud bell tolled its first note, the crowded assembly prostrated themselves on their knees. All was silence, save the quivering, half-stifled breath of the struggling spirit. The slow notes of the clock fell upon the multitude; peal on peal, peal on peal, rolled over the prostrate throng, in tones of angels' voices, thrilling among the desolate chords and weary heart-strings. Scarce had the clock sounded its last note, when the lightning flashed vividly around, and a loud peal of thunder roared along the sky—God's pillar of fire, and his trump of Jubilee! A moment of profoundest silence passed—then came the *burst*. They broke forth in prayer; they shouted; they sang, glory, alleluia; they clapped their hands, leaped up, fell down, clasped each other in their free arms, cried, laughed, and went to and fro, tossing upward their unfettered arms. But, high above the whole, there was a mighty sound, which ever and anon swelled,—it was the utterings, in broken negro dialect, of gratitude to God."

This is the *doctrine*, and this the *practice*, of immediate abolitionism — principles which shall spread until the

whole earth shall acknowledge their influence; "truth shall
spring out of the earth, and righteousness shall look down
from heaven." And that prophetic song of the Bethlehem
angels shall be realized in history, " Glory to God in the
highest; on earth peace, and good will toward man."

Before this emancipation took place, all evil auguries were
rife respecting the results; but, so far, only good has resulted. By thousands, the poor creatures flocked to the
churches to be joined in marriage; no white man has been
injured; no sheriff or constable has been resisted in executing the laws, and no complaints of the working of this
emancipation has yet been heard, except from a few, who
weigh sugar and tobacco and coffee against the inalienable
rights of immortal man.   [*Time expired.*

[MR. RICE'S NINTH SPEECH.]

Gentlemen Moderators, and Fellow Citizens:

I shall have something, presently, to say, which will greatly change the aspect of things in relation to West India
emancipation. I have facts to adduce which will shew that
it is not to modern abolition, or abolitionists, that that emancipation is to be attributed.

My friend thinks the views of Dr. Cunningham and Dr.
Chalmers, are entitled to no weight or consideration in this
discussion, because, until very recently, they were opposed
to free churches! Truly, he puts forth singular logic, the
amount of which is, that no man who is wrong on *one
point*, can possibly be right on any other! Yet, in a few
moments after urging this objection, he, himself, appealed to
the opinion of Pope Gregory! He objects to any reference
to the opinions or testimony of such divines as Cunningham
and Chalmers, yet immediately contends that the opinions
of the " Man of Sin," (who was also a political despot,) in
the sixth century, are worth a great deal! If he quotes
Pope Gregory, I think he should not, for shame's sake, object

to my quoting Drs. Cunningham and Chalmers, two of the best and most distinguished men of our own day.

How, I ask, does a man's being in favor of a church establishment, hinder him from seeing the evils of slavery? What is there, in his notions of church government, to blind his eyes on this question? How is the logic of a man who is wrong on the subject of ecclesiastical establishments, necessarily bad on the subject of slave-holding? I should like to hear the process by which the gentleman has reached this conclusion.

But when Dr. Chalmers states *matters of fact*, is he not to be trusted? He is a wise man, and a man of veracity. Shall we not, then, hear and candidly weigh his testimony concerning an important matter of fact? Now, what does he say, touching the history of abolitionism? In his letter on this subject, recently published, he says:

" But again, not only is there a wrong principle involved in the demand which these abolitionists now make on the Free Church of Scotland: it is in itself a wrong procedure for hastening forward that object, for the accomplishment of which we are alike desirous with themselves; or, in other words, it is not only wrong in principle, but hurtful in effect. Should we concede to their demands, then, speaking in the terms of our opinion, we incur the discredit (and in proportion to that discredit we damage our usefulness as a church, of having given in—and that at the bidding of another party —to a factitious and new principle, which not only wants, but which is contrary to the authority of Scripture and Apostolic example, and, indeed, has only been heard of in christendom within these few years; as if gotten up for an occasion, instead of being drawn from the repositories of that truth which is immutable and eternal—even the principle, that no slave-holder should be admitted to a participation in the sacraments."

Now, if slave-holding is in itself a heinous sin—a gross violation of the law of God, as abolitionists affirm, the Scriptures must clearly condemn it, and clearly teach the doctrine advocatèd by them. And if the Scriptures do so teach, surely it is to be supposed, that wise and good men, at least many of them, have so understood them. Now, Chalmers asserts not only that, in his opinion, the principles of the abolitionists are false; but he states it as a *fact,* that they are *new*, and such as have " *only been heard of in christendom within these few years,* as if gotten up for an occasion, instead of being drawn from the repositories of that truth which is immutable and eternal." It is true, Dr. Chalmers has been in favor of church establishments; but, it is also true, that he is most decidedly and strongly opposed to slavery; and, therefore, however blinded by his prejudices on the former subject, he is just the man who would be likely to see the truth on the latter. On this his eyes were not blinded by pro-slavery prejudices. At any rate, he is certainly capable of testifying to a historical fact, such as he states. These remarks apply with equal force to Dr. Cunningham. The United Associate Synod of Scotland, the gentleman says, expressed themselves as amazed and grieved to ascertain that ministers of the gospel, and officers in the church in America, held slaves. Well, their amazement only proves how little they had examined the subject of which they wrote; for, as learned men, they might have known, that such has been the fact ever since our church was organized; that the same is true of almost every church in the world, not only in modern, but ancient times.

But the gentleman quotes the report of the Free Church of Scotland, which he says, was approved by Drs. Chalmers and Cunningham, as if it condemned the doctrine of the last General Assembly of our church on this subject. So it appears, they can see, at last. The gentleman first tells us, that Dr. Cunningham and Dr. Chalmers, are blind on the subject of slavery; and then he insists, and attempts to prove, that they are both abolitionists! [Laughter.] When he commenced his speech, it seems, he did not think they were abolitionists, but before the end of the same speech, he is convinced that they are! Well, what does the report of the Free Church say on the subject? It says that it is a sin to regard and treat slaves "*as mere chattels personal.*" This, Mr. B. thinks, is contrary to the sentiments expressed in the report of our General Assembly. I will take the liberty of reading to the gentleman a sentence or two from that report, which, indeed, he seems never to have read at all.

"Nor is this Assembly to be understood as countenancing the idea, that masters may regard their servants as *mere property*, and not as human beings, rational, accountable, immortal. The Scriptures prescribe not only the duty of servants, but of masters also, warning the latter to discharge those duties, 'knowing that their master is in heaven, neither is there respect of persons with him.'"

Does not this report represent it as a sin to regard slaves as "*mere property?*" Does it not teach, that masters are bound to regard and treat them "as rational, accountable and immortal beings?" Our report and theirs thus agree perfectly in sentiment: and yet Mr. B. holds them up as diametrically opposite to each other!

But he says, this doctrine is hateful at the South; for those men hold slaves merely as property. I am not here to please the North or the South, the East or the West. It is my duty to advocate and defend *Bible doctrine* because it is Bible doctrine, and not to please either North or South. If it be true that southern slave-holders do not love our doctrine; then, surely, it is not "pro-slavery," as the abolitionists assert that it is; else they would like it. Last night my friend told us the South were well pleased with our doctrine; but, now he says, the South cannot endure it. Here is a flat contradiction. Which of his contradictory assertions are we to believe? He says, that slave-holders must and do regard their slaves as property: aye, but do they regard them *simply as property?*—as "*mere* chattels personal?" Certainly Christian masters do not; and this is precisely what both the Scotch report and ours condemn.

But let us hear the opinion of Dr. Cunningham as to the character of slave-holding as it exists amongst Christians in

these United States. He visited the slave-holding States;
and his testimony is that of an eminently wise and good man
who first examined for himself, and not of one who sees
slavery only as it is caricatured in the books and speeches
of abolitionists. When he returned to Scotland, he found
the abolitionists urging the church in Scotland to hold no
communion with the Presbyterian church in America, unless the latter would agree forthwith to exclude from her
communion all slave-holders. In a reply to their speeches
in Presbytery he thus remarks:

" We have to do with the churches. It is important to
view this question in relation to the churches, just because
there are churches of Christ, in that country. It is absolutely necessary to examine this question with candor and
fairness, that we may seek to realize the fact, that there are
churches of Christ, which, in regard to all matters, except
slavery, are just as well entitled to be regarded as respectable, useful, honored churches of Christ, as the evangelical
churches here ; and numbers of ministers, the most of them
just as fairly entitled to be regarded as ministers of Christ,
living under the power of the truth, laboring faithfully, and
serving God in the Gospel of his Son. And whatever motives abolitionists and other slanderers may ascribe to me, I
believe myself, if my views and feelings are in any way
different from those obtaining among my brethren, it arises
from this, that I realize more distinctly the character of these
men and churches. I know something of them from personal intercourse ; and therefore I feel myself constrained,
in common fairness, to begin the investigation of the question with the assured conviction, that as a whole, they are just
as well entitled to be regarded as Christian men, ministers and
churches discharging their duty to Christ, and honored by
Him, as any, generally speaking, in this country. The
ground taken on the other side comes to this, that whatever
appearance of piety, worth, and excellence the churches may
possess, their conduct and views in regard to slavery deprive
them of all right to this character. Many slur over the

thing in this way; and according to the general purport of of Mr. Grey's speech, you would come to this conclusion. I expected to hear more discussion of the scriptural principles which are ordinarily brought to bear on the settlement of this question. Practically and substantially, the controversy virtually lies there; and the point on which the decision will mainly hinge is this—Is the Church of Christ bound, as a matter of imperative duty, to exclude every man, who stands in the relation of a master to a slave, from office and ordinances in the Church of Christ? There occurs here the obvious and undoubted fact, that the Apostles admitted them to office and ordinances, and I hold this upon this ground, that in a question somewhat analogous, the Apostles made monogamy a qualification for office; a precept which clearly establishes,—1. That monogamy was not then a qualification for ordinances in the church. 2. That non-slave-holding was not a qualification for office. Slave-holders were members and ministers of the Church in the apostolic times; and it is somewhat strange, that in the discussion of a question turning mainly on that point, we should not have one single syllable on the conduct of the churches then. It is said, however, that slavery is a sin, therefore every slave-holder is a great sinner, and ought to be treated as the abolitionists do, as thieves and robbers, and at once expelled. Even if one were to concede that slavery is a sin, it would not follow that every slave-holder ought to be excluded from the Christian Church, because the conduct of the Apostles proves that that is not a general or universal law. And whatever view you take as to the sinfulness of slavery, you must thread your way through the conduct of the apostolic churches. If slavery is a sin in such a sense, as that every slave-holder is a sinner, and ought to be expelled, you are landed in this principle, that, under the authority of the Apostles, the churches connived at slavery—at sin—because of the peculiarity of their position—because of the difficulties of their situation. If not on this ground, then you must admit that slavery is not a sin, or not in such a sense as that every man connected with it is to be counted as a heinous sinner. I have no doubt as to which alternative we ought to take. Slavery, as a system, is sinful, inconsistent with the ordinary rights of man—the moral bearing and general spirit of the Word of God—and injurious to the interests of religion ; but there are some difficulties which must be disposed of. A man, may lean either to the side of denying that, and adduce the conduct of the Apostles, or admit all that, and endeavor to explain the conduct of the Apostles, in consistency with the admission of that great truth, as to the character of slavery. The Apostles' conduct may be explained in consistency with the general position I hold as to slavery, but I cannot see how it can be reconciled with one which slipped in as if it were identical, that slavery is a sin in such a sense that every man who stands in the relation of a master to a slave is thereby guilty of a great and heinous sin, just as a man guilty of robbery and murder, and ought to be denounced and treated as such."

" We may imagine in this country that a man need not be a slave-holder unless he pleases ; but this is gross ignorance. If a man takes his slaves to the door, and says, ' You may go about your business, you are free men,' they would be instantly seized, and sold for the benefit of the State. There are possibilities of emancipation, but that is the law. The way they are legally emancipated is, that the slaves must be expelled from the State altogether, and, in addition to that, he must give positive security for the maintainance of these slaves all their days, which is a virtual prohibition of manumission. There are hundreds of slave-holders who would give their slaves liberty to-morrow, if the law of the land would allow it. These laws indicate the condition in which the churches are placed, and we should make use of them first for increasing our horror of the system, and then to realize the true state of these churches in the difficulties with which they have to contend. A man may be placed in such a condition, as that the only act of humanity he can discharge is just to buy a man, and make him his slave. He acquires a legal right to him, and may do injury according to the law; but this does not follow. In general, men of Christian feeling are desirous to avoid standing in the relation of masters to slaves as far as they can, though their feeling is not so strong as it ought to be. In many parts of the slave States they have just this alternative, either to become the proprietor of two or three slaves, or be destitute of every thing in the shape of domestic servants. In some of the northern States they have to contend with the absolute impossibility of getting any person for a servant except an Irish Papist. Ministers have told me that this was literally the case. Many of us would think that to bring an Irish Papist into our family was something like a sin; yet there it is rendered a matter of necessity. In the southern States slaveholding is matter of necessity, because there is no other way of getting domestic servants. Though Christian men prefer hiring slaves, the property of another, they cannot always do it. A minister who lived in a slave State made it his business not to acquire property in slaves, but to hire them. He lived in a town where that could be easily done. One woman he hired. Her owner's circumstances became embarrassed. This woman came to her master, not her owner, and told him she had reason to think she would be sold, and besought him to buy her. He replied he did not wish to buy slaves. The woman, who was a religious person, took it so much to heart, that she could not do her work, nor take any meat, lying about her kitchen crying and howling, till at last he was obliged to borrow money and buy this woman, as the only way in which he could really perform an act of humanity towards her. An anti-slavery gentleman in one of the northern States, who succeeded by inheritance to a plantation and a number of slaves in the south, shuddered at the idea, and wrote down there to tell them that they must dispose of the slaves, for that he would not become their master. They wrote back telling him what were the conditions, that he must not only give bond for their support all their days, but expel them from that State, and that otherwise they must be sold for the benefit of the State. He came to this conclusion, that since he could not get quit of the duty, he would just give up his business, and go down to reside on the plantation, and labor it with these slaves; and there he is, I believe, at this moment, the owner of a considerable number of slaves, just as fully discharging the duties of a Christian man and a 'believing master,' as it is possible for any man to do."

Here is his testimony, given in view of what he saw of slavery, as existing among the Presbyterians of the southern States; and his opinion that such men were not to be turned out of the church.

My friend felt constrained, in his last speech, to give the audience some reasons for the singular course he has chosen to pursue, in failing, during a debate of thirteen hours, to produce evidence from the Bible in support of his affirmative proposition. And what are his reasons? The first is, that all his arguments were intended to be Bible arguments. Indeed! Then how has it happened, that he has not given us *Bible language*—quotations from the inspired word? It is truly singular, that in a discussion like this he should give us Bible arguments, and yet make not an effort to sustain them with quotations from the Bible. Or does he expect the audience to take it as granted, that all his assertions are in accordance with the Scriptures? Besides, he himself made the distinction between "the *direct* argument" for abolitionism and the Bible argument. When, on last evening, I stated that he had given notice of his intention to present the Bible argument, he corrected me by saying, it was the *direct* argument, not the *Bible* argument. And after having made the distinction, he now, with marvellous inconsistency, asserts that all his arguments are Bible arguments! Such are the inconsistencies and contradictions into which men advocating error are driven.

His second reason is, that the long discussion with which he has occupied the time, was necessary, in order to show what slavery is. Now, I thought that that was a matter

understood by every body before he began. There is no
mystery about it. But it did require a very long discussion
indeed to show, that the relation of master and slave is identical with the laws made in all times and countries to regulate that relation. That, I confess, would require a much
longer and much more convincing argument than any we
have yet heard. Marriage, according to my friend's logic,
is just what human laws define it to be; and, according to
the same authority (which is the gentleman's simple assertion) slavery is identical with the laws made for the regulation of the relation. A slave-holder, in other words, is
necessarily as bad a man as the laws allow him to be!
This, it would require a long argument indeed to establish.
I am persuaded, that intelligent men never will believe doctrine so palpably absurd as this, even after they have listened
to his seven hours' argument. No one admits the correctness of the principles of his reasoning.

The good brother charges me with having brought against
him a railing accusation. Will he have the goodness to state
what I have said, that deserves such an appellation? I am
not conscious of having laid myself liable to such a charge.
Besides, here are moderators presiding over the debate,
whose office and duty it is to prevent any such indecorum,
should it be attempted by either party. Certainly, in making such a charge, he pays them a poor compliment.

The gentleman says, he is determined not to plunge into
the labyrinths of Hebrew and Greek; and he discourses eloquently of a certain class of men, *whom the world could well
spare,* who are great sticklers for lexicons and commentaries;
men who, like bats around the top of a tower, aspire to the
high places in the church; and who, like rats, are ever de-
scending into dark cellars! These men, he says, are fond
of going back into remote and despotic ages to find arguments to sustain slavery. Truly, there is something strange
in all this. I had really supposed, that the Hebrew of the
Old Testament, and the Greek of the New, contained the inspired words of the Holy Ghost; and that to plunge into the

Hebrew and Greek, was to plunge into the clear light of divine truth. Moreover, the Confession of Faith which he has solemnly adopted, declares, that "in all controversies of religion, the church is finally to appeal unto them." But if we are to believe the gentleman, he who appeals to the original languages in which the Scriptures were inspired, is plunging into mists and profound darkness! Our Saviour tells us, that "he that doeth the truth, cometh to the light," and that only those who perform evil works, hate the light, and refuse to approach to it, lest their deeds should be reproved. But the nature of men, it would seem, is now changed; for Mr. B. assures us, that the "pro-slavery men," who love darkness, and whose deeds are evil, insist on coming directly to the pure light—to the precise words of inspiration! Strange indeed!—yet not more strange than his description of them. He says, they are like bats flying about lofty towers, and like rats retreating to dark cellars. Curious men these—like bats that *fly up*, and like rats that *run down!* [laughter.] Surely, if there are such men, the world, as Mr. B. says, might well spare them. One thing, however, I think most unaccountable,—viz: though like bats and rats, both of which love darkness, they insist on running directly into the light; and even the gentleman, with all his efforts, cannot prevent them doing so!

The gentleman reminds me of a certain class of preachers, very zealous, though ignorant men, who are accustomed in their discourses, to thank God that they never rubbed their backs against a college.—They profess to get all their divinity by inspiration. Like them, my brother seems to thank God, that in discussing a question of Christian morals and faith, he has not run, where I have pressed him to go, *into the Hebrew Bible and the Greek Testament.* Yet he has promised to go into both. Yes: he is going, it seems, to run into this very region of darkness, after condemning me for being disposed to do so! How very consistent.

But he says, if you take me off of my beaten track, I can do nothing. Well, I confess that in moral and religious questions, I have but one path, and that is illumined by the Bible, which "is a light to my feet, and a lamp to my path." I plead guilty: take me from this, and I can do nothing. [Applause.]

An inspired prophet, I remember, exhorts men to "inquire for the old paths," and to walk therein; and I am the more inclined solemnly to regard the exhortation, because I have seen whither a contrary course has led men. I see where Garrison, and Leavitt, and Smith have got to, by striking out new paths, and turning from the good old way of Bible truth. No longer guided by the word of God, they are boldly denouncing the church of Jesus Christ, and with vain efforts laboring for its overthrow. The brightness of their new light has quite dazzled, if not absolutely deranged them. I desire not to follow in their footsteps.

As to Constantine's ratifying the manumissions of the church, he was perfectly right in so doing; and the Legislature of Kentucky does the same, though the members of that body do not, generally, profess to be pious men. But the request of the slaves, if they made it, that the church funds might be applied to their ransom from *heathen masters*, and the refusal of the church to comply with their request, is, to say the least, a very inconclusive evidence, that the *church-members*, in that day, were all abolitionists! But Pope Gregory is quoted as saying, it is a wholesome act to restore to liberty men by nature free. So say I. Most heartily do I desire that every slave on earth should enjoy liberty; and I should truly rejoice to see the slaves of our country liberated and placed in Africa, the land of their fathers. There they can be free indeed, and their character can be elevated. In Liberia are found flourishing colonies of emancipated slaves, who have flourishing churches, and schools of their own. They are not in the condition of the free negroes of Ohio, who have the *name* of liberty, but know little of the blessings of freedom. They are deprived (and with the consent of the gentleman and his abolition friends) of the right to a voice in the making of the laws by which they are gov-

erned; degraded and down-trodden, having the *name* of freedom without the thing itself. I oppose abolitionism, as I
before remarked, precisely because I believe that it post-
pones and hinders a consummation so devoutly to be wished.
If the course pursued by the abolitionists would, indeed, free
the blacks, and improve their condition, I would be the last
to oppose them. But with Dr. Chalmers, with Dr. Cunningham, with Dr. Griffin, with Dr. Spring, and many
other eminent men—the true friends of the slaves—I believe, most firmly, that the tendency of their principles, and
of their whole course, is to perpetuate slavery, and to aggravate all its evils.

What, then, is the doctrine I advocate? That the slaves
should be manumitted as speedily as this object can be
effected without upturning the foundations of society. And
I conscientiously believe that the course pursued by the
abolitionists, has prevented the manumission of hundreds on
hundreds of slaves in the southern States.

But it is not sufficient for these modern reformers, that
men should liberate all their slaves. They must adopt their
views, refuse fellowship with all slave-holders, and denounce
them; or they will be denounced and excommunicated.
Rev. Mr. Graham, now of Kentucky, did liberate all his
slaves; yet he is now on trial before the New-School Synod
of Cincinnati, for venturing to publish a speech against the
peculiar views of abolitionists!

I cheerfully concur in the sentiment quoted from Gregory,
though he was a *pope*. But let it be remembered, that in
the Roman empire there existed no such difficulties in the
way of emancipation and of the elevation of the slave, as
arise in our country from the difference of complexion.
Call the strong aversion of the white man to the black, prejudice; still it exists; and with the complexion of the negro
is associated the idea of degradation. And so long as the
negro lives in our country, he will be degraded. It was
the prejudice of which I am speaking, which occasioned the

death of the poor negro in Indianapolis. His murderers, nevertheless, deserve to meet the full penalty of the law.

Even in Ohio, the negro is deeply degraded, in consequence of the deep-rooted prejudice against his color. He is not allowed to vote in the State elections; he cannot vote in your city elections; you deprive him of these important rights, not because he is really more ignorant and degraded than multitudes of white men, but simply on account of his color. But in Liberia, the colored man does enjoy liberty. There all are placed upon a perfect equality. Black men are their governors, their legislators, their judges, their military officers, their merchants, &c. Yet the abolitionists have done their utmost to prevent the emancipated negroes from going thither, and to cripple the efforts of the Colonization Society.

But I must again remind the audience, that the question under discussion is not, whether the slaves should be manumitted so soon as this object can be effected with safety to the parties concerned; but whether every man who is a slaveholder, is to be denounced as a heinous sinner, and excluded from the church of Christ. He has told us, that from the sixth to the thirteenth century the doctrine of the abolitionists prevailed, and that by it slavery was abolished. Will he point us to a single instance, during that period, in which a man was excluded from the fellowship of the church, simply because he was a slave-holder? He has given instances in which the Christian feelings of men induced them voluntarily to liberate their slaves; but he gave none in which any portion of the church *required* this; and, I presume, he cannot. He has failed, therefore, in proving, that, during that period, the doctrines of abolitionism prevailed.

It is curious to observe how, with this worthy brother, the same doctrine is abolition, or pro-slavery, just as it suits his argument. What was abolitionism in the sixth and following centuries, is pro-slavery now. Dr. Chalmers is most decidedly opposed to slavery, and in favor of manumission; he has published to the world his sentiments on this subject; yet he is denounced as pro-slavery: but Pope Gregory is a very good abolitionist, who held the self same sentiment, but in a different age and country. Thus "the legs of the lame are not equal."

And now, I have something to submit on the subject of the liberation of slaves in the West Indies. I rejoiced, and do rejoice, in that event. I hope it may prove a blessing to the negro population; but that, time must prove. Meanwhile, I deny that it was brought about by the doctrines of modern abolitionism.

Clarkson, to whom the gentleman refers so triumphantly, was not, at first, in favor of immediate, but of gradual, emancipation. The gentleman tells us, however, that it was a book written by a certain lady, in favor of immediatism, that did the work. If so, the world has, to this hour, been under a great mistake: they never knew it before. I ask, did Clarkson and Wilberforce, in pleading for emancipation, ever denounce those who hold slaves, as kidnappers and man-stealers, and call upon the church to turn them out of her·communion? Never. They held the system to be wrong, and earnestly maintained that it ought never to have existed; and who disputes this? But one generation can often bring difficulties on society, which the efforts of six generations cannot remove. We have inherited a great evil, and the query now is, how shall we get rid of it?

The gentleman gloried much over West India emancipation; but he omitted to tell how much the British Parliament gave to the planters as a compensation for the loss of their slaves. Our abolition friends, I believe, have never given any such proof of their zeal in the cause—probably from the fear of sanctioning the right of the slave-holder in his slaves as property. Pity the parliament had not been as cautious. But they so far sanctioned the "chattel principle" as to pay twenty millions sterling for the slaves; and even then they were not immediately set free, but were placed under a system of apprenticeship for *seven years*, remaining, during the whole of that period, still under a master. Thus the relation of master and servant continued for seven years. Emancipation there was gradual. Time was allowed, to prepare the slaves, in some measure, for the change in their condition. I would rejoice to see the slave-holding States devise some plan of gradual emancipation. Kentucky would have done so, I believe, ere this, but for the agitation caused by the abolitionists. By their indiscriminate and intemperate abuse of all slave-holders, they excited the worst passions of men, and put it in the power of demagogues to defeat the election of a candidate who would avow himself a gradual emancipationist, by representing him, to the ignorant and unreflecting, as an abolitionist. Time was, a few years since, when Judge Green, now, I trust, in heaven, and others of similar views, could be elected from year to year, though they failed not to agitate the subject in the legislature; but few politicians, if any, would venture upon such a course now. For this unfavorable change, we are indebted to the ceaseless agitations of abolitionism. However, a reaction, I believe, has commenced; and I hope, that, at no distant day, Kentucky will adopt some such plan of gradual emancipation as was adopted by New Jersey, New York, and Pennsylvania, and the older free States.

I sympathize with my zealous friend in all his persecutions, of which he has given a touching account. Stones and brickbats, it seems, were hurled at him, thick and fast; (I rejoice that not one of them hit him.) I will not call him a coward, exactly—but I must believe that he won't go across the river and preach abolitionism to the slave-holders, till I see him attempt it.

It is truly remarkable, that although abolitionist ministers feel themselves standing in the clear light; and though they so much deplore the condition of the people in Kentucky and other slave-holding States, as groping in midnight darkness; none of them have ever felt providentially called to go and preach the truth to them. They felt their souls stirred within them in view of the hard bondage of the poor slaves; and they have talked much, and talked stoutly, and written and *resolved* much; but not one of them has been called to go and preach on the south side of the Ohio river. I cannot, for the life of me, understand it. [Much laughter.]

The gentleman tells you that according to our Standards the infant of a slave, being illegitimate, cannot be baptized. This is news to me. I have seen nothing in our book forbidding it. On the contrary, the decisions of our General Assemblies have been precisely the opposite; and I have, myself, baptized several. True, the laws of Georgia and of some others of the southern States forbid slaves being taught to read; but I should not feel bound to regard such a law. No legislature has the right to forbid me to teach my family to read the word of God. In the meeting recently held in Charleston, to devise means to extend religious instruction more generally to the slaves, I noticed, it was stated, in several letters, how many of them could read. And from information to be relied upon, the law forbidding the slaves being taught to read, in some of the States, is practically a dead letter—public sentiment being against it.

I am very happy to percive that my good friend has himself become a gradual emancipationist. He says a "reasonable time" must be allowed for a man to rid himself of slavery. But if slave-holding is a sin in itself, worse than stealing or blasphemy; and if hell is not hot enough to punish it, then, surely, it must be abandoned at once—instantly. A man may not continue in known and flagrant sin one hour, one moment. A reasonable time! He says, by way of illustration, that he would allow the owner of a distillery a reasonable time to wind up his business. But if distilling ardent spirits is in itself sinful, we dare not say to him who manufactures the poison, that he may continue it one hour. If a man were engaged extensively in mixing arsenic with food for the market, would the gentleman give him a "reasonable time" to cease his business? No—he would insist on his immediately "ceasing to do evil." A reasonable time for a kidnapper to cease kidnapping! Who ever heard of such morals? There are not a few slave-holders who would ask no better license to continue holding their slaves, than this. For they think it most unreasonable to manumit them, to remain amongst the whites. No: either it is sinful in itself, or it is not. If it is, let us hear no more about a reasonable time to abandon it. I do not believe it to be in itself sinful, though it is a great evil, and, therefore, I can consistently go for its *gradual removal*.

But I gave notice, last evening, that I intended to go, without farther delay, more directly into the Bible argument of the question before us; and I shall do so, though the gentleman may regard me as rushing into darkness!

I have presented *five* arguments, preliminary to the principal argument from the Bible (which I call the direct argument) to show that slave-holding is not, in itself, sinful, and that the relation of master and slave is not a sinful relation.

Let me recapitulate them.

1. The great principles of the moral law are so written upon the hearts of men, that when presented they do commend themselves to the understandings and consciences of all, unless we except the most degraded. Slave-holding, according to abolitionists, is one of the grossest and most aggravated violations of that law; and, consequently, the proposition that slave-holding is in itself sinful, if true, must so commend itself to the minds of men. But it has not so commended itself, even to the wise and good generally: therefore, it is not true.

2. No man, or society of men, ever were, or ever will be found, to be heretical on one fundamental point of Christian doctrine, or one fundamental principle of morals, and yet sound on all the rest. The rejection of one fundamental doctrine of Christianity, necessarily leads to the rejection of others; and the rejection of a fundamental principle of morals, betrays a destitution of principle which will inevitably lead to the rejection of others. The gentleman, as you remember, attempted to disprove this admitted principle, by referring to the Pharisees: but it is notorious that they

were in error as to all the fundamental and distinguishing doctrines of Christianity, and rotten in morals, like "whited sepulchres."

3. It is admitted by some abolitionists, and even by the gentleman himself, that there are Christians and Christian churches in the slave-holding States; and that they sometimes enjoy seasons of religious reviving from the presence of the Lord. But it is a Scripture truth, that God does not answer the prayers and bless the labors of men living in heinous and scandalous sin. He does hear and bless those involved in slave-holding; therefore, if it is not a heinous sin, as abolitionists affirm.

4. The faith of abolitionists leads them to pursue a course wholly different from that pursued by the apostles of Christ —a course, the tendency of which is to perpetuate slavery, and to aggravate all its evils. 1st, They denounce and vilify slave-holders, thus irritating them to the highest degree. The apostles went amongst men and *reasoned* with them. 2d, They steal the slaves, and run them off to Canada. The apostles, so far from pursuing such a course, exhorted slaves to honor their masters, and serve them with all fidelity. 3d, The abolitionists, by their course, take from masters the glorious gospel, the only influence by which the condition of the slaves can be ameliorated, and by which it can be peaceably abolished. Thus do they rivet the chains upon the slaves. 4th, Their course takes from the slaves that gospel which they especially need to elevate their character and render them happy, even in bondage; and thus, whilst abolitionists denounce the master, they leave the souls of the slaves to perish in their sins. The apostles of Christ went forth preaching, both to masters and slaves, "the unsearchable riches of Christ." Since then, the works of abolitionists are so different from, and even opposite to the works of the apostles, under similar circumstances, it is evident that their faith is equally different and opposite.

5th, The *golden rule*—"Whatsoever ye would that men should do to you, do ye even so to them"—though it requires us to improve the condition of our fellow-men, so far as we can, without disregarding other paramount duties, does not forbid slave-holding under all circumstances. On the contrary, there are not a few instances in which it makes men slave-holders; because by becoming such, they can greatly improve the condition of a suffering fellow-creature. To this argument, as to most of the others, the gentleman has attempted no reply.

And here, before I proceed, let me call your attention to one striking fact. Many odious charges, as you know, were brought against the apostles of Christ: and yet, though slavery existed in its most odious form throughout all parts of the Roman Empire, *they never were charged with being abolitionists.* Now I ask, and I put it to the candor of the brother opposed to me, and to the common sense of every man that hears me, if they had preached and acted as modern abolitionists do, is it possible that no such charge would have been made by any one of the innumerable slave-holders with whom they came in contact? The apostles, it will not be denied, were as faithful in preaching what they believed to be truth, as our abolition friends, yet not a word of reproach was cast on them by any slave-holder, as if they had preached abolitionism. How is this fact to be accounted for?

But, to the Bible argument.

My first position is this: God did recognize the relation of master and slave among the Patriarchs of the Old Testatament; and did give express permission to the Jewish church to form that relation.—But God who is infinitely holy, could not recognize a relation in itself wrong, or give men permission to form such a relation. Therefore the relation of master and slave is not in itself sinful.

I presume the brother will not maintain, that God can ever, under any circumstances, give men permission to commit sin. The question, then, is whether God did give permission to the Jews to form the relation in question? If he did, and it is in itself a sinful relation, then he did give them express permission to commit abominable sin. I affirm that he did give such permission, and will proceed to prove it from the clear and unequivocal declarations of the Bible.

1. God recognized the relation of master and slave among the patriarchs.

My first proof is, that Hagar was the female slave of Abraham and Sarah. The abolitionists tell us that word "*servant*" in our English version of the Bible, does not mean *slave*. This word is derived from the Latin word *servus*, the literal and proper meaning of which, as every Latin scholar knows, is *slave*. The Romans had two words which they used to signify slave; one was *servus*, the other, *mancipium*. In the passage, however, where Hagar is first named, *Gen.* xvi. 1, she is called " an handmaid"—and in the 2d, 3d, 5th, 6th and 8th verses she is called Sarah's " maid." Sarah calls her "my maid." The Hebrew word *shifha* translated "maid" signifies a female slave. When the Jews spoke of a female slave, that was the word they generally employed. So it is understood by the best Hebrew scholars and lexicographers. Gessenius defines it by the Latin words *famula, ancilla:* both of which mean a female slave, a maid-servant, or waiting woman.

2. The Septuagint version, which is a translation of the Hebrew Scriptures into the Greek language, and which was made by Hebrews, renders the word in the Hebrew by *paidiske* which, my brother will scarcely deny, means a female slave.

3. But that Hagar was a *slave* is proved beyond contradiction by the language of the apostle Paul, in Galatians, 4th chapter, and 22d and following verses. " For it is written, that Abraham had two sons, the one by a bond-maid, the other by a free woman—which things are an allegory : for these are the two covenants; the one from the mount Sinai, which gendereth to bondage, which is Agar. For this Agar is mount Sinai in Arabia, and answereth to Jerusalem which now is, and is in bondage with her children. But Jerusalem which is above is free. which is the mother of us all. Nev-

ertheless what saith the Scripture ? Cast out the bondwoman and her son ; for the son of the bondwoman shall not be heir with the son of the free." Several things are worthy of remark in this portion of Scripture. 1st. The two mothers are here placed in contrast ; the one called a *free woman*, the other a *bondwoman*. Now if Hagar was a *hired* servant, if she was not a *slave*, she was as truly *free*, as Sarah, who is called her "mistress," and with whose condition in this respect hers is contrasted. 2d. The great truth the apostle designed to illustrate, requires, that we should understand Hagar to have been a slave. These things, he says, are an allegory ; the condition of Hagar the bondwoman illustrating the condition of the Jews who had rejected Christ, and were in spiritual bondage or slavery ; the condition of Sarah the free woman illustrating the happy condition of true Christians, whom Christ made free. 3d. The Greek word in this passage, translated bondwoman, is *paidiske*—the same word used by the Septuagint in translating the Hebrew word *shifha;* and as it here stands in contrast with the word *eleuthera, free*, it must be understood to mean a female slave. It is impossible, without the grossest perversion of language, so to interpret this passage, as to make it consist with Hagar's being a *hired* servant, or any thing but a *slave*. The man whom I hire to labor for me, is as free as I am. Every hireling is a free man. He gives his labor for his wages, and receives, as a free man, *quid pro quo*. Common sense is all that is requisite to enable us to understand the passage under consideration.

4. Hagar was punished by Sarah for contemptuous behavior. "When she saw that she had conceived, her mistress was despised in her eyes." Sarah remonstrating with her husband, "Abraham said unto Sarai, Behold *thy maid is in thy hand,—do to her as it pleaseth thee*. And when Sarai *dealt hardly* with her, she fled from her face." Does this language suit the condition of a free hired servant? Is a hired servant at the absolute disposal of the party hiring, so that he may do as he pleases to him? Is such the

condition of hired servants in Ohio? And do hired servants
run away from their employers? *Apprentices*, I admit,
sometimes do, but they are under indentures for a time set
by law, and they are never spoken of as *servants* in contrast
with *free persons*, as Hagar is with Sarah. When Hagar
had fled as far as to a fountain in the wilderness, the angel
of the Lord found her; and what advice did he give her?
" Flee, Hagar, as fast as you can, or Abraham will be after
you?" No, nothing of the kind. "And the angel of the
Lord said unto her, *return to thy mistress*, and submit thyself
under her hands." It is plain, the good angel was no abolitionist. What abolitionist, now on earth, would have given
her such advice? But the angel was not then in the light
of the nineteenth century. He was still in the "darkness of
remote ages of despotism," of which the brother told us.
Had he lived in the nineteenth century, he would doubtless
have known better! So we are obliged to suppose, if the
doctrines of the abolitionists are true.

My second proof, that God recognized the relation of master and slave among the patriarchs, is drawn from the 17th
chapter of Genesis, which contains the institution of circumcision. We read the 12th and 13th verses. "He that is
eight days old shall be circumcised among you, every man
child in your generation, he that is born in the house, or
bought with money of any stranger, which is not of thy seed.
He that is born in thy house, and he that is *bought with
money*, must needs be circumcised." Does not this divine
provision prove, that at that time Abraham had servants,
who were bought with his money, as well as such as were
born in his house?—and were not servants bought with
money slaves? If not, what were they? Who would so describe a hired servant? And can we believe, that, if slave-
holding were in itself sinful, God could have entered into a
covenant with Abraham, requiring him not to liberate his
slaves, but to circumcise them?

2. Again, in the 20th chapter of Genesis and 14th verse,
it is said: " and Abimelech took sheep, and oxen, and

men servants, and women servants, and gave unto them Abraham." Did he make a present to Abraham of *free hired servants?* Will my brother say this? No: they were slaves; and as slaves they were transferred by free gift, from one master to another, just as slaves are now given away in the southern States. Abimelech gave, and Abraham received them. If Abraham had been an abolitionist in sentiment, would he have received such a present? Would he not have rebuked Abimelech for offering it to him?

A third passage, to the same effect, is found in the 24th chapter of Genesis, and at the 35th verse. Abraham's pious, confidential servant was trusted to go and bring a wife for his son Isaac, and in executing his commission, he said to Rebekah's relatives, "and the Lord hath blessed my master greatly; and he is become great: and he hath given him flocks and herds, and silver and gold, and men servants and maid servants, and camels and asses." (The brother is much scandalized at the manner in which slave-holders are wont to speak of their slaves, in the same breath with their horses and mules: here they are numbered in the same catalogue with camels and asses: but this I notice in passing.) Abraham's servant says, "THE LORD hath given my master men servants and maid servants." God gave them to him as his own. Now, either this pious man blasphemed God, or slave-holding is no such sin as the brother maintains it to be. That these servants of Abraham were slaves, is evident, not only from the fact, that some of them were bought with money, that they were received as a present, and that they are enumerated as part of his possessions which the Lord has given him, but from the words employed to designate them. *Shifha*, the word translated "*maid servant*," as we have already seen, means a female slave. And the word *eved*, translated man servant, means literally and properly a male slave. This is the word always used by the Hebrews, when they wished to speak definitely of a male slave. Gessenius, one of the most celebrated lexicographers, defines it thus: "Servus quo apud Hebræos mancipium esse solebat." *A servant, one who used to be among the Hebrews a slave.* *Servus* and *mancipium* were the two Latin words commonly used to signify a slave. Every Hebrew scholar will admit, that the Hebrew word for a male slave, is *eved.* If the gentleman should deny it, will he be kind enough to tell us, what word the Hebrews used, when they wished to speak of *slaves?* And since they were surrounded by slaves and slave-holders, it will not be denied, that they had occasion to speak of them.

But in Leviticus, 25th chapter, and 39th and following verses, we have not only the word which definitely means *slave;* but we have *the thing itself* so completely described, that there can be no room either for argument or for evasion.

" And if thy brother that dwelleth by thee, be waxen poor, and be sold unto thee; thou shalt not *compel* him to serve as a *bond servant.* But as a hired servant, and as a sojourner, he shall be with thee, and shall serve thee *unto the year of Jubilee:* and then shall he depart from thee, both he and his children with him, and shall return unto his own family, and unto the possession of his fathers shall he return. For they are my servants, which I brought forth out of the land of Egypt: they shall not be sold as *bondmen.* Thou shalt not rule over him with rigor; but shalt fear thy God.

" Both thy *bondmen* and thy *bondmaids*, which thou shalt have, shall be of the heathen that are round about you: of them *shall ye buy bondmen and bondmaids.* Moreover, of the children of the strangers that do sojourn among you, of them *shall ye buy*, and of their families that are with you, which they begat in your land; and *they shall be your possession.* And ye shall take them *as an inheritance* for your children after you, to *inherit them for a possession: they shall be your bondmen* FOREVER: but over your brethren the children of Israel ye shall not rule one over another with rigor."

I venture to say, there is not language more clearly and unequivocally describing slaves in any slave code on earth, than is found in this chapter. Indeed I know not what phraseology more unequivocal could be employed. Let us carefully examine it.

There were among the Hebrews, several classes of servants distinct from each other.

1. There was the hired servant, who was called *sakir.* He was a free man, and his wages were to be paid promptly. " The wages of him that is hired shall not abide with thee all night until the morning." Levit. xix: 13.

2. The Jew who had become poor and sold himself for six years, and who was to be treated, not as a slave, but as a hired servant. Levit. xxv: 40. This class is spoken of also in Exod. xxi: 2, as follows : "If thou buy an Hebrew servant, six years he shall serve : and in the seventh he shall go out free for nothing. If he came in by himself, he shall go out by himself: if he were married, then his wife shall go out with him. If her master have given him a wife, and she have borne him sons or daughters : the wife and her children shall be his master's, and he shall go out by himself." Here, by the way, we find the legal principle so abused by the gentleman, " *partus sequiter ventrem.*"—the state of the offspring is governed by the state of the mother.

A servant of this class, though originally bought only for six years, might voluntarily become a bondservant during life. The law is as follows :

" And if the servant shall plainly say, I love my master, my wife, and my children ; I will not go out free. Then his master shall bring him unto the judges ; he shall also bring him to the door, or unto the door-post ; and his master shall bore his ear through with an awl ; and he shall serve him *forever.*" Exod. xxi : 5, 6.

The same law is repeated, more fully, in Deut. xv : 12. " And if thy brother, an Hebrew man, or an Hebrew woman, be sold unto thee, and serve thee six years : then in the seventh year thou shalt let him go free from thee. And when thou sendest him out free from thee, thou shalt not let him go away empty : thou shalt furnish him liberally out of thy flock, and out of thy floor, and out of thy wine-press : of

266   DISCUSSION

that wherewith the Lord thy God hath blessed thee thou
shalt give unto him.   And thou shalt remember that thou
was a bondman in the land of Egypt, and the Lord thy God
redeemed thee : therefore I command thee this thing to-day.
And it shall be, if he say unto thee, I will not go away from
thee ; because he loveth thee and thine house, because he is
well with thee : then thou shalt take an awl, and thrust it
through his ear unto the door, and he shall be thy servant
forever.   And also unto thy maidservant thou shalt do
likewise."

3. The Gibeonites, who by treachery had obtained an
oath from the children of Israel to spare their lives, were, for
their deceit, made "hewers of wood and drawers of water to
the congregation, and for the altar of the Lord, even unto
this day, in the place which he should choose."   I do not
say, they were slaves in the same sense with others ; but
they were condemned to involuntary servitude.   The principle of bond-service was there.

4. There was still a fourth class of servants, who were
bought of the heathen.   These were all *slaves* during life.
"Both thy bondmen and thy bondmaids, which thou shalt
have, shall be of the heathen that are round about you : of
them shall buy bondmen and bondmaids, &c."

It is evident, that these were slaves, from several considerations :—

1. They were *bought with money*, which certainly was
not the case with hired servants.   My brother will here tell
you, that the Hebrews were accustomed, sometimes, to buy
their wives.   I do not deny that they sometimes did so, but
when a man bought a woman as a *wife*, she was *his* wife;
and when a man bought persons, male or female, for *servants*, or *bondmen*, they were *his* bondmen or slaves.   The
bondmen here spoken of, were bought for *servants*.

2. The bondmen and bondmaids here spoken of, are not
only distinguished from, but put in contrast with *hired servants* ; "And if thy brother that dwelleth by thee be waxen
poor, and be sold unto thee, thou shalt not compel him to

serve as a *bond servant*, but as an *hired servant*, and as a sojourner shall he be with thee." The words used to designate these two classes of servants, are different. The hired
servant is called *sakir*; and the bond servant, or slave, is called *eved*.

3. The contrast in which the hired servant is here placed
with reference to the bondservant, as well as the words by
which the two are respectively designated, proves beyond
question, that the latter was a slave. For if both were hired servants, how could Moses command that the Jewish servant should be treated, not as a *bond servant*, but as a *hired
servant*? Will the gentleman please to explain?

The same contrast is found in Exod. xii. 44, 45, where
Moses gives directions concerning those who might or
might not partake of the Passover. "But every man
servant that is *bought for money*, when thou hast circumcised him, then shall he eat thereof. A foreigner and an
hired servant shall not eat thereof." The servant *bought
with money*, belonged to the family, and might, therefore,
partake of the Passover ; but the *hired* servant, temporarily
in the family, could not.

4. The servants thus bought, are declared to be the POS-
SESSION of their masters, and the INHERITANCE of their children. The words here translated *possession* and *inheritance*,
are constantly used with reference to landed estate, or any
other property. No stronger expression can be found in the
Hebrew language, to express the claim of the master to the
services of those bought with his money.

5. It is further evident that these servants were slaves, because they might be compelled to obey their masters, not by
law, as a debtor might be compelled to pay his debts, but by
chastisement; and that might be very severe without exposing
the master to the penalty of the civil law. The law on this subject is in Exod. xxi: 20. "And if a man smite his servant, or
his maid, with a rod, and he die under his hand : he shall
be surely punished : notwithstanding, if he continue a
day or two he shall not be punished ; *for he is his money.*"

Can any one believe that this language was meant to apply to a free man, hired for his labor? Do you call your hired servants *your money?* Or do you claim authority tŏ punish them with a *rod?*

6. That these servants were not free men, is equally manifest from Exodus xxi: 26. "If a man smite the eye of his servant, or the eye of his maid, that it perish; he shall let him go free, for his eye's sake; and if he smite out his man servant's tooth, he shall let him go free for his tooth's sake."

How could liberty be granted to them in consequence of the loss of a tooth or of an eye, if they were free before?

[*Time expired.*

Friday, 4 o'clock, P. M., Oct. 3, 1845.

[MR. BLANCHARD'S TENTH SPEECH.]

Gentlemen Moderators, and Gentlemen and Ladies, Fellow-Citizens:

While the house is getting quiet I will glance hastily at some points which my friend has raised. I request your careful attention while I do so.

My brother would have you think that the action of the Scotch General Assembly is the same in principle with the action of the Old School Assembly, which lately met in this city—whose report, written by Dr. Rice himself, contains not one word condemnatory of slavery or of those who practice it. I will read one part of the Scotch Assembly's Report which brother Rice omitted.

"All must agree that whatever rights the civil law may give a master over his slaves as 'chattels personal,' it cannot but be *a sin of the deepest dye in him to regard* or treat them as such : and whosoever commits that sin *in any sense,* or deals otherwise with his fellow men, whatever power the law may give him over them, *ought to be held disqualified for Christian communion.*"

That is far enough from his Assembly's action.

He has presented for the third or fourth time, the proposition that men are not fundamentally wrong on one point, and fundamentally sound on all others. He evidently attaches some importance to this point, from which affirmation (for it is but assertion) he wishes to infer that slave-holders, being admitted to be sound on other points, cannot be sinning in holding slaves.

In answer, I observe that Rev. John Newton, while right in every other point of faith and practice, was engaged in the slave-trade on the coast of Africa. We all agree that the slave-trade is piracy. He therefore was unsound on one point while sound on all others.

Moreover, sinners commonly become blind to the truth point by point. They fall before some one temptation, and seek to find a creed which will fit that one indulgence ; so that his argument does not hold, being defective in his main proposition. It is not true that men are never found sound on all points but one and defective in that.

He seemed to say something in reply to what I advanced showing that the doctrine, that slave-holding is sin, was the potent principle which abolished Roman slavery. His remark was, I think, that there was no comparison between Roman slavery and ours because Roman slaves were not colored persons. In this he is mistaken, as to fact, Africa was one chief source of slaves sold in the Roman market. And great numbers of African females especially, were kidnapped and sold in the Balerian Isles, at the highest price commanded by Roman slaves.

I was glad to hear my brother avow himself a gradualist, opposed to slavery, and approving of its abolition in New Jersey and other northern States, where it is either abolished or fast perishing by the operation of anti-slavery laws. I could not help reflecting, however, that an expression of his deep hostility to slavery would have been highly appropriate in his report to his last General Assembly. But no, not one sentence or word or syllable does that report contain calculated to lead any one to conjecture that strong opposition which its author finds it proper to express here, against slavery.

I could not help remembering too, as I heard his warm zeal for gradual emancipation declared, that there is another Kentuckian who is a gradualist; I allude to Cassius M. Clay, before whose intellect common minds do homage, and acknowledging the superiority of his genius, cordially love the warm and honest sincerity of his heart. Yet we have heard from Kentucky lips—aye, from clerical lips, a sneer at Cassius M. Clay on account of one single expression, for which he was made an offender and his press mobbed down. The phrase was an over-ardent depicting of the dangers of men of wealth—from slavery; warning them that "but a single pane of glass intervened between the smooth skinned woman on the Ottoman," and the hard hands in the streets which the slave-system makes and keeps poor and poverty makes desperate.

I considered it an unfortunate expression, though in an ordinary political paper, and on any other subject, it would have excited no special alarm, and passed as the eloquent rounding of a period. No human creature, not absolutely insane, would suspect him for a moment, of a desire to stimulate slavery to cut the throats of the ladies of Kentucky. C. M. Clay is in favor of gradual emancipation, and proves it by earnest efforts to bring it about. Dr. Rice is a gradualist also, and evinces his zeal in the cause of gradual destruction of slavery by attempting to prove slave-holding to be no sin, denouncing abolitionists, and sneering at the writings of C. M. Clay. His words *at least in this debate* look toward emancipation but his deeds all run toward slavery.

For the fifth or sixth time he has arraigned the abolitionists for "*running off slaves*," that is, for aiding those who are running off; and he seeks to make the impression upon your minds that the angel who sent back Hagar, (whom he considers a runaway slave) to Abraham, was really an instance of arresting and sending back fugitives from slavery to their owners. This he says, proves abolition principles to be wrong, because they lead them not to follow this angel's example in sending back runaways; but to an opposite course, viz: running them off to Canada. Yet when I urged him, he himself declared that he would not help take up runaways — and I say he would be a ruffian if he would. [Applause.] But how is it that this angel's example binds abolitionists and not Dr. Rice? The whole point of his oft-repeated argument is that abolition principles are wrong because they lead to a practice different from this angel's: yet in almost the same breath he tells us that he himself will not follow this angel's example in sending fugitive slaves back to their masters. If he means this argument for an argument; the next time Betsey or Sue or Peggy sets out for Canada through Ohio, my friend is bound by the rules which he seeks to enforce on others, to call on God to send this angel or some other along with him and scratch gravel after her as she dashes away for the land of freedom. [A laugh.] Let him stand up to his own principles or cease to upbraid abolitionists for not following an example which he rejects. Consistency is indeed a jewel.

The fact is, abolitionists are not the only ones who aid slaves to escape. I stood in the window of an inn one bright night, and saw some two thousand men gathered in the town square at the door, swearing they would raze the house unless the landlord gave me up to be murdered or insulted as an abolitionist. And I was amused at the trick, when unbeknown to me, the landlord sent some person, by a back way into the skirt of the crowd, who ran down a street crying, " Here he goes!" " Here he goes!" when the whole crowd ran off at full speed in the pursuit.

This inn-keeper, though a genuine latitudinarian landlord, in favor of no particular principles, and, especially, no abolitionist, yet would help off runaway slaves. He told me about 12 o'clock that night, when all was quiet, how he found two in his wheatfield who had come from Georgia, near 400 miles, all the way by night. He noticed something had trailed down the young green wheat and followed them under an apple tree where they lay hid in a little ravine, with eighteen green apples which they had stolen for food, each about as large as the end of your thumb. They had divided them equally, nine apiece. When the poor creatures saw they were discovered they ran off to a saw-mill pond, and dived among the logs and slabs, down into the muddy water like "black ducks." And, "do you think," said the landlord, "when I got them by the feet to pull them out (for they seemed determined to drown themselves,) I saw that the poor creatures had worn almost every particle of skin off the bottoms of their feet in travelling. When I got them out, they fell on their knees crying 'Oh God-a-mercy massa, we be no thieves, we be only runaways, massa! Oh God-a-mercy massa!' 'Never mind,' said I, 'if that's all, you shant be hurt.'" He then went to a paper-rag warehouse and from the cast off rags got them tolerable suits of clothes, and, aided by another benevolent man of the village, concealed them, and finally bought one for a nominal price of the master who came in pursuit. "But," said my landlord, with a rueful look; "He would'nt sell the other for love or money, and so we were obliged to slip him off. The one we bought has paid his purchase money, works up here, and is doing well."

Now can any minister of Christ condemn and denounce that inn-keeper for the part he took in aiding those wretched men. If he can, be he who he may, I say again, though he may have the exterior of a preacher, he has a ruffian's heart!

My friend still insists that I bring no argument from the Bible. I have already told you that I have prepared a speech, of an hour and a half of the kind he calls for; and I intend by the help of God, in due time to give that branch of my subject a full and fair consideration; and to show that the apostolic or New Testament churches did not receive slave-holders to their communion. Meantime, I will, in passing, give him a slight taste of the argument, as he seems famishing for it.

You know how anxious he has all along seemed, to put slave-holding upon a level with marriage. "Both," he argues are liable to abuses; but one is no more wrong than the other, nor is there more harm in the relation of master and slave, than in that of husband and wife. So I understand my friend, and if I state him wrong I hope he will put me right:—

MR. RICE. I have put the gentleman right more than once, but I have little hope that he will stay right. I said no such thing. I said that he has no right to urge arguments against the relation of master and slave which would do away the marriage relation.

MR. BLANCHARD. I thank him for his explanation but not for the sneer "that I will not *stay* right."

MR. RICE. It is the third time I have put you right upon this point.

MR. BLANCHARD. May be so. That is not according to my recollection of it, but if so, let my brother remember "*errare est humanum, ignoscere divinum.*"

I will take him where he now stands if I can get there. He holds that the same arguments which would prove slavery sinful, would also prove marriage sinful. No. I am wrong. " The arguments which I use would prove marriage sinful: That is, I appeal to you all, that, *in point of not being sinful, the relation of slavery is on a level with marriage.*" Slavery, like marriage, is a non-sinful relation. To establish this, he says that the apostle did not denounce slavery but regulated it as he did marriage. Now to show you that this, which he and his friends rely upon as a chief point in their argument, is an utter fallacy, you have but to apply the advice of Paul respecting the slave relation to that of marriage. Thus, he says, "Art thou called being a servant care not for it, but if thou mayest be made free, use it rather." Now apply this to the marriage relation ; " Art thou called being a husband, care not for it, but if thou mayest be made free, use it rather." [Laughter.] Ecce humbug! No man on earth would ever have thought of comparing slavery with mar-

riage if slavery had not first existed, an abuse requiring defence, and blinding with its rewards, the minds of the wise.

I say of the Mosaic bond service, which he adduces as a
pattern and precedent for American slavery, in the words of
a father now in my eye, (Dr. Beecher,) "it was'nt slavery:"—
"It is a mockery to call it so."

And as to the ear-bored servant who was to remain with
his master "forever:"—My friend seemed to rejoice as if he
had found great spoil, when he quoted this case, which after
all, is simply that of a man, who, after long acquaintance,
wished to live with his master, and came voluntarily before
the judges, and had his ear bored that he might remain till
the next jubilee.

He cited also the case where the servant coming into service and going out at the end of six years, if he married
while in service, his wife was not to go out with him. I
looked narrowly here, and was glad to miss that cold corpse-
like smile; that fiend-like grin, which I saw on the lips of
a minister of twenty years standing in his Presbytery, who
brought up the case as one where God had sanctioned the
separation of slave-husband and wife—a minister to whom
brother Rice has seen fit to refer as a man persecuted
by his synod, who are trying him for pro-slavery teaching.
But at any rate Dr. Rice thinks this a case of a six years
slave who went out while his wife, being a life-slave, stayed
behind. Nevertheless, it is true that some servants were
brought in from the heathen, and if they were not converted
in one year they were sent back. If one of these had married a Hebrew wife, God would not let him take her back
into idolatry.

This was a good reason, a merciful, missionary, and glorious reason: a reason as wide of the spirit of the slave-
coffle relation as heaven is wide of hell. The law merely
exempts a pious woman from the necessity of following à
worthless husband into idolatry and want. If the woman
wish to go with her husband, she had nothing to do but run

away with him and the law of God forbid the sending her back.

My friend must now consent to wait for my Bible argument, seeing I have given him a taste of it just by way of spice.

But he meets my argument showing that the principles of abolitionism have abolished slavery, by declaring that British emancipation was not immediate abolition, nor its authors modern abolitionists. So in his printed lectures, he tells us that " *Wilberforce, Clarkson and others, were far from being abolitionists in the modern sense.*"—*Rice's Lectures*, p. 67. His design is to prove that West India emancipation was not a triumph of the principle that immediate emancipation is a duty, and slave-holding a sin. I beg you will remember his printed statement that Clarkson and company were not abolitionists in the modern sense, for I wish to test this statement by facts. You will mark that the point between us is, whether the principles of abolitionists have, as he says, abolished slavery "*nowhere on earth;*" or "everywhere," where it has perished without bloodshed, as I say.

Let us now see whether the authors of the West Indian emancipation of August, 1834 ; were "far from being abolitionists in the modern sense."

I hold in my hand an "Essay on Slavery, by *Thomas Clarkson*" who is still living, and well known on both sides of the Atlantic, to be, so far as one man can be, the very life and heart's blood of the English abolition movement. And where think you, was this book printed, when, and by whom? It was published in 1816, *at Georgetown, Kentucky*, by the *Rev. David Barrow.* So the doctrines of Clarkson, which I will read, were once popular in Kentucky, before the gold of her piety became dim, and her fine gold changed. Surely some must have favored his views to warrant the publication there of his book.

Now what are Clarkson's doctrines on slavery, laid down in this book, the writing of which led him, then a university student, to resolve on devoting his life to the cause of humanity against slavery?

Before reading, I must remark that I never said, as brother R. stated, that the pamphlet called " *Immediate not gradual Abolition*" changed the principles of English abolitionists, but that it contributed to change their mode of operation—to produce a new *application* of their principles. Clarkson's principles were the principles of British abolition. This essay was written when he was a young man. He has now labored, as his last letter in my desk shows, more than fifty-nine years, exclusively in this cause. He was the means of bringing to its aid the talents of Wilberforce, Pitt and Fox, and of organizing the committee of which *Granville Sharp* was chairman and *Macauley* an active member. He was, as I said, the soul of the English anti-slavery movement; and this essay, which he wrote at the instance of Dr. Peckard, and which gained the prize at Cambridge University, sixty-five years ago; was his first essay on the subject, and has been the chart of his principles ever since, and of those of the English abolitionists;—and this is the summing up of his doctrines on the last page at the end of the book;—

" But this is sufficient. For if liberty is only an advantitious right; if men are by no means superior to brutes; if every social duty is a curse; if cruelty is highly to be esteemed: if murder is strictly honorable; and Christianity is a lie; then it is evident that African slavery may be pursued without either remorse of conscience or the imputation of a crime. But if the contrary of this is true, which reason must immediately evince, it is evident that no custom established among men was ever more impious; since it is contrary to reason, justice, nature, the principles of law and government, the whole doctrine, in short, of natural religion, and the revealed voice of God."—*Clarkson's Essay. Kentucky Ed.* p. 175.

That was Clarkson's doctrine sixty-nine ago; and it was the doctrine which has wrought out the English abolition. What then becomes of Dr. Chalmers, and his declaration that ours is a new dogma? What of Dr. Rice and his published assertion that Clarkson is "far from being an abolitionist in the modern sense?"

My brother, anxious to prove that abolitionists hold horrible doctrines, refers again to the book of Rev. James Duncan, and not to the book only but to the man, who, he says, "was as crazy as Foster."

MR. RICE *explained.* That is a mistake. I said that Foster was not a whit more crazy than Duncan.

MR. BLANCHARD. I accept the correction. He did not say that "Duncan was as crazy as Foster;" but that "Foster was not more crazy than Duncan." [A laugh.]

Now what is his chief accusation against this pious missionary and man of God, whose life was devoted to preaching Christ in the early log cabins of Kentucky, Ohio, Indiana and Illinois; and who died on a missionary tour? The head and front of Duncan's offending in his book is, that he teaches that " *slaves have a right to resist their enslavement by force.*"

Now, in respect to this doctrine, though we, as abolitionists, do not undertake to disprove the right of force, commonly called the right of revolution; yet, we do not give such advice to the slaves, but the contrary. We tell them, as Paul told the Christian slaves of heathen masters, to submit cheerfully and patiently to their condition, but if they may be made free to "use it rather." To

" Wait for the dawning of a brighter day,

" And snap the bond the moment when they may."

We have other motives beside our principles, in teaching slaves to endure their burdens, though heavy—never to rise in warfare, but to wait. Many of our parents, sons, brothers, sisters and other relatives, live in the South. Many have gone down and married plantations of slaves, particularly ministers' sons, and we do not wish to have these killed in a general massacre. We are moralists, and we leave politicians to regulate questions of force.

Yet, see what language this book of Mr. Clarkson—published in Kentucky—holds on this very point, which he brings against Duncan, viz: the right of slaves to resist by force:

"Let us suppose, then, that in consequence of the commerce, you were forced into a ship: that you were conveyed to another country; that you were sold there; that you were confined to incessant labor there; that you were pinched by continued hunger and thirst, and subject to be whipped, cut, and mangled at discretion, and all this at the hands of those whom you had never offended; *would you not think that you had a right to resist their treatment? Would you not resist with a safe conscience?* And would you not be surprised if your resistance should be termed rebellion? By the former premises you must answer, yes. Such, then, is the case with the wretched Africans. *They have a right to resist your proceedings. They can resist them, and yet they cannot be justly termed rebellious.* You have no right to touch even the hair of their heads without their own consent. It is not your money that can invest you with a right. Human liberty can neither be bought nor sold. Every lash you give them is unjust. It is a lash against nature and religion, and will surely stand recorded against you, since they are all, with respect to your impious selves, in a state of nature; in a state of original dissociation, perfectly free."—*Clarkson's Essay, Ky. Ed., p.* 166.

This book is of Kentucky manufacture, published at Georgetown, by Rev. David Barrow, in 1816, and must have found some circulation there to pay the printer. I hope my friend will not blame me for quoting Kentucky doctrines from Kentucky books.

For myself, I am a minister of the peaceful gospel of the Prince of Peace. Though not strictly a non-resistant, I would say to every slave,

> " ———— 'Tis better, to bear the ills we have,
> " Than fly to others which we know not of."

But my friend may take it into his head that these sentiments of Clarkson were errors of his youth, and that he had changed his opinions before the first of August Abolition of 1834. Let us see.

Here is a work of Clarkson, published by *Johnston & Barrett*, LONDON, 1841. Let us read and see if fifty-nine years service in the cause of the slave, has not softened down and changed the sentiments of this venerable patriarch and apostle of human liberty. It is a "*Letter to the clergy of the various denominations, and to the planters in the southern parts of the United States of America.*" This is to the clergy:

"I fear, gentlemen, that this is the case with you, that you have become gradually more hardened, and that you are not the men you once were. Indeed, I have been informed that you make no scruple to declare, both in public and private, and even in your pulpits, that *the practice of slavery is no sin*. But if you cannot see sin in the monstrous oppression of your fellow creatures which is going on daily before your eyes, I do not see *where sin is to be found at all*, or that you can impute it to any actions of men, however gross or injurious. Perhaps your ideas of sin may be different from mine. My notion of sin is that it is a "*transgression of the law of God.*" * * * * Do you agree with me in the representations now made to you? Do you allow that any one transgression of the divine commandments, which are solely of a moral nature, is sin? If you do, I shall have no difficulty of proving to you, that *slavery is a sin of the deepest dye.*"—*Clarkson's letter to clergy, p.* 8.

Mr. Rice distinguishes between *slavery* and slave-holding. But when Clarkson says that "*slavery is sin*," he means that *slave-holding is sin.* Thus, on page 15, of this letter:

"I come to a very serious and awful part of the subject; that is, I am to prove to you that you are *guilty of sin in holding them in bondage,* or *that slavery is sin in the sight of God,* of the deepest dye."

And again on page 22: "It is *sin* in its *root, sin* in its *branches,* and *sin* in its *fruit.* And yet, living where all those evil practices are going on, you can see no evil or sin in slavery. May God, of his mercy, provided your day of visitation be not over, grant you to see slavery in its true light, before your "houses are left unto you desolate."— *Matt.* xxiii. 38.

Now, remember that the question between Dr. Rice and us, is, "*Is slave-holding sinful?*" I have read you Clarkson's opinion on the point; yet, my friend has printed, in his lectures, that Clarkson is "far from being an abolitionist in the modern sense."

But, beside our doctrine that "slave-holding is sin," we are for turning unrepenting slave-holders out of the church, and the refusing our pulpits to slave-holding ministers. Perhaps brother Rice means that Clarkson is "far from being an abolitionist in this sense." Let us see what he holds as to this practical application of our principles. I still read from page 22d, of his letter:

"And now, gentlemen, (the southern clergy,) I am going to address you on a different branch of the subject and in a manner somewhat different from that before. I feel it my duty to *warn you,* if you be honorable men, that you ought *to withdraw yourselves* from the sacred office of ministers of the gospel of Christ, since your doctrines, as they relate to slavery, are *at variance* with the *revealed word of God.* You are doing no good, with your present sentiments, to genuine Christianity, but lowering the excellence of its standard, and leading your flocks astray."

Amen and amen, to these just and honest sentiments. I wonder if my friend will confess that Clarkson is an abolitionist?   *[Time expired.*

[MR. RICE'S TENTH SPEECH.]

Gentlemen Moderators, and Fellow Citizens:

[I am happy to observe, that those of the audience who hear me, usually hear the brother who is opposed to me. I desire that all who have thought with me, and those, even, whose minds are fully made up upon the question, would remain, in quiet and respectful attention, and listen to every word he has to say.]

The truth never gains, nor seeks to gain, any thing by misrepresentation. There are causes, however, which never gain much in any other way; and, if I mistake not, abolitionism is of this class. I have remarked, that when any thing occurs bearing on the subject of slavery, the gentleman is sure to get hold of that end of the story, which suits his views, and equally sure never to hear the other end. In the progress of this discussion, he told us of a colored man, a member of the Presbyterian Church, in Danville, Ky., who was sold by his master, a member of the same church, so as to be removed to a distance from his wife. So much of the story was adapted to promote abolitionism, and bring reproach upon a church of Christ. But he was careful not to tell the whole truth on the subject. Now it so happens, that there is in this house a minister of the gospel who resided in Danville at the time, and who received that colored man into the church; and he informs me, that the church session did take cognizance of the case, and enforce the discipline of the church against the master. To tell only a part of the truth, is often the most effectual method of telling a falsehood. The impression made upon the audience, by the gentleman's statement, was wholly at war with the truth in the case. I have little doubt that the other facts of the same character, which he has so eloquently detailed, are equally incorrect.

He told you that the Church of Scotland had declared, that whoever regarded his slaves as mere property, ought to be turned out of the church; but that our Assembly, at its late meeting, did not express this sentiment. I have already proved, that the Assembly strongly condemned the sin of regarding and treating men as mere property; and he knows it to be a law of our church, declared by the Assembly of 1818, that any member of the church who is guilty of cruelty toward his slaves in any way, especially by traffic for gain, and the separation of husbands and wives, shall be excluded from the church. Is it necessary, that the same law should be declared every year, in order to satisfy the gentleman? None are so blind as those who are resolved not to see.

In attempting to reply to my argument, founded on the fact, that no man or body of men was ever known to be heretical on any one fundamental point of morality, or of Christian faith, and sound on all others, Mr. Blanchard referred us to the Pharisees, who, as he informed us, were quite orthodox on all points except one, viz.: they rejected Christ, and regarded him as an impostor !

Driven from that refuge, he now refers us to John Newton, as a case in point. Newton, he informs us, wrote excellent hymns at the very time he was engaged in the slave trade on the coast of Africa. I do not know precisely the time when he commenced writing his hymns, but I do know, that he himself informs us, that the light entered his mind very gradually and almost imperceptibly; and at the time to which the gentleman refers, he was in such darkness, that he could afterwards scarcely determine whether he was a converted man or not. We know also how the early period of Newton's life was spent; that his mind was enveloped in midnight darkness on the whole subject of religion; and that he was most hardened in sin, and degraded in moral character. Yet, this man, just emerging from the midnight gloom, is brought forward to prove that the Christian ministers and churches in the slave-holding States, may be orthodox on all other points of faith and morals, and yet fundamentally erroneous in regard to the horrible sin of slave-holding!—to prove, that such men as Chalmers, and Cunningham, of Scotland, and Tyler, of Connecticut, and the great body of eminently wise and good men, may be in the same predicament! ! !

The brother says, that most of the slaves at Rome were Africans.

[Mr. Blanchard here rose to explain. I said that Africa

was one of the *chief* sources from which they were drawn, but not that a majority came from there.]

Well, be it so. I will not inquire, whether all slaves born in Africa were black: whether they were or not, my remark will hold good, that there did not exist, at Rome, in that day, the same prejudice in regard to slaves which exists at this day and in this country. In the Roman empire, as he very well knows, slaves generally did not differ in complexion from their masters, and therefore they were required to wear a cap and a coat of a peculiar shape, to distinguish them from free citizens. The slave had only to change his cap and his coat, and wear the dress of a free man; and he would stand on a perfect equality with other citizens. It could not be known that he had ever been a slave. But with us, the color of the slave creates a prejudice against him; and so strong is that prejudice, that even a free colored man is not, in fact, free. He does not, and cannot, enjoy the privileges of a white man. There are insuperable difficulties in the way of his enjoying all the rights and privileges of a free man. As I have said before, I am in favor of the gradual emancipation of the slaves, and of having them placed, with their own consent, where these difficulties do not exist—where they will be free, not in *name*, but in reality.

I will here notice the statement of the gentleman, that in the Report adopted by the General Assembly, there is no intimation of a wish that slavery should ever be abolished at all. What is the language of that Report? I will read it:

" We feel constrained further to say, *that however desirable it may be to ameliorate the condition of the slaves in the Southern and Western States*, or TO REMOVE SLAVERY FROM OUR COUNTRY, these objects, we are fully persuaded, can never be secured by ecclesiastical legislation. Much less can they be attained by those indiscriminate denunciations against slave-holders, without regard to their character or circumstances, which have, to so great an extent, characterized the movements of the modern abolitionists, *which*, *so*

*far from removing the evils complained of, tend only to
perpetuate and aggravate them.* The apostles of Christ
sought to ameliorate the condition of slaves, not by denouncing and excommunicating their masters, but by teaching
both masters and slaves the glorious doctrines of the gospel, and enjoining upon each the charge of their relative
duties. Thus only can the church of Christ, as such, now
improve the condition of the slaves in our country."

Did not the Assembly intend to say, and does not their
language clearly express the idea, that it is desirable to
ameliorate the condition of the slaves? and did they not
immediately add, in precisely the same connection, and in
the same sentence, "or to *remove* slavery from our coun-
~v?" There stand the words in the printed report; yet my
urate brother tells us, that it says nothing on the subject;
.atains not even an *intimation* of the faintest wish upon the
Subject! I will not charge him with a deliberate purpose
to misrepresent; but the truth is, that he reads, and sees,
and feels, and talks one-sided—*he is one-sided all over.*
[Laughter.]

The gentleman says, that my words look one way, and
my actions the other—that I am anti-slavery in words, but
pro-slavery in deeds. I now challenge him to refer to one
single action of my life which shows that I am opposed to
what I advocate in words, viz.: the gradual emancipation
of every slave in the land; or which can afford the least
justification of his ungenerous charge. He cannot point to
one; unless, indeed, he chooses to consider the colonization
of free blacks, with their own consent, opposed to emancipation.

The gentleman is very indignant at the removal of Cassius M. Clay's paper from Lexington, which, he tells us,
was done simply because of an unfortunate expression—a
mere flourish, to turn a period. I know Mr. Clay. We
were, for a short time, school-fellows; and I regard him as
a man of talents. But it is not true, that the tremendous excitement which resulted in the removal of his paper, was

caused by a single expression—a mere rhetorical flourish. It is truly a singular method of rounding a period, to tell slave-holders that there are spikes in the streets, and only panes of glass between them and your "smooth-skinned" wives and daughters! The obvious meaning of such language is—"take care, or the slaves will rise and murder your families;" and the direct tendency of such language is, to produce a servile insurrection.

But Mr. B. has great facility in concealing the odious features of abolitionism. When in the early part of this discussion I read the intemperate and disgusting language of Foster on this subject, he told us, that some considered him insane. And when I read paragraphs from Duncan's pamphlet, republished by the Cincinnati Abolition Society, containing sentiments equally abhorrent, he coolly remarked, that he did not approve of every *comma* and *semi-colon* in it! I replied, that the justification of slave insurrections and murders were something more than either commas or semi-colons. And then he urged me just to let "father Duncan's pamphlet alone; he was a very good man, and is gone to his rest." I shall not deny that he had piety; but whether he had or not, he published doctrines not only false, but of the most ruinous tendency; and the Cincinnati Abolition Society have endorsed them. That society, therefore, stands before the public, chargeable with sending forth the most incendiary publications. The gentleman himself was most active, as he has informed us, in having it republished. He and his society, therefore, are fully responsible for all its abominable sentiments; for in having it reprinted they did not disclaim one sentiment it contains. But this by the way.

I am not here to justify the course pursued toward Mr. Clay. I cannot justify it; but no man, who knows anything of human nature, can be surprised at it. In the articles which produced the excitement, it cannot be denied, that there were sentiments of dangerous tendency; and it is worse than vain for the gentleman to attempt to cover them over by representing them as mere rhetorical flourishes without meaning. I was truly glad when Mr. Clay proposed to publish his paper. I did hope that he would calmly and prudently plead the cause of gradual emancipation, and that great good would result. Had he done so, I believe he might have gone forward without interruption; but his language was violent and intemperate, and the result is known. Although I cannot justify the course pursued against him, I cannot condemn it without first condemning him as the aggressor.

The gentleman says, I condemn abolitionists for *helping* runaway slaves, and yet I have said, I would not force them back. No—I have not condemned them simply for helping those who have run from their masters, but for sending emissaries into the slave-holding States, to render the slaves discontented, and induce them to run. And I condemn them for publishing papers and pamphlets urging them to leave their masters, and even encouraging insurrection and murder. I condemn them for publishing addresses to the slaves, as did Gerrit Smith, and the New York anti-slavery nominating convention, advising them not only to run from their masters, but to *steal*, along their route, in the free as well as the slave States, "the horse, the boat, the food, the clothing," which they need! Conduct and sentiments of this character are unscriptural and abominable. True, I do not regard it as my duty to be a catcher of fugitive slaves, or to force such to return to their masters; but if I were to see a slave leaving a good master, I should *advise* him, as the angel advised Hagar, to return and faithfully discharge his duty. Most assuredly I would never be found engaged in the pitiful business of running a few slaves to Canada, to starve and freeze; but the gentleman's fraternity will. [A laugh.]

I do not say, that every abolitionist will do this thing; but I do say, that Duncan's pamphlet, endorsed by the Cincinnati Abolition Society, urges it as the solemn duty of slaves to embrace the first opportunity to escape; and Gerrit Smith and his party advise them not only to run, but to *steal !* But there are amongst abolitionists so many parties, that I do not well know what is orthodoxy and what is heterodoxy amongst them.

I do, indeed, most strongly condemn both the principles and the conduct of the abolitionists; but I have also uniformly condemned all violence toward them. When Mr. Birney's press was destroyed in Cincinnati, I as editor of a religious paper, condemned the course of his opponents in language as strong as I could command; and I took the same course in regard to the violence against Lovejoy, in Illinois. I go for freedom of speech and of the press, even though in some instances, evils grow out of it.

The brother says that I am anxious to put slavery on a par with marriage. Such, however, is not the fact, as I have repeatedly explained. I have said that he has not the right to bring an argument against slave-holding, which would be of equal force against marriage. An argument that proves too much, proves nothing. This all logicians maintain, and the gentleman will not deny.

He says, farther, that I affirmed that the apostles treated the relation of master and slave, and husband and wife, alike. I never said so. I have said that they did not treat the slave relation as the abolitionists do; but enjoined upon master and slave the discharge of their respective duties. I did not say they treated the two relations alike.

Having thus misrepresented my views he attempted to ridicule them by applying to the husband, Paul's language to the slave—"Art thou called being an *husband*, care not for it," &c. It is often easier to misrepresent, and then ridicule the sentiments of an opponent, than to prove them erroneous. Slavery is an evil; and liberty, to those who can appreciate and improve it, is a blessing. So poverty is an evil; and to possess a competency of the good things of this world, is desirable. The language of Paul to the slave, suffering under an evil, might be addressed to a man suffering from poverty—"Art thou called, being *poor*, care not for it; but if thou mayest be made comfortable, choose it rather." As a state of slavery is attended with many evils, its removal is desirable. So say I; and so say all anti-slavery men, who are not abolitionists.

He reminds me, that when the Bible says that the slave shall go out, but his wife and his children shall remain and be his master's, it does not imply that the man was driven out of the house: he might "go out" of a state of bondage and yet remain in the house, and not be separated from his wife. But I did not say, that he was separated from his wife, but that although he went free, his wife and children remained slaves, the children following the condition of the mother, and not receiving liberty with the father.

The gentleman attempts to explain the fact, that the wife of the servant who went out free, under certain circumstances, did not go out with him, but remained in servitude, by stating it as one of the laws of Moses, that a servant bought of the heathen, if not converted in one year, was to be sent back to the heathen, but was not permitted to take with him his wife and children. There are two difficulties attending this explanation, viz: 1st. There is no such law as that of which he speaks. On what authority he has made the assertion, I cannot imagine. 2nd. The law of which I was speaking, relates to a Jew who had been sold for six years, not to a man bought from the heathen. If such a Jew married a servant of his purchaser, (one perhaps bought from the heathen) and had children by her; at the end of the six years, he went out free; but his wife, given him by his master, and the children born in the master's house, did not go out with him, but continued in servitude. Since, therefore, the law in question related exclusively to Jews, (not at all to servants bought of pagans) and to a term of service of six years, not of one, the gentleman's reply is a perfect failure.

I shall not detain the audience to discuss the views of Clarkson on slavery; because it is unnecessary. But let it be remembered, that the British Parliament adopted the plan of West India emancipation, not at the suggestion of Clarkson, but under the influence of a public sentiment created by the great body of Philanthropists and Christians in England and Scotland. Were they abolitionists? Were slave-holders denounced, without regard to character or circumstances, as heinous sinners? Were the churches called upon to exclude all the slave-holders from their communion? These questions must be answered in the negative. The Christians and churches in England and Scotland generally, believed no such doctrine, and therefore resorted to no such practice. No man was excommunicated simply because he was a slave-holder. The slaves in the West Indies, then, were not emancipated by the principles of modern abolitionists, but by the principles of anti-slavery men whom they denounce. Under the influence of such men the British Parliament paid to the owners of slaves twenty millions of pounds, and placed the slaves under an apprenticeship of seven years.

I ought to notice, for a moment, the gentleman's remark that I represented Mr. Duncan as crazy. I did not say so. He excused the intemperate language and abominable sentiments of Foster on the ground that he was partially deranged. In reply to this, I said that his friend Mr. Duncan was at least as crazy as Foster, for his pamphlet contained precisely the same sentiments. But I hold neither of them to have been insane, nor do I charge the Cincinnati Abolition Society with being madmen because they sanctioned and reprinted Duncan's book. All I said, and now say, is that the one writer was as much a crazy man as the other, and both were about as sane as men can be, who hold the doctrines of abolitionism.

I have proved by language too plain to be misunderstood, that Hagar was the slave of Sarah; nor will all the gentleman has said or can say by way of ridicule, prove that she was any thing else. That she was a *bondwoman*, a slave, and that she fled from her mistress, because she punished her, are facts plainly stated in the Bible. If she was free, there was no sense in her running into the wilderness from her mistress. Nor was the angel a " ruffian " because he advised and directed her to return. He well knew, that her

condition was far better in the family of Abraham, than
in the wilderness. The running off of slaves does not
always better their condition. A man residing at Vicks-
burgh had a slave who left him, and succeeded in getting safely to Canada; but he was so far from experiencing
the advantages he had expected, and which had been promised by his abolition advisers, that he voluntarily returned to
his master. Other fugitive slaves have done the same thing.
Our friends may yet learn, that by tempting slaves to run
away they often place them in a worse condition, than that
from which they have induced them to escape.

I will close this speech with a very brief recapitulation of
the evidence proving the bondmen bought of the heathen by
the Jews, to have been *slaves*, in the proper sense of the
word. 1. They were bought with money. When the gentleman reads in the newspapers, that a certain man in Kentucky bought a servant with money; does he not at once
conclude, that the servant bought is a slave? 2. The master was permitted by Moses' law to enforce obedience on
the part of the servant by *chastisement;* and the reason
given why the master should not be punished, if the servant survived a day or two after the chastisement, was, that
" *he is his money.*" Here the property relation is recognized, and is regarded as a protection of the slave, and as evidence that it was not the design of the master to kill him;
for it is not to be supposed, that in any ordinary case a man
would deliberately aim to kill the servant who was his money Such are the facts as they stand recorded in the word of
God. The gentleman may, if he is so disposed, pronounce
this law cruel and inhuman; but he cannot erase it from the
volume which he professes to regard as inspired by God.
Is such language as we find here employed, applicable to
hired servants? Do men in Ohio regard their hired servants
as *their money?* Do they claim the right to enforce obedience by chastisement with the rod. 3. The word used, and
translated *servant* and *bondman* is the proper Hebrew word
for *slave;* it is the word the Hebrews uniformly used, when

they spoke of slaves. If the gentleman should deny this, will he please to tell us what is the proper word for slave in the Hebrew language? I affirm, that if the word *eved* does not mean *slave*, the Hebrews, though surrounded by slavery, had no word in their language by which they could designate it. 4. The Hebrew has a word which definitely signifies a *hired* servant; and that word is placed in contrast with the *eved* or bondman. The *sakir* is the hired servant; and the *eved* is the bondman or slave. 5. Finally those servants are declared to be the *possession* of their owners, and *inheritence* of their children—language never employed concerning hired servants, but constantly employed with regard to *land* and other property.

The fact, then, is clearly established, if language can establish it, that God did recognize the relation of master and slave as, under the circumstances, lawful, and did give express permission to the Jews to purchase slaves from the heathen, and hold them. To understand the language on which I have been remarking, as descriptive of hired servants, is to disregard the plainest principles of language. The gentleman must admit, that God gave the Jews permission, under certain circumstances, to form the relation which he denounces as in itself sinful; or he must deny that the Old Testament is the word of God. [*Time expired.*

Friday Evening, 7 o'clock.

[MR. BLANCHARD'S ELEVENTH SPEECH.]

Gentlemen Moderators, and Gentlemen and Ladies, Fellow-Citizens:

At the commencement of my remarks, it is proper for me to say that I render cordial thanks to the brother opposed to me, for his kindness in consenting to adjourn this discussion till Monday. I have asked this, in consequence of my health, which is infirm from a cold contracted a few days before the debate began.

In my last speech of the afternoon, I said that the abolition of slavery in the British colonies, was the fruit of the
principles of abolitionism: and my quoted proofs fully sustained my proposition.   My brother objects that the abolition
of West India slavery was not immediate, but that an apprenticeship of seven years was substituted for slavery.
This is partly true, and partly erroneous.   In Antigua, and
the Bermudas, emancipation was immediate, and took instant effect, August 1st, 1834.   It is true, that against the
wishes of many leaders of the abolition movement in Great
Britain, Parliament refused to grant immediate abolition
throughout the colonies, and substituted a clumsy apprenticeship of seven years, which, however, worked so badly,
that they were glad to abolish it two years before the legal
time expired.

My friend also tells you that a hundred thousand dollars
were paid as a compensation to the owners for their slaves.
This, also, was not in accordance with the views of many
leading abolitionists.   They said that if slavery had been
profitable, the slave-holders had enjoyed the profits of it long
enough—if not profitable, abolition was no sacrifice to them.
They, however, were willing to accept the bill enacted by
Parliament, seeing it struck out at once, the principle of
chattelism, and speedily resulted in perfect emancipation.

I now call your attention to what I call the direct argument (and all my arguments are from the Bible, or are intended
to be) to show that the *relation* of master and slave is *a sinful relation.* I have showed (I think) slave-holding to be " in
itself sinful," which was the first part of the question.   The
latter part of the question respects the RELATION.   I wish
therefore, to show that the *relation,*—not the practice, only,
of slave-holding, but the *relation of master and slave* is sinful.   I have duly advertised the audience of my one and a
half hours' speech in the Old Testament servitude and a
speech of similar length on the New Testament view of
slavery.   Mr. Rice will have an opportunity to reply to

them, for he has the closing speeches, both afternoon and evening, in each day of debate.

Now I beg you to bear in mind, my object, now in hand, is not to arraign every man who is sinfully or unfortunately connected with the slave system. But if I show the *relation* to be a sinful relation, it will follow that it is the duty of every church to tell its candidates for membership, to come out of it, that God may receive them. A HUMAN RELATION *is that connexion between two persons which creates mutual rights and obligations.* As the relation of husband and wife. That is based upon a certain principle, and vests certain claims in the wife upon the husband, and certain claims in the husband upon the wife; and these rights and obligations take root in the principle which lies at the foundation of the relation.

Let us analyze this thing which is called a relation. There are three things constituting a relation. 1. The principle on which it is based. 2. The claims which it creates; And 3. The obligations it imposes. If we consider any good and wholesome relation, say a partnership in business, we find first the principle in which it rests, is the *mutual* wants of men. One man may know more than the other; the other may be physically stronger than he. Their relation rests on this natural foundation; the mutual dependence of men upon one another, and because it rests on this true principle, the relation, thus formed, gives rise to certain claims which are just claims, and certain obligations, which are right obligations. *Marriage* is susceptible of the same analysis. The principle on which it rests, is the mutual affection of the opposite sexes. This is a natural principle. God laid the foundation of marriage in the constitution of man. He is the author of nature, or rather nature is the rule by which God works. The claims of the husband on the wife, and of the wife upon her husband are right and just, because they are rooted in a right relation. So of the relation and mutual claims of parent and child. But look now at the relation of a gypsy to the child which she has stolen; that is, the relation of false parentage. The principle of the relation is wrong at bottom. The relation is forced and unnatural. It is unwarranted by scripture, having no foundation in the word of God. Hence it can give rise to no just claims nor obligations, because the relation itself is void in equity, *ab initio*, and, whatever claims exist, are rooted in a relation which is false.

Now, take the relation of master and slave, and test it by this same analysis. Has God fitted one man to be *property*, and adapted another to be the *property-holder of men?* is one man formed for fetters and a yoke, and another with a whip in his hand, and a spur on his heel? Will my brother tell me, as the southern defenders of slavery argue in Congress, that the wise are the natural owners of the foolish, and the strong of the weak. Mr. Pickens, of South Carolina, stated in his place, in Congress, that *" when once society is pressed down into its classifications, one class will always hold the other as property, in some form or other."* Is that doctrine to find advocates in free Ohio? Sirs, if it be true that the strong are born to own the weak, why not put the weak slave-holder into slavery, and make the strong slave his master? If the unwise and the untalented are the natural slaves of the wise and capable, the moment when, by causes inseparable from slavery, the owner becomes the slave's inferior, that moment your rule gives the slave of strong and vigorous mind and athletic muscles, dominion over the master of weak intellect and emasculate person; and it is well understood that slavery deteriorates both the mind and body of the owner class. If the silly and weak are to be enslaved by the wise and strong, God help the cripple, the idiot, and the weak-minded child! No, gentlemen, no, never. I will never admit the doctrine of the inequality of man, by nature, while I am told in God's word, that *" He has made of one blood all nations of men to dwell on all the face of the earth."* And *if of " one blood," then equal, because one.*

The doctrine that the relation of slavery is an unnatural

relation, is not a new doctrine. It is laid down in the code of Justinian, which has been the fountain and spring-head of the civil law since A. D. 527. This code declares that slavery has no foundation in natural justice. "SERVITUS EST CONSTITUTIO JURIS GENTIUM, *qua quis domino* CONTRA NATURAM *subjicitur.*"—(*Just. code, L.* 1. *Title* 3.)—which, translated, is "Slavery is a *constitution of the law of nations,* whereby a man is subjected to a foreign master *against natural right.*" Every lawyer knows that "contra naturam" means against natural equity. And slavery is said to be a creation of "*positive law,*" because the relation has no archetype in nature, and hence, all the claims arising out of it, perish, because rooted in a vicious relation, and all its obligations are void, because its claims are unjust; that is, the relation is wrong in itself.

Now, again: The relation is sinful, because every act which it warrants, is something which my brother himself calls sinful. I know well what I say, and I will prove it. I say, *the relation itself is sinful, because every act which it warrants is a sinful act.* What acts does it warrant?

1. It warrants the taking of a man's labor without wages. My brother has almost said that the master is bound in justice to give his slave wages. He ought to say so. But what becomes of slavery when you compel wages? It has perished and the slave becomes a hired servant. Slavery excludes wages, and if withholding wages is sin, then is slave-holding sin.

2. Another act which this relation of master and slave warrants, is the separation of man and wife. My brother says, he is opposed to that. So when he has given the slave-holder a property power over mankind, by the permission of God, the Father, Son, and the Holy Ghost; (for he does this if he proves slave-holding not sinful;) he then turns round and forbids him to use the power which he has thus given. The first property-holding act which the slave-holder puts forth, my friend tells him is *an abuse of the relation.* I argue from that, that the power to hold slaves—the

relation itself, is sinful. Can the fountain be pure, if all the streams flowing from it are corrupt? Suppose a man has a spring on his land, from which flows water which kills the grass of the sod which it irrigates, and the cattle which drink of it. I tell him his spring is poisonous; and he admits that all the water which comes from it is poison, but stoutly denies that the spring is a poisonous spring, and yet agrees to stop up the well and prevent its flowing, in order to prevent its doing damage. He certainly admits his spring to be poisonous. So I say that the relation which cannot be carried out in practice without *abuse*, is an *abusive* relation. *It is abusive in itself.* What sort of a relation is that which cannot be acted out without sin, unless it be a *sinful* relation? Assuredly, it is not a holy relation. A smuggler may be a man who has never yet handled contraband goods, yet, being connected with smugglers—standing in a criminal relation, he ought to come out of it. He may say: "I have never run goods across the line." But you tell him; "you are in a wicked relation, you ought to come out of it." So I say to the slave-holder; lay down the mischievous power which you have assumed. Come out of the relation, for it is a relation wrong in itself. Who does not see that, that is a poisonous fountain, which, to prevent its pestilent and destructive effects, must be perpetually and forever damned up?

My brother declares for the gradual abolition of slavery; he would kill it off by degrees. But why abolish slaveholding gradually, unless it is unjust? and if it be unjust, why continue it one hour? Do you not see that in admitting that it ought to be abolished, he admits it to be wrong?

But he will have us to abolish safely. Let us lop off one abuse after another. Let us pluck out one strand after another until this scourge of the human race is taken wholly away. But why, when he arises to demolish one bad thing in it, does he not strike off the whole? is not the whole thing bad? Most evidently, the same reasons which require abolition at all call for it *now*. In the name of the God of truth and in the living light of truth, I say, abolish it at once if it be wicked. Why should injustice live one hour? There is another inquiry of serious practical moment here. Why do those men who say they are opposed to slavery, and desire its speedy gradual abolition, stand so well with incorrigible slave-holders? My brother boasts that he preaches to slave-holders, enjoys their full confidence, and yet that he is opposed to slavery. Yes, somebody has committed an immense amount of sin in the slave-system, if we could come at it. There is a forbidden part of the hog, but nobody has found out where or which it is. He is opposed to slavery.

But, if he is actually opposed to slavery, how does his doctrine happen to be acceptable to every one who is irrecoverably wedded in the slave-holding interest? The answer is:—Because it justifies slavery as a divine institution. It can be no other.

You may read his allegation to the soul-driver at the head of the slave coffle; "that God permitted his ancient people to hold slaves." "Ah," says the driver, "that is the doctrine for me. I am one of Abraham's descendants in line direct. I am the good old patriarch's agent. My employer stands in the place of principal, and I as agent, and we shall both go to Abraham's bosom together." Oh! gentlemen, the reason why his doctrine is so popular with the slave men, is, that they well know that if *ministers give them God's permission to hold men as property*, they will easily get man's permission to use them as such. That is the reason that my brother's popularity will carry the book South. Slavery never will be put down in this way. My brother is *pro-slavery*, and they know it. He gives them God's permission to hold slaves, and that is all they want of him. He tells *them* they may hold slaves without sin, but tells *us* that he is opposed to their using their slaves as their property. He puts a saddle on a man's back, and the bit in his mouth, vaults the slave-holder into the saddle, and as he places the reins in his hand, cries, "Easy, sir, I never meant you should ride." [A laugh.]

I have also proved slave-holding relation sinful, because where slavery goes into a family at one door, every God-ordained relation goes out at the other. I know my friend tells you that it is not slavery that separates man and wife; that they are not separated till the master sells the husband into Georgia, and the wife to Alabama. Is it the mere placing a man and woman at a distance, that dissolves marriage? Is it miles and leagues that tear and separate heart from heart, whom God has pronounced one? No! It is not distance. It is slavery. A relation which has no sanction in Heaven, and will have no place on earth when God's "kingdom is come, and his will done on earth as it is in heaven."

I say, therefore, that when slavery goes to a house, and constitutes the husband property, the wife property, and the child property; every God-ordained relation has perished out of that house. All that is wanting to complete the ruin is the will of the master to separate them actually, as they are virtually taken apart by the slave-making statute.

I have one more point to make, and then, after adverting to my friend's golden rule argument, I shall proceed in the course which I have prescribed.

I will here make one observation, which is this: Though I might, as my friend suggests, flinch in the trial, if actually called to lay down my life; yet, I solemnly aver that I should esteem my life a profitable outlay, if by death I could convince every person in this assembly of the truth which I am here to sustain. I am at least sincere in this. Though I will not say but that if put to the test I might shrink from the sacrifice, as many good men have done. But, Kentuckians, I call upon you; I address you with the utmost solemnity as *men*, as men who are soon to die. I beseech you, let us reason together. Take what course you may in practice, I know you must abhor, you cannot help abhorring slavery in your understandings and hearts. Its foul deformities are so obvious in every joint and limb and feature, that when once your attention is fairly directed to them, you can never, go where you will, and do what you may,

shake off your impressions of disgust. Do not make me
your enemy because I tell you the truth. I speak in the
spirit of humility. I am willing to wash your feet. My
master did the like, and I am content if I may but be as he.
I am sincere and solemnly earnest in the position I take. I
am willing to sacrifice to it whatever I must. I did not embrace this cause when a young man, and incur obloquy on
account of it, because I loved ignominy and reproach. I was
not then reckoned inferior to my equals in age, in scholarship and the hope of usefulness, and. I have not been insensible to the desire of popularity with good men. But in
the course I have taken I followed what I thought my duty,
and I well knew what I was to meet in discharging it.
While yet a student, I was preaching in a church where the
salary was a thousand dollars, and where to oppose slavery
was to be unacceptable. But I told them I was an abolitionist. I knew no pettifogging distinctions by which to
reconcile the conscience to slavery, while condemning it in
words; and I determined to take the consequences of a
straightforward and honest utterance of correct principles,
derived, not from collating the opinions of men, but by listening
to the voice of God. Do not therefore, make me your enemy
because I speak plainly, and tell you the truth. My labors
are almost done in Cincinnati I am about to leave the
church of my first labor and first love, to live in an interior
town of Illinois, where I have little to expect from your approbation or esteem. But I beseech you, Kentuckians, to
remember *David Rice;* to remember *Barlow*, and listen
with candor and patience while I seek to show you, *that, if
slave-holding is not sinful then I can justify all those acts
which my brother calls the " abuses of slavery," and prove
them innocent and good.*

*My first proposition is this ; if slave-holding is not sinful,
then kidnapping is right.* For what is the moral difference ?
Suppose one man snares and steals your game, and another
man knowing the fact, eats it; where is the difference in their
guilt ? Now the kidnapper is the hunter for the slave-holder,

if slave-holding is not sinful, the slave-trade is not sinful, for certainly the slave-holder is a *particeps criminis.* He is a partner in the concern, for what are kidnapping and the slave trade to slave-holding, but the jackal to the lion. They are the lion's providers, and the slave-holder has the lion's share of the spoil, the largest part of the profits. You will not find a slave-driver but will tell you the slave-holder is as wicked as he. "They curse us, and abuse us, and we must bear the odium of this business," says the slave-driver, "but when they want slaves to fill their gangs, they accost us politely and offer us a second glass:—yet they affect to call us pirates, and while they are regaling themselves with their segars, their mint juleps, the product of the labor of their slaves, they can talk about 'the wicked soul-driver.' Now where is the equality and justice of this." Tell me, in God's name, is it not true either that slave-holding is sinful, or the slave trade justified? He heaps abuse upon his own servants. He betrays the hand that feeds him. We furnish oil for the wheels of the system, and they curse the hand that brings it. Truly the slave-holder

> "Atones for sins he is inclined to,
> "By damning those he has no mind to."

There is no reply to a soul-driver, speaking thus, but to confess that he utters truth. But you not only justify kidnapping and the slave-trade, by denying that slavery is not sinful, but also all the other "*abuses of slavery*," as my brother calls them; such as THE PARTING OF MAN AND WIFE.

This is my second point, under this head. God has made one man to be the husband of one woman. "For this cause he shall forsake father and mother and shall cleave unto his WIFE"—not to his WIVES. But the slave-holder, who has the husband or the wife for his property, can say, give me the husband or the wife, and none can gainsay him, simply because property is his property; this, *slavery* authorizes him to do, and defends him in doing; thus putting asunder whom God has joined. Now, to rebut this, you are gravely told, "this is an abuse of slavery, not slavery itself." But,

I ask, by what rule does a man who receives slaves, understand the nature of the purchase or gift made him. Suppose a man, dying, bequeaths slaves to his heirs, and they wish to know, being strangers to slavery, what is the nature of the gift; what do they do? They can go nowhere but to the slave code. And what do they see in the slave code? Why, the chattelizing statute; and they then say, *we get these slaves as* OUR PROPERTY, *by* THESE LAWS. My brother Rice, standing by, tells them, that it is not wrong—not sinful—to hold them. Now Dr. Rice gives them these slaves as their property, and yet, in his argument here, he annexes a condition to it, destroying its value as property, viz.: that they shall not sell the man without his wife and children, &c. Such ethics remind one of Hudibras's philosopher, who,

> "By metaphysics, could divide,
> A hair 'twixt North and North-west side."

A sort of moral bodkin which he can thrust in between the theory and practice of the same thing, which are all of a piece, and separating them where there is neither fissure nor seam, justify, christianize, baptise the principle of slavery into the name of God; and yet condemn every part of the practice as an abuse. [Applause.]

Sirs; this is the very anchor ground of the friends of slavery, and I mean with God's help, to test it thoroughly and well, and see if it is safe. My third point is this:—*If slave-holding is not sinful, then the separation of parent and child is not sinful.* The same argument lies to show this. My brother gives the slave-holder permission to *hold his human property*, but affects to deny the right to use it. His ground is, slave-holding is not sinful, but certain laws, regulating slavery, are: but the slave-holder says he does not understand this sort of gift. You teach us that it is "not sinful to hold slaves as property." Seeing then that slavery itself is right, why couple it with a condition which destroys its value? Why, like Macbeth's witches;

> "Keep the word of promise to the ear,
> "And break it to the heart:—"

Why abuse men by giving them a right in theory, which you deny them in practice? Why insult the slave-holder? God knows he has a hard enough time of it with all the evils of the system working with his own corruptions, and those of his slaves. Let us rather pray for them,—and be faithful to them. Why not be frank and say to them "You are certainly sinning; *come now out of your sin* and find peace." This is the way we treat other vices. Shall we cower before this difficulty? Has this one evil a claim above all others? Nay, rather why abuse slave-holders by giving them God's permission to hold slaves as property, and denying them the use of that property?

Suppose, in illustration, that a man sells another a herd of cattle, and after sale, annexes a condition that he shall never sell the dam without a whole string of young cattle, would not the buyer justly hold himself insulted, and imposed upon? Would not such a sale be but a different phase of the one principle on which Dr. Rice's whole argument rests; vindicating slave-holding, yet pretending to oppose separating families? Do you not see the palpable absurdity of the doctrine which he has been teaching ever since this debate opened? A slave-holder may be honestly opposed to selling slaves away from their families, and while his circumstances are good, he may be able to act up to his principle. But by-and-by his sons gamble, his daughters die after expensive sickness, and he is reduced to poverty—and he says to himself, "There's Betsey, I must sell her, and there's Jane, I must let her go also:" and so his slaves go one by one, to pay honest debts, and keep off starvation. Now, can you excommunicate him for this, and yet tell him he had a property right to those slaves. Why should you turn him out of a church conducted upon Dr. Rice's principle, that slave-holding is not sin? Now were I a member of such a church he should never be put out by my voice. I would plead for him till I died. I would say, "Hands off!" You are wrong: You have first taught him that he had the right, and now you would punish him for using it. You are guilty of the most arrant hypocrisy in so doing." Meet the question like men. "Slavery or no slavery." Come out honorably and tell the slave-holder. " Sir you cannot commune with the church while you hold slaves: or else cease from the wretched pretence that you would excommunicate for selling slaves irrespective of family ties. *It is not wrong* to do so, if SLAVE-HOLDING IS NOT SIN. I would then say to the slave-holder; I will then help you. I will part with my coat. I will sell my property and divide it with you; you shall not want while I have, provided you first do justice by freeing your slaves."

No: this does not suit them. They choose to "put evil for good, and good for evil, light for darkness and darkness for light." *They forsake the way of just and holy and plain principles, for the sake of a wicked practice—plain principles for the sake of a wretched practice which one class are unwilling to condemn because another is unwilling to give up.*

I show, in the next place, that *if slave-holding is not sinful, the working of men without wages is right.* What does Dr. Rice say in his pamphlet. " IF I BUY A MAN HE IS MINE, *so far as his services are concerned;*" though he adds, " and I am solemnly bound to treat him as a man," that is, as MY *man!* Treat him how? Why, if he is mine, he must work for me. His services are mine because HE is mine. (See Rice's Lectures, page 17.)

This is put forth by him as a well considered doctrine, because it was first delivered at the first Presbyterian church, and afterwards published. I should not have stood here against him if he had not delivered those lectures. I refused when they first came to me, to enter on this discussion with a Presbyterian minister, because I felt for the honor of Christianity—the Christian ministry, and the ark of my God. But when I saw him come out in public as the charioteer in the very front of the car of despotism, as it rides over the wrecks of human beings, I determined to withstand him and his error if I died in the gap. [Applause.]

If slave-holding be not sinful, though it seems hard that the

hand made hard with toil should not feel the cash it earns, yet
it is not wrong to withhold wages from the laborer, but right
perfectly right. When a boy, I heard of the effects of the em-
bargo law in eastern towns and cities. The hammer of the
smith was idle. The chisel of the artizan was not heard upon
the wall. The cry of the children was heard for bread, when
three mouths were to be fed and but two mouthfuls to give
them. It seemed hard that the laborer could not be fed by
his toil : for the wages principle—that " The laborer is worthy of his hire," blazes from every page of God's Book
which is a wall of fire around the rights of the poor. But
there is no hardship, no injustice in withholding wages—*if
slave-holding be not sin.*

My brother has told us that slaves do not earn more than
they receive. They should be the judges of that themselves. We have no right to judge for them what is best for
their interest.

If I know how to manage property better than my neighbor, does it give me a right to take the management of his
property ? If I know how to manage his wife or his child,
better than he ; does that entitle me to take possession of
and manage them?

My friend's doctrine is that they should be paid no wages,
except what masters see fit to allow them, excluding hiring
and fixed wages; but the Bible says, "the laborer is *worthy*
of HIS HIRE." The daughter of Pharaoh did not dare compel a Hebrew servant to nurse Moses for her without promi-
sing her wages. This common, house-hold equity ; this simple justice to the laboring poor, blazes on every page of the
Bible from Genesis to Revelation, yet he vaunts his eagerness to bring this discussion to the words of Holy
Scripture, as if that blessed book contained no justice for
men compelled to work without hire! Oh thou blessed charter of human hope ! Thou sweet pole-star to the
voyager of life! (addressing the Bible which lay on the
stand before the speakers,) thou bright beam of the ineffa-
ble effulgence of God! would they dive into thy glorious

brightness to draw from this charter of human liberty, their title deed of slavery? Gracious and compassionate God! they vaunt that they will thrust their hand into this blessed book, (holding up the Bible,) to fetch hence fetters for our feet, and manacles for our minds! And are these the vaunted triumphs of all my brother's Hebrew and Greek?

> "Oh star-eyed science, hast thou wandered there,
> To bring us back these tidings of despair!"

Then, let the laurel and olive branch be laid aside, and all the insignia of erudition be changed: let the scholar put off his cap, and the professor his gown. Henceforth, let the scepter of science be a whip, and her chaplet a chain!

But shall they prosper who do such things? Never! Never!! That impious hand which is thrust into God's word to bring out chains and fetters for our race, shall yet be as the hand of Jeroboam, at the altar of Bethel, when he stretched it forth against the prophet of God. And the day cometh, when the light daily increasing from this blessed page, piercing and dispersing the mists they have cast around it, shall so dazzle and confound their vision, that they shall grope at Reason's noonday, and, like Elymas the sorcerer, "go about seeking some one to lead them by the hand." Oh, if she were but here, who once washed her Master's feet, she would wash out their foul aspersions from this His book, with her tears, and wipe them away with the hairs of her head! Let us emulate her wisdom and copy the piety of her example.

I now, inly imploring aid, proceed in proving that, if slave-holding be not sinful, then there is no abuse, nor law, nor anything sinful about it. And my next point is, that, *if slave-holding be not sinful, the master has a right to whip the slave inhumanly,* till he submits, as the Kentucky synod, already quoted, states, slavery takes away from the slave all right to hold property, all chance of character, all the ties of family, and all the motives by which God meant to propel the human machinery of free agents, and substitutes *force* in their stead. Thus far, all is sinless, says Dr.

Rice. But he is opposed to anything cruel or wrong in the masters' treatment of slaves, or in the laws regulating slavery. I know that in words, he does not mean to stop the wheels of God's administration over mind and intellect, and cut off His action upon man as a free agent; but this is what he does in giving permission to hold men as slaves, thus stripping their souls of God's motives. He only proposes to take away the water that turns the wheel, not to destroy the wheel itself; not to brutify the slave, but strip his soul of human motives. Aye, but when you have taken away all other motives to exertion, and still wish action, you have left only force by which to produce it. And when you have put the whip in the place of God's motives to human action, what can you do with your man but the same that is done to a horse—whip him, or sell him? The man is become an animal.

Bartholomew Las Casas, under that doctrine of expediency which has been the dry-rot and curse of the church ever since; reasoning against Indian slavery, was induced, it is said, to sanction the enslavement of the Africans, because he thought the curse of Canaan had fallen upon them, as the progeny of Ham. All the other commentators who have defended slavery upon Bible principles, have adopted more or less of his ideas. They all hang to each other, *each* copying from his predecessor, like the Welshmen in the story, who, in passing a bridge, saw the moon shining in the water, and fancying it a green cheese, they took hold of each others legs to form a string to reach it, and when the upper one gave way, they all fell into the water together.

Sirs, you can do nothing with a slave, after you hold him, but whip him, till he obeys. A Baptist minister said, in convention, "sir, *we have to be cruel.*" If I were a slave, you would have to be cruel to me. A command against my conscience I would not obey. I would die in the furrow, before I would be driven like the ox. A man in the lowest slavery, still retains a spark of that *Promethean* fire which distinguishes men from brutes. As long as he retains the intellectual image of his God, slavery has not entirely stamped it out; and hence cruelty follows, and is part of slavery, as murder is of robbery on the highway.

I make one point more. *If slavery be not sinful, it is not sinful to murder slaves, under certain circumstances.* This you may consider a strong assertion. But I desire to be put upon trial upon it; and I pledge myself to make it good. Suppose there are given me fifty slaves. I am merciful. I wish to do the best I can for them. God has cast my lot in Mississippi or Alabama, whither, Cassius M. Clay tells you, all the rascally slaves are sold—all those who cannot be kept under proper discipline in the upper country. My heart bleeds for the conscientious slave-holder, whose lot is cast in the extreme South. It is true, though that does not excuse them, that British policy kept standing, if it did not originate, southern slavery. It is true, also, that conscientious slave-masters are in terrible difficulty. In Maryland and Virginia, a part of the value of slave-property consists in slave-breeding for the South. So, in a late paper, says the junior editor of the Louisville Journal. Now, then, suppose I have fifty slaves in Alabama or Mississippi, the Botany-Bay of the American slave-system, and my slaves are men who are made brutes by slavery, and rendered fierce by oppression. I say to them, some morning, 'come, boys, to work.' One is lazy and idle, and refuses to work. When I order him to march, he stands up, and, in presence of the gang, gives me words. I have been kind to him; but he resists. I threaten him with the whip; for if I do not enforce obedience, in this instance, I breed insurrection. Besides, the slave-holders around me would not allow of such dangerous mercy. They will say, I am a poltroon, and a deserter of southern institutions. They will not endure my neighborhood, unless I use force. Say I, 'You must submit;' and my slave replies, "I will not." What have I left but to raw-hide him till he yields? Well, I roll up my sleeves and go at it: the negro runs into a stream or thicket, turns round, and curses me to my teeth. What am I to do? The penal code does not help me. There is no other Botany-Bay, no Georgia or Carolina, south of me, whither to sell him. I have undertaken the care of rascals myself; there is no penitentiary for slaves; they are not allowed to go there—if they were, they would be so thickly crowded that their arms and legs would stick out through the prison grates. The criminal code, therefore, does not allow imprisonment to slaves. *There is no resort left but to kill him, unless he surrenders; and slave-holders do it!* I can show you plenty of instances, where masters have killed their slaves, under similar circumstances; and there is no candid slave-holder, of information, but will tell you, that it must and may be done. They call it pure self-defence, though the negro has not raised a hand! The system drives you to that extremity. The root of the evil lies not in the killing, but back of it. You cannot keep up discipline without it; and hence, *to murder is right, according to the law of slavery, and the teaching of Dr. Rice, that slave-holding is not sin.* If you give me God's permission to be a slave-holder, then you give me his permission to take all the steps necessary to enforce the powers with which you have clothed me, and

"Things bad begun make strong themselves by ill."

When once you have, by your teaching, saddled the system of slave-holding upon me, you lay me under obligations to carry out that system, by such means as the system furnishes and allows. All the wrong roots there.

My brother complains that we apply to him the word "pro-slavery." And he complains of Dr. Bailey, the editor of the Herald, whose "Facts for the People," he says, contain but few facts. As to *Dr. Bailey*, I will lay my judgment in pledge with your good opinion, on the fact that there is not an editor in Cincinnati, or elsewhere, (and I mean no disparagement to the gentlemen of the press, when I say it,) more disposed to do justice to his fellow-men, and there are few men more able to do it than he. Is he a liar and a publisher of lies because he calls men "*pro-slavery men*," who give the slave-holder God's permission to hold slaves, when that permission includes all things necessary to carry out the system?

I must beg permission not to take up the argument on the golden rule, here, as my strength is exhausted. I wish to say that the word pro-slavery is not a slander upon those men who advocate slavery as right. Suppose a colony of men go to settle in Oregon Territory, and you wish to set up slavery there. All you have to do is to give to the colony the law by which "slaves shall be deemed and taken in the law to be chattels personal," and you give them all the slavery which has ever existed since the time of Aristotle:—all the slavery that existed in Rome during the twelve hundred years of that mighty Republic. You send over the Rocky mountains, the very same system which obtained in Britain when our British ancestors were shipped like brutes to be sold in the Roman markets. The same identical system which has existed in the United States of America, since the first ill-freighted bark brought twenty slaves to our shores, in the year 1620, the very year of the landing of the Pilgrims upon the Plymouth Rock. It was in that year that Dutch merchants, under the protection of England, sowed the first seeds of that dreadful system in our country, whose fruitage now poisons the very air. You have, I say, only to give your Oregon colony the chattel law, and to teach them, as my brother does, that slave-holding is not sinful, to introduce into Oregon the whole system of Greek, Roman, British and American slavery. Does not my brother know it? Yet he preaches these doctrines. He reiterates them to-day. Why suffer your judgments to be abused, Oh, Kentuckians! In the name of God, and your holy dead, I invoke you to hear the man who is now among you, toiling to persuade you to abandon this accursed and ruinous system. Stand by your countryman, Clay, whose only offence is the fault of Kentuckians, a slight excess of ardor, and desert the man who, in the garb of God's minister, would give you God's permission to enslave your race. Humanity with her bleeding bosom, and fettered hands, and brow, branded with the brand mark of brutes, implores you to spare her the degradation, and yourselves the sin of upholding a system like this. To my unfortunate brother, who feels slandered by the term " pro-slavery," I have no advice to give, but to throw down his idols, and return to his God. Let him forsake his way and his thoughts, and let him return unto God who will have mercy upon him, and to our God who will abundantly pardon.   [*Time expired.*

[MR. RICE'S ELEVENTH SPEECH.]

Gentlemen Moderators, and Fellow-Citizens:

I should be grateful if those who entertain the views I advocate, would abstain from applauding. A good cause does not require aids of this kind to sustain it; a bad one may.

I do not intend to imitate the example of the gentleman by telling you how much I have *prayed* on this subject. It is right to pray; but whilst listening to his numerous incorrect statements, especially those bearing on the character of ministers of the gospel, I could not help thinking, he would better pray less and examine more. And I would venture to suggest, that whilst praying for light on this subject, he would do well to look a little into the Scriptures, through which light is to be obtained, and by which alone the question before us can be satisfactorily settled. I have another objection to telling the audience how much I pray, viz: I have observed that generally those who talk most of their praying, give least evidence that they have prayed so as to *be* improved thereby.

Mr. B. asks, what is a *relation?* He answers by telling us, that a relation, a lawful relation, implies mutual rights and obligations; and he infers, that the relation of master and slave is sinful, because, as he affirms, the slave has no rights, and the master no obligations. In this case, as in many others, he differs from Paul the apostle. He evidently

believed, that this relation has connected with it mutual duties and obligations; and, therefore, in his epistles he points
out the duties of the master, as well as those of the slave,
and enjoins upon each the discharge of their respective duties, and upon each to regard the rights of the other. According to the doctrine of the gentleman, however, the
master has no rights and the servants no duties. I hope to
be pardoned for being, on this subject, as blind as Paul, and
as foolish as Peter!

He asks rather triumphantly, who are to be the slaves,
and who, the masters—whether those superior in intellect
and physical strength may rightly reduce their inferiors to
servitude.

And here, before answering this question, it occurs to me
to say a word or two with regard to the adjournment of the
debate till Monday afternoon. The gentleman complains
of illness; and, therefore, in accommodation to him I have
reluctantly consented to the arrangement. I say *reluctantly;*
for although eighteen hours have been consumed, the gentleman has not yet touched the question he stands pledged to
debate. What he has thus far advanced, is, almost the
whole of it, as distant from the question, as the moon from
the earth. He has abounded in *assertion,* but failed to adduce anything like scriptural evidence in favor of his proposition. Last evening, he gave us notice, that he would offer
"the *direct* argument for abolitionism:" we looked for a *Bible
argument,* but in vain. Now if a man cannot prove slave-
holding sinful in *nine hours,* I think he would better quit.
[A laugh.] I regret that he has made the request, particularly because many who have come from a distance, expecting the debate to close on to-morrow, will probably be obliged
to leave without hearing the most interesting part of it. As
to the question, whether superiors may enslave those inferior
to them, I reply: 1st. It has nothing to do with the subject
we are discussing. As I have repeatedly remarked, we are
not discussing the question, whether it is right to *enslave
free men.* The question before us, which the gentleman

stands pledged to discuss, relates to our duty to a class of men reduced to slavery by others. Is it the duty of those who inherited this evil, to rid themselves of it by an immediate emancipation, without regard to circumstances? This is the question. And if the brother felt himself able to support his affirmative proposition, would he be continually speaking to something else? I presume not. He cannot avoid seeing and feeling that there is a difficulty in maintaining his side of the real question: and he therefore tries to divert our attention to a different issue. Is this candid?

But with what propriety does he ask the question, since he himself has said, that the negroes, if liberated, might with propriety be prevented from voting, and subjected to laws made for them; because in some respects they are inferior to the whites? If he does not advocate the depriving them of the right to vote and to hold civil offices; he certainly considers such a course not wrong, since he proposes to leave it to politicians to do as they think proper. He holds, that superiors may not enslave inferiors, nor under any circumstances hold them in bondage; but they may deprive them of some of the dearest rights of freemen! The propriety of his question will not appear, at least, till he is more consistent.

To prove the sinfulness of the relation between master and slave, he tells us, that every act authorized by the relation, is a sinful act. To prove this assertion, he selects one particular: he says, that the slave-holder exacts the service of the slave without allowing him wages.

I have repeatedly presented for his consideration the case of the Presbyterian elder in Kentucky, who had become heir to a large number of slaves, of different ages—some old and infirm, others women and children. He asked the Synod what he ought to do. As for paying them wages, he said, taking them altogether, "*they are eating me up.*" They were an expense to him. Will the gentleman tell us, how much he owed them? Dr. Cunningham, who had paid particular attention to this subject, says, truly, that the worth of labor depends upon circumstances; and he states, that in

Great Britain there are many persons who are obliged to labor *twenty hours* out of the twenty-four, and even then they cannot secure a support for themselves and their families. I presume, the gentleman had not heard of these facts. He is slow to hear what makes against his favorite doctrines. I affirm, that if any slave-holder in Kentucky should require his slaves to labor *twenty hours* in twenty-four, he would be drummed out of the State; he would be regarded as a monster of cruelty. It is absolutely certain, that the slaves in our country do receive generally better wages, than multitudes of the free laborers in England and Scotland. The amount justly due, as wages, must depend upon many circumstances. I can truly say, that if a family of slaves were offered me to-morrow, as a present, on condition that I should take care of the aged, feed and clothe the children, pay doctor's bills, &c., I would not, as a mere matter of pecuniary consideration, accept the gift. (I mean as a matter of profit and loss.) If I were obliged to maintain the old who are past work, and the children who are not yet able, and to pay the doctor's bills for the whole, I would not take the family as a free gift.

Doubtless great injustice is often done in the slave relation, as in the married relation. Oppression and cruelty may be practiced in both, but that does not prove either of the relations to be in itself sinful. Paul thought (but he was no abolitionist,) that the relation might continue and yet the master give to his slave "that which is just and equal." He does not require the relation to be dissolved; nor does he require wages to be paid *in money.*

The brother says, the slave-holder has a right to separate husband and wife. How does he prove it? By the Bible? No: but by *the Rev. Mr. Blanchard's assertion!* No doubt, the master can do it; he has the physical power to separate them. So he may beat his slave to death, or knock him down with an ax; but who recognizes his moral right to do so? No man ever asserted it.

If the gentleman's assertion be true, Constantine must,

after all, have been a great fool in making laws that no master should separate husband and wife.

It is vain for Mr. B. to assert that every slave-holder can do what in some countries the law of the State forbids, and what in this country the law of the Presbyterian church expressly prohibits him from doing. Men own horses; and the gentleman will scarcely deny that a man's horses are, in the fullest sense of the word, *his property*. But does it follow, that he may treat them as cruelly as his passions may prompt him to do? May he cut them up by peacemeal, allowing them still to live? The Bible teaches, that "a righteous man regardeth the life of his beast;" and even the civil law punishes a man proved guilty of cruel treatment of his horse. And yet the gentleman would have us believe, that because a man claims the services of his fellow man under certain circumstances, he may treat him as a brute, may inflict on him all the suffering he can endure! Such logic may satisfy those who are already ardent abolitionists; but cannot convince the unprejudiced.

Why only look at it. He urges, as an argument against slave-holding, that which, if valid, would destroy the marriage relation. He says, that slave-holding is a deadly sin, because a master may separate a wife from her husband. Granting that he can, (though certainly the relation does not authorize him to do so,) cannot a husband prevent his wife from going to church? Has he not the physical power? And cannot a father, so long as his son is under age, prevent him from attending any place of worship? or from joining any church? Certainly, the husband and the father may thus tyrannize over the wife and the child, but is this a valid argument against the relation of husband and wife?—of parent and child? What does his argument amount to? It amounts just to this, that if a man has power over another, he may abuse it as much as he pleases. The gentleman is arguing against principles which are avowed by no man under the sun.

Then he asks, " But why seek to free a slave, if the relation is not sinful?" In reply, I ask, 'why seek to relieve a man's poverty, if poverty be not sinful?' Wonderful logic, this.

Again, he asks, "why is it, if Dr. Rice is so much opposed to slave-holding, that his doctrines are so popular among rampant slave-holders?" A little while ago, he told you, that my doctrines were most unpalatable at the South— that slave-holders could not endure them; and, behold, he now asserts directly the contrary. Ought not a man, who will assert, in the space of two hours, two propositions, the very reverse of each other, to have till Monday to adjust his ideas? [A laugh.]

He inquires how, if I am opposed to slavery, I can preach to persevering slave-holders in Kentucky—how it happens, that my doctrines are so acceptable to them. I ask him, how he can preach the truth to sinners in Cincinnati? [A laugh.] He really seems to think that no man can preach the truth to sinners without being stoned. I think it probable, that when the stones flew so thickly around him, as he told us they once did, that he provoked opposition by some such incorrect statements as he has repeatedly made here.

By the way, I will not say how much I have been praised, or how much popularity I have sacrificed, for what I believe to be the truth, as the gentleman has done. I have nothing of the kind to communicate.

There is in the house a number of Kentuckians, who came to this place to hear all the gentleman had to offer in proof of his doctrine, that slave-holding is in itself sinful; but they have been disappointed. They have heard him *nine* hours, and have heard him advance nothing like a scriptural argument. They would doubtless hear him patiently, if he would *reason;* but I venture to say, they will regard all his declamation and attacks upon personal character, as the idle wind.

But slave-holding, he thinks, must be in itself sinful, because it hinders the coming of the Millenium. Facts, however, contradict his assertion; for it is well known, that the churches in the slave-holding States—those, for example, in Kentucky, are quite as prosperous as those in Ohio, or any of the free States. This the abolitionists cannot deny. I could easily point to many churches in Kentucky, far more prosperous than that to which the gentleman ministers in this city, which, if I am correctly informed, he has preached almost to death.

The brother insists, that slave-holding is kidnapping continued—kidnapping "stretched out." This is but a repetition of his former argument. He seems about to begin *de novo.* Then, he says again, that it abolishes marriage, but brings not a word from the Bible to prove it. Perhaps he is going to "keep saying" it, like his friend, Mr. Leavitt! [A laugh.]

But I shall now leave such arguments as these, and return "to the law and to the testimony."

The brother has pronounced a most eloquent eulogium upon the Bible. I cannot pretend to repeat it; yet he attempted to cast no little odium upon me because I insisted upon going directly to the Bible. How shall I please the gentleman?

He would fain excite prejudice against me, because I said that if I buy a man he is *mine.* But what does the Bible say to slaves? "Obey *your* masters in all things." If the man is *his* master, then he is *his* servant. And I simply said, if I buy a man, he is mine, *so far as his services are concerned.* This is Paul's doctrine, but if Paul were on earth to-day the abolitionists would excommunicate him! [A laugh.]

"Oh thou most blessed book," exclaims the gentleman. Yes: and oh that the gentleman would but get into the blessed book. [Renewed laughter.] But he won't, and I can't get him there. He comes no nearer than to cry, "oh blessed book."

The gentleman says, if the slave is his master's, then he may beat him at pleasure, and exercise all cruelty toward him, just as he may the log of wood he owns. But, unhappily, the Bible admits the one, and forbids the other. "Oh, blessed book!" A man's child is his; may he knock its brains out? If the gentleman's argument is good for anything, he may kill it, or do anything else to it he pleases. I cannot detain, to answer such logic.

I now, resume the Bible argument; and as there are many persons present now, who did not hear me this afternoon, you will bear with me whilst, for the satisfaction of such, I briefly recapitulate.

It is a truth which the gentleman will scarcely deny, that God, who is infinitely holy, and "of purer eyes than to look on sin," never did, and never could, give men permission to form a relation in itself sinful, or sinful in the circumstances in which it is formed. In other words, God cannot grant to men permission to commit sin. Now, if I prove, that God did recognize the relation of master and slave as lawful, and did give express permission to the Jews to purchase slaves; it will follow, inevitably, that the relation between master and slave is not in itself sinful. I go, then, directly to the "blessed book," as Mr. B. very appropriately styles it.

1. I have proved, as I think, beyond a doubt, that Hagar was Abraham's slave; for in the first place, the Hebrew word *shifha*, translated "maid," properly means a female slave. Gessonius defines it *ancilla, famula*, which words in the Latin tongue, mean a female slave. The Septuagint translates it by the Greek word, *paidiske*, a word of the same meaning as *ancilla* and *famula* in Latin. In the second place, I showed, that in the 4th chapter of the epistle to the Gallatians, Hagar is called a "*bondwoman*," (*paidiske*) in contrast with Sarah, who was *free—eleuthera*. If she was not a slave, there was no contrast such as Paul draws, between her condition and that of Sarah. Thirdly, Abraham told Sarah, her maid was in her hand, and she could do with her as she pleased; and when Sarah punished her, she fled from her, and was found in the wilderness. Those who have hired servants, do not claim authority to punish

them; nor do they *run* from their employers. The angel of God found her in the wilderness, and admonished her to return and submit to her mistress. Would he have done so, if the relation of master and slave had been in itself sinful? Would Mr. Blanchard give such advice to a fugitive slave? Did God denounce Abraham as "a kidnapper," because Hagar was his slave?

2. Abraham, as I proved from the 17th chapter of Genesis, had servants *bought with his money*, as well as servants *born in his house;* and so far from requiring him to liberate them, or denouncing him for holding them, God required him to administer to them the ordinance of circumcision. Moreover, Abimelech gave bond-servants of both sexes to Abraham, and he received them. Is not the receiver as bad as the thief? If they were kidnapped, (as my friend maintains,) and were "found in Abraham's hand," he was worthy of death. Once more, Abraham's pious servant told Laban, that the Lord himself had given his master men-servants and maid-servants, as well as camels and asses. Was it a sin in Abraham to hold what God had given?

3. I gave the Hebrew words which signify *slave* and hired servant viz: *eved,* a slave, and *sakir,* a hired servant. The Hebrew servant, sold for six years, was not to be treated as an *eved,* a slave, but as a *sakir,* a hired servant. I read in Leviticus, ch. 25, the express permission given the Jews to buy bondmen and bondmaids from the heathen; and if the gentleman denies, that the word *eved,* here translated *bondman,* means *slave,* I earnestly request him, as I did this afternoon, to tell us what word in the Hebrew language does have that meaning. Moreover, not only were these bondmen bought with money; but they are called the *possession* of the man who bought them, and the *inheritance* of his children *forever.* The Jew, sold for six years, might also voluntarily become a servant for life, having his ear bored. But if they were *bought,* were they not his for the purpose for which he bought them?

4. There were also hired servants; and the law required that their wages should be promptly paid, but said nothing concerning the wages of *bondmen.* The bondmen were distinguished from the hired servants, in that the former were permitted to partake of the passover, but the latter, not being permanently connected with the family, were not. 5. As a further and conclusive evidence that the bondmen spoken of in the law of Moses, were slaves, I proved that the master was permitted to enforce their obedience by chastisement, which was never done in the case of hired servants; and that the master was not subject to punishment if his servant lived a day or two after the chastisement, because *"he was his money."* I have stated, and I repeat it, that all commentators, critics and theologians of any note, understand the word *eved* to mean a slave, and the bondmen of the Jews to have been real slaves. Indeed, stronger language to establish this fact, could not be used.

The fact, then, is clearly established, that God recognized as lawful, the relation of master and slave in the case of the patriarchs, and that he gave express permission to the Jews, to form the relation by purchasing slaves from the heathen. The conclusion is inevitable, that the relation is not in itself sinful.

How do the abolitionists attempt to escape the force of this evidence? I will pay my respects to their replies to it.

1. They say, the servants bought by the Jews, *sold themselves.* To this I reply—1st, It cannot be proved. Whatever might be true of adults, it is certain that *children* did not sell themselves; and they were permitted to purchase "children of the strangers." 2d, If the relation is in itself sinful, they had no right to sell themselves into it; nor had any man the right to purchase them, and thus to form a relation in itself sinful. No consent of parties can make that right, which is in itself wrong. A woman may consent to be a concubine; but her consent will not make the relation thus constituted, lawful. 3d, But Rev. T. E. Thomas, a zealous and

influential abolitionist, says—" The advocates of slavery can devise but one answer, accordant with their views; namely, that the heathen round about were slave-holders, that they had captives taken in war, and whom they might sell to the Jewish purchaser. *We admit that some servants of this sort might be bought of the heathen, who claimed to be their masters,* and shall prove, presently, that even such persons could not be held by the Hebrews, without their consent." *Review of Junkin,* p. 23. It is admitted, then, the slaves did not always *sell themselves,* but were, at least sometimes, sold by their masters.

2. But it is said, the Jews could not purchase servants *without their consent.* To this I reply, that no Christian would be willing to purchase an adult slave without his consent, nor to sell an obedient slave to a master with whom he is unwilling to live. If a professing Christian were known to purchase adult slaves, contrary to their wish, and to compel them to live with him, I admit, that he would thus manifest a spirit so inconsistent with Christianity, as to deserve the discipline of the church. But suppose I buy a slave at his own earnest request, do I buy him without his consent? Yet abolitionists denounce the slave-holder who has formed the relation with the consent, and at the request of the slave, whilst they are constrained to admit, that the Jews purchased in this way!

3. It is alleged, that the term of service of the servants bought of the heathen, was *limited.* Of this class of servants, Mr. Thomas says—" They were never purchased for six years; *but always till the jubilee.*" For argument's sake, we will admit the truth of this statement; and now, let me ask, what proportion of those purchased in this way, would live to enjoy the freedom proclaimed at the jubilee? Suppose a man thirty years of age, bought by a Jew immediately after the jubilee, he would be a slave *forty-nine* years, and would become free at the age of *seventy-nine.* Of what advantage would his liberty be to him at that age. How many live to

four-score years? But it may be said, his children will, at any rate, be free. Suppose we admit this, it does not affect the question before us. We are discussing the question, whether slave-holding is in itself sinful, and the relation between master and slave a sinful relation. If it is in itself sinful, it is a sin to hold a man in that relation one day, as truly as to hold him forty-nine years ; and if it be lawful to hold a slave five years, or fifty years, he may be held a longer time, if there be no law against it. But the argument I am considering, admits that the relation might lawfully exist till the year of jubilee. This admission is all I ask ; for it concedes that the relation is not in itself sinful. I thank no man for making this concession ; because it is perfectly easy to prove the fact, whether it is admitted or not.

4. It is alleged, that the bondmen of the Jews *received wages.* I demand the proof; and I venture to say it will not be produced. The law (*Levit.* xix, 13) required the wages of the *hired servant* to be promptly paid; but where does it say a word concerning the wages of the bondman ? But let it be remembered, that unrequited labor is only *one* of the sinful features of slave-holding, mentioned by abolitionists. If the relation was sinful, the fact that the slave received wages, would not make it right.

5. It is said that though the Jews might buy servants, they might not *sell.* Admitting this too, for the argument's sake, will it follow that the *holding* of a slave is sinful? The controversy between us and the abolitionists, is not about *slave-selling*, but about *slave-holding.* But where is his proof that they might not sell ? The law expressly permitted them to buy slaves, and did not forbid them to *sell.* There is, indeed a law forbiding a master to sell a Jewish servant to *strangers;* but they might sell to their *brethren. Exceptio probat regulam :* the exception confirms the rule.

6. It is alleged, that some of the old patriarchs had several wives, and the same arguments which prove slave-holding not in itself sinful, prove that polygamy and concubinage are

right.   It is admitted, that some pious men, at an early day, had a plurality of wives; but let the gentleman, if he can, produce the divine permission given to any man to marry more than one wife. Polygamy and concubinage are wrong; but God never gave permission to any man to form such relations.   But I have proved, that he did give the Jews express permission to buy and hold slaves.

I am under no obligation to assign the reason why God gave the Jews permission to purchase and hold slaves.   I have proved the fact; and that is sufficient to prove the doctine of the abolitionists false.   Yet I will give what was, as I suppose, the reason.   Doubtless he intended that in this way degraded heathen should be made acquainted with that blessed religion by which they might be made happier on earth, and might secure eternal life.   Those who were purchased by the Jews, were not, I suppose, thereby reduced to slavery.   They were already slaves to degraded and cruel heathen masters, held in a state of bondage compared with which slavery under the Mosaic law, was almost freedom.   God's permission to the Jews to purchase them, was therefore, benevolent; for their condition was greatly improved by the change.

In view of this whole argument we are forced to the solemn conclusion that one of two things are true: either God gave permission to men to form a sinful relation, and to become according to our brother, kidnappers and man-stealers— or, it is not true, that the relation of master and slave is in itself sinful.

The gentleman who imagines himself peculiarly illumined, pours upon me his denunciations, and calls upon all Kentuckians to abandon such a man.   In the fulness of his compassion he commisserates my blindness and moral degradation; and his abolition brethren may sympathise with him.   But after all, I am inclined to think, he will find himself in the condition of a certain monomaniac of whom I have somewhere heard.   A visitor asked him how it happened

that he had become an inmate in the Asylum. He answered—" The world said, I was deranged; and I said, the
world was deranged ; and they outvoted me." [A laugh.]

Suppose the question put to vote, how many of the eminently wise and good, in past time and at the present day,
would be found with the gentleman ? Doubtless, he feels
deep commisseration for such men as poor blinded Dr. Scott,
the Commentator! for his views concerning Jewish servitude precisely accord with mine. I will read a single extract from his commentary on Levit. xxv, 44,—46. " The
Israelites were *permitted* to keep SLAVES of other nations ;
perhaps in order to testify, that none but the true Israel of
God participated of that liberty with which Christ hath made
his people free. But it was also allowed, in order that in
this manner the Gentiles might become acquainted with true
religion, (Gen. xvii, 10—13. xviii, 19,) and when the Israelites copied the example of their pious progenitors, there can
be no reasonable doubt, that it was overruled for the eternal
salvation of many souls," &c.

Poor ignorant Dr. Scott! how our abolitionist friends
must pity him!

Bishop Horne, too, the author of the celebrated " Introduction to the study of the Scriptures," in 4 volumes—one
of the most learned men of his day, takes precisely the same
view of the subject. He says. (Vol. 3, p. 419.

" Slavery is of very remote antiquity. It existed before
the flood, (*Gen* ix, 25 ;) and when Moses gave his laws to
the Jews, finding it already established, though he could not
abolish it, yet he enacted various salutary laws and regulations. The Israelites indeed might have Hebrew servants or
slaves, as well as alien-born persons, but these were to be
circumcised," &c. After stating the various ways in which
slaves might be acquired, he says :—" Slaves received both
food and clothing, for the most part of the meanest quality,
but whatever property they acquired, belonged to their lords :
hence, they are said to be worth double the value of a hired
servant. (*Deut.* xv, 18.) They formed marriages at the will

of the master; but their children were slaves, who, though they could not call him a father, (*Gal.* iv, 6. Rom. viii, 15,) yet they were attached and faithful to him as to a father, on which account the patriarchs trusted them with arms. If a married Hebrew sold himself, he was to serve for six years, &c., but, if his master had given one of his slaves to him as a wife, she was to remain, with his children, *as the property of her master.*"

The compassionate brother no doubt is all this while pitying blinded Dr. Scott, and blinded Dr. Horne, and poor blinded Dr. Chalmers and poor stone-blind Matthew Poole, (the author of the Synopsis and Annotations,) who fell into the same heresy : and while he is weeping, he may as well include, at once, all the best critics on the Old Testament who have enlightened and blessed the church of God. I defy the gentleman to show a single commentator, critic, or theologian of any admitted pretensions to scholarship, who does not give the same exposition which I have given of the passages in relation to servitude among the Jews. That an overwhelming majority of the wisest and best men the church ever saw, agree with me in this view of those scriptures, I am prepared to prove.

The brother wants very much to show that Dr. Cunningham is an abolitionist, and is with him in sentiment. I will therefore quote a little from his testimony, just to show that he is as blind, as stupid, or as corrupt, as I am, and as all other Bible critics and commentators.

"They [slave-holding Christians,] submit to what they cannot help. Slavery is sinful as a system, but not necessarily in those who stand related to it. A very little consideration of the whole state of things, then, would show, that this is really the case. A man may be a slave-holder innocently. Every man of right feeling, who has true notions of what man is, as made in the image of God, and of man's duties and obligations, would, as much as possible, avoid ever coming into such a relation.   * But then we ought to make distinctions, and enter into the position in which we perceive they are placed. The slave laws are, beyond all question, most infamous. They do treat them as " brute beasts" or " chattels personal." On the majority of the community there rests a fearful amount of guilt, which could scarcely be exaggerated, &c. The law makes the slaves chattels personal. The necessary consequence is, that a man becomes, whether he will or not, the possessor of slaves. They are his, and he cannot get rid of them. * * * The sum and substance of what is commonly asserted by the church, is just a denial of the abolition principle that slavery is sinful in such a sense, that mere slave-holding in all circumstances is a crime, and an adequate ground for expulsion from the Lord's table: *and they have beyond all question, the example of the apostles and apostolic churches to justify them.*" Again— " I have not the slightest hesitation in repudiating American abolitionism."

You observe, when speaking of abolitionists, he speaks of them as on " the other side." Is he one of them? Or does he not hold my principles precisely? I told you that the slave laws were many of them infamous. Dr. Cunningham says the same. He says, the law makes them chattels personal; but, he also says, concerning many masters, their slaves are theirs, and he cannot get rid of them.

[*Time expired.*

———

Friday Evening, 9 o'clock.

[MR. BLANCHARD'S TWELFTH SPEECH.]

Gentlemen Moderators, and Gentlemen and Ladies, Fellow-Citizens:

My whole speech, fortunately, will be in reply to the one just fallen from my brother, without departing from my prescribed course. It will be, throughout, upon the scripture argument, after about five minutes' reply to what he said before he himself came to the scriptures.

When he said that the Sixth Presbyterian Church, of which I am pastor, "*was preached almost to death*," I felt sorry that such a remark should have escaped him, first, because my success as a pastor has nothing to do with the truth of my arguments here, and therefore the charge was entirely gratuitous; and secondly, I do not like to say a word in my own case, in reply to such a remark, nor would I (for my work, as a pastor, is with God,) but for the sake of a beloved church, which has been faithful to me: and for the sake of those theological students in the audience, who might be misled, by his remark, to suppose that opposing slave-holding is against pastoral success.

When I took charge of the church, seven years ago last March, I was inexperienced and unpopular with those who hate all religion, except that which, like the piety of Mr. By-ends in Bunyan's Pilgrim's Progress, " always jumps with the times." We had then but one hundred and twenty members, and have since been bereaved of several leading members by death. We have, through the mercy of God, enjoyed frequent revivals, and as the fruits of about seven years' labor, have received more than four hundred members. Through the rapid multiplication of new churches of the same order to which colonies we have largely contributed, the number of dismissions have been large, so that our present number is about two hundred and fifty, or about double that with which we commenced. A debt of *five thousand dollars*, incurred in the purchase of a house of worship, during the times of pecuniary pressure, was, on the first day of January last, entirely cancelled, being paid down, or assumed by responsible men, and the church and congregation were never more united, prosperous and happy, than at present. I shall not bring my brother's want of pastoral ability to refute his arguments in this debate, nor go into Kentucky to enquire whether he has preached his former churches into death or into life.

My brother thinks me guilty of an inconsistency in saying that his doctrine was *acceptable* to slave-holders; and saying, also, that it was unacceptable to them. I did utter both those remarks, and both are true, and both consistent. The explanation is simply this, that like all defenders of error, his arguments are inconsistent with, and destroy each other, one part being acceptable to slave-holders, the other, not. What he said, declaring that "slave-holders have no right to hold their slaves, as property, for gain," they will not thank him for saying; but the vilest of them will own him as their champion, while contending that "slave-holding is not sin." So that, as I said, what he teaches is unacceptable to slave-holders, and what he teaches is acceptable to them.

Again: He says that I, in the figure of the rats, represented, that to go to Hebrew and Greek is to go into darkness. But he is mistaken. I said no such thing. This is what I said. That there is a class of men who seek to climb by sectarian services to the top of old ecclesiastical establishments founded by the piety of past generations:—that these men are slaves to authorities, weighing men's opinions against plain justice :—that they dive into the lumber-room of antiquity to fetch out what instances they can find of the curtailment of human freedom in dark and despotic ages, before the empire of force had yielded to that of reason; and twist them into a coil of precedents, to bind American Christianity to the toleration of American despotism in an age of liberty and light. That is what I said ; and not that Hebrew and Greek, the original tongues of the scriptures, were a source of darkness. Much good may his Hebrew and Greek do him ; I apprehend he will have need of all he is master of, before he gets through this debate. He further remarked that there could not be found one respectable commentator who did not hold that slave-holding is not sinful, " he will confess that he could find none." I have an argument upon commentators which I will introduce in its place. Meantime I observe that Dr. Adam Clarke, whom Methodists at least will respect, in commenting upon the Ephesians vi, 5, says, that; " In heathen countries slavery had some sort of excuse.

Among Christians it is a crime, and an outrage *for which perdition has scarcely an adequate punishment!"*

There is one commentator at least who does not quite agree with my brother.

Mr. Rice rose. I will beg leave to correct the gentleman. I said he could not find one respectable commentator who ever gave a different interpretation to the passages of scripture which I quoted, from mine.

Mr. Blanchard. Perhaps you are right. I will however, give other commentators in their place. I thought I would read this just here by way of spice. [Great laughter.]

Now, Gentlemen Moderators, and Fellow-Citizens. I am happy to be in a situation to follow my brother *pari passu* in his scripture argument. His first main argument was from authorities. That I shall hereafter consider. His second was from scripture language, and that I am to consider now.

In the scripture argument for slavery, there are two texts so much relied on by slave-holders, and their apologists, that (if any part of the Bible could be) they might be called "the slave-holders, texts;" as their whole Bible argument hangs on their understanding of them. If these are taken from under them, their whole argument drops to the ground. They are Leviticus, chapter, xxv, 45, and Exodus, xxi, 21.

It is not pretended by them that the general principles of the Bible give the slightest countenance to slavery. They therefore do not attempt to show, by reference to the whole scope of the Bible, that slavery is consistent with its principles, for the principles of the Bible are justice and righteousness. But they rely upon individual texts and parts of texts, which, taken out from the connexion, seem to teach that slavery was not a sin under the circumstances there found. Though their texts by no means prove their doctrine when an enlightened and just criticism is applied to them. As I have observed, their whole argument radiates from these two texts as from a centre, while all their subordinate and inferior inferences, drawn from other texts, as well as from these, are founded upon the same false view of the Bible, and are chickens of the same brood of error. I will come now; though contrary to the usual course pursued in forensic argument, (which is, to prove your proposition before stating and answering objections; so as to arm your hearers with truth, before staggering them with errors which you have not yet prepared them to meet.) I will come first to the very heart and core of their "Bible argument," reading the texts on which they mainly rely, and on which they are harping from July to June. The first is Levit. xxv, 45.

"Moreover, of the children of the strangers (*i. e.* Canaanites,) that do sojourn among you, of them shall ye buy, and of their families that are with you; which they beget in your land: and they shall be your possession, and ye shall take them as an inheritance for your children after you, to inherit them for a possession: they shall be your bondmen forever: but over your brethren, the children of Israel, ye shall not rule, one over another with rigor."

I have an hour and a half speech, to prove that these bondmen or bound-men were not slaves. But I am now simply replying to his arguments. His position is that this passage proves that the Hebrews held slaves, and that by God's permission.

I wish here, in the outset, to protest against being understood, even if I admitted the Hebrew bond-servants to be slaves, as also admitting that their slavery could sanction ours. (But I do not admit that those bond-servants were slaves, and my main argument will be, to prove that they were not.) For even if they had been slaves, they were Canaanites, a race of men accursed of God, having filled the measure of their iniquities, and doomed to extermination from the earth. Surely, if God saw fit to enslave these people for their crimes, and commanded his people to execute this wrath upon them, that would not justify an American in enslaving indifferent, unoffending persons. This must be clear to every understanding If the court issue a war-

rant to the sheriff of your county to hang a convicted criminal, that warrant does not authorize any man to go out and
hang any man in any other county who has been illegally
seized.   Supposing the Canaanites were really enslaved,
with God's permission, for their sins, it does not give Dr.
Rice, or his slave-holding friends, a right to enslave any
person in the State of Kentucky, be it negro, mulatto, or
white woman, the child of German, Irish, or Italian parents.
I do not therefore admit, that, if those Hebrew bond-servants
were slaves, that it does any thing towards maintaining his
argument, that "slave-holding is no sin."   This argument
depends on the assumption, that God never can permit, for
any purpose, punitive or otherwise, that which is wrong in
itself.   But God certainly permitted the Jews to divorce for
hatred; and divorce for hatred is wrong in itself.   See *Deut.*
xxiv. 3.   "If the latter husband hate her, and write her
a bill of divorcement, and giveth it in her hand, and sendeth her out of the house," &c., her former husband may
not again take her to wife.   Thus by the Jewish code,
authorized by God, and given by Moses, men were allowed to divorce their wives for hatred, so far as regulating and restricting a vile practice allows it.   Does
that justify American husbands in turning the mothers of
their children out of doors, in every family quarrel, weeping
and friendless, because hated?

Admit his inference from Jewish bond-service—(Jewish
slavery if he will) to American, and you admit a principle by
which every husband who hates his wife may drive her
from his door.   The teaching of Christ is explicit on the
subject of divorce for hatred, showing that it is contrary to the
original constitutions of God.   When the Pharisees, asked
him, "Is it lawful for a man to put away his wife for every
cause?"   His reply was "*From the beginning it was not
so.*"   "What therefore God hath joined together, let not man
put assunder."   "Moses because of the hardness of your hearts
gave you that precept."   *Mat.* xix.   Yet in Deut. xxiv, 3, it
is said, "And if the latter husband hate her and write a bill

of divorcement and giveth it in her hand and sendeth her out of his house; or if the latter husband die, which took her to be his wife, her former husband which sent her away, may not take her again to be his wife," &c.

We see therefore that divorce for hatred was permitted—and yet the same thing is not permitted now, but expressly forbidden as sinful by Christ himself. So if, in despotic countries, and in ages when as yet the law of force had not given way before the empire of reason, slavery had been permitted; it does not help the argument for American slaveholding.

But again. This text, itself the very sheet anchor of the slave-holding doctrine, is misinterpreted to make it yield those inferences in favor of slavery which they draw from it. It positively does not mean, and can be shown not to mean what they say and suppose it to mean.

My brother told you that my argument on a certain point, proving to much, proved nothing; I grant that if an argument proves too much, it proves nothing. I deny however, that mine was of that class. But let us apply that logical test to his main argument from Levit. xxv, 45. "Of them shall ye buy bondmen," etc., "and they shall be your possession."

Is not the slave-trade justified here?

Now if their understanding of this text be correct, that those bondmen bought, were slaves; was not the business of buying them from the heathen tribes, the slave trade? And if this verse proves that God permitted slavery, does it not also prove that he permitted the slave trade? This certainly is proving too much; more even than Dr. Rice wishes to prove, that God permitted, nay commanded them to drive a slave trade with heathen nations—a traffic which consigns the trader caught on the African coast to be hung as a pirate? If you take this text in their sense; it is a complete justification of the slave trade; far more clear than it is of slavery. For: "Of them shall ye buy," etc., not them shall ye hold. Certainly his interpretation of this text proves too much, and, therefore, by his own quoted canon proves nothing. For my brother himself roundly denounces the slave trade as an "infernal traffic."

Mr. Rice. I did not denounce the buying of slaves: we are under obligations of humanity often to do that; but the speculating in them for money—the tearing apart of families, &c.

Mr. Blanchard. You hear the brother's explanation, and I desire you should allow it all the force which it deserves.

I now resume the argument—with this remark, that, if you buy a slave only to set him free, your act is not slave-holding; it is an act of redemption. When the United States bought Americans from the Algerines, it was not slave-trading. We bought them to set them free. Now the whole question is simply this: were those bondmen which were bought by the Jews, *slaves* in the hands of their Hebrew masters or not? If they were not, then there was no slavery among the Jews, and his whole vaunted Bible argument is founded in and drawn from a mistake. But if they were slaves to the Jews, then the text justifies, not only slavery, but the slave trade, the original kidnapping, middle-passage, auction mart, coffle and all. He can no more escape from this than he can from the gripe of death. So truly as that text justifies holding slaves, in Kentucky or Virginia or Tennessee; so truly is it a warrant for the slave trade by which those slaves are procured; for its leading idea and object, is to direct the Jews to buy their bondmen of heathen nations, nations which were to them what Africans are to us. And when Sir John Hawkins, under Elizabeth, commenced the slave trade, it was founded and defended upon this very text. And, according to Dr. Rice's interpretation, Hawkins was right. They reasoned fairly, from my friend's premises; for if it authorises the holding, it authorises the trading, in slaves. *But it does neither*—blessed be God— *it does neither!*

Nor does his argument hold good if it did both. There is not in the text a sprinkling of American slave-holding and

American slave trading. The American slaves were *stolen* in the persons of their ancestors, and are held by the title by which men hold stolen goods. I remember, when a student, the account given by one who had been in the slave trade. He said he had been a seaman before the mast upon the African coast, in a vessel engaged in this traffic ; and that their custom was to take out boxes of muskets, powder, gun-flints, and whiskey, and distribute them among the petty kings along the coast ; and, at night, they could see the flaming villages, fired by these chiefs, in their savage marauds upon each other's territory, for slaves to freight the vessel in the offing; that they could sometimes hear the shouts of the conflict, and see the naked and affrighted wretches by the light of their flaming dwellings, flying from immediate death, or, what is worse, an eternal slavery in an unknown land. These wretches, captured in this revolting manner, in wars, stimulated and set on by the traders, were the ancestors of our slaves. That is the way, and such the title we have obtained to them. More than this, multitudes are now kidnapped, thus, brought direct to the United States, and " broken in" upon our plantations, being introduced in contempt of the law making it piracy, through Florida, and, at points along the coast of the Gulf of Mexico. The number thus introduced has been variously estimated, by speakers in Congress, but never lower than 13,-000 per annum, besides the multitudes smuggled into Texas from the Island of Cuba, or openly received in some instances, as has been stated, in contempt of law. *Thus* ALL *our slaves were stolen from Africa, directly in their own persons, or in the persons of their ancestors, and doubly stolen when infants at their birth : for human beings are* BORN *free.*

Now, with these facts kept in view, what does my brother's text say? "From the heathen ye shall *steal ?* No! "From them shall ye BUY bondmen," etc. Thus his own text, with his own interpretation, will not justify American slave-holding; for our slaves were stolen—stolen in their persons or their parents—stolen by the aid of boxes of muskets, powder, gunflints, and savage chiefs made drunk and employed as agents to steal them. Now his text has not a word about stealing. And my brother himself, does not go quite so far as to say that it is no sin to *steal* slaves; he only contends that it is right *to hold* them after they are stolen. Thus, even his own text with his own interpretation yields no justification to American slavery, without grossly perverting his own meaning of it.

But I now proceed to my brother's entrenchments—to his main grand proposition: *Did God permit the Jews to hold slaves?* I deny it. And if he fails here, his whole argument fails; for it all depends on God's permission to the Jews to hold slaves.

This whole question turns on the *status*, the civil and social condition of the Hebrew "*bondmen*" named in his text. Were they slaves or not? I shall not here stop to go into Hebrew criticism with my brother. It is easily shown, taking a common Hebrew Bible and Gesenius's Lexicon, that the phrase, (*Lev.* xxv, 46.) "*they shall be your bond-men forever*," does not mean, that each man of them should be a slave during his life; but, "they," *i. e.*, that sort of people, "shall be your bondmen forever"—that is, that sort of people shall always supply your bond-servants. Thus it is in the Hebrew—"*Forever of them shall ye serve yourselves.*" 'You shall always get that sort of servants from that sort of people.' The Hebrew word, translated "buy," meaning, "*get*," "*obtain*," "*procure*," "*buy*." I shall not, however, stop, to translate Hebrew, or read commentators; but shall inquire directly, *into what state were those servants, thus procured of the heathen, brought*, WHEN THEY CAME AMONG THE JEWS?

And, in the first place, they were brought into a country, and among a people, who possessed, like Ohio, a free constitution. They were brought from slave States into what I shall show was a free State: it was as if the people of Ohio were allowed to procure servants from the people of Kentucky, and when thus procured, they were free, after paying their redemption-money, by serving you six years. The soil of Ohio has never been legally defiled by slavery. If a slave is brought here by his master's consent, he is, from that moment, a free man—though that unhappy clause respecting fugitives from service still exists—a provision perfectly anomalous in such a government as ours; and though certain odious and unconstitutional State statutes have been enacted to carry it out.

If a Hebrew bought a bond-servant from the heathen, and brought him into the Jews' land, and if he was not kept in slavery there; their taking slave-men into a free land is not, cannot be, any justification for taking *free* men into a *slave* land. By the Jewish constitution, the status into which the servant was brought, was nothing like the status into which the African slave is brought, when introduced into our country. The pith and point of the whole question turns on what was this *status?* It is of no use, in this question, to peddle commentaries, and criticise words and marshal and march such witnesses as mere verbal critics, who are such thorough-paced slaves to authority, whose ideas have been baked so stiff by half a century spent in their study, that they can hardly go to bed without the concurrence of a committee. [A laugh.] But, for the settlement of this question, we must go to the history of the times, and consider the *facts* connected with the whole case, and draw just conclusions from known principles and admitted facts. It is wholly a practical question. The testimony of mere verbal commentators, and lexicographers, and grammarians ought not to decide in a question like this. Men of mere learning, for the most part, are timid drudges, useful and indispensable in their place, but they should not be brought to decide questions of this kind. They cannot be expected to study them profoundly as broad practical questions affecting the human race should be studied. It is not in their profession. They are commentators upon the language of scripture, and they are obliged to consider every question that can arise relating to the interests of mankind, in all time and in all eternity; and to consider perfectly an infinite range of topics, they must have a mind like God's. It would be a miracle, if they could enter into a thorough practical consideration of every subject which they are obliged, as commentators, to write about. They are men who, like almanac-makers, take the tables which have been prepared by other men, and adopt them as authority in their own works. It is no reproach to them to say so. They would not feel it such. And for my brother to stand here quoting them as absolute authority, upon the great moral and practical question of slavery, is, in my view, "*operose agere nihil.*"

The whole question turns on the single question what was the *status* of these Hebrew bond-servants? And I shall show you that, whatever it was, it was not slavery. My first argument, and one which I beg you to weigh with great attention, is this. *If they were slaves, the translators* of our Bible *would have called them so.* They have never in one instance, translated the Hebrew word "*ebedh?*" (which my brother pronounces ebed, though he says, in his pamphlet, that abolitionists have little learning, and perhaps, I have no right, and ought not to criticise him) by the English word *slaves.* Our version of the Bible was issued by royal authority, in the year of our Lord, 1607; the year of the first settlement of the United States, at Jamestown, Virginia: in an age of Biblical study, and by forty-seven men learned, not only in books, but in affairs. Now in only two places in the Old and New Testament, have the translators used the word slaves. One is Jeremiah, ii, 14, in which instance it is put in Italics, showing there is no corresponding word for it in the Hebrew. And the other is Revelation, xviii, 13, (where the original Greek is not "*Doulos*" but "*Somaton*" the genitive plural of "*Soma*"—"a human body.") Where "slaves and *souls of men*" are spoken of as the traffic of the mother of harlots.

[*Time expired.*

[MR. RICE'S TWELFTH SPEECH.]

Gentlemen Moderators, and Fellow Citizens:

I perceive that my friend is determined to occupy my time as far as possible in correcting his statements. He first misrepresents even my pronunciation of a Hebrew word, and then sneers at my mispronunciation!

The gentleman complains of my remark concerning the state of his church. I should not have said a word concerning it, had he not told us, that the churches in the slave-holding States were withering under the influence of slavery: my reply was designed to prove by facts that his representation is not correct, but that, on the contrary, there are multitudes of churches at the South and West more flourishing than his. It was a fair reply, because those churches are involved in the sin, (if it be in itself a sin,) of slave-holding, and his church is under the influence of the purest abolitionism. The Second Presbyterian church in St. Louis, for example, which was organized in 1836, as a small colony, has grown in the space of seven years to the number of about 450 members; and in the mean time, has sent out one or two colonies to organize new churches. Thus it is proved by facts, the best kind of evidence, that slave-holding is not so heinous a sin as to wither the piety of the churches, and provoke God to withhold his spirit and blessing.

My brother says he would not have invited the present discussion, but for my lectures recently delivered in this city; but he took care not to tell you, that those lectures were delivered in consequence of the violent attacks made upon report of the last General Assembly by the *Watchman of the Valley*, and the Morning Herald, abolitionist papers of this city. The attack began on the part of the abolitionists themselves; yet now he would represent himself in this debate, as acting only on the defensive!

Mr. B. attempts to escape from the contradiction in which he involved himself, by saying, that a *part* of my doctrine is quite acceptable to pro-slavery men in the South. This fact, however, is a poor argument to prove it false; for he will admit, that many parts of even the Bible itself, are acceptable to ungodly men. What thief or drunkard objects to the declaration that "God is love?" or to the truth, that God forgives "iniquity, transgression and sin?" But shall we reject the scriptures because they contain truths which even the most ungodly men do not object to? The gentleman would condemn my views on the subject of slavery, because, as he affirms, southern slave-holders are pleased with a part of them. Then must he not for the same reason, condemn the gospel itself?

The gentleman says, he did not object to an appeal to the Greek and Hebrew scriptures to settle this controversy; but he said, that certain men go back to the dark, despotic ages to support slavery. But the audience have not forgotten, that he represented those who insist on going to the original languages, as bats that flutter about the tops of high towers, and as rats that retreat into dark cellars. They remember, too, how he sneered at Dr. Junkin for pursuing this very course, and told us that he "*Junkinized*" the people who heard him, with his Greek and Hebrew, till they had no sense left!

[Mr. BLANCHARD explained—I said that he *Junkinized* them, till they had not two substantial ideas left in their heads on the subject he was discussing!]

The gentleman, then, from his own account of the matter, said, the audience had not two ideas on the subject of slavery, because Dr. Junkin appealed, in his discussion of it, to the Greek and Hebrew; and yet he now admits the propriety of doing the very same thing!

He quoted Dr. Adam Clarke's opinion of slavery "*for spice.*" But all the spice was created by his own mistake: it would have been more poignant, and would have had a better relish, had it been a reply to what I had said. It is true that Dr. Clarke did denounce slavery as my brother says; yet as a commentator, he was compelled by the force of truth to give the same explanation of slave-holding among the Jews, which I have given; and his testimony is the more important from the fact that he was a most decided anti-slavery man. He was one of the men who go back into the dark and despotic ages of antiquity, and though he sought nothing there to justify slavery, he found the same proof with me that it was permitted by God himself. The opinion of such a man greatly strengthens my argument.

My friend says, that the " pro-slavery men," (as he calls those who differ from the abolitionists) do not reason from general principles, but run to isolated texts of the Bible. Now this audience knows better; for they have listened attentively to a long argument I offered from the *golden rule* —an argument to which, as yet, he has attempted no reply. My brother forgets. We do go to general principles, as well as to Bible texts. And Dr. Cunningham, to whom I have so often referred, does the same. For example:

" A man may be placed in such a condition as that the only act of humanity he can discharge, is just to buy a man, and make him his slave. He acquires a legal right to him, and may do injury according to the law ; but this does not follow. * * * A minister who lived in a slave State made it his business not to acquire property in slaves, but to hire them. One woman he hired. Her owner's circumstances became embarrassed. This woman came to her master not her owner, and told him, she had reason to think she would be sold, and besought him to buy her. He replied, that he did not wish to buy slaves. The woman, who was a religious person took it so much to heart that she could not do her work, nor take any meat, lying about her kitchen, crying and howling, till at last he was obliged to borrow money and buy the woman, as the only way in which he could really perform an act of humanity towards her. * * * It is utter folly and sheer madness to be denouncing every man, simply because he stands in the relation of a master to a slave, as a man-stealer ; &c. * * * What has been the great source of all the evil, is, that the abolitionists, *finding they could not answer the scriptural argument*, have made it their busi-

ness just to slander and calumniate the American churches."
This is the writer who my brother says, agrees with him.
He makes his appeal to general principles of benevolence,
to justify a man's purchasing a slave to better his condition.
This case I have presented again and again, but I cannot
induce my friend to touch it.

The gentleman affects great contempt for German critics,
men, as he informs us, of timid and narrow minds, who
" can hardly get to bed without a committee ;" and he ridi-
cules verbal criticism as a means of arriving at the truth.   I
had really supposed, that words were *signs of ideas ;* and
that the only method of getting the ideas of an author, was
by understanding his *words.* Will the gentleman be good
enough to inform us, how we can get at the *ideas* presented in
the Bible, except by inquiring into the meaning of the *words*
used ?   I did quote one, and only one, German lexicographer, viz : Gesenius, whose reputation as a learned man and
a standard authority, is too well established to be affected by
the ridicule of Mr. Blanchard.   He only exposes himself
by affecting to laugh at such men.   But since he has so little respect for the authorities I have quoted, *I challenge him
once more to produce one respectable commentator or critic
who gives to the scriptures to which I have referred, a different interpretation from that which I have given.*   He has
studied and discussed this subject for years past ; and therefore he is just the man to produce such authorities, if they
exist.

I will now pay my respects to his answer to my arguments, so far as he has attempted to answer them. He says,
in the first place, admitting the bondmen of the Jews to
have been slaves, this fact does not authorize *American slavery.*   We are not discussing the question, whether American
slavery is right.   The question proposed by the friends of
the gentleman, relates simply to the morality of the relation
between master and slave.   Let us settle the *principle,* and
we can then *apply* it. But he attempts to escape the difficulty
in which he is involved by the clear declarations of the Bible

by bringing forward a particular kind of slavery, of which the question before us, says nothing.

But why would not the fact, that the Jews were permitted to hold slaves, justify others in doing the same? Because, as Mr. B. says—those whom the Jews were permitted to purchase, were under the curse of God. Admit this statement to be strictly true; will he maintain, that the Jews were at liberty to form a relation in itself sinful, because the person sustaining the relation of slaves, were under the curse of God? If so, he goes very far toward fully justifying American slavery; for Canaan, from whom the Africans descended, was not only cursed of God, but expressly doomed, to be "servant of servants." Does this fact justify men in making slaves of the Africans? If so, surely the question must be given up. If not, how can the fact that the Canaanites were cursed, justify the Jews in holding them as slaves? To say in one breath, that slave-holding is in itself sinful, and consequently sinful under all circumstances; and in the next, that in cases where nations are under the curse of God, men may be justified in reducing them to slavery, is to be chargeable with a flat contradiction.

The gentleman's second answer is, that God may permit that which is in itself sinful, and that he did so in granting to the Jews permission to divorce their wives, "because of the hardness of their hearts." I answer, God did not give such permission for the sake of hard-hearted men, but for the sake of their wives, whom their wickedness lead them to treat cruelly. The husband might greatly sin in making a divorce desired; but it was not in itself wrong that the oppressed wife should be released from her obligations to a cruel husband. The doctrine, that God may give men permission to do that which is in itself sinful, appears to me near of kin to blasphemy. I find nothing in the Bible to countenance such an idea; nor have I ever before heard it advanced.

But he tells us that God permitted slavery in the sense of not hindering it. But was that my argument? Did I. contend that God only permitted the Jews to form the relation of master and slave by not hindering it? I said, *and I proved*, that He gave *express permission* to form the relation; and therefore it could not be sinful. Has he replied to this argument, and proved that such permission was not given? He has not, and he cannot. The argument, therefore, remains unanswered.

But if, as the gentlemen contends, God may permit a relation in itself sinful, why cannot abolitionists do the same? Are they holier than God? Do they feel themselves in conscience bound to oppose and denounce what He permitted, and to purify the church from that which He permitted to remain in it?

But the brother says that buying slaves is *slave trading*, which "Dr. Rice" himself denounces; and if God permitted it, he sanctioned the *slave trade!* Not at all: to buy a slave, with a view to improve his condition, is not slave trading. *Speculating in slaves*, for the sake of gain, is slave trading. Can the brother's discriminating mind discover no difference between them? The difference is as obvious as between light and darkness. Those purchased by the Jews, as I said, were generally already in slavery— in cruel bondage; and God, as I suppose, permitted the Jews to buy them in order that their condition might be mitigated, and that they might come to the knowledge of the true religion.

Again, he says, my argument fails, because the Africans were all originally stolen; and, if we buy them, we are guilty of the sin of man-stealing. I reply, that if this principle is sound, there is not a man in Ohio who can, honestly and innocently, hold the farm he owns: for the land was, most of it, originally taken by force or fraud from the Indians. Besides, did not the heathen masters of whom the Israelites were permitted to buy, obtain their slaves by war and violence? And if so, where is the difference between their case and that of our negroes? Abolitionists labor hard when they get near the Bible. Again, if the relation be in itself wrong, the manner of forming it can never make it right. And, by admitting that the sinfulness of slave-holding depends upon the manner of our getting slaves, the gentleman virtually gives up the question in dispute, and admits that the relation is not wrong in itself, but is only made wrong by circumstances.

But the brother reminds us that God never said, the Israelites might *steal* slaves. That again, is not the question we are debating. Who, in his senses, would debate it? Every body knows that to buy, is to obtain something, by giving a consideration for it. Is this stealing?

But he tells us, the Jews bought their wives. This argument has been anticipated and answered. When a man bought a woman for a *wife*, she became his wife; but when he bought a man or woman for a *servant*, such persons became his servants. What, then, has the fact that men sometimes purchased *wives*, to do with the subject before us?

Again, Mr. B. seeks to evade the argument by informing us, that the Hebrew word translated "*buy*," sometimes signifies simply, to acquire, no matter by what means. I admit it; but unfortunately for his reply, the bondmen of Jews, we are distinctly informed, were bought "*with money.*" Now I suppose, to get, to obtain a thing "with money," is to buy it; and when it is bought, it is mine for the purposes for which it is bought.

The gentleman says, if a man buy a slave *for the purpose of liberating* him, he commits no sin. The abolitionists, I believe, show very little disposition to liberate slaves in this way. But did God give the Jews permission to buy slaves, on condition that they should liberate them? He passed a law that if a man smote out his servant's tooth or his eye, he should let him go free for the sake of his tooth or his eye. Would God have passed a law requiring a servant to be liberated on a certain condition, if he were already free? But God said of the servant, *he is his master's money*. Would this be true, if he had only redeemed him from slavery, and liberated him? Why, the gentleman's doctrine makes the Bible speak contradictions and nonsense. It represents God as commanding a man under certain circumstances to *liber-ate a free man!* Such are the arguments by which the gentleman expects to persuade Kentuckians to abandon the man who denies that slave-holding is in itself sinful!

But the argument which he seems to think conclusive on this subject, is this: If the word *eved* meant *slave*, the transla-tors of our English Bible would have so rendered it. This is indeed a miserable evasion. They translated it *servant* and *bond-servant*. Does not Mr. B. know, that the Latin word *servus*, from which the English word *servant* is derived, sig-nifies *slave*, and that the word servant, when our translation was made, had its literal and proper meaning. But if the word *servant* does not mean *slave*, will he tell us the mean-ing of *bond-servant*, by which the word *eved* is translated? Does it not mean *slave?*

His last argument is blown to the winds; and I now cheerfully leave the audience to decide, whether his replies to my arguments from the Bible, are of any force. Have they overthrown one position I have taken?

I will now read another extract from Dr. Cunningham's letter. He says—" In three of the leading slave States, con-taining one-fourth of the whole slave population of the Union, there are only eight settled Presbyterian ministers; and the churches in the country are very much in the same position as the missionaries we send to the West Indies, *and whom we strictly enjoin not to open their mouths on slavery. This, in* 1834, *we regarded as the right way of dealing with that question, in certain circumstances; and the case is similar in America. Notwithstanding, there have some people, in ten years, gone into the opposite extreme of re-fusing to hold communion with churches that practically do what we expressly enjoined our missionaries to do.* This is clear proof that there is gross ignorance, or great prejudice. The churches in the slave States must take their choice, be-tween virtually letting this matter alone, or taking it up, and being expelled."

The gentleman has been anxious to make the impression,

that the Church of Scotland had adopted, substantially, abolition principles. But Dr. Cunningham informs us, that, in 1834, she forbade her missionaries to the West Indies to open their mouths on this subject; and thus he exposes the inconsistency of the abolitionists who urged that church to hold no fellowship with ours, unless she would exclude all slaveholders from her communion.

I am now done with that part of my argument, which is derived from the Old Testament. I am also prepared to hear the gentleman's hour-and-a-half argument, with which he has so repeatedly threatened me; and it is my purpose fairly to meet and refute it. Having done this, I purpose to inquire into the teachings of the New Testament; and I will not only prove from the New Testament, that slave-holding is not in itself sinful, but that every respectable critic and commentator sustains fully my interpretation of the passages in which the subject of slave-holding is brought to view. Mr. Blanchard, I am aware, holds commentators and critics in great contempt; but perhaps this intelligent audience do not view them in the same light. I expect to prove, that the primitive churches took the same view of slavery, and pursued the same course of conduct in regard to it, that we do. Finally, I expect to prove, that the views we take, are those which have abolished slavery wherever it has been peaceably abolished. [*Time expired.*

Monday Afternoon, 2 o'clock.

[MR. BLANCHARD'S THIRTEENTH SPEECH.]

Gentlemen Moderators, and Gentlemen and Ladies, Fellow-Citizens:

While the house is getting still, and to close up what of this debate precedes my Old Testament argument; I will notice some of those points which my brother has brought forward in this discussion, and to which he seems to attach importance. I have written down for the sake of condensing, brief replies on several points which I will read :—not because I deem the points important, but that I may not seem to leave anything without attempting a candid and clear answer. The following are all the points hitherto unanswered that I can recollect, which I have considered deserving of notice; excepting some personalities which it is not worth while to reply to.

1. He asks : " When an elder of the church was implored to buy a slave to save him from being sold from his family ; did the elder sin in buying that slave ?"

Answer. If he bought him to free him ; No—that is redemption. If he kept him as his slave ; Yes : he did sin : because he has no right to keep slaves or concubines in order to keep them from being abused. Slavery and concubinage being unscriptural relations. 2. He sinned because he still held the slave under all the horrid liabilities of slavery. He might die the hour after he bought him, and the slave is sold from his family for a division among merciless heirs ; or he might become a bankrupt, and the slave is sold by creditors. Thus to do an uncertain good to one suffering slave, he commits the sin of sanctioning the whole slave system by himself holding slaves. He thus does a general evil that a particular good may come. Being a pious man, his example leads a thousand young men, who had scruples, to become slave-holders. They go into slavery, fall before its temptations, and sink to endless ruin, holding on to this one pious man's skirts. If he bought the slave to keep him as his property he certainly sinned.

2d Case, " A pious elder asked his synod what he should do with some 70 slaves or more, who were a bill of cost to him, altogether earning less than they consumed ?"

Answer. Free them by all means, or, in a little while, they will run him so in debt that the sheriff will sell them in lots or individually, to satisfy creditors, and suit purchasers. Surely 70 persons earning less than they cost must soon eat up his estate. If he can remove to a free State, do so. If this is not convenient, let him do as an infidel sheriff in Virginia did—call his slaves into the house—tell them solemnly they are free—that he will pay them fair wages for fair work—and that they must maintain their own wives, children and old people ; and he will find they will earn more for "cash" than for " lash." Then let him take the " *True American*," and begin to persuade his neighbors to do likewise.

3. When urged with the fact that slave-holders have no title to their slaves but that which they bought of kidnappers and traders ; and therefore in justice do not own them. He says ; that argument would destroy our title to lands which were by force or fraud wrested from the Indians.

Answer. Law and justice give stolen property to the true owner, when he can be found. But if no owner is found, occupancy and possession give title. If an Indian can show as good a title to a piece of land as a slave can to his head, hands, feet, and person, which God gave to *him*, and not to another man, let that Indian have the land, by all means. If he can show an equitable right to it, though less strong, than the slave's right to himself, still let him have it. But it is a capital error, in Mr. Rice, to bring the title acquired to the land of dead Indians, whose heirs are unknown, to justify the holding of living stolen men, who are always present to claim themselves ; and who do claim themselves every time they say, in human speech, " *my head*," " *my hands*," " *my body*," &c.; thus showing, that, under God, whose mark and image are upon him, the man belongs to himself. There was a law in England, which provided that the king's goods should be marked with the figure of an arrow—and if goods having this mark were found in the possession of a man, without the king's authority, he was, by that single mark, convicted of having stolen the king's goods, and punished accordingly. Every human being has God's mark upon him, and belongs to God first, and, under God, to himself. The mark of the King of Kings is his own image, and the man who has in his possession a human being, is, by the mark of God upon him,

convicted of robbing the Almighty—that he may oppress
his fellow man.

4. My opponent still reasons about "Hagar," as though
she was not only the bondwoman, or *bound-woman* of Abraham, but the actual slave or property of Abraham.

Answer. If Hagar was Abraham's property, and if she
was sent back by the angel as Abraham's slave, then Dr.
Rice is bound, by every principle of justice, and by this
angel's example, to help to take and send back runaway
slaves to their owners. But he has told us that he has seen
slaves running away, but never would do any thing to send
them back—thus showing, that he, in heart, does not believe
in his own argument—that he knows that Hagar was not
a slave, and that Kentucky slaves are not justly the property
of their masters. For if they are the just property of their
masters, then Dr. Rice is wicked to see them running off,
without trying to send them back. For, "If thou seest
thine enemy's ox, or his ass, going astray, thou shalt surely
bring it back to him again." *Exod.* xxiii, 40. He draws a
distinction, however, between *not preventing* the escape of
a slave, and aiding him to escape—condemning abolitionists
for the latter, while he practices the former. But the distance between "*not preventing*," and *actually aiding*, escaping slaves is so short, that I commend my brother to the
careful watching of the southern slave-holders, lest, in a little while, he be found actually helping slaves to run away.
[A laugh.]

5. Again. A Massachusetts man went to South Carolina
to live with certain slaves who fell to him, as the best plan
he could devise to do them (the slaves) good. Was he a
sinner?

Answer. If he went there, and honestly told the negroes
they were free, and avoided the appearance of evil, by letting his neighbors know that he was no slave-holder, but
had simply come to help the negroes out of difficulty, he was
no sinner ; but if not—if he simply set down among them
as a slave-holder—he was a gross sinner. For he left a

free State, where he and his family were surrounded by the influences of freedom, for a slave land, and a practice of slavery and its corrupting influences. He made himself and family props to support the rotting fabric of slavery, to the injury of millions, with the precarious and uncertain hope of benefitting a few slaves.

6. He says Constantine made a law forbidding to separate husband and wife, and yet slavery still existed. He argues thence that separating husband and wife is not an ingredient part of slavery.

Answer. In forbidding the separation of families, Constantine was destroying slavery. He was driving his legislative axe into the very meat and bones of slavery. He was a wise legislator and knew what he was doing. He knew that a repeal of the family state was of the essence of slavery; and therefore began his work of destroying slavery by stopping family separation. If Constantine had added legal personality and wages, his law would have been an immediate abolition law. As it was it stabbed slavery to the heart.

"Then," replies he, "Kentucky Presbyterians do not hold slaves in full, for they do not separate families, and the law of the church forbids it."

Answer. Kentucky Presbyterians do hold slaves in full, for they hold them by a tenure which denies marriage and parentage to them, which Constantine did not. They hold them in a state of virtual and real separation, hourly ready for actual separation; and their slaves are constantly separated by sheriffs for debts and by administrators for a division, which division the heirs have a right to order, and Presbyterians, when dead, cannot prevent. Witness the slave coffles or gangs annually driven from the upper slave States to the lower, and who pass by our city. They used to *land* here, but blessed be God, such is the state of feeling now, that they do this seldom or no more. The law of the church against it is but an inoperative conscience-plaster. Kentucky Presbyterians holding slaves, are *slave-holders.*

7. Again, he says. "True moral principles strike every honest mind, as true, and, by their own force, command assent." And he asks, "if the doctrine be true that slave-holding is sin, why does it not so strike every mind?"

Answer. It does strike every mind when themselves or their families are concerned. No sane man is willing that himself and posterity, in all time, should be slaves. Do unto others as you would have them do unto you. Let the slave law strike one of Dr. Rice's children, and the wickedness of it would certainly strike him.

8. He told you I was willing to "keep the slaves from voting, after they are emancipated." What I said upon that point was, that I leave their political rights to political men, to be determined by exact political justice. Abolition has done with them when they are free as unnaturalized foreigners, who are free, though they cannot vote.

Tell an Irishman, before he is entitled to vote, that he is a slave, and my word for it, Patrick will show that his fist is free, at least. [A laugh.]

If he made any other points which my present arguments do not answer, I am willing he should have all the benefit of their going unanswered, and that they may have, with you whatever weight they deserve. I hope now, that my brother will not continue to complain of me, as if I were unwilling to answer him to the best of my ability. Of course, it is not to be expected that I would set my ability in competition with so grave and learned a Doctor of Divinity, but I mean not to be outdone by him in candor, and an honest desire to vindicate the truth.

I must now be excused from noticing further his line of argument, and be permitted to go straight through with my own. Yet, if my brother is very anxious that I should answer any questions I may possibly turn aside for a few minutes, to do so. I will notice briefly his "golden rule" argument, and then consider the Old Testament bond service. This argument of Dr. Rice may be found in his printed pamphlet, pages 39, and 41. He says of Christ's command requiring us to do to others as we would they should do to us ;—" *Evidently it requires us to treat others, as we would reasonably expect and desire them to treat us,* IF WE WERE IN THEIR SITUATION." (*Lect.* p. 39.)

That is, the "golden rule" only requires the slave-holder to treat his slave as he might reasonably expect to be treated *if he were in that slave's condition.* The fact that the slave is a slave, is taken for granted to be right, so far as the owner is concerned. Then he says on page 41. That the golden rule requires a man to become a slave-holder, who buys a slave to keep him from suffering a worse fate. " *The truth is in such cases* THE GOLDEN RULE MAKES THE CHRISTIAN THE OWNER OF A SLAVE." (*Lect.* p. 41.,

I think I shall be able to show you that this exposition, which deserves to be called the " *slave-holder's golden rule,*" in the first place, proceeds upon a plain denial of God's golden rule. 2nd, That it contains a logical error. 3d, That it contains a gross immorality.

The reason on which the rules rests, which requires men to do to others as they would have others do to them, is, that *men are equal.* But this slave-holder's rule contradicts this fundamental truth of God's word, that " *God has made of one blood all the nations of men,*" and if of *one blood,* they are of equal blood. This exposition of Dr. Rice, assumes that there is one blood of the slave-holder ; another blood of the slave ; and they are of different conditions instead of being by nature on the same footing. It *assumes* the inequality of the human race to be right, *which is the very question in dispute.* It goes upon the supposition that one man is naturally a slave-holder, and another a slave. The question lies back of this. Abolitionists claim that injury is done in making a man a slave, or, in assuming towards a man the relation of his OWNER, and keeping him a slave. Dr. Rice *assumes* that men are by God's law divided into two classes, master and slave ; and says that the whole duty required of the master class, by the golden rule is, to treat slaves " *as we might reasonably expect to be treated, if we were slaves !*

Suppose that my father, caught a boy and put him in a dungeon, and gave me the key. I put the key in my pocket and keep the boy in the dungeon. My father in this case is the kidnapper and I am the slave-holder. Dr. Rice, we will say, is defining my duty under his golden rule towards that imprisoned boy. Doctor, I ask, "what, say you, is my duty to the boy imprisoned by my father?" He replies;—"*Do unto others as you would have others do unto you if you were in their situation.*" "Well, but, Doctor, how do you understand that rule? Shall I let him out?" "By no means" says he;—"All you are required to do, is to keep him there for life, and treat him just as kindly as *you might reasonably expect to be treated if you were in his place.* That is, as men who are shut up in dungeons may reasonably expect to be treated by those who keep them there."

Is there a man on earth capable of knowing right and wrong who would not instantly feel that such an exposition of the golden rule carries a monstrous fraud in it, if applied to himself. It denies that "God has made of one blood (and equal because one) all nations of men." Dr. Rice's religion *is the religion of a privileged class.* And it is so with every religion which is based on radical error. Puseyism, and Popery, &c., withhold from the common mass in favor of their priesthood, rights which God has given alike to all men. Dr. Rice allows the slave-holders to hold the slaves, before he begins to apply the golden rule to them; and his exposition, like Puseyism, is based upon a denial of the law of human equality. It takes for granted that God has made it the destiny of one portion of his creatures to be slaves and another portion masters, and that masters fulfil their duty to the slaves by treating them according to that destiny. And this monstrous perversion of this holy and beautiful law of Christ, is preached in nearly the same words by professed ministers of the gospel, throughout the South, perverting slaveholders' consciences, sinking the rights of the slaves—and dimming and diminishing the light of justice in the word of God.

2. In the second place, I observe, that my friend's exposi-

tion contains a logical error. It is a clear *petitio principii* —a begging of the question in debate.

He *assumes* there is nothing against the golden rule, in keeping men in a state of slavery. But that is the very thing abolitionists deny, and the very question we are here to debate. And there is no other way for Dr. Rice to get his vindication of slavery over the golden rule, but to take the question, whether slave-holding is according to it, for granted; and apply the rule to master and slave as to men in different situations, *equally innocent.*

3. But there is a worse than logical error in this slave-holder's golden rule, manufactured by Dr. Rice. It contains a gross immorality.

The original precept, as it stands in the New Testament, is the most precious of all the practical rules which our Saviour taught, and is justly called "golden," from the most precious of metals. Yet, in Dr. Rice's hands, *it sanctions an immorality, by giving to the slave-holder the benefit of his own, and his father's wrong.* My father wickedly locks a man up in a dungeon, and I keep him there. His exposition allows me to keep him in that " situation," and only requires me to treat him as I might reasonably expect an indifferent man to treat me, who should find me in a dungeon through no fault of his own, without his connivance, and against his consent. He thus gives me the benefit of my father's wrong. Or to drop the figure: Dr. Rice allows the present slave-holders, whose ancestors wickedly enslaved the present slaves, to adopt the sin of their fathers—to stand in it—to take the benefit of it, and yet stand on a moral equality with their slaves; applying the golden rule to them both as equally right in the eye of God's law.

Now it is a principle, not only of common justice, but of the common law, that "no man shall take the benefit of his own wrong." If, for instance, you pull down the fence, and let your neighbor's cattle upon your own crops, in order to get damages; the law gives you no damages, because your crime is a part of the case, and you shall not have the benefit of your own wrong. But my brother gives the slave-holder the benefit of his own wrong in keeping the man in slavery, and of the wrong act by which the kidnapper first placed him there: thus sanctioning, by Christianity, and the voice of a minister of Christ, a principle which is cast out of the court-house, as polluting the fountains of justice, and perverting and destroying men's rights. Thus he places Christianity in a position to be despised and trampled beneath the hoofs of the State, as having a lower standard of rectitude, than that by which civil judges, advocates, and juries are bound, in trying the most paltry interests and questions of right.

Contrast now, Dr. Rice's vindication of the present slave-holders, on the ground that they did not make men slaves, but only kept those in slavery who were enslaved by their fathers; with the ground which Christ took, in a like case, against those who condemned their fathers for killing the prophets; yet kept up the spirit of their fathers' crime, by persecuting the prophets of their own day, saying:—" *If we had lived in the days of our fathers we would not have been partakers with them in the blood of the prophets:*" precisely as Dr. Rice, and his friends, the slave-holders, pretend to condemn the enslaving of freemen, while they agree in justifying the continuance of the crime upon the persons and descendants of the enslaved. What did the Saviour do, in adjusting the balance-sheet of sin with those Pharisees? Did he give them the slave-holders' exposition of the golden rule, which blinks the sin of both sire and son? Did he tell them that "they found the prophets a persecuted, hated, despised race; and they fulfilled the law of love by treating them as well as a persecuted race can reasonably expect to be treated? No: never. Instead of justifying the continuers of persecution who condemned its beginners, as Dr. Rice justifies the continuers of slavery who condemn the first enslavers: *he took the sins of all the former generations, and laid them over upon the heads of the present.* Christ took precisely the opposite ground to Dr.

Rice. Instead of giving that generation the benefit of the fathers' wrong, and their own, He laid upon it the woes of both:—"Fill ye up then the measure of your fathers. That upon you may come all the righteous blood shed upon the earth from the blood of righteous Abel unto the blood of Zacharias, son of Barachias, whom ye slew between the temple and 'the altar." " *Verily, I say unto you all these things shall come upon this generation.*" Such is Dr. Rice's golden rule, and such its contrast with the teachings of Christ.

I now speak directly and distinctly to the question:— *What was this ancient Hebrew bond-service upon which, as precedent,* the justification of modern slavery is built. The discussion which we now enter upon may seem dry to some, but this subject, at least, is not dry in itself; and I earnestly commend it to your consciences for a patient hearing, as in the sight of God.

The ground which they take respecting the Old Testament bond-service is succinctly this:

1. " That God did expressly give permission to his people under the Old Dispensation to hold slaves."

2. " That he could not have done this if slave-holding had been sinful in itself."

3. " That therefore, American slave-holding is not in itself sinful, and those who would treat it as sinful by setting church discipline against it are in error."

Now it would seem obvious, at a glance, that this reasoning carries some fatal defect in it. God gave the Israelites " express permission" to borrow jewels from the Egyptians, expecting not to return them. Therefore, according to my brother's argument, it cannot be sinful in itself to borrow without intending to return.

So God gave permission to buy free laborers in Judea who had become poor : " If thy brother be waxen poor and be sold unto thee." *Levit.* xxv, 39. Therefore, according to my friend's reasoning, the Bible sanctions the buying of free laborers who have waxen poor in Ohio at this day.

How can he manifest such horror at taking a free man and reducing him to slavery ; (which he seems almost to make a merit of condemning ;) when if his doctrine be true that Jewish bond-servants were slaves, then God permitted this very thing—to reduce a freeman who had waxed poor to slavery?

But I object formally to the sum total of the ground which they take.

I object to their main proposition: "*That God did expressly give permission to his people under the Old Dispensation to hold slaves;*" That it is equivocal; and that it is not true. I object to their second proposition to wit: "That slave-holding cannot be sinful in itself because God once permitted it ;" as false, so far as derived from the first ; and also as not true in the absolute sense in which they use it. And I object to their practical inference in favor of American slavery, as drawn from two errors, and like its parents, itself erroneous. And I further object to their whole position as essentially pro-slavery—and as meaning nothing unless it means to vindicate oppression from the Word of God.

I have objected to their main proposition; "That God permitted slavery, as equivocal. It may mean that God permitted slavery with approbation ; or that He permitted it as He does murder, merely in the sense of *not hindering it.* Why not say, "justify" if he means it ; and certainly you justify, in court, the man whom you pronounce " not guilty." If he proves slave-holding to be not sinful in itself, does he not *justify* it? Why then say " permit?" Why not say at once, " *God did expressly justify slavery under the Old Dispensation?*" O, but that would not please the North. Well, then : why not say that God "*permitted slavery*" merely in the sense of " not hindering," as he does other crimes ; and this permission can give no possible sanction to Kentucky slavery? That, again, would not please the South. So the equivocal word " *permit*" is chosen, if not to please both North and South, at least, to displease neither.

The northern man takes up this Debate and reads from

Dr. Rice, " *that God expressly permitted slavery ;*" and he understands it to mean, some such permission as he gave to recorded evils—that is, in the sense of not hindering a qualified slavery for temporary purposes; while the southern man will think that the same words mean, that the Bible justifies slavery, out and out. I deeply disapprove of an equivocal expression, selected to hit the whole United States' population right between wind and water—a word which lies midway between right and wrong—a phrase lodged in the vacuum of betweenity, on no side of nothing.

I have heard that there is a little prairie animal, of the gopher species, which has a northern and a southern end to his hole, so that in sultry and hot weather, when it is desirable to "raise the wind," if it blows north, he opens the south end of his burrow; and when south, the north end; and, besides the advantage of shifting his position to suit the wind, such an arrangement, in case of pursuit, is marvelously convenient for the purpose of dodging responsibility. [A laugh.]

My friend's position seems to me to have a northern and southern end, so that the occupant can have the advantage of standing in either, as it suits the exigencies of his case. With his southern brethren, "God permitted slave-holding," is to mean, that he permitted it as a worthy practice of worthy men; but at the north end, only that God permitted slave-holding, as he directed wars of extermination against the Canaanites, or some like event, which ended long ago, with its divine license.

I object, therefore, to this half-and-half phrase—" *God permitted slavery*"—that it is equivocal. When a southern man, like J. C. Postell, says, that the Bible justifies slavery, I understand him. Every body understands him. When an abolitionist says, that God condemns slave-holding, he is equally explicit. But when a man, somewhere between North and South, says, that " *God permitted slavery,*" he may mean, that He *permitted it as an evil ;* or he may mean, that He *permitted it approvingly, as what was fit to be done.*

Professor J. H. Thornwell, with his "*Slavery-no-evil*" doctrine, swallows this proposition of Dr. Rice, and finds it excellently palatable, that "*God expressly permitted his people to hold slaves;*" while the good pious northern lady who reads it, may wipe her spectacles and think—"Oh, well, God has permitted strange things, in old times; Dr. Rice does not go so far out of the way, after all."

That you may see what tone of sentiment, and what sort of principles prevail at the extreme South, and which meet and harmonize with northern opinion, in the sentiments of Dr. Rice, I will read from a southern religious paper, "*The Alabama Baptist,*" the editor of which, replying to a Vermont paper, says:—

"The editor of the Vermont Observer honors us with the sentiment, that 'we are in a fair way to become as rabid in support of slavery as the Index of Georgia.' We are much obliged to him for placing us in such good company. *We came into this station* with the determination that no one should surpass us in the ardor of our devotion to, *and the boldness of our defence of, southern institutions,* and we think we have fulfilled that determination. He says that we endorse the sentiment of George McDuffie—'*slavery is the best possible relation between the employer and the laborer,*' and '*we repudiate that old-fashioned doctrine, that all* MEN *are born equal.*' THIS IS EXACTLY OUR POSITION: and we will state also that our motto is, DEATH to abolitionism, and confusion to the enemies of the South."

This main proposition of Dr. Rice will be palatable to that man, while at the same time the good old mother, in his church here, will not dream that her beloved pastor is defending slavery.

But I further object to their equivocal main position, that "*God expressly permitted his people to hold slaves under the Old Dispensation,*" THAT IT IS NOT TRUE.

I am fully aware that we are now in the Thermopylæ of this discussion, and that the liberties not of Greece, but of mankind are bound up, not (I am thankful) in the ability with which it is conducted, but in the principles of which it takes hold.

There are two chief sources of argument appealed to by Dr. Rice in support of his main position *that God did expressly permit slavery to the Jews.* The first is *the authority of Divines and Commentators.* The second is scripture itself. As to the first, he has asked, repeatedly, during this debate, as if he thought it conclusive of the whole subject, " Why have learned and godly men *thought* that God permitted slavery in the Old Dispensation if it be not true ? Meaning, it would seem, that it must be true if good and wise men think so. Whereas the whole difficulty is solved by simply supposing that his good and wise men are in a mistake. There are several reasons why those wise and godly men have thought so. One is that Dr. Paley's definition of slavery has been adopted, even by anti-slavery men, instead of a true definition—and hundreds of speculative minds have been misled by his definition instead of looking at the thing as it actually exists. Paley defines slavery to be merely, " *an obligation to labor without contract or consent.*" *That is, mere compulsory labor.* And *such labor* is found in the Bible, and in every family, and prison, and press-gang, and poor-house. But children, and paupers, and prisoners, though compelled to labor are not slaves ; for they have rights. Slaves have none. But actual, veritable slavery ; viz: "men made property :"—bereft of self-ownership, marriage, property, liberty, for no crime ; this is not in the Bible. This ownership of the blood and bones of human beings is not there.

2. Another reason why some classes of commentators have thought that slavery was in the Bible, is, that their opinions and feelings on the subject were influenced by the slave-hold ing spirit of the age. They have seen the Bible through slave-holding spectacles ; and have interpreted Hebrew words by European and American practices. Successful commentators prove by their very success that they are more or less the exponents of the sentiments of the age in which they

wrote. If no body believed them, no body would buy them. And though able commentators may have moulded the public mind to their own or a few points, no mere human being can revolutionize the sentiments of his age throughout. I did not say that the German commentators were stupid men, but I said, that the ideas of some of them were baked stiff in the oven of German hermeneutics. And there is a race of literary drudges, who write in their books what they find in others. And one great source of error, with minds of a higher sort, on the subject of slavery, is, that they have interpreted Hebrew words by European and American practices. Take Matthew Henry for an instance of this. He was the pastor of a taxed, tolerated, and licenced church; and wrote his commentaries at a small town not twenty miles from Liverpool, while a hundred ships, engaged in the slave-trade, sailed from that single port.

Liverpool itself was built by the profits of this traffic: in allusion to which, Brooke, the comedian, when he appeared in their theatre, and, for some reason or other, was hissed; in the indignation of the moment, told them that "every brick of their town was laid in human blood." Matthew Henry wrote his commentaries near this town, in an age and country where the slave-trade was not deemed inconsistent with a Christian profession. But neither he, nor any other Bible commentator has taken up the subject of slavery as a topic for distinct and thorough investigation; but they have incorporated into their works the ideas current among good men at the time they wrote. It is no reproach that they have done so.

To understand thoroughly all the topics which come within his range, a commentator must have a mind infinite, like God's: for his profession calls him to write about all that is in the Bible, and hence, to treat of all the principles which belong both to time and eternity. If Henry's subject had been slavery, and he had written against it as John Wesley did, his book would have sold no farther than he could create a party to buy it.

The man who undertakes to settle great moral questions

by scraps from Biblical commentators and definitions of lexicographers, acts on precisely the same principles of investigation with the man who should undertake to master the
Constitution of the United States, by looking out the meaning
of every word in that instrument in Perry's Dictionary, instead of explaining the document by its own great principles,
and the history of its times, and the known facts which bear
upon the case to be examined.

Yet there are not wanting authorities for the contrary
interpretation of the scripture passages, in question, from
that given by my friend. Whether there are more for his
view, than against it, is more than I can tell. Authorities
upon the subject may be divided into two classes. First,
timid, and book-bound minds, such as commentators and
lexicographers are apt to be, who depend largely for what
they write, upon what others have written. These can generally be quoted in favor of slavery. Bartholomew Las
Casas, a pious Roman Catholic, who, I have no doubt—but
no matter whether he has gone to Heaven or not—[a laugh]
(not that I wish to doubt he is there, only that is nothing to
the point,)—his heart was so grieved to see the poor Indians
toiling and perishing in the Peruvian mines, that, observing
the patient, much-enduring habits of the negro, he is said
to have written an argument to show that it was the will of
God, that Africans should be enslaved, as the cursed progeny
of Ham. Other commentators have taken up their opinions
after him, or some vindicator of the slave trade, like the
story of the Welshman and the bridge; so that you may go
through a dozen of these " *authorities*," and you will, perhaps, read in all of them, but the opinions of one man from
whom they have all copied, taking his opinions upon trust,
and putting them into their books, to be in turn quoted as
authority by others, *verbatim et literatim*. Break the hold
of one of these authorities upon my brother's text, and they
all fall into the river with him. But there is another class of
authorities, viz : men marked for originality and independence,
thought and investigation. These writers are generally

clear on the subject of human rights.   Grotius, a name that all respect, as a scholar, a lawyer, and a divine, concerning whom, his biographer has said, that he was "*master of all that is worth knowing* in sacred or profane literature,"—a man whom lawyers quote as a jurisconsult of the highest authority, and whose work, "De veritate Chris. Relig.," is still commonly referred to by Divines.   Grotius says, " *Hominum fures, qui servos vel liberos abducunt,* RETINENT, *vendunt vel emunt.*"   That is, " *They are men-stealers, who bring off slaves or free men ; who retain, buy or sell them.*" So, according to this high authority, every man who buys, sells, or *retains* a slave, is *a man thief.* And the General Assembly of the Presbyterian church, for the space of twenty-two years, from 1794 to 1816, used an edition of their Confession of Faith, which contained this opinion of *Grotius,* in a note, explaining the meaning of the word "*men stealers,*" used by the apostle Paul, in I. Timothy i, 10.

John Wesley, whom our Methodist brethren delight to honor, a clear-thinking, independent and apostolic man, says, " *I strike at the root of this complicated villany.   I utterly deny all slave-holding to be consistent with any degree of natural justice.*"

In a letter written by John Wesley to Mr. Wilberforce, dated February 24th, 1791 ; supposed to be the last, or one of the last, he ever wrote ; he declares his opinion ; unless God had raised him (Wilberforce) up for the very purpose of destroying slavery, he would be worn down by the opposition of men and devils ; and he exhorts him to go on in his work until even " *American slavery, the* VILEST THAT EVER SAW THE SUN " shall be no more.

I will now quote some authorities from Presbyterians, the first of whom stands as high with his denomination as John Wesley does with Methodists.

PRESIDENT EDWARDS is a man who will be admitted to stand second to no other on questions of morals.   His father was the first American whom European divines would acknowledge to be a theologian.   They seemed scarcely to suppose there was such a thing as theology in America until he wrote his treatise on the Will, the Affections, etc. President Edwards, the younger, in a sermon preached in New Haven, Ct., in 1791, before a society of which Dr. Stiles, (then President of Yale College,) was president;—says " *It is as really wicked to rob a man of his liberty, as to rob him of his life, and much more wicked than to rob him of his property.*" "·He who holds a slave, continues to deprive him of that liberty which was taken from him on the coast of Africa, and if it was wrong to deprive him of it in the first instance, why not in the second?" (This is putting slave-holding on a level with man-stealing. We now go on with the quotation.)

" *The consequence is inevitable, that other things being the same, to hold a negro slave unless he have forfeited his liberty, is a greater sin in the sight of God than concubinage or fornication.*" And again, "*if we may judge of the future from the past, within fifty years from this time, it will be as disgraceful for a man to hold a negro slave, as to be guilty of common robbery or theft!*"

This was in 1791. Fifty-four years ago, and the prophecy was as true as the logic of the discourse was sound. And the day is at the door when it will be literally verified.

I will quote another authority. The "*Philadelphian,*" (newspaper) of June 23, 1834. The Editor (Mr. Engles?) who was clerk to the General Assembly, (Old School,) says in answer to the man who propounded certain questions to his paper;—

" *He who steals a man and makes him a slave, is one of the* WORST THIEVES, *and oppressors. He who* PURCHASES *a man thus enslaved is as great a criminal as the man-stealer*

So far the stated clerk of Dr. Rice's General Assembly. Let us next hear the Rev. Dr. Breckenridge, President of Washington College, Pennsylvania; who also belongs to the same church as my brother. He is a Kentuckian, and Kentuckians are not in the habit of stopping half way. He says; "*Out upon such folly! The man who cannot see that involuntary domestic slavery, as it exists among us, is founded upon the principle of taking by force that which is anothers,* HAS SIMPLY NO MORAL SENSE."

Gentlemen, and fellow-citizens: I know that reading is tiresome to an audience, and I shall spare you. Statesmen, jurists, divines, and eminent men of every class, of the Presbyterian, and other churches, might be adduced, and their sentiments quoted, to fill the time allotted to this debate. I have already quoted the learned and humane Clarkson, who holds that, "if Christianity is not a lie," slave-holding must be a "sin of the deepest dye." I might quote the celebrated law professor, MILLER, of Glasgow, who lays it down, that "it is impossible for a man to sell himself into slavery, seeing such a bargain is without consideration." If I give a man five hundred dollars for himself, I can, the next minute, take it away from him, because, when the bargain is concluded, the man reverts to me, and I own him, and all that he owns, the 500 dollars that I paid for him included. So that he has got nothing for himself. It is therefore utterly impossible for such a contract to be binding, because it is essential to a contract that there be some consideration.

Montesquieu, author of " *The Spirit of Laws,*" adds his testimony to the same effect.

Patrick Henry said, " We owe it to the purity of our holy religion to show that its precepts are opposed to slavery."

The testimony of such men as Patrick Henry is not to be thrown away, because they did not practice their doctrines. Washington regarded slavery as an evil, which ought to be abolished, and declared himself ready to vote for its abolition. Jefferson spoke of the abolition of slavery, as an event which he ardently desired; but said, (he was then an old man,) that it would require some young Eneas to bear the burden of this reform, instead of the trembling shoulders of the old Anchises. He must devolve the burden upon younger shoulders. These were professed statesmen, and felt no inconsistency in holding slaves themselves, while willing to co-operate with their fellow-citizens for the destruction of the system. Had they been moralists, or ministers of Christ, their practice might affect the value of their testimony.

I have now done with *authorities.* If the gentleman reads any more, I advise you to consider, well, who is the author of the book from which he reads, and to what class of writers he belongs, that you may know what consideration his opinion deserves.

I now come to the last argument, which, if I had placed them in the order of their importance, would have been first. With God's help, I mean not to leave one stone upon another of his argument from scripture which shall not be thrown down. I have once read the texts upon which he founds his doctrine, and it is not necessary to re-read them. I attempted to show, first, that, even though the Hebrew bond-servants had been slaves, that would not answer the purpose of justifying Kentucky slavery, any more than would the fact that the Israelites were permitted to borrow jewels from the Egyptians without returning them, justify modern swindling or stealing. I will now state my reasons for my belief, that *the Hebrew bond-servants were not slaves.*

It is plain that they were not slaves from the fact that they were not hereditary or perpetual bondsmen. Slaves are men held in hereditary and perpetual bondage: they are "*property to all intents and purposes forever. That is slavery.* Slaves are *property,* as cattle are property, and the progeny of cattle are perpetually the property of him who owns the dam. "*Partus sequitur ventrem.*" I will refer you to a pamphlet by Dr. J. L. Wilson, the venerable pastor of the First Presbyterian church in this city, and a man who, when right, is very hard to get wrong, and when wrong— I will not say whether he is hard to get right or not. [A laugh.]

Dr. Wilson, in his pamphlet on the "*Relation of Master and Servant,*" declares in his own decided manner, that "he must be a blind guide," who supposes that the Hebrew servants, obtained from foreign tribes, were held in perpetual bondage—and that the jubilee of the 50th year did not apply to them.   And the same doctrine, that the jubilee freed all the Hebrew servants, the ear-bored bondmen and all, has been laid down by one of the Bench of Bishops, speaking in the English House of Lords, and nowhere, so far as I know, successfully contradicted.   And because they were not perpetual and hereditary bondmen, they were certainly not slaves.

Again: It is plain that they were not slaves, *because the law of returning property did not apply to them.* "If thou see thine enemy's ox or his ass go astray, thou shalt surely fetch him back to him," but, if a slave were to run into their nation from the tribes outside of Judea, they were to permit him to dwell with them.   This law shows that slaves were not considered the propety of their masters.   And Dr. Rice says, by his practice, amen to this law.   For, says he, " *I have* SEEN SLAVES RUNNING AWAY *from their masters, and I would not interfere to send them* BACK.   But why, if the slave is the just property of the master, he must send him back when he sees him running off, or else he is neither an honest Christian, or Christian minister.   But whatever be true of Dr. Rice, this law, given of God to the Jews, shows that these servants were not slaves in God's account.   See Deut. **xxiii,** 15.   " Thou shalt not deliver unto his master the servant that is escaped," etc.

Another important fact, showing that the Hebrew bondmen were not slaves, is the one already once referred to; that the forty-seven learned and pious translators of tho Bible, in 1607, (the year that Jamestown, Va., was settled,) at a time when our forefathers were driven by religious persecution, to seek an asylum for liberty in the wilderness of America, a time of great religious agitation throughout Christendom, and when the Bible was eagerly and very generally studied, never once called the Hebrew bond-servants, *slaves.*

Forty-seven of the ablest men, and the best Hebrew and Greek scholars that could be found in that age, were set to translate the Bible into English.   They met together, divided the original Hebrew and Greek text into parts, each taking his portion; and when they met again, each read his part, while the rest criticised his translation. There never was such a translation made of a book. It may be said of it, that, like God's works, "it is good," for I believe that He aided by his spirit the men who made it. It will stand as long as the pillars of the earth stand. Now, what I wish to fasten on your memories is, the fact that they *never once* translate the Hebrew word "*ebedh*," A SLAVE!—never once in the whole book. Yet, Dr. Rice says, "it is the very word for slave," and that there is another word ("*saukir*,") which is the word for hired servant. Nor did they translate the Greek word (doulos) "*slave*,"in the whole of the New Testament.

Dr. Rice against our Bible translation!   [*Time expired.*

[MR. RICE'S THIRTEENTH SPEECH.]

Gentlemen Moderators, and Fellow-Citizens:

I am truly gratified to perceive that my friend, by having had time allowed him to recruit his bodily powers, has likewise, gained time to recruit his ideas, and has come here with *a written reply to my arguments*, (either prepared by himself or supplied by some other hand,) carefully drawn out. I will attend to its leading points before I enter on the Bible argument from the New Testament.

He first replies to my argument showing that the relation between master and slave is not in itself sinful, because it is often formed at the earnest request of the slave, and so as really to improve his condition. His answer is—if a man buy a slave for the purpose of liberating him, he does not sin; but if this be not the object, he does sin. He, then, admits, that the legal relation may be formed, and may exist for the time being, and yet not be sinful. But his assertion that if it be not the object of the purchaser to liberate the man, he sins, labors under this very important difficulty, viz: *it is without proof,* unless his mere assertion be regarded as proof, as it might be, if the Rev. Mr. Blanchard were Pope!

But he says, the purchaser holds the slave in a condition in which he is liable to be sold into merciless hands. And I ask, whether a man's own children, should he die, may not suffer a like misfortune by being put under the care of wicked men? If I buy a slave at his own request, thereby improving his condition, I am not responsible for any misfortune which may afterwards befall him, and which I could not prevent. When I have purchased such a slave, I have certainly, at least for the present, improved his condition, so far as other paramount duties will permit; and it will require something more than the gentleman's assertion to prove, that in so doing I am guilty of sin. If, in such a case, I have committed sin, it is in taking a fellow-man out of bad hands, or in preventing him from falling into such. This, if I have sinned, is my crime!

In regard to the duty of the Presbyterian elder and the Boston man to whom fell a large number of slaves of different ages and conditions, he says, they ought by all means to have manumitted them. What, then, I ask, as I have before asked, would become of the aged who could not support themselves by labor, and of the women and children in a similar condition?

But if they could not free them legally, they were bound, he says, to have called them in, and told them, they were free, and paid them wages. He did not tell us, however, what amount of wages would be due to that company of them who, as the elder said, were *eating him up.* Besides, all this is mere *assertion,* wholly unreasonable. Suppose a master in one of the slave States should call in his servants, and tell them they are free; would this make them free? It would not; for the laws of the State say, they shall not be liberated in the State, or at any rate, not until bond and security are given for their future support. They would be liable, therefore, immediately to be taken up, and sold, and might be sold into cruel hands. As to wages, that matter must depend upon circumstances. It is clear, that in the cases referred to, and in all similar cases, masters are doing their duty, when they live with their slaves, and do what they can for their present and future happiness.

In reply to his assertion, that slave-holding is but kidnapping "stretched out," I remarked, that such a principle, if admitted, would require all those farmers who own lands taken from the Indians by fraud or force, to restore them to their original owners. But he says, the original owners cannot be found. This, however, is not precisely true; for a number of the Indian tribes from whom land has been taken unjustly, *can be found*—especially the Cherokees in the South, concerning whose wrongs so much excitement prevailed a few years ago.

Will the gentleman, then, set out on a crusade in behalf of Indian rights, with the same zeal he manifests in the cause of abolition, and urge the owners of their lands to turn themselves out of house and home, because they have got only a "kidnapper's and robber's title" to their land? Will he carry out his own principle? It would be a curious spectacle: I do not think he would be quite as popular with the abolitionist farmers, as he is at present.

There is a distinction between the sins of a nation, and the sins of individuals in that nation. Individuals cannot help the sins which the nation, of which they form a component part, has committed; and how great soever they may be, every individual citizen is not to be held responsible for them.

He says, that if Hagar was Abraham's property, and, when running away from her mistress, was advised by an angel to return, I am bound to follow the angel's example, and turn back all runaways. I reply, that, when they are running from masters like Abraham, I would give them the same advice the angel gave to Hagar. I would tell them, what I sincerely believe, that their condition was not likely to be bettered by their flight to Canada. But even if it were, all who so run off make the condition of their brethren, remaining in slavery, so much the harder; and, therefore, a regard for those in bondage with them, should prevent them from taking this course.

The brother tells you, that when Constantine enacted the laws I read, against separating married slaves from each other, he was engaged in " killing slavery " throughout the Roman empire. I ask where is his proof of this? At all events, slavery did not die in the empire for centuries after; no, not till the thirteenth century, as the gentleman himself admits. This was, to say the least, a very slow death.

He says, again, that the law of the Presbyterian church, forbidding the separation of husband and wife in the sale of slaves, is a dead letter, and totally inoperative. He asserts this; I deny it. He has told us of the Danville case; but in that case the law was fully operative, for the church session did discipline the member so offending.

He proves slavery to be sinful by the fact, that the Kentuckian holds his slaves by a law that does not recognize their marriage as valid. Very well: the Hindoo holds his wife under a law which does not recognize women as having souls, and which treats them as incapable of religion. Is marriage, therefore, among the Hindoos, in itself a sin? The Roman law gave a father the right of life and death over his child: was it sin, therefore, in a Roman to have a son? The argument is just as logical in the one case as in the othar.

I pressed him with the inconsistency of his abolitionist friends in insisting with such uncompromising zeal on setting the slave free from his master, and then stopping short and refusing him the boon of a freeman in the right of suffrage; and how does he reply? Oh, he leaves all that to the politicians! he has nothing to do with that. Nothing to do with it? As an abolitionist, pleading for human freedom, he has much to do with it. Does he call him a free man for whom others make laws at their pleasure, he having no voice in the enactment of the laws or in the choice of the law-makers? Yet where is the abolitionist press in Ohio that pleads for this vital element of freedom in the case of the colored man? If he must be set free, why not make him free indeed? Ah, that would not do: and so that is none of their concern—they leave that to the politicians!

The gentleman has at last made one attempt to answer my argument based on the truth, that the great principles of the moral code are obvious, and commend themselves at once to the conscience of every enlightened man; connected with the fact, that men the most enlightened have failed to see or feel that slave-holding is in itself sinful. And what is his answer? Why, he says, all do see it to be wrong, when brought home to themselves; for, if a man should seize on one of my daughters, and make a slave of her, I would instantly feel that the act was a heinous sin. And does the brother really regard this as an answer? He offers it as an answer to my argument. But are we discussing the question, whether seizing on a free human being and reducing him by force to a state of slavery, is sinful? Who would argue such a question for one moment? I certainly would not. Yet that is his only answer! We are not enquiring whether it is sin to reduce men to slavery, but what a man is bound to do with those who are in slavery already, and were born slaves. What has this to do with the act of a man who would seize on my daughter, born free, in a land of freedom, and by force make a slave of her? Suppose I could show that the wise and good, of all ages and lands, thought *stealing* not to be wrong; would it be an answer to say, "ah, but if a man should rob you, you would then think it a sin?"

My friend has made a brief reply to my argument on the golden rule. He says that God has made of one blood all men to dwell under the face of the whole heaven; and as they are of one blood, they are by nature equal, and so must be equal in their condition; and therefore it is a sin, under any circumstances, for one to hold another as a slave. Admitting the inference to be sound, it is against himself and his friends, who assert that the politicians may deprive one class of men, on account of their color, of all political rights.

[Mr. BLANCHARD rose to explain. I never said that. I said that, as moralists, and as ministers of Christ, when we have freed the slaves from their masters, abolitionists have done with them.]

Yes, that is, when, as moralists, and ministers, and zealous abolitionists, they have restored to the slave one half his rights, they have done with him, and very coolly leave the rest to politicians! They do not even aim to secure, or pretend to claim, for him, all his rights. The gentleman is prudent. He saw the trouble into which his doctrine would plunge him, if he took another step, and he stops short. Oh, prudent abolitionists! Then complete freedom, it seems, belongs to privileged classes only. He admits that politicians may deprive the slave of some of the dearest of his rights all his life long, and yet their task as advocates of human liberty, will have been fully accomplished. "Abolitionists have done with them." If he were the African, would he be satisfied with such principles?

Again, he says, my argument from the *golden rule*, is a *petitio principii*—a begging of the question—that it assumes that there is nothing wrong in holding a man in slavery. It assumes no such thing. If I purchase a slave at his own earnest request, that his condition may be improved, I do not thereby say, that he, or his ancestors were justly enslaved. But I do deny, that I have violated that rule, when I comply with his request, and so place him in a better condition; or that I am bound to make him a present of four or six hundred dollars. If I purchase him at his own request, I confer on him a favor; he so regards it. I may not be able, without disregarding other paramout duties, to set him free; but I do for him the best that, under the circumstances, I am able. Is it begging the question to say, that in so doing, I commit no sin?

But the brother says, my argument gives me the benefit of my own wrong. I deny it. I have done the man, whom I purchase, no wrong. Admitting that, in some cases, a man may be responsible for the wrong done by his father,—

my father has done this man no wrong. The original wrong was committed long ago. What can we now do to remedy all the evils of generations gone by? They who enslaved our blacks, had gone to their account, long before we were born. We find them in slavery; what ought we to do for them? That is the question, and the only question.

The brother applies to slave-holders the language of our Lord to the Jews, where He told them that their fathers killed the prophets, and they garnished their sepulchres. But the cases are not analogous. They would be if we were answering those who stole and enslaved the blacks, or if we ourselves were to steal and enslave others. The Jews said, if they had lived in the days of their fathers, they would not have slain the prophets; while they themselves persecuted and put to death Christ and his apostles. Thus, they did indeed fill up the measure of their fathers. But what analogy is there between this case, and that of a man who buys a slave at his own earnest request? Did a prophet ever come to a Jew, and say,—"pray, do persecute me a little?" [A laugh.] I do not claim the right of going to Africa and purchasing slaves on speculation. The case the brother has brought, is as far from ours as the poles.

And now for his replies to my argument from the Old Testament.

He says my argument is bad, because the position I take is equivocal: at the North it is understood, that slavery is not wrong because God *permitted*, that, is, did not hinder it among the Jews; while at the South, it goes the whole length of maintaining that God *sanctioned* slavery among them. Is this a candid statement? Have I ever said that God permitted slave-buying to the Jews, in the sense of not hindering it, as he did not hinder polygamy? Never. The brother knows, and you know better. My position was, and is, that God *expressly* permitted it in the words of the Jewish law, given from himself by Moses. No man, in his senses, could understand the argument as meaning simply that God did not hinder the Jews from buying and holding slaves. No, my position is not equivocal; it is plain, open, and above board. It means at the North what it means at the South: it means at the South just what it means at the North, and no more, viz: that God gave the Jews permission to buy and hold slaves, because, as I suppose, their condition would be thereby improved.

As to the brother's quotation from the Alabama Baptist, I have only to say, I have nothing to do with it. I never have said that slavery is no evil; nor is that my belief. But on this subject the gentleman flatly contradicted himself, by saying, at one time, that my doctrine was highly agreeable to southern slave-holders, and at another, that they could not endure it. He changes his position more frequently than the wind changes its course.

In reply to my argument from authority, he says that the able scholars and critics to whom I referred, were misled by Dr. Paley. Now it happens, somewhat unfortunately for this reply, that they lived, (at least many of them,) before Paley. [A laugh.] And besides, Dr. Paley himself, though a pleasant and ingenious writer, never was regarded as a giant on questions of morals. There is no evidence that the eminent and able men, with whom I agree, and from whom Mr. Blanchard differs, in their exposition of the passages I quoted from the Old Testament, were misled, or in the least influenced by Dr. Paley.

But he says, that they looked at slavery through "slaveholding spectacles." Well, and where is the evidence of this? Why, Matthew Henry wrote his Commentary not more than 30 miles from Liverpool, where slave-ships were fitted out for the African trade; and he was afraid to speak out his real sentiments on the subject! The gentleman pays quite a compliment to that eminently good and wise man! But there may have been much sin beside slave-dealing committed in less than thirty miles of him. Was he afraid to expose this? But he has told us what persecution he endured in consequence of his fidelity to the truth. How faithful he was! How much more fearless than poor Matthew Henry! [A laugh.]

But he has a general reply, which sets aside forever the authority of critics and commentators. He says, they are generally men of *timid minds.* And, pray, what causes exist to make them more timid than others ? It is the business of lexicographers and commentators not to engage in any exciting controversies, but to define words, and expound the Word of God. Moreover, their reputation depends upon their accuracy and ability in their work. What, then, should cause them, more than others, to depart from known truth! The reply is simply nonsensical. The gentleman feels the difficulty in which he and his cause are involved, from the fact that all learned men, commentators, critics, and lexicographers give to the language of the Bible, on the subject before us, an interpretation widely different from his ; and he would fain destroy their influence by simply saying— "O, they are timid-minded men—they do'nt know every thing—they are mere babes—can't go to bed without a committee ! " Such an attempt cannot succeed with intelligent men.

He quoted the opinion of "the clear-headed" Grotius, concerning slavery. *Now will he please inform us whether Grotius gave to the scriptures I have quoted an interpretation different from that which I have given?*

The opinion of John Wesley has also been quoted. Did Wesley speak of the injustice of slavery as a *system,* or of the sin of *individuals* involved in the evil? Did he denounce and excommunicate men, simply because they were slave-holders? If he did, why have not his followers done the same? Does the Methodist Church in these United States make slave-holding a bar to Christian fellowship? It does not:

Dr. Engles has also been quoted. Now I happen to know something of the views of that gentleman on the subject of slavery; and I know, that, though opposed to slavery, he is no less opposed to abolitionism, in theory and in practice. It is by quoting isolated passages from the writings of men, without regard to the connection, they are made to utter sentiments they never held. For example, what they say of slavery as a system, or of traffic in slaves for gain, is applied to individuals involved in slave-holding. The gentleman has quoted Dr. R. J. Breckenridge. He is indeed one of the last men whom I should have expected to hear quoted in favor of modern abolitionism. He is well known as an anti-slavery man; but it is equally well known, that he engaged in a public debate of several days' continuance, with Thompson, a rampant abolitionist of Scotland, and it is said, that he effectually *used him up.*

We have also been treated to the opinions of George Washington, and Patrick Henry, both of whom held just about as much abolitionism as your humble servant.

Thus far has the gentleman got on, and *no Bible.* All he has done, or tried to do, is to defend himself *against* the Bible. In attempting to do this, he says:

1. The bondmen of the Jews, were not slaves, because their servitude was not *perpetual.* We are not discussing the question whether *perpetual* slave-holding is sinful—whether the relation of master and slave is sinful, if it continue perpetually. If the gentleman desired to discuss this question; why did he not say so? We are discussing the question, whether the relation of master and slave is in itself sinful; for if it is, it is sinful to have it continue *one hour.* Then, if we admit, that Jewish servitude was not perpetual, but ceased at the fiftieth year—the jubilee; what does it prove in favor of my opponent? It is certain, that they were *bought* with money; that they were declared to be their master's money; that the master claimed their services, and might enforce obedience by severe chastisement. It is certain that those purchased immediately after the jubilee, might be held in bondage *forty-nine years,* and that to a large portion of them, bondage would be perpetual; for they would not live till the year of release. And to many who would live to see the time, their freedom would be a poor boon;

for their advanced age and infirmities would disqualify them for the enjoyment of it. But the duration of the servitude, does not affect the *principle*. If I may hold a man in servitude forty-nine years, I may hold him longer, if there be no express law against it?

2. But the law concerning returning property, Mr. B. tells us, did not apply to the Jewish bond-servants, and, hence he infers that they were not slaves. I answer, that the law which forbade the Jews to return a slave who had escaped from his master, and required them to allow him to dwell where he pleased amongst them, related not to Jewish bondmen, but to the slaves of cruel heathen masters, who had escaped into the land of Judea, and who, if forced back, would not only be forced into pagan darkness, but might meet a cruel death on their return.

The law was, indeed, a merciful one. If I were to see a child escaping from a cruel father, who was accustomed to treat him unmercifully, I would not think of forcing him back. But does this law prove, that the bond-servants of the Jews, bought with their money, liable to be chastised, if they disobeyed their masters, were not slaves? Surely, we have singular logic from the gentleman.

The brother urges again his crowning argument, that if the Hebrew word meant slave, our English translators would have rendered it slave. I have asked him, in reply, what was the meaning of the English word *servant* in England, at the time our translation was made, under James I? I have reminded him that *servus* is the Latin word for slave, and *mancipium* for a man caught and enslaved. *Servant* is but *servus*, with an English termination. Besides did they not render the word by the word *bondman*? What, I ask, does the word *bondman* mean? Does it mean a free man?

How does the gentleman understand those passages of scripture, where the *bond* and the *free* are placed in contrast with each other? For example, God calls the fowls of the heaven to come, " That they may eat the flesh of kings, and the flesh of captains, &c., and the flesh of all men, *both free and bond*, both small and great." Rev. ix, 12. Again, "There is neither Jew nor Greek, there is neither *bond nor free*, &c., Gal. iii, 26. Away with such quibbling. Everybody knows, that a *bondman* is a slave. When, therefore, our translators rendered the word *eved* by the English word *bondman*, they employed as strong a term as the word *slave*.

Still, the gentleman insists that *eved* does not mean *slave*. I have asked him, when the Hebrews talked about a slave, what word they used? It is a fair question: I have put it to him again and again. He has not answered. I ask him once more, when the Jews wished to speak of slaves, did they use the word *eved*, or not? If not, will he please to tell us what word they did use. I hope he will give us some light upon this subject. I must insist upon his answering the question. I have paid due attention to the gentleman's replies, and now, according to promise, I enter upon the argument from the New Testament.

And here I cannot but express my regret that the discussion of the whole of the remaining scripture evidence, is confined to so short a time as the remaining hours of this day. Late as it is, in the afternoon of the last day of the debate, we have heard no Bible argument from our friend. Mark that.

1. In the commencement of this argument I state it as a fact, admitted by the abolitionists, as well as all others conversant with history, that in the days of Christ and his apostles, not only did slavery exist every where, but the slaves were as numerous throughout the Roman empire, as the freemen. My brother will not deny this.

[Mr. Blanchard. I admit that they were as numerous, and more so.]

Very well. In some instances from one hundred to ten thousand slaves were owned by a single man.

2. And I state it as a second fact, that the piety of a man was never called in question by the apostles because he was

a slave-holder, but slave-holders were freely admitted to membership in the primitive church; and though professing Christians were required to treat their slaves with all kindness, they never were called upon to set them free; as they certainly would have been, had slave-holding been in itself sinful.

This is our ground; and if it is true, we are forced to the conclusion, that either the doctrine of abolitionists is untrue, or the apostles of Jesus Christ did admit to the communion of his church, and that without reproof, or requiring them to quit their sin, the most heinous and scandalous offenders, men (according to our brother) chargeable with the greatest abomination of heathenism.

The proof of this fact rests on a few passages of the New Testament, familiar, as I presume, to most of those who hear me. I will read, in the first place, from Ephesians, VI, 5:

"Servants be obedient to them that are your masters according to the flesh, with fear and trembling, in singleness of heart, as unto Christ. Not with eye service, as men pleasers; but as the servants of Christ, doing the will of God from the heart;—with good will doing service, as to the Lord, and not to men:—knowing that whatsoever good thing any man doeth, the same shall he receive of the Lord, whether he be bond or free. And ye masters, do the same things unto them, forbearing threatening: knowing that your master also is in heaven; neither is there respect of persons with him."

Again: Colossians, iii, 22:

"Servants, obey in all things your masters according to the flesh; not with eye service as, men pleasers; but in singleness of heart, fearing God: and whatsoever ye do, do it heartily, as to the Lord, and not unto men; knowing that of the Lord ye shall receive the reward of the inheritance: for ye serve the Lord Christ. But he that doeth wrong shall receive for the wrong which he hath done: and there is no respect of persons."

I read again from 1. Timothy, vi, 1, 2:

"Let as many servants as are under the yoke count their own masters worthy of all honor, that the name of God and his doctrine be not blasphemed. And they that have believing masters, let them not despise them because they are brethren: but rather do them service, because they are faithful and beloved, partakers of the benefit."

Once more: 1. Peter, ii, 18;

"Servants be subject to your masters with all fear; not only to the good and gentle, but also to the froward. For this is thank-worthy, if a man for conscience toward God endure grief, suffering wrongfully."

Now the question arises, were the "masters" here referred to, slave-holders? The word *kurios*, translated *master*, signifies possessor, owner, master. When used, as here, in connexion with servant, it means "owner or possessor of servants, or slaves." In its proper sense it always implies authority, arising from an existing relation. Let me read you a brief quotation from an article in the *Biblical Repository*, from the pen of Professor Stuart, pages **737**, and **741.**

In his remarks on the meaning of the word *kurios* in the Septuagint, he says—"1. *Kurios*, then, means, *owner, possessor;* e. g. Ex. xxi, 28, and xxi, 29, 34. 2. It signifies *husband, lord*, in the sense of being the head of a family; e. g. Gen. xviii, 12, &c. 3. It is used as an appellation of respect and civility. 4. *Kurios* is very frequently employed to designate *the relation of a master to his servants or slaves;* e. g. Gen. xxiv, 9, 10, 12, 14, &c. In this sense the word is employed many scores of times in the Septuagint; as may be seen in Tromme's Concordance. Indeed, so far were the Seventy from recognizing the usual classic distinction between *despotes* and *kurios*, as stated by Passow, that they have scarcely used *despotes* at all in the sense to which I now advert, &c. 5. It is employed, in numberless instances, *to designate the only living and true God, the King of Kings and Lord of Lords*, as the supreme ruler, governor, master, owner, and rightful lord and possessor of all things, having them all under his control," &c.

Professor Stuart, one of the ablest critics and most learned expositors in this country, or in any other, says,

"As used in the New Testament, the word *kurios* has the following meanings: 1. It designates the *owner* or *possessor* of any thing; as Matt. xx, 8, &c. 2. It signifies the *head* or *master of a family* or *household;* e. g. Mark xiii, 35, &c. 3. It is used as an appellation of respect and civility; Matt. xviii, 21, &c. 4. *It is employed as designating the relation of a master to a servant or slave;* Matt. xxiv, 45, 46, 48, 50, Eph. vi, 5, 9, Col. iv. 1, iii, 32, *and often elsewhere."*

Abolitionists tell us, that *despotes* is the proper Greek word to signify an owner of slaves, but that *kurios* has not commonly this meaning. Professor Stuart, however, who is one of the ablest critics in our country, states, that the authors of the Greek translation of the Old Testament, called the Septuagint, do not make any distinction between these words, but that they almost uniformly use the word *kurios*, when they mean the master of slaves. On page 758 he says—"I proceed to note a few other instances, in which Paul used the word *kurios* in the common secular sense, as denoting the *master* of servants. Thus Rom. xiv, 4, Eph. vi, 5, and vi, 0, Col. iii, 22, and iv, 1, are plain instances of this nature; and I may add, these are among the very numerous class of examples in the Septuagint and New Testament, which go to show that the classical distinction made between *despotes* and *kurios* was not at all regarded by the Hellenistic writers."

It appears, then, that the Hellenistic writers—of whom were the apostles of Christ—did not make a distinction between the words *kurios* and *despotes*, but that they generally used *kurios* to signify a *master* or owner of slaves. In the Septuagint translation, Potiphar is called Joseph's *kurios* or master. Will the gentleman inform us, whether Joseph was Potiphar's slave?

Robertson, who is a lexicographer of standard authority, defines *kurios* thus: " *lord, master, owner*—generally as the *possessor, owner, master,* of property; Matt. xx, 8, xxi, 40, &c. The *master* or *possessor* of persons, servants, slaves; Matt. x, 24, xxiv, 45, &c."

It is clear, then, that the word *kurios,* translated *master,* does commonly signify an owner of slaves. And now I proceed to prove, that the corresponding word, *doulos,* translated *servant,* means a slave; or that the persons addressed by the apostles as *servants,* were *slaves.*

To satisfy the minds of the unprejudiced on this point, I will refer to some standard authorities; for I pretend not to such learning as to expect the audience to depend upon my assertions.

Robertson defines *doulos*—"a *slave,* a *servant*—spoken of involuntary service, e. g. a slave in opposition to *eleutheros,* free." *Douleia,* he defines, slavery, bondage. *Douleuo*—to be a slave or servant, to serve. *Douloo*—to make a slave, to bring into bondage.

Bretschneider, one of the most learned German lexicographers, defines *doulos*—"*servus,* qui sui juris non est, cui opponitur *ho eleutheros*; 1 Cor. vii. 21 "—a SLAVE, *one who is not under his own control,* to which is opposed HO ELEUTHEROS, *free.* *Douloo*—to make a slave, reduce to slavery.

Donnegan defines *doulos,* "a slave, a servant, as opposed to *despotes*—a master. *Douloo,* to reduce to slavery," &c.

Groves defines *doule,* a female slave; *doulos,* a slave, a servant; *douloo,* to enslave, reduce to slavery.

Greenfield defines *doulos,* a man in a servile state, male slave, or servant. *Douloo*—to reduce to servitude, enslave, oppress by retaining in servitude.

Such are the definitions of *doulos,* and its cognate terms, given by lexicographers of standard authority; men who, though regarded by the gentleman as weak and timid, may, nevertheless, be supposed to have some considerable acquaintance with the Greek language. They all agree, that the primary, proper, and ordinary meaning of the word *doulos*, is *slave*.

It is important here to remark, that the Greek language has a word which does definitely signify a *hired* servant, viz., *misthotos*—a word commonly used in this sense, both in the Septuagint and the New Testament; but this word is never used by the apostles addressing servants.

Having thus ascertained how the lexicographers understand the word *doulos*, I now invite your attention to a few quotations from the classics, showing that profane Greek writers uniformly used it to mean a *slave*.

Herodotus—"Rhodope was born in Thrace. She was the *slave* (*doule*) of Jadmon—the fellow-slave (*sundoule*) of Æsop," b. ii, sec. 134. Again—"Our affairs have come to this crisis, O Ionians, that we must be either *free* (*eleutheroi*) or *slaves*, (*douloi*,") b. vi, sec. 11. Again—"Argos was deprived of so many men, that the *slaves* (*douloi*) usurped the government. The expelled *slaves* (*douloi*) seized Terinthe. Cleander persuaded these *slaves* (*doulois*) to attack their *masters*, (*despotais*,) *ib.* sec. 83.

Plato—"As to the things connected with tame living animals, the rearing and managing of flocks embraces all except *slaves*, (*doulous*.") There remains, then, the class of *slaves*, (*doulon*,) and all other servants (*hupereton*.) What servants do you mean? Those that have been purchased or made property in any other way, whom we may unquestionably call slaves, (*doulous*.)

Harpocration, speaking of the Helots, says, "they were not naturally the *slaves* (*douloi*) of the Lacedemonians, but were the first of the inhabitants of Helos subdued." *Pausanias* says, "They were the first *slaves* (*douloi*) of the Lacedemonians." *Eustathius* says, "The Helots labored for the Lacedemonians, and were *slaves* (*douloi*)." *Julius Pollux* says, "They were not *slaves*, (*douloi*) but in a condition between *slaves* and *free men*, (*eleutheron kai doulon*.") Xenophon says, "Certainly, it is necessary, that a sufficiency of heat and cold, of food and drink, of labor and sleep, be allowed to *slaves, (doulois.")* *Cyrop,* ch. vi, p. 423. Again, " Or because we have now obtained *slaves (doulous)* shall we punish them, if they be dishonest?" Again, " It is proper that there should be this difference between us and *slaves (doulon)* that, as *slaves (douloi)* unwillingly obey their masters, *(despotais,)* we, if we deem ourselves worthy to be free men, *(eleutheroi,)* should willingly do that which is most praiseworthy."—*Ibid.* ch. vii, p. 430.

I have read these quotations to prove to the unlearned, as well as to the learned, that the ancient Greek writers used the word *doulos,* as the proper word for *slave.* And can any one doubt it, after hearing these passages from their writings?

I now proceed to prove, that the inspired writers used this word in the same sense in which it was employed by the Greek writers. For this purpose I will quote some passages in which it occurs. John viii, 31, " Then said Jesus to those Jews which believed on him, If ye continue in my word, then are ye my disciples indeed; and ye shall know the truth, and the truth shall make you free. They answered him, we be Abraham's seed, and were never in bondage *(dedouleukamen)* to any man : how sayest thou, ye shall be made free ? Jesus answered them, Verily, verily, I say unto you, whosoever committeth sin, is the *servant (doulos)* of sin. And the *servant (doulos)* abideth not in the house," &c. In this passage it is evident that the Saviour represents wicked men as the *slaves* of sin ; and truly the service of sin and of the Devil, is a most degrading slavery.

In the same sense the word is used by Paul the Apostle. Rom. vi, 17, 18. " But God be thanked that we were the *servants (douloi)* of sin : but ye have obeyed from the heart that form of doctrine which was delivered you. Being then *made free* from sin, ye became the servants of righteousness." In 1. Cor. xii, 13, it is used literally for *slaves,* thus: " For by one spirit are we all baptized into one body, whether we be Jews or gentiles, whether we be *bond or free (eite douloi, eite eleutheroi")*—that is, whether we be *slaves or freemen.* We find the word used in precisely the same sense, in Collos. iii,

11. "Where there is neither Greek nor Jew, circumcision nor uncircumcision, Barbarian, Scythian, *bond or free* (*doulos, eleutheros*) but Christ is all and in all." Again, we find the word *doulos* in 1 Cor. vii, 21, where even the abolitionists admit, that it means *slave:* "Let every man abide in the same calling wherein he was called. Art thou called being a *servant* (*doulos,*) care not for it; but if thou mayest be made free, use it rather." The last passage to which I shall now refer, in order to show the Bible usage of the word in question, is Rev. xiii, 16. "And he caused all both small and great, rich and poor, *free and bond* (*eleutherous kar doulous*) to receive a mark in their right hand, or in their foreheads."

Thus it is clear, that the word *doulos* is used in the New Testament, as it is in the writings of the ancient Greeks, to signify a *slave.* It is the appropriate Greek word by which to designate a common slave. If the Apostles, then, in the passages I have read, had been addressing *hired* servants, they would undoubtedly have used the word *misthotos,* which properly means a hired servant, as distinguished from a slave. Indeed, there is no controversy amongst learned men concerning the meaning of *doulos.* All agree, that its literal, ordinary and proper meaning is *slave.* I challenge the gentleman to disprove this statement. But perhaps, all men of learning are *timid,* as he says, afraid to utter their real sentiments!—though he has not informed us of whom they are afraid.

We will now turn to a passage, in which, the Abolitionists themselves admit, slaves and slave-holders are spoken of, viz: 1 Tim. vi, 1, 2. "Let as many servants as are under the yoke count their own masters worthy of all honor, that the name of God and his doctrine be not blasphemed." Here we have not only servants under the yoke, admitted to be slaves, but the word *despotes,* admitted to be the appropriate word to designate a master of slaves; so that the exhortation would literally read thus: Let as many slaves as are under the yoke count their owners or masters worthy of all honor. These, however, it is said, were *heathen* masters;

but here abolitionism gets into trouble, for in the second verse we read, "And they that have *believing masters*, (*despotas*,) let them not despise them, because they are brethren; but rather do them service, because they are faithful and beloved, partakers of the benefit." Here, we have not only *despotai*, owners of slaves, but *believing* slave-holders, that is, *pious* slave-holders—Christian slave-holders—"faithful and beloved, partakers of the benefit." And the slaves, who are also believers, are exhorted not to despise their masters, because as Christians they are brethren, but to serve them the more faithfully. These servants are admitted to be slaves, and the word translated *masters*, is admitted to mean slave-holder; and Paul, the inspired apostle, acknowledges them as believers, as faithful Christians.

How do you suppose, abolitionists attempt to escape the force of this argument? Why, they say, the phrase "believing master," is understood just as the expression, "reformed drunkard." And as the latter phrase means a man who has ceased to be a drunkard, though he has been such; so the former means a believer, who, before he became such, was a slave-holder, but has since liberated all his slaves? Truly, the cause must be sorely pressed, which cannot be sustained but by resorting to such perversion of the plainest language. No one can misunderstand such a phrase, as *reformed drunkard;* but suppose we should read of a reformed *husband*, would we understand by such language a man who *had* been, but was no longer, a husband? We read in 1 Cor. vii, 14, of "the unbelieving husband," and the "unbelieving wife," and by these phrases every person of common sense understands a real husband or wife, who is an unbeliever; and the phrase, "believing husband," would, of course, mean a husband who is a believer—a Christian. It is equally obvious, that when the apostle speaks of "believing masters," or slave-holders, he means real masters who are believers or Christians. Accordingly, the slaves are addressed as those who "*have*," not *have had*, believing owners, and are exhorted not to despise them because they are *breth-*

ren—on an equality as Christians—but to serve them the more faithfully; and the reason why they should do so, is plainly given, viz.: "*because they are faithful and beloved, partakers of the benefit.*"

Yet, this language, according to abolitionism, means nothing more than we mean when we speak of *reformed drunkards!* Is this its obvious meaning? Was it ever so understood until the rise of modern abolitionism? Was there ever the least controversy on this subject? Has not the phrase, "believing masters," been universally understood to mean, real masters, who are pious men.

But let us look again at the text I quoted from the first epistle of Peter. "Servants—(*oiketai*)—be subject to your masters, with all fear: not only to the good and gentle, but also to the froward." *Oiketai* means household slaves; it is so understood even by abolitionists; and the word here translated *masters*, is DESPOTAI—which, as already remarked, the abolitionists say, is the proper word to designate owners of slaves. In the passage just examined, we found "believing masters," "faithful and beloved:" here we find "*good and gentle*" masters. Is it possible?—good and gentle robbers!—good and gentle man-stealers!—believing murderers!—faithful and beloved, partakers of the benefit!!! Should he not have written—partakers of the plunder? What?—a good and gentle slave-holder? The word *good*, as used in the Bible, expresses moral quality; and the word translated *gentle*, is used by Paul to express one of the moral qualifications for the ministerial office (1 Tim. iii, 3). It is used to characterize the wisdom which is from above (James iii, 17); and to express Christian moderation (Phil. iv, 5). Will the gentleman say, that a kidnapper, a man-stealer, a robber, can possess moral qualities which fit a man to be a minister of Jesus Christ? In the mind and mouth of abolitionists, it is synonymous with the vilest monster—one who lives in "kidnapping stretched out"—who holds his servants "by a kidnapper's title"—and whose existence on the earth is among the strongest proofs of the necessity of a hell! Yet he is here called "good and gentle," "faithful and beloved." Ought a true believer, a man faithful and beloved, good and gentle, to be excommunicated from the church?

I have proved, as I think, that the word *kurios*, which signifies literally *owner, possessor*, when used in connection with *servants*, means a real master. It uniformly conveys the idea of one possessing absolute authority; and in this sense it is used as a name of God. It is also used for the head of a family. But the argument does not depend upon the word *kurios;* for the apostle spoke of masters as *despotai*—a word which, even abolitionists admit, means slave-holders.

The abolitionists, however, ask us, with an air of triumph, whether, when Christ is called *Kurios*, Lord, we are to understand that he is a *slave-holder*, and that all his people are *slaves?* Not so fast, gentlemen; you forget, that the word *despotes*, which, as you admit, means a slave-holder, when used with reference to men, is applied also to God. Good old Simeon, as he held in his arms the infant Saviour, said— "Now Lord (*Despote*) lettest thou thy servant depart in peace," &c. As applied to God, both *kurios* and *despotes* express his ownership of men, and his absolute authority over them. As applied to the master of servants, they mean the owner of slaves—a man who has authority to control them.

I think, I have now proved, that the word *doulos*, translated *servant*, means, in the New Testament, what it means in the writings of the ancient Greeks—a *slave*, and consequently that the servants addressed by the apostles, were slaves; and that the *kurioi* and *despotai* were slave-holders. The conclusion is inevitable, that the apostles of Christ did receive slave-holders into the churches organized by them, as worthy and faithful Christians, and did not require them to liberate their slaves, but to treat them with all kindness. Yet we are called upon to exclude such men from the church, and are denounced because we refuse to do so!

Our abolitionist reformers, it seems, are better than the Bible—more holy and faithful than the apostles of Christ! Nay, they are more benevolent, if we are to credit their professions, than the Son of God! A centurion came to Jesus, in Capernaum, told him that his servant, (*doulos, slave,*) "who was dear to him," was very ill, and besought him to heal him. What was the Saviour's reply? Did he denounce him as a man-stealer, a robber? No—he not only complied with his request, but said to those who followed him, "*I have not found so great faith, no, not in Israel.*" Ah, our modern abolitionists would denounce such a man as a hypocrite, and have him out of the church without delay! Verily, we have fallen on glorious times! We are likely soon to have the church so pure, that the very best of men cannot live in it. [A laugh.] [*Time expired.*

Monday, 4 o'clock, P. M.

[MR. BLANCHARD'S FOURTEENTH SPEECH.]

Gentlemen Moderators, and Gentlemen and Ladies, Fellow-Citizens:

My argument on the New Testament view of servitude will be the opening speech to-night. I have received a letter from Mr. J. R. Alexander, a respectable man, complaining that I did Dr. Stiles injustice in my remarks of yesterday. I would remark that Mr. Alexander is mistaken as to what I said. If the moderators will give me time after recess, I will show him his mistake, but it does not belong to the present argument.

Dr. Rice has told you that the word "servant" comes from the Latin "*servus*" which originally meant slave, and did so at the time the Bible was translated. This is an entire mistake, as you can all see from the fact that our translators do use the word *slave* in two places. The first is in Jer. ii, 14, where we read, "Is Israel a servant? is he a home born *slave?* and the second is in the 18th chapter of Rev. where the word *slaves* occurs as part of the traffic of the mother of harlots. This shows that when the Bible translators used the word "*servant*" they meant *servant*,—and where they used the word "*slave*," they meant *slave*. His assertion, therefore, that the word *servant* meant "*slave*" in England in the year 1607, is an entire mistake; as is perhaps two-thirds of all that he has asserted in a similar manner in your hearing, with an assurance to me perfectly unaccountable; using such expressions as, "There is no controversy about it; the abolitionists admit," &c. I said playfully, that 'I could not hope to compete with a Doctor of Divinity in ability' and talent; but I must candidly acknowledge that of the many whom I have met in conversation upon this subject within the past few years; Dr. Rice's defence of slavery (with the exception of some adroit and somewhat bitter replications which evince talent of a certain description) seems to me, decidedly the weakest I ever met. This much it is perhaps necessary to have said, as I have hitherto made no remark of the kind, while he has asserted so constantly that " I cannot meet his arguments;" that " I have not uttered one word on the question;" etc. etc. that I have feared he was in danger of scoffing.

There is one point more in his remarks that requires notice. He said he wished to know whether the Methodists excluded any body from their church for holding slaves. I am informed that the early Methodists did exclude slave-holders; (a voice: "they did.") A brother whose hairs are white, with years, and, though unknown to me, I trust venerable for righteousness, answers, " *they did*." I hold here the discipline of the " UNITED BRETHREN in Christ," whose origin and ways were the same with the early Methodists.

This denomination, eight years ago, had nine yearly Conferences, and the Pennsylvania conference with which I was most acquainted, had ninety preachers; many of them apparently (and I have attended their camp-meetings) very sincere, and pious Christians. OTTERBEIN, their founder, was ordained by Dr. Coke, the first Methodist Bishop sent out by Mr. Wesley to this country. Here is their discipline, which declares: "*All slavery shall be excluded from our church. If any of our preachers or members are found holding slaves, they shall be excluded from the church, unless they do personally manumit such slave or slaves within six months.*"—ART. SLAVERY.

Here is a large and respectable denomination of Christians, not, it is true, commonly, among the most educated classes, yet a laborious and God-serving people, who have acted from their origin upon the principle of John Wesley, respecting slavery. I saw a little short man, a bishop or presiding elder, among this sort of people in Pennsylvania, with whom I had much pleasant intercourse. He talked about half Dutch and half English, and rejoiced in the rise and progress of abolitionism, saying; "*Ven I vas in Virginia, I did think to get my pones out of a schlave schtate to die.*"

I have now informed my brother of one large class of Christians who, upon abolition principles, reject slave-holders from communion.

I will now refer him to another, viz: the American Presbyterian churches, which are of Scotch origin, "*Covenanters, Seceders,*" and "*Associate Reformed.*" Two of their ministers are in this house and one, the President moderator, (Rev. Mr. Prestly) now fills the chair.

Their preachers number about 300; and their united membership some **40 000** to **50,000** persons. As a people, they are remarkable for two things, adherence to their Bibles and their Catechism, studying the scriptures, probably more than any other denomination.

This scripturally educated class of Christians, as my brother now in the chair will tell you, totally excludes slaveholders both from their pulpits and communion tables. Dr. Claybaugh, the amiable and efficient President of their Theological Seminary at Oxford, Ohio, was the man who offered the excluding resolutions in his Synod.

Seventy years ago, the "FRIENDS" made it an article of their society to exclude slave-holders. I have seen something of the Quakers and have as good evidence of the personal piety of many of them, as I have of Christians in my own denomination, and have spent pleasant evenings with them in religious conversation.

Seventy years ago they decided that slave-holding was not a Christian practice, and when they freed their slaves in Maryland, I was informed by Mr. Russell, that they lost but one single member, who refused to obey the rule to free his slaves, and was read out of society. Many were offered as high as $700 each for their slaves, when they came to record their deeds of emancipation, BUT NONE SOLD : but paid, instead, from 5 to 7 dollars for making out the papers.

"THE HEBREW BONDMEN WERE NOT SLAVES." This is my position. I now proceed to prove it, by reference to the *patriarchical character of Jewish Society.* Their servants were clansmen, not slaves. Few comparatively, of all the ancient Jews were land-holders; they existed in tribes and sub-tribes, and the head man was a kind of sheik, like an Arabian satrap, uniting in his person the character of prince and priest. The bondmen were his clansmen, owing a sort of leige service to their chief.

Again; It is evident that those Hebrew bondmen were not slaves because *there is no trace of a system of legislative appliances necessary for keeping up a slave system,* like the American; where patrols are provided, informers and prosecutors paid, punishments by stripes ascertained; rewards provided for arresting fugitives; and sheriffs fined for not keeping slaves from all access to types and letters, as in South Carolina, and other States where the law whips the father upon the "bare back," for teaching his child to read the name of Christ. In the Mosaic code, there is no trace of all this. The whole spirit and letter of the laws were entirely different, by which Moses regulated the lowest classes of labor. When a land-holder gathered in his grain, a few handfuls were to be left for the poor to glean. And their servants were their poor, not *excepted* from the poor as our slaves are. They were not to deliver up to his master a servant who had escaped. There was no "fugitive" clause to catch runaways in their constitution. He who should steal and sell a man, (kidnapping,) or, if *the stolen man was* "FOUND IN HIS HAND," (slave-holding,) was put to death. Ex. xvi, 21. This was the law of Moses. There were, in the Jewish system, no Yankee overseers (the best drivers in the world,) to lash them to their work, nor any such provisions as belong to a slave system. Now in Greek, Roman, English, and American slavery, all these exist, *and they must necessarily exist wherever men are made the property of men.* Looking out of the Mosaic system into any one of these systems, is like looking out of the earth (where things are in a mixed and tolerable state,) into hell; which, like the slave code, is full of damnable appliances, and fell implements of torture, whose very nature and construction stamp every one with an evident design of some separate and peculiar mischief.

4. No: *Hebrew bondmen were* NOT *slaves.* Let every eye patiently behold me, and your " ear try my words, as the mouth tasteth meat," while I now show, that *Hebrew bondmen were not slaves, because the three leading human rights were secured to them by the law of God,* viz: LIFE, PROPERTY, and (strange as it may appear to my brother,) LIBERTY! Mark now, and let your ear try my words, and see if I prove what I affirm. I say that they had secured to them the three great rights of *life, property and liberty,* that is, civil liberty, with personal liberty, after short indentures. First, they were secured in their *life.* For this, I quote the law against murder found in Exodus xxi, 12, " *He that smiteth a* MAN so that he die, he shall surely be put to death."

The brother says my arguments from scripture, are "*half uttered.*' I will, therefore, utter with my whole voice, that this divine law, in Exodus xxi, 12, was a law passed for the benefit of the bondsman, against the master, as well as the master against bondsman. There was " *one manner of law,*" for those born in the land, and the stranger from other tribes. When we go farther down in the 21st chapter, we find, that

that much perverted passage, "*he is his money*," is only a merciful provision in the law, to guard against punishing a master capitally, when he did not kill his servant with malice aforethought. When a master killed his servant, he was put to death, but if, on his trial, it was found that he walked abroad a day or two after the assault, the master was not punished capitally, "*because he is his money.*" My brother will not take this, I hope literally. It did not mean that he was silver or gold coin. What, then, did it mean? It meant this. In the 12th verse, it is laid down, "*He that smiteth a man so that he die, he shall be surely put to death.*" Why? because "he that sheddeth MAN's blood, by *man* shall his blood be shed, for in the image of God, made he man."

A slave is as much a *man* made in the image of God as his master, and the reason given for this law by God himself, the same in both cases. Now then, after the law-giver had laid down this law, in tenderness for human life, he laid down the principle; that if the man died under circumstances which showed there was not an intention to kill, (such as whipping with a "rod" or stick, and the man's going abroad afterwards;) the killer's life was saved. The reasoning was this: if he intended to kill, why did he take a "rod" or stick? and not a bludgeon? Moreover, why did he not kill him while he had the man down? And in the third place, the *property* mentioned, is the property of the master *in the service of his bondman;* and not a property in his person. If you had an apprentice bound to you for seven years; your property in him in the sixth and seventh years would be greater than in the first years, because his services are more valuable; now if the master struck the servant with a "*rod,*" but the man afterwards went "abroad a day or two" the inference from these two considerations, added to the consideration that the servant was valuable to him, and his death a loss, was that the master did not mean to kill him, and therefore, was not guilty of murder; hence, although he was punished by the law of "an eye for an eye and a tooth for a tooth," yet the merciful law of God does not take away his life be-

cause there is no malice aforethought. It is therefore a gross
and palpable perversion of scripture to say that the phrase
"He is his money," shows that the Hebrew master owned
the body of his servant. You may, with strict propriety,
use the same phrase of a father and son; or of a master
cabinet-maker, who had taught a boy for four or five years.
Would he let that boy go away at the request of his father
or himself? No: he would say "*This boy is my money*: I
cannot spare him." Thus I have shown that Hebrew bondmen were secured in their *life*, the first of all human rights.
Let us now see how the slave code secures the life of the
slave.

My brother said that I, *or some one else* (!) had written out
a legal argument with great care; as though I had to get help
in constructing my 'arguments. I have, all along, taken my
authority from the slave laws of the States; which I have produced and read; and founded my arguments on the broad
principles of the word of God. And in this stage of the debate, and state of the argument, with this audience, it is a
truly pleasant insinuation of brother Rice that I lack talent
to meet HIM. [A laugh.]

By the law of murder in the Mississippi code, it appears
that if an "out-lying slave" is hailed and does not stop, and
is shot down, the law does not call the act in question, nor is
the shooter accounted a criminal. Thus while the slave's
security to life is taken away by his incapacity to testify, or
to be a party in court, the slave code expressly provides for
killing slaves if necessary to enforce its provisions. While
the Hebrew bondman had his life secured to him by the
statute of God. So that if a man laid his hand upon him
with intent to kill him, so that he died, he was put to death.

Secondly, *The property of the Hebrew bondman was
secured to him.* See Lev. xxv, 49. "Where the Hebrew
who had waxed poor," *and was "sold,"* might be redeemed
by his kindred, "*or if he is able he may redeem nimself."*
Thus, the law contemplated him as a property holder, who

might acquire enough to pay his debts, and "*redeem himself.*"
The word here used, to signify the bond service of the poor
Hebrew, is, "*ebedh,*" which, Dr. Rice says, "is the very word
for slave;" and this "ebedh" was a legal property holder.
Moreover, if he was sold one hour before the jubilee, he was
free at the hour's end; and if able to redeem himself before
the jubilee, that is, if he acquired property enough—if he
had made enough money in the "*ebedh*" condition, he could
redeem himself and go free. He was sold because he could
not pay his debts, like the German "redemptioners," who,
being too poor to pay their passage money to the United
States, were sold, when they arrived at this country, for a
term of years, for the amount of the debt, incurred to the
captain who brought them over.

But it is said that the Hebrew *bond service,* in the scriptures,
is opposed to "liberty" and "freedom." And it is true.
But does that prove it to have been slavery? Apprenticeship and all bond service, is spoken of as opposed to freedom, in the same way. We do not deny that there were
Hebrew servants. There was something there. There was
a bond service there, but no slavery. These Hebrew
"*slaves,*" as he calls them, had no property when they entered into service, but the law allowed them, *if able,* to redeem
themselves before their term of service expired; thus showing
that they could acquire and hold property *during their service.*
But "slaves can acquire nothing, can possess nothing but
what is their masters." In 2 Samuel, 9th, 10th, Ziba, the
servant of Mephibosheth, who was a Hebrew bondman or
"ebedh," had 20 "*ebedhs,*" and king David afterwards divided
the land between his master and himself. This Ziba was
a capable man and gained this property while a bondman
himself—an ebedh—"the very word for slave," as my
brother says, yet he had twenty ebedhs. So, 1 Samuel 9th
chap., Saul was directed by Kish his father, when a young
man, to go out and hunt for his asses. This was before Saul
was elected king. His father, Kish, told him to "take one
of the servants," and search for the animals. Saul, after

passing through many places, was afraid, from his long absence, that his father would leave caring for the asses, and begin to care for him. This servant, who was not a head-servant, but simply one of the rank and file; produced one-fourth part of a shekel of silver, to supply a gift to the man of God, in the neighborhood, who would tell them the way they should go. There are other instances where these ebedhs, had money, independent, and without the knowledge of their masters. The fact that they could redeem themselves, and the fact that Ziba had twenty (ebedhs,) and that this servant had a large sum, in silver, show that the Hebrew servant was a *legal property holder*, secured in this right, as their masters were, by the law of God. Not that every one actually had property, but every one might have, and it was as secure, and the courts were as open to them as to their masters. *They were not chattels.*

And, in the third place, *they had their liberty secured to them*, that is, their civil liberty, which was perfect, with personal liberty after short indentures. The reason of this bond service was simply that untaught heathen, brought among the Jews, might be kept steady until fully reclaimed from their savage ways and worship. It was a wise and good apprenticeship to the business of knowing and serving God. Meantime, having legal existence, they could punish their masters, if they were oppressed, and run away with impunity if they chose. The fundamental idea of the Hebrew bond service, and of slavery, *are* just as wide apart as heaven and hell, that is, they are exact moral opposites.

The very essence of civil liberty, is, that one man has the same chance of justice, by the laws, as another, provided, first, that *life* and *property*, are secured to them. This liberty the Hebrew bondmen had, though Cassius M. Clay has it not. They were more secure in the three principal human rights, than Cassius M. Clay is at this day, and yet, *C. M. Clay*, is a long way from the condition of a slave.

The proof that the laws were as free to the bondmen as to their masters, is the fact, that there was no disabling statute—that the men were not made chattels.   2. The frequent and terrible prohibitions against oppression: " *Wo to them who use their neighbor's service without wages,*" &c. " *Thou shalt not oppress a stranger, nor vex him. If thou afflict them in anywise, and they cry* at all unto me, I will surely hear their *cry, and my wrath shall wax hot, and I will kill you with the sword, and your wives shall be widows, and your children fatherless.*"   And if my brother is famishing for more scripture, I give him Prov. xxxi, 8, " *Open thy mouth for the dumb, in the cause of all such as are appointed to destruction. Open thy mouth, judge righteously, and plead the cause of the poor and needy.*"   *I give him* Lam. iii, 35, 36, " *To turn aside the right of a man before the face of the* Most High; *to subert a man in his cause the* Lord *approveth not.*"   If he still wishes more scripture, I will quote it.   The Word of God blazes from beginning to end with denunciations against those " whose treading is upon the poor ;" and who so destitute, who so poor, as the man who does not own his garments, his wife, his child, or even himself?   It is worthy of the most careful notice, the access which the most indigent and lowest people had to the person, not only of the judges, but of the monarch himself. Witness the two harlots who appeared before Solomon to dispute their claim to an illegitimate child.   The lowest and most wretched outcast thus had free access to their monarchs, who knew that God would judge them if they did not pronounce just judgments.   There were no grand juries intervening between the wronged man and the judge, and no such thing as advocates known in that day ; but justice was direct, and simple, and summary, without delay.

For these facts, I refer to "Jahn's Archaeology," and "Horne's Introduction," both of which my opponent will acknowledge to be good authority.   I refer also to the declaration of Job, himself a prince and a judge, "If I did despise *the cause* (suit) of my man-servant, or of my maid-servant, when they contended with me, what then shall I do when God riseth up? and when he visiteth, what shall I

answer him? Did not he that made me in the womb, make
him?" Job xxxi, 13—15. And I refer to the general de-
,nunciations of the Bible, against those judges who refused
the suits of those of low condition, all of whom had free
access to the courts of justice, and even to the ear of their
monarchs. I have referred to 1 Kings iii, 16—the case of
the two harlots before Solomon—and Deut. xvi, 18, " Thou
shalt not wrest judgment: thou shalt not respect persons:
neither take a gift: for a gift doth blind the eyes of the wise
and pervert the words of the righteous." In the same chapter it is provided, that judges shall daily sit in all the gates,
and hear the complaints of all, without respect of person.
There were six thousand of these judges in the time of David, the King. And this custom was adopted as the most
certain to bring the judges near to the people; because,
sleeping in the cities for safety at night, as they were an agricultural people, they passed through the gates in going
and returning from their labor. They were nomades, or
herdsmen, and in going to *their* flocks out of the city,
they passed directly by the judges seated upon the judgment seat. They were, moreover, as a people, well instructed in the law, and would know whether the judge decided
right or wrong; and the judges knew that if they judged
unrighteously, the vengeance of God would overtake them.
Such was the perfect civil liberty enjoyed by tho Hebrew
slaves. Slaves! That accursed system has so befouled language, that one can scarcely pick up a clean word!!—[A
laugh.]   [*Time expired.*

[MR. RICE'S FOURTEENTH SPEECH.]

Gentlemen Moderators, and Fellow-Citizens:

[We go for free discussion. We are neither afraid to discuss, or afraid to hear discussion. I observe that some are
in the habit of leaving the house as soon as the individual
with whom they agree has done speaking. I hope those
friends who happen to agree with me in sentiment, will not

imitate the example, but will remain and listen to the brother opposed to me.]

I certainly have never thought of calling in question the splendid talents, or the eminent attainments of my friend and brother, the Rev. Mr. Blanchard. I have known, for some time *how great* a man he is. But it will sometimes happen that the greatest men will fail successfully to defend a weak cause. I did not intend to represent Mr. Blanchard as a weak *man*, but as a man laboring to uphold a weak *cause*.

I did not come here to meet a weak man. I desired our abolition friends to select the strongest man they had; for I felt confident in the strength of the *doctrine I hold* on the subject. The brother seems to think that I insinuated, because he had not, for nearly a week, replied to my arguments from the Bible, that he was an incompetent debater. I insinuated no such thing. I meant to say, what I believed to be true, that he was oppressed with the difficulties which ever attend the defence of serious error; and I believe it now.

I enquired not whether any particular church, calling itself Methodist, had ever excluded slave-holders, as such, but whether John Wesley, whose opinion of slavery the gentleman quoted, took such ground. I have just received a note from a Methodist minister, worthy of confidence, stating that Wesley instructed missionaries to the West Indies, to preach the Gospel, but to avoid all interference with the subject of slavery. If it is asserted, that he attempted to make slave-holding a bar to communion, let the documentary evidence be produced. I maintain, that the Methodist church never has excluded men from the church, simply because they were slave-holders. Although that church has been divided by the question of slavery, even the northern division of it has not yet made slave-holding a bar to Christian fellowship. And the same may be said of every denomination of Christians of respectable size in our country. Some small churches have excluded slave-holders from their communion; but their numbers in the slave States, are extremely small. And this fact shows the tendency of abolitionism even in its mildest form to take the gospel from both masters and slaves. There are, at the present time, as I am informed by a Methodist minister who has made the calculation, near four hundred thousand negroes, (almost all of whom are slaves) members of different evangelical churches in the slave States—a number larger than all the churches that have made slave-holding a bar to communion!

The brother has at last approached my argument from the Old Testament; and he tells us that the bond-servants among the Jews were not slaves, but—what think you?—clansmen to a sheik! The Jews, he tells us, were sheiks—a sort of petty princes—and the bond-servants were their clansmen!

[MR. BLANCHARD rose to explain. I said that each head of a family was a sheik.]

It is notorious, that nothing of this kind ever existed among the Jews. Who does not know that they were, and that God designed they should be, an *agricultural* people—not living like roaming tribes of Arabs, but each family having their farm, and their home, and their servants? The Jewish heads of families shieks, followed by *clansmen!* Such an idea, I verily believe, was never heard of, till the dire necessity of abolitionism suggested it, as a desperate means of escaping from the plain declarations of the Bible. It is purely a fabrication of a fact which never existed. No respectable author ever suggested it; and precisely the opposite is true, if we are to believe the Bible. But the truth is, abolitionism can sustain itself only by outraging all rules of language, and all historical truth. Be it so; the candid will judge correctly of its character.

The gentleman says, the Jewish bond-servants were not slaves, because there is no trace of laws to sustain and carry out slavery. I affirm, that there are laws, so plain that he who runs may read. The law expressly permits the Jews to *buy* bondmen and bondmaids of the heathen. Who ever heard of buying *apprentices?* Moreover, the law permits the master not only to claim the services of the bondman, but to enforce obedience to his commands by chastisement. The Jews were permitted to buy bondmen, to hold them as a *possession*, to chastise them and thus enforce obedience, and to transmit them as an inheritance to children. What other laws were necessary?

Again, he argues, that the Jewish servants were not slaves, because, according to Jewish law, the man-stealer was to be put to death. Once more, I ask, is there no difference between stealing a freeman and forcing him into slavery, and purchasing a man already enslaved, so as really to improve his condition? Is there no difference between these two things?

But again, the Hebrew servants, he says, were not slaves, because the three great rights, life, liberty and property were secured to them. And he quotes the law which makes murder to be punished capitally, because man was made in the image of God. But Christians in the slave States believe that their servants were made in the image of God, and that he who kills one of them designedly, is a *murderer;* but this does not prevent them from claiming their obedience. Moreover, it is true, that the civil law protects the lives of slaves, about as well as did the law of Moses. The laws may not be always faithfully executed; but this circumstance does not affect the argument. I have already stated, that in Alabama a man was, not long since, sent to the penitentiary for *ten* years, because he was convicted of having murdered one of his slaves. The gentleman's argument amounts to this: no man can be a slave, whose life is protected by the law, who cannot be killed with impunity. If this be true, I say, there is not a slave in Kentucky; because the civil law does protect the life of the negroes. And with still greater propriety I may affirm, that there are no slave-holders in the Presbyterian church; for, as I have proved, the law of our church forbids any member to treat his slaves cruelly in any way. Yet Mr. B. not only denounces Kentucky as a slave State, but condemns the Presbyterian church as a slave-holding church. Truly, this is hard! The gentleman constantly reminds me of a certain mechanic whose sign over his door was in these words: " ALL SORTS OF TWISTING AND TURNING DONE HERE !" [Great laughter.]

But he condemns me for saying, that if I buy a man, he is *mine*, so far as his services are concerned. Yet the Bible says, that the servant is his master's " *money ;*" and is not a man's money his own? Did you ever hear a man say—I have *bought an apprentice* ? Or " I have *bought a hired* servant ?" Would one of your mechanics in Cincinnati say, " I have bought five apprentices, and they are my *money ?*" The gentleman has seemed particularly fond of telling us about the *fists* of emigrant Germans and Irish. I think I might say, the apprentices of Ohio would show him their *fists*, if he were to speak of them as *servants*, as the *money* of their purchasers ! [A laugh.]

But, if the Hebrew bond-servants were apprentices, how long did their indenture continue? Only six years, I think he said. It is true, that Hebrews who became poor and sold themselves, or were sold, went free at the end of six years. But we are speaking of the *bondmen* and *bondmaids*, bought from the heathen, from whom the Hebrew servant is expressly distinguished. The scriptures teach, that the Jews might buy them, hold them for a *possession*, and transmit them as an inheritance to their children. I should like to inquire of the gentleman, whether apprentices are bequeathed as an inheritance to the children of the man to whom they are bound? Is this the law of apprenticeship in Ohio? The ridiculous absurdity of the idea, shows how sorely abolitionism is pressed to support its claims, and how glaringly it is obliged to pervert God's word, that it may turn the edge of the sword of the Spirit.

As a further evidence of the truth of this remark, observe the course pursued by the gentleman in his reply. In attempting to prove, that there were no slaves among the Jews, he confined his remarks to the case of the Hebrew sold for six years, in consequence of poverty, and said nothing of the *bond-servants* bought of the heathen, who were slaves for life. The law itself, as I distinctly stated and proved, places the condition of the Hebrew servant in contrast with that of the bond-servant bought of the heathen, and forbids the latter to be treated as the former. I will again read the passage.

" And if thy brother that dwelleth by thee be waxen poor, and be sold unto thee, thou shalt *not* compel him to serve *as a bond-servant:* but as a hired servant, and as a sojourner, he shall be with thee, and shall serve thee unto the year of jubilee, * * * * for they are my servants, which I brought forth out of the land of Egypt: *they shall not be sold as bondmen.*"

Here the law distinctly states, that the Hebrew servant is not to be compelled to serve as a bondman, shall not be sold as a bondman; yet the brother presents the case of the Hebrew servant, sold for six years, as though it were identical with that of the bond-servants of the Hebrews!

Why does he not take up the case of the real bondman, bought from a heathen master, held as a possession, and bequeathed for an inheritance?—"for an inheritance for ever." Does this language mean a "short apprenticeship?" The Universalists tell us, that *forever* does not mean forever, but only a limited time; but I never heard before, that it signified so short a period as *five years!* [A laugh.] The term employed is the strongest word in the Hebrew language; yet it means *five years!* This is on a par with his assertion that the servants of the Hebrews were clansmen to Hebrew sheiks! Who ever heard of a sheik whipping the families under him? and buying them? and holding them as a possession? and bequeathing them as an inheritance?

If the gentleman can get over the difficulty placed in his way by the plain letter of the Bible, he must have far more talents, and learning too, than I can pretend to.

[MR. BLANCHARD.—I did not say five years—I said six years.]

Oh! yes—six years:—"forever" does not mean only five years—it means *six years.* I stand corrected! [Loud laughter.] If the Hebrew servant is bought one year before the jubilee, then "*forever*" means *one year!* If it was only three months, then three months was forever! Verily, if abolitionism continues much longer, I should not wonder if "forever" should come to mean nothing at all. [Laughter.]

But he tells us, that Ziba, the servant of Mephibosheth, had servants of his own. The probability is, that before having servants of his own, he had obtained his freedom. On this subject, however, we have no information; and, therefore, the fact stated is a poor offset to the plain declarations of the Bible I have produced.

Servants among the Jews, the gentleman tells us, owned property, and therefore were not slaves. And what evidence does he produce, that they held property? Why, the servant who accompanied Saul in searching for his father's asses, had "the fourth part of a shekel of silver," of which Saul had no knowledge!

This servant could not be a slave, because he had in his pocket the quarter of a silver shekel (worth about five cents). Indeed! Why, there is scarcely a slave in Kentucky, but has as much as that, and more. Some of them can show you laid up in a chest in their quarters, a hundred dollars, besides a horse and saddle of their own, purchased out of their little savings. They sometimes buy themselves and their wives too. Yet because this servant of Saul had a little bit of silver, unknown to his master, he was "protected in the sacred right of property," which is the mark of a free man, and he could therefore be no slave! Why the gentleman is proving, very fast, that there is no slavery in the United States, nor in the whole world.

Aye, but they enjoyed liberty! liberty! Yes; and so do the slaves in our country, about to the same extent. What liberty did they enjoy? What does the brother mean by the term? If he means, that the servant could go where he pleased, serve whom he pleased, and obey or not, as he pleased—then, I say, he had not his liberty. If a man can

buy me—if I am his possession—if he can bequeath me to
his children—if he can beat me with a rod, only so that I
do not die under his hand—will the gentleman say I am
free?

He says that the Jewish servant labored under no disabilities—he was a *man*. The truth, however, is, that the servants among the Jews were bought from the heathen—that
they were held as a possession—that they could be bequeathed, and be inherited—that they could be personally
chastised—and that they are designated by a word which
uniformly means slave. Whether, in view of these facts,
they were apprentices, hired servants, or slaves, I leave you
to judge.

The gentleman has been threatening us all along with
his two speeches of an hour-and-a-half, on the Bible argument; and when they come, he tells me, all my Hebrew
and Greek will be called into requisition. Well: I have
not had much use for the Hebrew and Greek as yet; but I
shall wait calmly and patiently for those powerful speeches.

He has repeatedly insisted, that the word *eved* does not
mean slave; because the translators of our English Bible
did not so render it. He says, they did use the word *slave*
twice. But does he not know, that the word *servant*, derived from the Latin—*servus*—a slave, originally, and at
the time our translation was made, signified a slave? True,
the translators use the word slave twice; but what does this
prove? Does not the word they have translated *slave*, occur more than twice? And did they not, in translating this
word, as in many others, render it by different words having
the same meaning? But the abolitionists admit, that *doulos*
is translated *servant*, when it means a slave; as in 1 Tim. vi, 1,
2. "Let as many *servants* (*doulous*) as are under the yoke,"
&c. "Art thou called being a servant (*doulos*), care not for it."
Now let me turn the gentleman's question against himself, by
asking,—if, as abolitionists admit, the word *doulos*, in these
passages, means *slave*, why was it not so translated? It
does mean *slave* in these passages, abolitionists themselves

being judges; the translators render it "servant," which, according to the gentleman, they never could have done, if it meant slave! Again, I am irresistably reminded of the sign— "*all sorts of twisting and turning done here.*" And is this the best that can be done to show that there was no such thing as slavery among the Jews?

In reply to Mr. B.'s denial, that the Hebrew word *eved* means slave, I asked him a plain question; he has not answered it; and I fear he won't. *When the Hebrews meant to speak of a slave, what word did they use?* I must insist upon an answer. I hope he will not refuse; yet, I do confess, I greatly fear he will forget it. I am really in earnest, and shall be truly gratified to hear his answer.

And now, let me urge my last argument from the scripture, to show, that the "servants" spoken of in the New Testament were slaves; and it is drawn from the directions which the apostles of Christ addressed to those persons. I say, they are directions suitable only to slaves: "Obey your own masters *with fear and trembling.*" "Be subject to your masters *with all fear;*" and that not only "to the good and gentle, but to the froward." And it is added—"for this is thankworthy, if a man, for conscience toward God, *endure grief, suffering wrongfully.*" Would the brother address exhortations like these to the hired servants in Ohio? Does he, as a minister, read to them those directions, as defining their duty? Would not any hired servant in the State, or in this country, deem it an insult to have such exhortations addressed to him? They are as free as their masters; they render *quid pro quo* for all they receive. Are they to obey "with all fear?"—to serve "with fear and trembling?" Are they bound to submit themselves to the froward, "enduring grief, suffering wrongfully?" If the gentleman's assertions be true, (for he says, these passages must apply fully and fairly to hired servants,) the apostles so exhorted such. Let this be known throughout free Ohio, as the abolitionist doctrine. I suspect, it will not be very palatable, at least to hired laborers. I say, these exhortations were addressed to slaves, and that they are applicable to slaves alone.   [*Time expired.*

[MR. BLANCHARD'S FIFTEENTH SPEECH.]

Gentlemen Moderators, and Gentlemen and Ladies, Fellow-Citizens:

I will answer the question which my brother has urged so frequently, since he evidently deems it important, viz: "If the Hebrews wished to say ' *slave*,' what word would they employ?" I do not think of any single word at present, but I suppose that they employed a circumlocution analagous to the Greek phrase used to designate a slave in the New Testament, as in 1 Timothy vi, 1, *doulos hupo zugon*, "*servants under the yoke*," or under bondage to heathen masters who held them as slaves, and not servants to the children of God. No single word in the New Testament necessarily means "*slave.*" It takes a "*doulos under the yoke*" to mean one.

When I sat down, I was in the midst of an argument to prove that the Hebrew bond-servants were not slaves because they had secured to them by law the three great fundamental rights of man; *life, liberty,* and *property.* I showed that they might be redeemed from their bond service by any of their relatives, or *might redeem themselves* if able, before the jubilee, and that they must therefore, (if allowed the latter privilege,) have held property while in their condition of bond-servants. In answer to this, my friend states that the negroes in Kentucky often have money and other property of their own, and sometimes purchase themselves and their families. This argument seems cruel and unfeeling in him, when my brother knows that if they have acquired five hundred or a thousand dollars by their owner's permission, or indeed, any sum whatever, their masters can, and often do take the whole from them and sell them South. It often happens that when a slave has agreed to pay six hundred dollars for his liberty, the master receives from him three, four or five hundred dollars of the amount, and afterwards sells him. And in doing this, the Kentucky master violates no law, but simply uses his slave-holding rights. If the poor slave has but a shilling it belongs to the master. Old Billy Cravens, a Methodist minister, who belonged, by family connexion, to the aristocracy of Virginia, and who preached many years against slavery to both slave-holders and slaves, had closed his sermon on one occasion ; and, when the collection was being taken up, he saw the stewards going up into the gallery to circulate the plates among the slaves ; " Stop !" cried Billy from the pulpit, with his stentorian lungs, " Stop !" " Dont go there ! *They* hav'nt got any thing : They don't own their hats, their coats, or their bodies. No," (said he, raising his voice to the top,) " there is not a louse in their garments that don't belong to their masters." This is literally true. The master owns the body and the garment and all that is in it or upon it. Though sometimes, kind masters will permit them to have money, yet that is granted as a *privilege* and not as a *right.*

But the Hebrew servant had a *right* to his property the same as his master, and if his master took it away from him he could recover it back by suit at law. That is, he was a *man*, with the rights and immunities of a man. While the slave has neither. You can all see the difference between a man's holding his money or his wife *as long as I permit him*, and holding them by a sacred right of which none can deprive him. One state is *slavery*, the other *liberty*. The slave is in the first condition. The Hebrew servant was, as I have shown in the last, moreover, the Hebrew servant not only was a legal property holder, having access to the courts of justice to secure him in his rights, and to punish aggressors, who should trespass upon his rights ; but, after his master's death, in certain cases a share of his goods fell to his servants. Abraham said, " I go childless, and one born in my house " (to wit : Eliezer) " is mine heir." So,

after he had taken Hagar to be his wife, the reason given by
Sarah, why Hagar should be put out of the house, was, that
Ishmael, the son of Hagar (who was a slave according to my
friend) *should not be heir (!) with Isaac.* (Gen. xxi, 10.)
Hagar went out, accordingly, because she was "*put forth.*"
Now if Hagar had been a slave, it would not have been necessary to put her out. She would have gone out very
willingly. They would have had but to open the door and
point to the north star, (if there were a Canada in the region)
and she would have gone out quickly enough of her own
accord. [A laugh] Slaves will always go free when permitted unless slavery has already broken their souls upon its
wheel. But the point is this; *Ishmael had a right to be co-
heir* with Isaac, otherwise there would have been no force in
Sarah's plea to expel her. But the merciful slave-holder
of the South, allows whatever he allows to slaves, as a *privilege,* not as a *right.* The slave cannot keep a shilling in
his pocket, one moment longer than until his owner sees fit
to take it from him. Why he may take all he has and sell
him too! the owner may sell *him* with his shilling in his
pocket. If the master dies, not a cent of his property goes
to his slave. But the slave is put up with the hogs and
sold for a division among heirs. My brother knows all
these facts, but I suppose he means to argue the best he can.
[A laugh.]

I have shown that the Hebrew servant has secured to him
as rights, his life, his property, and his civil liberty, with personal liberty after his indentures expire. "Oh but" says
Dr. Rice, "according to the gentleman; eternity means only
six years!"

Now Dr. Rice knows that Dr. Wilson, of this city, who
strenuously opposes abolition, teaches in his pamphlet, that
fifty years is the longest term the Hebrew bond service could
last, and my friend does not and dare not dispute the fact.
There was no perpetual servitude for the ear-bored servant.
Nor is fifty years any nearer a literal "forever," than six
years? I observed you smile at his reply to me on this

point, but I could not tell whether you laughed at the smartness of the joke or the folly of the argument. Both were somewhat marked.

The Hebrew servant was secured, I repeat, in life, liberty and property, in neither of which the American slave either was or is; and I have shown that Roman, Grecian, English, and American slavery are one and the same. Now if you wish to abolish slavery in Kentucky, what have you to do? Nothing, but to strike the chattel principle from the code, and then give the emancipated free access to the courts. Repealing the chattel principle turns the slaves into men, and giving them access to the courts, secures to them the rights of men. This sweeps slavery from the soil. There is no person in this audience but can see this. If you strike out the chattel principle and enable slaves to come into courts of justice and establish their rights to person, wife, children, property, and character—what is there left of American slavery? *Now these two things* THE MOSAIC CODE DID. No: I do not speak correctly. The Mosaic law did not *strike out* the chattel principle, *for it never was there.* There was, therefore, nothing of the kind to strike out. But it allowed the lowest order of servants free access to courts of justice; and these two things, viz: the absence of chattelism and legal security, show conclusively, that no such thing as slavery did or could exist in Judea. Give the Jewish law of bond service to Kentucky, and the thousands who lie down slaves to-night, will rise in the morning free men. Establish the Hebrew code throughout the States, and there will not be a slave left to wet the soil with the tears, and the sweat of his unpaid labor, in the whole country. So utterly false is it, that " *God did expressly permit his people to hold slaves.*"

Again:—All the Hebrew servants who were bought from the heathen, were to be circumcised. Gen. xvii, 13. " *He that is born in thy house, and he that is bought with thy money, must needs be circumcised.*" And this law of circumcision alone shows that THEY WERE NOT SLAVES. For they had nothing to do, to free themselves, but simply to refuse to be circumcised, unless you adopt the abominable and monstrous supposition that they might be *forced* to be circumcised and profess the true religion. Thus their relation to their master was *a voluntary condition*, while slavery is involuntary, hereditary and perpetual, in the slave and his posterity. Hebrew servitude was voluntary, and limited, ordinarily, to six years, and could never go beyond fifty: and even from this modified bond service, they could free themselves after they were bought from the heathen, by refusing circumcision.

Maimonides, contemporary with Jarki, (both writers of authority with Jews,) says, that the master who had bought a foreign servant, must win him over to the true religion in one year or send him back to his tribe. And his statement surely has reason to support it; seeing there is no other supposition possible, but the absurd one that the Jews filled their land with *forced* converts who were forced to undergo circumcision. If one of these servants bought of the heathen had disliked his condition, refused to be circumcised and become a Jew, what could they do ? Seize him and cut off his foreskin before the eyes of the people ! Surely it was not so that the Hebrews made converts to their religion.

Now Professor Jahn, in his Archaeology, a high authority in Jewish statistics, says that these bondmen "were circumcised," and that "*after circumcision* THEY WERE RECORDED AMONG THE HEBREWS."

Now in the light of all these facts, let us look into Judea, and see what sort of a thing this bond service, or religious serfdom was. Remember, that not only the Hebrew servant who was waxen poor and sold for debt, but the bond-servant bought from the heathen, was required to be circumcised, and all "*were reckoned among the Hebrews,*" and the law of the Hebrew servants was, that they should serve for six years and then go free. " What then," says one, " was the fifty-year jubilee for ?" It was to free any remnant who had waved their right to go out at six years, by having their ear bored before the judges and agreeing to remain until the next semi-centennial jubilee.

' But what was the Hebrew bond service instituted for ? Was it not founded on the same reason as slavery? Was it not indeed slavery for six years ?' No. The end proposed was to bring in heathen and convert them to God. If a servant relapsed into heathenism, his wife and children whom he had obtained while in service, he could not compel to follow him into idolatry and wretchedness. If they remained steadfast in the true religion; he might redeem himself as soon as he was able without waiting for the jubilee ; and he was, at all events free when jubilee came. For in that year, Hebrew bondmen, foreign servants, circumcised, ear-bored servants and all went free. *Lev.* xxv, 10.

The Jews were few land-holders, each land-holder owning a great tract, and each head-man was a priest-prince or sheik—a sheik is a sort of a head of families who unites the sacred and civil characters of priest and magistrate in his own person. These heads of tribes, called " *elders*" were general heads of families like Boaz the husband of Ruth. And their clan was their " house-hold," in registering which, the grandson is frequently called the son ; indeed, the descendants generally, were called children, and the head man the father, or prince. Such was the patriarchal state. If a servant at the end of six years was unwilling to leave his master, he was obliged to take his master before the judge and make that declaration in his presence. His ear was then bored, and he staid with his master till the fifty-years jubilee. The mass of servants were Hebrews by birth, and their servitude of course was only six years. Those who were bought from the heathen became Hebrews by circumcision, and says Jahn, " *were reckoned among the Hebrews;*" from that time. In consequence of this they came under the law of six years. The little remnant of ear-bored servants went free at the jubilee ; but the great mass went free in six years.

In object and effect it appears, that the Mosaic law of bond-service was a sort of missionary mill, to take up the servants of the heathen and grind them into children of God. A system of moral screw-blocks and pulleys, to elevate the heathen from their abject degradation, sunk to the lowest pitch by their worship of idols, to the pure and holy and elevated worship and service of the true God.

Is that system to be quoted here as authority for American slavery, which lays stripes on the back of a slave if he but teach his child to read the sacred name of Jesus?

Moreover, there was in Judea one manner of law for the stanger and him born in the land. But, you recollect, that in the Mississippi criminal code, an article reads thus, "The provisions of this act (the criminal code, condensed into 344 sections,) shall not be construed to apply to slaves." The same law, in principle, was adopted in Kentucky in 1802. The slave is, therefore, left under the brute's criminal code, to be whipped, sold, or killed, as the owner's exigencies may demand. But the Hebrew bond-servant had the same criminal law, the same judge, and the same free access to courts of justice, as his master had. The judges held their courts in the gates of all the cities and towns through which the population passed every morning and evening. In David's time, there were six thousand of these judges! See what ample provision they had for the administration of justice! You will read it in Chronicles xxiii, 4.

The people brought their causes before these judges, in person, as heretofore said, without intervention of advocate or jury. And before the manners of the people were corrupted, the men who were made judges were those most distinguished for wisdom, piety, and integrity. Job was one of these judges, as is evident, from his speaking of himself as "rising up to go to the gate." This wise, and cheap, and equitable administration of justice existed among a people who were better instructed in their laws, perhaps, than any other nation in any age: who, by the appointment of God, wrote their statutes upon the posts of their doors, the borders of their garments, and the frontlets of their foreheads. Judicial proceedings were all summary, as upon the complaints of orphans in the courts of Kentucky. And Horne informs us, in his *"Introduction to the Study of the Scriptures,"* where the matters above are explained in detail; " The Hebrew bondmen were required to be instructed in the laws, on the sabbaths and feast-days, equally with the rest of the inhabitants;" while our slaves are forbidden the language in which the laws are written—and, while slaves can never appear in courts as parties, or witnesses in their own case, the Hebrew bondmen had free access to the person of the judge, and brought their own suits in person, as the harlots came to king Solomon, and the woman deputed by Joab, for restoring Absalom, came to king David.

Thus the poorest poor, the meanest bondman in the whole land, if cruelly treated, could come at once to the judge, lodge his complaint; and the judge at once despatched an officer with him to bring the person whom he accused before him for judgment. The case between them was then heard and summarily determined by judges, subject to an immediate appeal to God, who had denounced and executed the direst judgments upon those who perverted the cause of the poor while sitting in the place of judgment.

Now to say that the condition of men, so circumstanced, was slavery, and, on the strength of such averment, to build the assumption, that " God permitted his people to hold slaves," betrays an entire want of acquaintance with the facts; or a total misapprehension of the bearing and connection of those facts with the principles and elements of civil and personal liberty; or, what is equally deplorable, an utter ignorance of the nature of human rights, and of liberty itself.

Behold, by contrasting the two, the exceeding unfairness of making the elevating and enlightening Hebrew bond-service, a justification and precedent for American slavery.

Moses instituted this legal bond service in an age when absoluteism was the rule in all civil and ecclesiastical matters. At the present day, in enlightened countries, liberty is the rule and restriction the exception. Moses brought men a step forward from an age of darkness toward one of light. Slavery takes society backward to maxims and principles which belong to an age of darkness. In other words—Hebrew bond service brought the race forward; slavery takes it backward.

You will, by an illustration, perceive the incongruity and unfairness of quoting the few restrictions which Mosaic bond service imposed on Hebrew servants, all of which were made necessary by merciful reasons in existing circumstances, to justify the entire deprivation of rights by American slavery, by chattelizing human beings, which no circumstances can make necessary, and against the spirit of surrounding institutions.

Suppose you had a family to rear in a prison-city.; and your yard was environed by other yards occupied by culprits, and men confined as such; the jail-yard on one side, the State's-prison-yard bounding you on another, the work-house on the third, and house of correction on the fourth.—To rear and conduct a family under such environment, many restrictions and impositions would be requisite, for security and morals, which would be arbitrary and impious, even, to lay upon the members of your household in a city like this we inhabit. And yet, to bring the restraints imposed upon a pious household, in the midst of a prison-city, to excuse parental cruelty, is a poor and weak incongruity and absurdity, compared with fetching Mosaic bond service to screen and justify American slavery. For in the supposed case, the *spirit* and object of the two families are the same, while their circumstances are opposite. But Hebrew bond service, and slavery have no one principle in common. The difference between them is the difference between taking fifty prisoners, in the midst of a vast prison, and, leaving some of the prison regulations unrepealed, yet putting your fifty into a system where they *instantly cease to be prisoners*, and gradually become perfectly free—and taking a class of persons and making them prisoners in the centre of a free population. Moses legislated when the world was a prison, and his laws made Judea a free State, in the midst of it. Slavery legislates in the heart of Christendom, and every spot which it regulates is a bastile. Moses was environed with slave States, and produced and conducted a free State in their midst. Slavery is surrounded by free States, whose polity it is all the while mastering and moulding to its own. In the Hebrew system, the utmost that can be said is, that Moses did not take away all restraints, which the world had imposed on human liberty, at once. Slavery invents and imposes restrictions which did not before exist. Every one knows that the Jews became a free nation. Between the Babylonish captivity and Christ, there is among them no trace of slave, though environed by a world full of slave States. It was the operation of the Mosaic code which made them free. Thus Mosaic bond service took those whom the world had made slaves, *i. e.*, servants " bought of the heathen," and turned them into freemen. Slavery takes those whom God made free and turns them into slaves! The restrictions of the bond service grew less and less, by its own legitimate operation, till the thing itself faded out and disappeared. Slavery is perpetually increasing its guards and fastenings, the longer it stands, and must do so from its own nature. And the reason is, that Hebrew bond service was a measure for freedom—the slave system a contrivance for despotism.

The friends of temperance in Ohio, are now asking their legislature to take the power licensing dram-bars, from those who now hold and exercise it to the injury of society; and put it into the hands of majorities of the people. The *reason* of this movement, is a temperance reason, and the movement itself a step toward destroying the dram-bar system. They hope the people will refuse licenses altogether. Therefore, they vote to place the license power in their own hands. Now if we were seeking to turn dram-sellers out of the church, and a vindicator of dram-bars as " not sinful," should quote this *temperance action* in support of their cause, saying: "See the best temperance men in Ohio voted to give majori-

ties power to license dram-bars ! Would they have done
this if they had thought dram-selling sinful ?" Such a man
would outrage fairness and truth, respecting temperance,
precisely as fairness and truth are outraged by quoting the
Mosaic bond service which killed slavery out of Judea, to
prove it not sinful in America! One would be quoting a
temperance measure to shield dram selling; the other, a lib-
erty-measure to vindicate slave-holding.

Whatever temporary restrictions Moses left upon bondmen, "bought of the heathen," by the Jews, every one of
his laws was a repeal of some principle of absolute despotism, in the midst of the world of slavery. Like this placing
the license law in the hands of the people, his servitude-
laws, were, every one of them, liberty movements. My opponent's doctrine, put in practice, is, in every part, a slavery
movement; and quoting Mosaic practice, for it, is a dreadful
perversion. Moses legislated mankind out of an enslaved
state into a free state; while *his* doctrine, that "slave-holding
is not sinful," would legislate men out of a free state, into a
slave! He thus, with terrible fatuity, brings the light of
God's word to conceal the darkness of slavery, and weaves
righteousness itself into a cloak to cover sin! by drawing
illogical inferences from just and necessary institutions of
past ages, and seeking out from antiquity, every restriction
upon human liberty he can find there, to weave them into a
snake coil of argument, wherewith to bind down American
Christianity, to tolerate American despotism, in an age of
reformation, and in a land of liberty and light. [Applause.]

I have done with the Old Testament; and I must tell my
brother that what I have now spoken is nothing which I
have written down since I was sick. [A laugh.]

Gentlemen Moderators, and Fellow-Citizens : I now commence my argument, to close the debate, upon the New Testament. I stand in the Gospel of Christ, to plead for my
clients, three millions of human beings, who cannot plead
for themselves, and I beg, in the name of God, who pities
them, and us all, that you will hear me with patience and

candor. But though I go into scripture, I am not going to turn this argument into a mere bandying of authorities, and a lecture on the interpretation of words. I am weary with this everlasting criticism upon Greek and Hebrew. I will, however, remark, as to one authority whom my opponent refers to, so perpetually. I mean Dr. Cunningham. I have shown you why he was not in a favorable situation, (ecclesiastically speaking,) to understand human rights. As to Dr. Cunningham, personally, I have nothing particular to say. I saw him pleading the cause of the *"Free Church of Scotland,"* standing near the seat of the chairman of the meeting, behind whose seat was placed, upon a small table, some decanters of choice liquors, surrounded, and as occasion required, tasted by his brother divines, doubtless, to keep up the inspiration, and sustain the fatigue of a long meeting in Exeter Hall; and I have occasion to know, that his Scotch authorities, the Cunningham fraternity, are as good against the cause of "total abstinence," as against that of the slave. I have neither time nor inclination to quote *such* authorities.

But I will give you one plain, easy rule, by which interpretations of scripture may be tested, to see if they are true interpretations or false. My friend told you, on Friday, that the Hebrew word *"ebedh," "is the very word for slave,"* while another word *"saukir,"* means "hired servants." As to *"doulos,"* he says, that *"the literal and ordinary meaning of the word doulos, is slave."* I take this from his printed pamphlet, page 177.

Now bear in mind, that if this be true, the translators of our English Bible never once, in the whole Bible, have given the word *" doulos"* its *" literal and ordinary meaning !"* See what a Bible according to Dr. Rice, we have got! The translators of which have never once given to the word *dou-los* its "literal and ordinary meaning" for *doulos* is not translated *slave* in the whole New Testament! and yet it is an important word, and one of frequent occurrence !! The only time the word *slave* occurs in the New Testament, is in Rev xviii, 13, where the Greek is "*somaton*" or *bodies.* If *ebedh* is the very word for *slave,* the translators have not in the Old Testament once translated "*ebedh*" by the word by which it should have been translated! What must become of people's confidence in our English Bible if such statements are to be believed! Gentlemen; there are other words than these used to express slavery. It takes a "*Doulos hupo zugon;*" a "servant under the yoke" to mean a slave. When the sacred writers wished to speak of a slave, they had no difficulty in describing one. But the ordinary meaning of these words is *not* slave.

His error in stating this, is the same as that of a man who should affirm that "*bird*" is "the very word" for "*owl;*" "*bird*" may mean "*owl;*" and so *doulos* may mean *slave;* but these are not their *ordinary meanings.* If one were telling a fable of the owl and spoke of it as "*the bird;*" the connection would show that the owl, was the bird meant. So the connection must show that "*ebedh*" and "*doulos*" mean "*slave*" or *they always mean* "*servant.*" They are generic words like "*bird,*" while "owl" and "slave" are specific words, having a specific meaning. "*Servant*" is the "ordinary and literal" meaning of both "*ebedh*" and "*doulos.*"

I was therefore amazed at my friend's assurance when, declaring "slave" to be the ordinary meaning of these words, he could add: "There is no controversy upon this point!" What! No controversy whether "*ebedh,*" and "*doulos*" ordinarily mean "*slave*" when that meaning is not once given to them by the translators in the whole word of God! Old Testament and New!

But I said I would give you a plain, easy rule, by which you can try his interpretation of these words, and see if it be true. The way to try it, is, to put his definition in place of the word itself, and see how it will read. "The 'literal and ordinary meaning' of 'ebedh' and 'doulos' is slave," says Dr. Rice. Now take this definition and go through the

Bible, putting his definition in place of the word, and if his definition be true it will not change the sense.

Take Psalms cxvi, 16, "*O Lord, truly I am thy servant; I am thy servant and the son of thy hand-maid.*" According to Dr. Rice, this will read—"*O Lord, truly I am thy* SLAVE; I AM THY SLAVE, *and the son of thy female* SLAVE!" The Hebrew word for hand-maid here, is not, however, as I have seen it stated in some abolition writings, "*abdah,*" but another word. Again, in Romans i, 1, *Paul, a servant of Jesus Christ,*" would read, "*Paul, a* 'SLAVE' *of Jesus Christ.*" Thus, my brother not only makes the Eternal God the Father, but Jesus Christ himself, a slave-holder; and all the apostles, who are called the "douloi" of Jesus Christ, his slaves! In Col. i, 7, and iv, 7, Epaphras and Tychicus are called "sun-douloi" of Paul, which Dr. Rice would call fellow-slaves of the apostle. I pause to say, also, that in the solemn address of the Judge at the last day—"*Well done, good and faithful servants*"—must be read, "*Well done, good and faithful* SLAVES!" Thus God and Christ are made slave-holders, and the apostles and ministers of his church, slaves! Not only so, but the angel who said to John, in Revelation, "I am thy sun-doulos," *was a fellow-slave* of God with John the Divine.

Thus his definition, carried through the whole Bible, makes a horrid havoc of its meaning, and turns the whole book into a Newgate calendar, where God is chief superintendent, and angels and apostles the turn-keys and slaves of his will.

So in Luke xvi, the case of the steward who had wasted his master's goods, and went to one and said, how much owest thou my lord? &c., that was a "doulos;" and these servants, or "douloi," are represented as owing, having running accounts, with their lord; that is, they were property-holders, having houses and accounts of their own. Does not this simple fact stultify and cast into utter error the doctrine founded upon the false assumption, that "doulos" is a slave? Remember, the steward says, "how much *owest* thou to my lord." Thus does his false definition make havoc of the meaning of the scripture, and prove itself false by clouding and confounding God's truth.

But the "New England divines!" the "New England clergy!" my brother is evermore backing and sustaining his sentiments and interpretations with opinions of the New England clergy.

It becomes necessary that I should say something of these divines; and, to prevent misconstruction, and charges of abuse, I wish to say, in the outset, that the mass of New England ministers, wherever found, East or West, in my deliberate judgment, for broadness of views and singleness and integrity of heart, will compare with any other class of men on earth of equal number; and that they will do more things in the course of a year for the sake of duty and conscience, without reference to their interest. Yet they are not all of this stamp; nor, unfortunately, the majority of those whom Dr. Rice has quoted in favor of his doctrine in this debate.

One, whom he has often quoted, is a natural born high churchman, the president of a high church seminary, and a fit representative of his class of New England clergy. By high churchman, I mean those men with whom the gospel is grown weak, and who are evermore bringing in church power, and the power of a technical orthodoxy to eke out the power of truth: and *high churchism*, being in its nature spiritual despotism, is perpetually bringing in the principles of other despotisms to justify and strengthen itself. Hence the leaning of this class of ecclesiastics to the doctrines of slavery.

Next to the high churchmen, are a class of men like Dr. Bacon of New Haven, who have some noble sentiments, and generous hearts, and who sincerely love the truth. Hence, like *Dr. Bacon*, when they freely utter themselves, they put forth sentiments which make a clean sweep of the whole doctrine of slavery. These men have a strong sense of justice, and a deep abhorrence of oppression, but stag-

gered by the overbearing influence of the high church party, and dreading to be deemed "ultra," by those who make
this party their standard of orthodoxy, and discretion; de-
terred, moreover, by the natural respect for established
errors of interpretation; and disgusted by the faults and
deficiencies of some leading abolitionists; this class seldom say a smart thing against slavery, but they utter something of another sort to balance it. They make progress,
but they move one step this way and one step that way : and
when, at length, the disturbing causes shall be removed,
they will be out-and-out abolitionists.

Next to these are the abolitionists themselves; honest, sim-
ple-hearted, and clear-sighted; but few of them dwellers in
high places; who take up the truth, and the cross with it, to
bear both after Christ. These give slavery no quarter, but
in principle and in fact, in doctrine and in practice, they
hold it doomed, and act accordingly.

The next large class of ministers are men who have the
minds of followers, and in their several locations do the best
they can. The prevailing element in the whole body of the
clergy of New England is decidedly abolitionist, when it
can be fairly brought out. The General Conference of
Maine Congregational churches, have unanimously condemned slavery, and Dr. Rice's report on the subject to his
last General Assembly. The Massachusetts General Association have done likewise, but with less specification and
point ; and others will follow in a little while.

Having spoken of the propensity of the high churchmen,
to walk softly beside, and look lovingly on civil despotism,
it is proper that I should not leave the subject without saying that there is one New England minister, who, I believe,
my brother has not yet quoted, and, who, through wariness,
is seldom quoted to his disadvantage, who, yet influences
the policy of the eastern churches towards slavery, at this
time, more, perhaps, than all others put together. Concerning this man, I will say nothing but that, if *Talleyrand
had been a Congregational minister, Talleyrand's history*

would have answered for his. I shall not name him, nor
need I, for, whenever you meet an intelligent New England
minister, give him this description, and he will tell you the
man.

But how long shall such men bear rule in the church of
Christ ? How long will intelligent and enlightened Christians for the seductive boon of sectarian quietude and temporary exoneration from self-denial in opposing slavery,
endure the leadership of those who are resolved to keep
them in church fellowship with those who deem no interest
or relation of time or eternity sacred, which stands in the
way of slavery ?—men in whose hands the gospel itself
becomes a yoke, and its blessed precepts fetters ; before whom
marriage, parentage and wages fade away as they are driving,
in their car of slavery, rough shod, over the hearth and
hearts of mankind !

Why do they do this ? Gracious and compassionate God !
What folly blinds them ! What have they done with our
free Bible ? Surely this is that blindness of a land which
precedes and presages destruction. " *Quem Deus vult per-
dere prius demental.*"

They have turned our Bible into a smith shop whence
consecrated hands bring fetters for the feet and manacles for
the mind. They make the Old and New Testament a pair
of hand cuffs ; and the whole book a straight jacket for the
soul ! They have transformed the Eternal Jehovah into a
slave-holder, and his holy inspired apostles into overseers
under him, and the ministers of Jesus Christ into book-
keepers, and drivers, set over separate gangs of men !

> " Just God ! O what must be thy look,
>   " When such a man before thee stands,
> " Unblushing with thy sacred book,
>   " Turning its leaves with haughty hands,
> " To wring from out its text sublime,
>   " This creed of blood and hate and crime !"

But shall they prosper who do this ? No, never ! The
light which beams from that burning page like the eye-
flash of God, piercing and dispersing the mists which they

have thrown around it, as has been already said, and shall
so dazzle and confound their vision, that like Elymas the
sorcerer, they shall seek at noonday some one to lead them
by the hand. Nay, that hand which has been thrust into
God's word, to bring out chains for his children shall be
smitten like the hand of Jeroboam at the altar of Bethel,
when it was stretched out for the destruction of the Prophet
of God. For those who teach the doctrine of slavery are
found in the very wickedness of Jeroboam who "made
Israel to sin." Those who say that the Hebrew servants
were slaves, and that God permitted the slavery of Hebrews,
thereby justify the general enslavement of their species, and
their principles if carried out, would lead to the sale of every poor insolvent laborer of Ohio. It is a Christian duty to
pray against their success ; Forbid it, O thou most merciful
God !

I come now to the direct argument from the New Testament. There are few whims more absurd than the notion
that slavery and slave-holding derive any sanction whatever from the New Testament. But I will take up one argument, which might produce some effect. My brother quotes
the passage containing the words, " believing masters"
1. Timothy vi, 2, and triumphantly asks, in what part of the
Bible are such things as " believing" villains, " believing"
and " faithful " murderers, &c. I answer thus: The apostles in planting churches outside of Judea, planted them in
Roman slave-holding countries. Some slaves came into the
church with their masters. Others had masters out of the
church. When Paul is instructing those who have masters out
of the church, he says to them " art thou called," (or converted,) " being a servant, care not for it, but if thou mayest be made
free, use it rather," precisely the sentiment expressed in the
paraphrase by a modern poet.

> " Wait for the dawning of a brighter day,
> " And snap the bond the moment when you may."

This was the sentiment of Paul, and was addressed to
Christian slaves who had heathen masters. The Roman

Empire extended throughout the world.   There was no Canada outside its border, where the fugitive was safe.   Judea, hitherto their refuge, was now a Roman province.

The Christian church did not wish to preach sedition and rebellion. If they recognized the right of war, in defence of life and liberty, they had no means. Hence, Paul gave such advice as we now would, to a slave in the heart of South Carolina. 1 Tim. vi, 1. "Let as many servants as are under the yoke, count their own masters worthy of all honor, that the name of God and his doctrine be not blasphemed." Here the Greek is "doulos hupo zugon," which is, "servants under the yoke," and is applied to those servants who have heathen masters, to distinguish them from servants who had believing masters, spoken of in the succeeding verse. I admit the *douloi hupo zugon* to have been slaves. And they were hereby advised to treat their masters with respect, that the reputation of the Christian church be not tarnished with the charge of preaching sedition, and the "*name of God and his doctrine blasphemed.*" The next verse is addressed to those who have believing, or Christian masters, "and they that have believing masters, *let them not despise them,* because they are brethren, but rather do them service, because they are faithful and beloved, partakers of the benefit." "These things teach and exhort." Mark the language of this text. "They that have believing masters *let them not despise them.*" Why? A slave despise his master, when that master can cowhide him at any moment, or send him to the jailer to be flogged, and hand-cuffed, or sell him. Ah, things had changed with those who had believing masters. They are all equal now. They are brethren. Servants must not therefore look with scorn upon their former masters, but rather do them service, for Christ's sake, and "because they are faithful and beloved;" not because they can compel them to work. Is that slavery? And these are the masters addressed in Col. iv, 1. "Masters give unto your servants that which is *just* and *equal,* (i. e. "justice and equality," gr.) knowing that ye also have a master in heaven." Is justice and equality slavery?

While heathen, they stood in the relation of master and slave. But now, that they have entered the fold of Christ, they are brethren—equal men. "You, therefore, that were servants, despise not your former masters. But rather do them service, for Christ's sake, and because they are faithful and beloved, partakers of the Gospel benefit with you." Onesimus was a slave, it would seem, when he entered the church, but afterwards became the Bishop of Ephesus. And Ignatius, in A. D. 107, writes concerning Onesimus, and blesses God they have so good a Bishop. You perceive, therefore, that not one of those passages upon which my friend relies to prove the point for which he adduces them, afford the least countenance to his doctrine.

Before I take up the direct argument on the New Testament, I wish to consider a few more points presented by my brother. He insists, and relies much upon the fact that Christ and his apostles did not denounce slave-holding, in so many words, or forbid it, though slavery was all around them.

I reply, that Christ and his apostles did not denounce gambling in so many words, though gambling was all around them. They did not say, "Thou shalt not gamble." Is gambling therefore not sinful?

Again: My friend said: "Is it not strange that slave-holding which is so great a sin, so much more aggravated than gambling, should not be denounced in terms?" I answer, No. There was no need of denouncing it among the Jews, because they held no slaves. "But why not in heathen countries?" I answer, that the whole heathen religion was, a religion of slavery, from beginning to end — from bow to stern. Their very gods and goddesses made slaves of one another. In demolishing paganism, they destroyed the slavery which was in it. Christianity turned the world upside down, and slavery was one of the things which fell out. Paul, when he stood upon Mar's Hill, uttered doctrines which swept from their pedestals the three thousand gods and goddesses of the Athenian calendar, and, with the destruction of heathenism, perished slavery, which was part and parcel of pagan society. This the extract from Ignatius, shows, A. D. 107. And it has crept again from paganism into the Christian church. We, ourselves have received it from the king of Dahomey or some pretty African prince, and have given him in return for this institution, "rum, gun flints," &c. &c. It is no wonder that this particular feature of paganism was not specially and verbally denounced, when they were sweeping away the whole system which contained it. In destroying the greater evil they were effectually destroying the less, which was included in it. For example, in receiving a new servant into your house, you do not take him from garret to cellar, and point out to him every article in the house, telling him "not to steal this," and "not to break that." No, we expect him to follow the great commandment, "Thou shalt not steal," and with that we rest content. It was thus, that the apostles swept off slavery. In the time of Ignatius, so far from holding slaves (though afterwards this came in with other corruptions,) we find they not only did not hold slaves themselves, but the Christian slaves, who had heathen masters were actually importuning the church to vote the church money to buy their freedom.

"But," asks my opponent for the fiftieth time, "*why don't the Bible condemn it?*" I answer, it does. What is that terrible denunciation of those who withhold the hire of the laborer by the apostle James, v, 4, but a stern and awful denunciation of slavery? Unless you make this denunciation to include slave-holders who work their slaves without pay, you charge the Bible with glaring injustice. For, in that case, all that a guilty rich man need to do to keep his crime, and escape its penalty, would be just to pay up his defrauded hired laborers, and then get some persons, whom others have reduced to slavery, and he may work them without wages and be guiltless. Thus, by doubling his guilt, he wholly escapes punishment.

The Bible also denounces slavery, whenever it denounces *oppression.*

Robbery is forcibly taking a man's earnings; theft is stealing them; and swindling is taking them by fraud. Neither of these is, strictly, "*oppression,*"—which is putting your hand through a man's earnings, and taking out of the man himself the right to acquire; and when you have stripped him, not only of the right to acquire, but of every other right, then you have made him a slave. This is oppression complete. And the Word of God is one blazing wall of fiery wrath against this oppression, from Genesis to Revelation. " Thou shalt not oppress the stranger, nor vex him." " Woe unto him that useth his neighbor's service without wages." " Ye make the poor to howl." " Do justly, love mercy, and walk humbly with thy God."

Does not the Bible condemn slave-holding, when it condemns, successively, every element and principle of it?

The Roman Catholics have the form of a curse which they employ in cursing heretics. They curse them in their head, (the curse, I believe, was made by the doctors of the Sorbonne,) in the neck, in the shoulders, in the bowels, in the arms, and legs and feet, and so in every limb and member. Now when they have thus gone through with the man, is not the whole man cursed?

All this the Bible does to slavery—condemning every element, principle, and part of it. Does it not therefore condemn slave-holding?

Again: I refer to 1 Tim. i, 10. " *The law was made for men-stealers,*" &c. In abolishing slavery, you abolish that calling of the men-stealer, and in abolishing that calling you abolish slavery.

My brother is a Presbyterian, after the most strictest sect, and I strive to keep along in his neighborhood. We must alike respect this good old Confession of Faith, which I hold in my hand, and which contains that far-famed note, inserted in 1794, under the 142d question of the Larger Catechism, where it stood, a part of the standard book of the church, unmolested, for twenty-two years. This note, as is well known, declares, explicitly, that the Greek word, "*andrapodistais*," translated "men-stealers," in 1 Tim. i, 10, includes "slave-holders,"—and quotes the Latin note of Grotius, already cited in this debate, to substantiate the fact. This book was used as the standard of the church for twenty-two years, with this note appended, (though it had not authority as an article of faith,)—and yet he tells us that the Bible does not denounce slavery

As I informed you, the last argument I have to produce is the direct argument from the New Testament, and I regret, on my brother's account, that I did not give him a syllabus of it at the opening of the debate, as it might have saved him some impatience. It is as follows:

1. *The constitution of Christianity destroyed slavery whenever and wherever enforced.* If this be made good, it sets the whole question at rest.

2. *The character and standing of the first Christians affords a sufficient guaranty against their members holding slaves.*

3. *The history of the formation of the first churches shows, that there could have been no slave-holding among them.*

4. *The discipline of the apostolic church destroyed slavery wherever it was enforced.*

The first of my propositions, you will observe, is, that *the consitution of Christianity destroyed slavery whenever and wherever it was enforced.* I wish you well to consider what a constitution is. It is the supreme law of the land, and lies lower than common law or statute in the polity of the community. The common law is silent when the statute speaks—the statute is silent when the constitution speaks. In England there was no statute abolishing slavery. In the Granville Sharpe case, the judges simply declared that it always was British law, that as soon as a slave touched English soil he was free—but that the law had merely lain dormant. So it was in Massachusetts: they never enacted a statute abolishing slavery; the Bill of Rights was incompatible with slavery—the enforcement of the one was the abolition of the other. It is so in my native State, and it is so in other States. I propose to show, that the constitution of Christianity was, and is, the abolition of slavery. And, as this is a hinge point of this whole argument, I hope you will follow me with patience and care through my remarks on this head.

What was the constitution of Christianity?

1. It was the constitution of the Jewish church revised, amended, and enlarged by Christ. It was a new edition of the Jews' religion, revised, enlarged, improved, and adapted to the condition of all mankind. By it the folding doors were opened, and the kingdom of God preached to all men, inviting all to press in and partake of its high privileges: "*The law and the prophets were until John; since that time the kingdom of God is preached, and every man presseth into it.*" Luke xvi, 16.

To know what is the constitution of Christianity, therefore, we must have in mind what was the constitution of the Jewish church.

I have already shown, that the Hebrew bond-servants were not slaves: and I am about to show, that the Jewish constitution was both a non-slave-holding and an anti-slave-holding constitution. It was non-slave-holding, so far as it regards *stealing men and holding stolen men.* Ex. xxi, 16, "*He that stealeth a man and selleth him, or if he be found in his hand, he shall surely be put to death!*" Again: the Jewish church was non-slave-holding, as to returning fugitive slaves from the heathen tribes. Deut. xxiii, 15, "*Thou shalt not deliver unto his master the servant which is escaped from his master unto thee.*"

But the Jewish community was not merely *non-slave-holding*, but an *anti-slave-holding* body; that is, they not only abstained *from slave-holding, but vigorously opposed it.* In the 34th chapter of Jeremiah, it appears, that the Jewish nation had relapsed into something like slave-holding in this way. They obeyed God's command, in letting go their servants at the end of six years, and then, under pretence that they had complied with the precept by leaving them free a single year, they laid hold of and reduced them to service for another six years : " *Therefore, thus saith the Lord, ye have not hearkened unto me, in proclaiming liberty, every one to his brother, and every man to his neighbor : behold I proclaim a liberty for you, saith the Lord, to the sword, to the pestilence, and to the famine : and I will make you to be removed into all the kingdoms of the earth.*" Jer. xxxiv, 17.

This struggle of the Jewish nation to expel and keep out *slavery* which had begun to insinuate itself through to the violated law of bond service, stamped their minds and measures as abolitionists : and made them known to neighboring tribes as a nation of abolitionists. And the surrounding nations knew that they were anti-slave-holding people, because they had always harbored their fugitive slaves, and refused to return them. Those towns along the Ohio River where the people harbor, and help off fugitive slaves, are known as anti-slavery towns throughout the entire slave-holding region. And as the law of God forbid the Jews to return fugitives to their masters; as the Jews had abolished the first elements of slavery which appeared among themselves ; and as they were surrounded by slave-holding nations; the Jewish church was known to be both a non-slave-holding and anti-slave-holding church.

The next question is : *what alterations did Christianity make in the Jewish constitution?* When Peter preached Christianity on the day of Pentecost he showed his auditors that it was *made out of the same promises* of which the Jews' religion was made. These same promises, made to the ancient Jews he told his hearers " were unto them and their children." But, though Peter and the other apostles, in founding the Christian church, preached out of the Old Testament, showing that, in substance, the new religion was the same with the old ; yet Christianity did make alterations in Judaism. What were they ?

1. In the first place the Jewish religion made distinctions

between male and female as to personal consideration and rights. Their women had almost no rights; they were menials to their husbands and parents. They had no name in the church rolls, and could take no part in their religious rites. It is so in Judaism to this day; if you go into the Jewish synagogue on Sycamore street, in this city, you will see the men conducting religious worship in the house, and the women looking from the lobby, or the gallery in the rear. Wives were bought and treated by the husband as serfs and dependents.

The first alteration which Christianity made in the polity of Judaism, was to abrogate this oppressive distinction of sexes; declaring that, while the husband is the head of the wife, yet in " Christ Jesus there is neither male nor female." The degrading serfdom of the woman to the man, was abolished. Christ declared the husband and wife to be " one flesh," and set the woman in the family, by the side of her husband, as she stood when first created his helpmeet, and not his menial dependent. This was one alteration which the constitution of Christianity made in that of the Jewish church. [*Time expired.*

[MR. RICE'S FIFTEENTH SPEECH.]

Gentlemen Moderators, and Fellow-Citizens:

[I wish to state, that I have received a note from the elders of the Sixth Presbyterian church in this city (to which my brother has been ministering) respecting what I said I had been told of its unprosperous condition, in which they desire me to recall the statement. They know perfectly well what called forth my remark; my opponent had spoken of the declining state of religion in southern churches.]

[MR. BLANCHARD.—I deny it.]

[The brother did certainly say, that the millenium was kept back by the existence of slavery in southern churches.]

[MR. BLANCHARD.—Yes, I did say so, the curse of slavery is on us all.]

Then, surely the Sixth church, having fully washed its hands of the sin, would, like Gideon's fleece, be wet with the dews of heaven! Surely we have the right to expect it to be prosperous beyond any other. Yet such, it appears, is not the fact. My remark was made, not in the absence of the persons concerned, as have been many of Mr. B.'s statements, but in the presence of the pastor, who, if my information was incorrect, could have at once corrected me. He replied, stating all the facts deemed important. There is, of course, no necessity of my saying anything more on the subject.]

I will here notice one of the gentleman's arguments to prove, that God has given men permission to do that which is in itself sinful, which I forgot at the proper time. He says, God directed the Jews, when about to leave Egypt, to *borrow* of the Egyptians articles which they were not to return.

This I deny. The word translated "*borrow*," signifies *to ask;* and it is so explained, if I rightly remember, by Dr. Adam Clarke. I utterly deny, that God directed them to practice deception, and thus commit sin. The Egyptians, trembling under the judgments of God, were anxious to have the Jews depart from the country; and God directed them to *ask* of them such articles as they needed.

The gentleman's argument seems to be this: it is vain to argue that slave-holding is not in itself sinful from the fact that God gave the Jews the permission to form the relation; because he directed them to borrow what they never meant to return, which according to every code of morals is a sin. I deny that they did so borrow, or that God gave them direction or permission to do so; and if he did not, his argument falls to the ground. I take the ground, the correctness of which is too obvious to require argument in its support, that God never, at any time, under any circumstances, did give men permission to do what is in itself sinful. And I say, the fact that he did give express permission to the Jews to hold slaves, proves, that there were, and again may be, circumstances under which it is not wrong.

I have proved from the text of the New Testament, that the servants there spoken of were slaves, and the masters there referred to, slave-holders; and I have given for that opinion the following reasons.

1. The word *kurios*, translated *master*, properly signifies possessor, owner, master—one possessing absolute authority. This being its meaning, when employed to designate master of servants, it means an owner of slaves, over whom he has positive authority. 2. The word *doulos*, translated *servant*, properly and literally translated, means *slave.*—The lexicographers uniformly so define it. 3. The Greeks had a word which properly and literally means a *hired* servant, viz; *misthotos*; but it is not used by the apostles in addressing servants concerning their duties to their masters. 4. The classical usage of the word *doulos*, as I proved, shows conclusively, that its proper and ordinary meaning is slave. It is so used by Herodotus, Plato, Harpocation, Pausanias, Eaustathius, Julius Pollux, Xenophon, and others. 5. The Bible usage was proved to be the same. There *doulos* stands, in contrast with *eleutheros*, free.. 6. Besides, the word occurs in connection with the word *despotes*, which is admitted to mean *slaveholder*; and we read of " believing masters" or slave-holders, "faithful and beloved, partakers of the benefit"—"good and gentle" "slave-holders."—And the slaves are exhorted to obey them the more cheerfully, because they are pious men. 7. And finally, the directions given to servants, are such as to apply only to slaves.

I wish now to strengthen my argument by quoting several of the most celebrated commentators and critics—those men so complimented by the gentleman, as weak and of timid minds· I wish to show the audience, that eminently wise and good men are unanimous in giving to the scriptures I have quoted, the same interpretation for which I have contended. We will first examine the views of a few of them on the slavery which existed amongst the Jews.

Matthew Pool, the learned author of the *Synopsis Criticorum*, in his comments on Gen. xvi, 6. *In manu tua*, sub potestate tua, a qua eam non liberavi accipiendo in uxorem secundum. *Utere ut libet*, non permittit saevire (maxime in gravidam) sed compescere. Jus vitae et necis tum habebant domini et dominae. *In thy hand*—under thy power, from which I did not liberate her by receiving her (Hagar) as a second wife. *Do to her as it pleaseth thee.* He does not permit her (Sarah) to treat her with severity, (especially as she was pregnant) but to restrain her. Masters and mistresses then had power of life and death [over the slave.] Again, on Exod. xxi, 21. *Quia pecunia illius est*—Possessio. Comparatus est pecunia ejus. Ergo jure moderate castigare poterat Consequentea duplex est. Non debet puniri—1. Quia amisit quod suum erat, et in eo satis punitus est, quod pecuniae suæ jacturam feccit. *Because he is his money*—his possession. He was bought with his money. Then he might justly inflict upon him moderate chastisement. The consequence is twofold. He ought not to be punished; 1. Because he had lost what was his own, and was sufficiently punished in the loss of his money, &c.

Dr. Clarke, on Gen. xvi. "As Hagar was an Egyptian, St. Chrysostom's conjecture is very probable, that she was one of those *female slaves*, which Pharaoh gave to Abraham, &c. The slave being the *absolute property* of the mistress, not only her person, but the fruits of her labor, with all her children, were the owner's property also. *"Sarah's maid'* —This mode of address is used to show her that she was *known*, and to remind her, *that she was the property of another."* Again, on Gen. xvii. *"He that is born in thy house*, the son of a servant—*bought with thy money*—a *slave*—on his coming into the family. According to the Jewish writers, the father was to circumcise his son, and the master the servant born in his house, or the slave bought with money."

In view of these extracts from Clarke, I make two re-

marks: 1. The audience will remember, that when I challenged the gentleman to produce one respectable commentator or critic who differed from me in the exposition of these
scriptures, he triumphantly adduced Dr. Clarke. You now
see not only that he agrees with my exposition, but that his
language is stronger than I have used. Hagar, he says,
was reminded by the angel, "*that she was the property of
another,*" &c. 2. Clarke, you observe, appeals to the Jewish
writers, who say, the master was to circumcise "*the slave*
bought with money." Yet the gentleman gravely tells us,
the Jews had no slaves bought with money. How, then,
happened the Jewish writers so to understand this law?
Either Mr. Blanchard is in error, or the Jewish writers
were strangely mistaken.

Let us hear *Dr. Thomas Scott,* one of the best commentators in the world.   On Levit. xxv, 44—46, he says—"The
Israelites were permitted to keep slaves of other nations; perhaps in order to typify, that none but the true Israel of God
participated of that liberty with which Christ hath made his
people free.   But it was also allowed, in order that in this
manner the gentiles might become acquainted with true
religion."

We will now consult the excellent *Matthew Henry.*   On
Levit. xxv, 44, he says—"That they [Jews] might purchase bondmen of the heathen nations that were round
about them, or of those strangers that sojourned among
them, (except those seven nations that were to be destroyed,)
and might claim a dominion over them, and entail them
upon their families, as an inheritance; for the year of jubilee should give no discharge to them."

You remember, the gentleman told us, the Jews were
permitted to buy servants only of the *seven* nations of Canaanites, devoted to destruction.   Henry tells us, they were
allowed to buy, not of those nations, but of all others.   Again:
Mr. B. told us, *six years* was the duration of the labor of the
bond-servant bought of the heathen.   Henry tells us, even

the year of jubilee, the fiftieth year, gave no release to them. Professor Bush, whom the gentleman will scarcely charge with being a man of timid mind, or of walking in the old beaten paths, takes the same view of this subject as the authors already quoted.

We will now hear from Professor Stuart, of Andover, one of the most learned critics of the age. In a letter addressed to a friend, who has kindly allowed me to use it, he says:— " Levit. xxv, 46, decides, that the Hebrews might not only procure HEATHEN SLAVES, but pass them, as a part of their *inheritance*, to their children. *Laresheth ahuzza* can mean nothing else. The next clause decides the *perpetuity* of this inheritance. *Leolom behem taavodoo*, literally translated, means—*ye shall do service by them forever;* which can mean neither more nor less than that they might be servants perpetually, *i, e.*, as long as they lived. The case of the Hebrew servant is made expressly different, by the context, and is recognized at the close of v. 46. It is impossible to doubt, *exegetically*, what this means."

Observe, Stuart (who, by the by, is an anti-slavery man) does not only say, that the language *will bear* the interpretation he gives, nor that such is its obvious meaning; but he asserts, *that it can mean nothing else—that it is impossible to doubt what it means*—there can be no controversy on the subject. This is strong language.

But let us hear him on the teaching of the New Testament, on precisely the question now under discussion. He says: "As to the question—*whether the bare relation of a* MASTER *to a* SLAVE *is sin*, Paul has settled this. He never once bids the master *dissolve* it, nor liberate the slave from it; but always gives precepts regulating the demeanor of both in this relation. What hinders a Christian master from treating his slaves well? Nothing but cupidity or cruelty; both of which are sins. Paul would not break, by *violence*, the civil relation. But Paul himself gave precepts, in abundance, which, if obeyed, would bring all slavery, ere long, to an end."

Professor Stuart thinks that the Gospel, embraced by master and slave, contains precepts which, if obeyed, would, ere long, bring slavery to an end; but he holds, nevertheless, that the thing itself is not sin. We are blamed as being behind the age, and we have been charged with seeking to drive from our church "the New England spirit." Behold the language of one of New England's wisest sons! He sustains fully the position for which I am contending.

What says the brother to John Locke, one of the greatest friends of human freedom. He was not, I presume, among the gentleman's timid, narrow-minded commentators. He was not under the influence of German critics, whose ideas are "baked stiff" in the oven of German hermaneutics; yet he in his paraphrase of the Epistle to the Ephesians, speaks of the servants addressed by the apostles, and held by pious masters, as "*bondmen*" and "*bond-slaves.*" I might also quote Gill and Bloomfield, (that acute and learned critic,) Chalmers and Cunningham, men revered throughout Scotland, and through the christian church. I may also, with propriety, appeal to the General Asembly of the church of Scotland; for that learned and venerable body has recently, with great unanimity, adopted a report, in which the ground is distinctly taken, that the relation between master and slave is not to be regarded as a sin, excluding the master from church fellowship.

The American Board of Commissioners for Foreign Missions—almost all of them New England men—take the same ground I am contending for. They were petitioned by certain abolitionists, to take the ground that slave-holding was in itself a sin, and must be made a bar to communion in all the churches organized by the missionaries, under the care and control of the Board; but they refused. And what reasons do they give.

"Strongly as your committee are convinced of the wrongfulness and evil tendencies of slave-holding, and ardently as they desire its speedy and universal termination, they still cannot think that in all cases individual guilt exists in such a manner that every person implicated in it can, on scriptural grounds, be excluded from Christian fellowship. In the language of Dr. Chalmers, when treating on this point in a recent letter—the committee would say, 'Distinction ought to be made between the character of a system, and the character of the persons whose circumstances have implicated them with it. Nor would it always be just if all the recoil and horror, wherewith the former is contemplated, were visited in the form of condemnation and moral indignancy upon the latter.'

"Dr. Chalmers proceeds to apply this distinction to the subject now under consideration in the following manner, in which sentiments substantially Drs. Candlish and 'Cunningham, with the whole General Assembly of the Free Church of Scotland, unanimously concurred: 'Slavery,' says he, 'we hold to be a system chargeable with atrocities and evils, often the most hideous and appalling, which have either afflicted or deformed our species. Yet we must not, therefore, say, of every man born within its territory, who has grown up familiar with its sickening spectacles, and not only by his habits been inured to its transactions and sights, but who by inheritance is himself the owner of slaves, that unless he make the resolute sacrifice and renounce his property in slaves, he is therefore not a Christian—and should be treated as an outcast from all the distinctions and privileges of Christian society.'

"Such substantially are the views of your committee, and tho more thoy otudy God's method of proceeding in regard to slavery, polygamy, and other kindred social wrongs, as it is unfolded in the Bible, the more they are convinced that in dealing with individuals implicated in these wrongs of long standing, and intimately interwoven with the relations and movements of the social system, the utmost kindness and forbearance are to be exercised, which are compatible with steady adherence to right principles."

This report was drawn up by Dr. Woods, one of the ablest and most godly men who live to adorn the American church of Christ; or, at any rate, he was chairman of the committee. Such is the ground taken by the American Board. They approve, as you perceive, the opinion of Dr. Chalmers, that the principles and practice contended for by modern abolitionism, are novelties in the church.

I propose now to read a few extracts from the speeches made by members of the Board, as published in the New York Observer, that we may know their sentiments on the question before us. I will, first, read from the speech of Dr. Bacon, of New Haven; and I do so the more readily, because in the notice taken of the action of the Connecticut Association, by the *Watchman of the Valley*, Dr. Bacon was paraded boastfully as an abolitionist, and the representation I had made of the action of that body was thereon pronounced incorrect. We will now hear Dr. Bacon speak for himself.

"We are all agreed that the system and the laws that sustain it are an abomination in the sight of God and the nations of the earth. But these memorialists contend that no man having the relation of a slave-holder, can give evidence of piety. But if there is one thing plain on the face of the New Testament, beyond all dispute, it is that in the churches formed by the apostles, there were *believing masters*, slaveholders, and I will never consent to put the Bible under my feet to accommodate the views of any man.

"I would like the report better if it contained a distinct avowal that slave-holding is not a sin in itself, in such a sense as to disqualify a man for church membership, and on the other hand if these missionaries fail of doing their duty in inculcating the truth on this subject, they should be called to account by the Board."

I will now read a little from Professor Stowe, a first rate abolitionist, and one whom the brother will hardly call weak minded or timid. He has bitterly denounced the report adopted by our General Assembly; but, with singular inconsistency, he warmly defends that of the American Board, which embodies the same great principle, that slave-holding is not in itself a sin which should exclude any one from the church of Christ.

"Dr. Stowe said he had conned this report over and over again, and he had heard all the objections to the report, and he knew they all proceeded from ignorance of it. With this prefatory remark he read the report, after which he continued to say that it was the desire of the committee to express the most decided and fullest condemnation of slavery in all its bearings. And as to the evils enumerated as connected with slavery, every member would say they demanded immediate discipline. The point where they differed from the memorialists was on the question, whether slave-holding is a sin *per se*. Here they did differ."

Dr. Williston, and Dr. Tyler, of the Connecticut Association, asserted the doctrine put forth by the Assembly.

"Rev. Dr. Tyler said, after all the discussion, he was more and more convinced of the wisdom of the report. This he inferred from the directly opposite character of the objections urged against it. It is objected to by the gentlemen from the South because it denounces slavery, and by our abolition brethren because it does not. I therefore think we have hit upon the happy *mean* where the truth lies. He then showed the views of the committee to be, that the apostles did admit slave-holders to the church, and for us to decide against it would be to impeach the apostles. We are conscientious in this opinion. Dr. T. then reviewed the report and expressed the hope that it would be unanimously adopted."

Dr. Wisner takes the same ground:

"Dr. Wisner lamented this discussion. He said that it was evidently directed, not at slavery in mission churches, but at southern slavery. He spoke of the general discord produced by this subject, and said he had hoped this Board would be left free from it, especially when there was already another Board organized for the very persons who were urging this on us. Let the Union Missionary Board take its own course, in its own way; and may we not be permitted to pursue ours in the way that our charter prescribes. If a rumor had come to us, that in the churches in some mission field intemperance was prevailing, would this course have been pursued by these persons. What would have been done? Discuss the merits of drunkenness and temperance societies! No sir. I am constrained to believe that the object of all this is abolitionism in its general bearings, and not the good of the poor Cherokee. But can we satisfy these gentlemen? One of the last speakers told us there was no common ground unless we go the whole length. Common ground, if we come over to them! And this common ground is to give up the Bible, and rely on some principle back of and independent of it. Can we find this common ground? Yes, by asking these brethren what they claim and come to it. But next year there will be another common ground. Yield, and you must yield. I would as soon undertake to fill the bottomless pit as to satisfy men who have their minds fixed on this one absorbing idea."

Such are some of the views entertained by distinguished members of the American Board. Much as the brother said against commentators, he will scarcely say, that these are weak-minded and timid men.

The same views are entertained by Doddridge, Dr. Mc-Night, Bloomfield, Scott, Gill, and in a word, by every respectable commentator and critic, and theologian, I ever read.

I will now take up my opponent's last speech, and reply with as much rapidity as possible.

I had asked the gentleman whether the Hebrew word *eved*, rendered bond-servant, did not mean slave, and if not, what Hebrew word did express an idea which could not but be familiar to the Jewish mind, since the nation was surrounded by slavery in its worst forms: that is, when an Israelite wished to speak of a *slave*, what word he used? I have at length, been favored with a reply. He says, he supposes they used some words analagous to the Greek phrase in 1 Tim. vi, 1, *doulos hupo zugon*, "servant under the yoke."

That is, *he supposes the Hebrews had no word for slave*, a thing known throughout the earth and having its title in every tongue.   No man can believe this, unless he is resolved to take leave of common sense.   I will venture to say, the gentleman cannot get a Hebrew scholar in the land to sustain him in his opinion.   It is given up, then, either that the word *eved* means slave, or that the Hebrews had no word for that idea.   He did, indeed, tell us in a previous speech, that the Hebrew servant sold for six years, is called *eved;* but such is not the fact.   On the contrary, that class of servants is contrasted with the *eved.*

The gentleman tries to get out of the difficulty, in which he involved himself, by attempting to prove by the fact that Saul's servant had a little piece of silver in his pocket without his master's knowledge, that there were no slaves among the Jews, by saying, whatever the slave has, his master can take away from him.   Yes—we know that the slave laws permit him to do so; and so the civil laws would permit a father to take away every cent his son might have labored for, and saved, even the day before he came of age; but what does that prove?   That masters never allow a slave to have a sixpence in his pocket?   Or that if a slave has so large a sum by him unknown to his master, he is no slave?   Or that my son is a slave, because I can take from him all his little savings?

But the gentleman asserts, that the Hebrew bond-servants might be and were property-holders; and that Sarah was afraid that Ishmael, Hagar's son, should be co-heir with her own son Isaac.   I call for the evidence of the truth of this assertion.   Let him if he can, point to the provision in the Jewish law, authorizing *bond-servants* to hold property.   (I am not speaking of poor Israelites, but of bondmen bought of the heathen, or the strangers living amongst the Jews.)   If there is any such provision in the law, my brother is the very man to find it.   Let it be produced.

As to Sarah's fear that Ishmael might be heir with Isaac; has the gentleman forgotten, that Ishmael was Abraham's *son?* That was the ground of her fear, and not because Hagar was free.

The gentleman would make the impression, that the slaves generally bear a mortal enmity against their masters, and are ready to embrace the first opportunity to run from them. By way of replying to this representation, I will tell you an anecdote. Some years ago, a gentleman who had been a resident in Alabama, and who owned a number of slaves, on his way to Philadelphia, met on the steam boat a very zealous abolitionist preacher. In conversation he assured him, that in a multitude of instances, slaves were very strongly attached to their masters, and could not be easily induced to leave them. The abolitionist replied, that slave-holders might tell such stories; but he believed not a word of them. "Well," said the southern gentleman, "you shall have the opportunity of testing the truth of my statement. One of my colored men, reared in the family, is on board. I will call him up; and you shall be at full liberty to take him with you to Ohio." The man was called; and his master said to him: "This gentleman is a minister of the gospel. He is opposed to slavery, and desires you to go with him to Ohio, and be free." The negro considered the proposition seriously for a few moments, and then replied: "Ah, massa, I know you; I don't know dat gentleman. I'll stay with you." So he went to Philadelphia, and lived happily in the family of his old master, where I saw him a short time after this occurrence. And I can point you to negroes in this city, now living in the family of their old master, who is no abolitionist, and whom it might be difficult for the abolitionists with all their zeal, to induce to leave him. Facts like these do afford an edifying evidence of the truth of the assertions of abolitionists, that the slaves bear a mortal enmity to their masters, and only want an opportunity to escape from them.

The gentleman tells us, that all slaves among the Jews were free at the end of six years. Now it is a little hard that abolitionists in their great zeal for whatever is black, should run directly against each other. Yet so it is. Hear Mr. Thomas, a very staunch abolitionist.

He says—" It is but candid to admit, before leaving this topic, that Gentile servants seem to have been in a condition, in some respects inferior to that of Hebrew servants. 1. They were never purchased for six years; but always till the jubilee. 2. No mention is made of Hebrew servants, even when their ears were bored, laboring for the children of their master; whereas if the master of a Gentile died before the jubilee, he was inherited by the children, and retained until his whole time of service expired." (Lev. xxv, 46.) *Review of Junkin*, p. 90.

Thus does an abolitionist of the first water flatly contradict the gentleman, and assert that Gentile servants were never bought for six years, but always till the jubilee.

Now if we admit this statement of Mr. Thomas, though it is not true; what proportion of the bond-servants bought of the heathen, would live to be free? The man of thirty years of age, bought immediately after the jubilee, would be *eighty years* old, if he should live to see the day of freedom. To a considerable proportion of those servants the period of bondage would be during life. But the *principle*, as already remarked, is not affected by the *duration* of the servitude. If the relation of master and slave is in itself sinful, it was wicked to have it continue five years, as truly as during life. So we are forced to the conclusion, that, if abolitionism is true, God gave the Jews express permission to commit sin and oppress their fellow men for *forty-nine* years!

He says the Jewish law struck out the chattel principle. But what does he mean by the chattel principle? Is it embraced in the permission to buy servants, possess them, bequeath them, and compel them even by chastisement, to serve? Were not all these elements in the bond service of slaves whom the Jews were permitted to purchase from the Gentiles? If he says, that is liberty, I have no earthly objection. If a man who can be bought, and held, and forced to serve, and bequeathed as an inheritance to children *forever*, is a free man;—very well. Then the slaves in the United States are all free; and the abolitionist society have nothing to do! Such, however, is not my notion of liberty.

As to access to the courts, which, he says the Jewish bond-servants had, (because they passed by the place where the court was held) might not the slaves in our country have the same rights without destroying the relation? If they are treated with cruelty, and can prove the wrong, they can have redress even now, at least in Kentucky. But does the enjoyment of this right, destroy the relation, or prove they never were slaves, but only hired servants?

Again—the logical gentleman told us, the Hebrew bond-servants were not slaves, because, in the first place, they could refuse to be circumcised; and then they could not be held as slaves; and, in the second place, if they were circumcised, they became Jews, and their term of service continued only *six years*. And, in proof of this last statement, he refers to Jahn, a learned Papist. This is, indeed, a curious jumble to come from so learned a gentleman as my opponent. It is true, that *adult* persons might refuse to be circumcised, and thus avoid being bought by a Jew; for it was not the purpose of God, that the servants of his people should be pagans. But, as slavery in its worst form existed amongst all the nations around the Jews, multitudes of the slaves would desire to exchange their severe servitude for that amongst the Jews, which was comparative freedom.

But Jahn does not say, that the bondmen bought of the Gentiles, were free at the close of six years. He does, probably, say, that they, on being circumcised, enjoyed all the privileges of the Jewish church. This is true. But he says, the Jewish bondmen were slaves, in the true sense of the word. It matters little, however, what Jahn says. The question for us to determine, is—what says the law? The gentleman's statement places two of the divine laws in flat contradiction to each other. One law, forbids the Jewish servant, sold for six years, to be treated as a *bond-servant.*

Levit. xxv, 39—43. And the reason given is: "For they are my servants, which I brought forth out of the land of Egypt." The other law, if we are to believe Mr. B., requires the bondmen, bought of the heathen, to be circumcised, and then requires them to be treated precisely as a Jewish servant, because they have become Jews! That is, the law forbids the Jewish servant to be treated as the bondservant; and then makes the bond-servant a Jewish servant!!

There is not a scholar of any standing to be found, who will confirm the gentleman's assertion, that the bondmen among the Jews went free at the end of six years. Even his own friends, the abolitionists, will not assert it.

The brother, however, tells us, that there was one law for the stranger, and for him that was born in the land. And by the stranger he understands these bondmen who came from the heathen, and who, according to him, were not slaves. Strangers might, indeed, reside among the Jews, either as "proselytes of the gate," or "proselytes of righteousness;" and to these there was the same law as to Israelites, though, to the former, not the same privileges. But they were not servants at all, but were wholly a different class from the bondmen bought with money, who were never called "strangers."

He represents the laws of Moses, concerning servitude, as designed to keep the servants, bought of pagans, within bounds, till they became converted, and joined themselves to God's people. This, however, is but a flight of his imagination. For servants, when purchased, were to be circumcised immediately. There is not one intimation, that pagans might be bought as bondmen, and circumcised, if, after a time, they became converts.

All the laws of Moses, he asserts, tended toward liberty. This is true, though not in the sense which he gives the language. Those laws, so far from forbidding the existence of the relation between master and slave, did give express permission for it to be formed. But by its formation, the condition of the slaves was greatly improved. Their liberty

ON SLAVERY. 449

was far greater under the Jewish law; and, which is still better, their minds were delivered from the degrading slavery of ignorance, superstition and vice.

There were some of the gentleman's very eloquent appeals, which I cannot fully answer. He represents himself as pleading the cause of his colored clients, consisting of three millions of his fellow men, who cannot be heard. I can only say, that if ever any people on earth had occasion to offer the prayer—"deliver us from our friends," they are that people! [A laugh.] The only good as yet accomplished, by the advocacy of the gentleman and his friends, in their behalf, has been to rivet their chains upon them!

But now, after so long a time, my worthy friend has been forced to reply to my argument from the New Testament. We will now see how far he has succeeded in replying to it.

He tells us, first, that if the word *doulos*, translated *servant*, does mean *slave*, our translators were most unfaithful, for they never once so rendered it. To this argument I have, once and again, replied, that the word *servant*, derived from the Latin *servus*, means literally a slave, and that it had this meaning when our translation was made. You observe how carefully he avoids meeting this question. I have replied, in the second place, that those translators, on whose knowledge and fidelity he pronounced so eloquent an eulogium, did translate this word *servant*, in passages where the gentleman himself admits, that it means *slave*. In 1 Tim. vi, 1, 2, we have the word *despotes*, which, according to his own admission, means a slave-holder; and yet the corresponding word, *doulos*, which, he acknowledges, in this passage, means slave, is translated *servant*. But I am not particular about the word *slave*. I am quite as well pleased with "*servant.*" But the question is, what kind of servants were those addressed by the apostles, whose masters were believing members of the church? I maintain, and I have proved by arguments he has not met, that they were slaves. He asserts that they were hired servants. All I ask of him, is to produce his evidence.

But the gentleman seems to think, he has discovered a method of proving, triumphantly, that the Hebrew word *eved* and the Greek word *doulos* do not mean *slave*. He says let us test the question, whether *slave* is a correct translation of the words *eved* and *doulos*, by substituting that word for *servant;* and with an air of triumph, he quotes the language of David—"O, Lord, I am thy SLAVE," &c. Well, I should like to ask him, what he understands the Psalmist to mean, when he says, "O, Lord, I am thy servant"? Did he not design to acknowledge God as his rightful owner and absolute sovereign? Does not God claim the entire services of all men? And does He not punish all who rebel against Him? What more would any slave-holder on earth ask, than to own the slave, and control his entire services? But he also quoted the language of Paul, who calls himself "the servant (*doulos*) of Christ;" and he asks, whether Paul was the *slave* of Christ. I answer, the apostles addressed Christ as Lord (*kurios*) and Master (*despotes*); and in so doing, they recognized his unbounded authority over them. They called themselves His *servants*, (*douloi*,) thus acknowledging their obligations to serve Him perpetually, with all their powers of soul and body. Would any slave-holder claim greater authority, than the gentleman's own illustration gives him? So his triumphant answer to my argument is calculated very much to strengthen it!

His second evidence that *doulos* does not mean *slave*, is found in Luke xvi. The steward, he tells us, went to his *fellow-servants* (*sun-douloi*) and reduced the amount of their respective debts to his lord; and he is quite confident that the servant placed in so responsible a station, could not have been a slave. There are two capital faults in this argument, viz : 1. neither *doulos*, nor *sun-doulos*, occurs in the passage referred to. The steward went to his lord's "debtors," not to his fellow-servants. 2d. If these words were there, the fact that a master placed a servant in whom he had confidence, over a portion of his business, would by no means prove him not a slave. I should be pleased to hear the gentleman explain how it is to be inferred that a servant is not a slave, because his master places great confidence in him.

But my principles, Mr. B. says, would justify a rich land-holder in Ohio, in buying poor free laborers, and holding them as slaves. My doctrine authorizes no man to force a free man into slavery. The Jewish law permitted the wealthy Jew to buy, for a term of six years, the brother Jew who had become poor, and could do no better, though not without his consent. And where is the injustice, if God chose to permit a poor man to recruit his shattered fortunes, by selling himself for six years? Was this arrangement sinful in itself?

Such appeals to mere prejudice are unworthy of a good cause. Declamation like this may make a momentary impression with persons of unreflecting minds; but with men of sense they will not weigh a feather.

The gentleman refers me to a note appended by the committee of publication to the Confession of Faith, the amount of which is, that they who are concerned in *retaining* men in slavery, are guilty of a violation of the eighth commandment. This note was no part of the Confession of Faith of the Presbyterian Church; and it was expunged from the Confession long ago. But, if it were still in it, what does it amount to? It testifies against those who are concerned in *retaining* men in slavery. And are we in favor of retaining them in this condition? Have I not stated over and over, that I desire and seek their restoration to freedom, as soon as it can be done safely, and consistently with other paramount duties? But I am not for tearing up the very foundations of society, to effect an object not now practicable. I am not for spilling floods of human blood, and rending this happy Union asunder, to effect what one would think is the sum of all human duty in my brother's estimation—the liberation, at one sweep, of every slave in the country. I will not do evil, that good may come. I go for liberating the blacks as soon as it can be done according to the Bible; but I will not trample the Bible under my feet, to effect that object.

Having now paid due attention to the gentleman's speech, I propose briefly to recapitulate, that the audience may have the whole ground over which I have passed, distinctly before them. And I will commence by, once more, stating the question under discussion, viz.: *Is slave-holding in itself sinful, and the relation between master and slave, a sinful relation?* In other words, is every slave-holder necessarily a transgressor, to be denounced and excluded from the church, without regard to circumstances? If the relation is in itself sinful, it is sinful under all circumstances, and must, therefore, be at once abandoned, without regard to circumstances? It is as truly sinful to hold a slave one hour, as fifty years. The duration of the servitude does not affect the morality of the relation.

Slave-holding I have defined to be, the claim of one man, under certain circumstances, to the services of another, with the corresponding obligation, on the part of the master, to provide comfortable food and raiment, and suitable religious instruction, for the slave, whose services he claims. The whole argument of the gentleman has been founded upon two false assumptions, viz.: 1. That the question in debate, is, whether it is sinful to force a free man, charged with no crime, into slavery. Who denies that it is? Who would, for one moment, discuss such a question? 2. His second false assumption is, that all the defective and cruel laws which have, at any time or anywhere, been enacted for the regulation of slavery, and the injustice and cruelty which have been inflicted by wicked men upon slaves, are part and parcel of slavery itself, and are essential to the existence of the relation between master and slave. That this assumption is false, I think, has been made perfectly apparent, if indeed it be not self-evident. No master, as every one knows, is obliged to treat his servant as badly as the civil laws permit him. No matter how defective and cruel the laws are, the religious master, governed in his treatment of them by the divine law, may treat them with all kindness, and pay constant regard to their happiness, present and future.

The conjugal relation is of divine institution; but it is also regarded as a civil institution, and is regulated by the civil law. Many of the laws enacted for its regulation, have been, and still are, most unjust and oppressive; and indeed over a great portion of the world, the wife has been the degraded slave of the husband. But who, in his senses, would argue against the relation as in itself sinful, on the assumption, that all those bad laws are part and parcel of the relation, and are essential to its existence? The same remarks hold good concerning the parental relation. The authority of the father over the child, has been very different in different ages and countries; but the relation itself has always been the same. The laws made by human legislators, for its regulation, are one thing; the relation itself quite another. The former may vary almost endlessly without at all affecting the latter. It is right for men to be land-holders; and yet most unjust and oppressive laws have been enacted for the regulation of that matter, say, in England. I may with perfect consistency denounce the laws which any particular government may pass relative to land-holding, without admitting the thing to be in itself wrong. So the relation between ruler and subject is not sinful; for human government is recognized by God himself. But multitudes of most iniquitous laws have been passed, and do now exist, for the regulation of that relation. I may consistently denounce the bad laws, whilst I defend the relation.

Precisely so, the relation between master and slave has always been the same; though the laws regulating it, have been widely different in different countries, and in the same country at different times. Who, then, unless his judgment is completely warped by inveterate prejudice, would think of confounding the relation itself with all those different laws?

Who would think seriously of charging any relation among men, with all the crimes committed in that relation? Yet this is the amount of a great part of the gentleman's argument. Take away the two assumptions I have pointed out, and what remains but declamation? You may put all the rest of what the gentleman has occupied so many hours in saying, into a thimble.

Again I ask, what is slave-holding ? It is the claiming, under certain circumstances, of the services of a man, with the corresponding obligation of providing abundant food, raiment and religious   nstruction ; in a word, of treating him with all kindness, as a rational, accountable, immortal being.

This is the slavery which I say is not, in itself sinful. Oou abolitionist friends really do not seem to know what slavery is, nor what we are met to discuss.   They propose one question for debate, challenge me to discuss it, and then spend the whole time in discussing other matters.

We are not debating, let me say once for all, whether it is a sin to reduce a free man to slavery.

We are not debating whether slavery, as a system is a righteous thing.   An institution which ought to be perpetuated.

We are not debating whether all the laws which have ever been enacted regulating slavery, in our country or in others, are just, humane or wise.

We are not debating whether slavery is an evil, the removal of which is to be ardently desired and promoted by all wise and lawful means.

Neither of these questions did I come here to argue : yet my opponent has argued little else.   We live in a country where slavery has long existed.   I regard it as a great evil, and desire its removal , but the question is, how this is to be accomplished ? and what is the duty of men living in slave States, so long as the system continues.   Is every slaveholder obliged either instantly to free his slaves regardless of consequences ; or live in heinous sin against God ?

[*Time expired.*

Monday Evening, 9 o'clock, P. M.

[MR. BLANCHARD'S SIXTEENTH SPEECH.]

Gentlemen Moderators, and Gentlemen and Ladies, Fellow-Citizens:

I shall briefly advert to some things which have fallen from my brother, and then close my argument.

In respect to one reference which I made when last up, I was a very little at fault, quoting from memory and in haste. It was the passage in 16th Luke, 1st verse; the word was "*oikonomos*," and not "*doulos*," as I intimated. Though the *relation* of the wasteful steward was the same with that of the person called "doulos" in other places.

The reference which I intended to have made, was to Matthew xviii, 28, the case of that "*doulos*" whom his lord had forgiven his own debt of one thousand talents; but the same "*doulos*" went out and took by the throat one of his "*sun-douloi*," or fellow servants, who owed him only one hundred pence, and cast him into prison till he should pay the uttermost farthing. This scripture shows, that the New Testament *douloi* were business men, property-holders, having accounts current with their lord; and is alone sufficient to overthrow Dr. Rice's extraordinary assertion, that the "*douloi*" were slaves.

The wasteful steward, and his fellow debtors, however, were in the same condition and relations, so there was no mistake in the argument, but a slight one in the reference.

My friend asks me to show authority for the Hebrew bond-servants holding property in their own right. Jahn, (Archaeol. 181,) says, that when a bond-servant was circumcised, he was reckoned among the Hebrews. The law of the Hebrews attached to them, and of course they were entitled to hold property. The scripture also necessarily implies the same—Lev. xxv, 49, "*If he (the ebedh) be* ABLE, *he may redeem himself.*" As to the commentators and other authorities whom he has presented from an early stage of this debate, oft times repeating the same names, as in his view so weighty and conclusive of the matter in question, I simply observe that, I attach but little weight to them in settling this great practical question. So I have said, and so think; and, therefore, I have preferred presenting slavery to you in its elements and practice, its roots, limbs, and branches, that you might behold and condemn it for yourselves, rather than to vex your understandings with the quoted or garbled opinions of fifty different men, who, perhaps, copied their opinions from one another, and of whom, perhaps, not one is better capable of judging than many here. There is nothing novel in his course. Authorities and interpretations are the common refuge of every cause which cannot stand by the principles of reason and justice. I have often met the arguments which he has adduced here, and I can sincerely assure you, that they are steadily and rapidly giving way and disappearing before the increasing light of truth in this country, like snow before the sun. But, if I had left my prescribed course to follow him at his request, we should have had nothing but " *doulos* " and " *ebedh*," with commentators and criticisms through the whole four days of the debate. Besides, I thought that by taking him off his beaten track, where other minds had passed before him, he would be at a loss what to say in vindication of slavery; and so, as you have seen, it turned out: and this was what worried him so sadly during the first days of the debate.

My friend parades with much pomp the names of Clarke, Stuart, etc. etc. etc., and God forbid that I should depreciate the holy dead or disparage the memory of the learned Dr. Adam Clarke. He is said to have originated the opinion that the serpent who beguiled Eve was a monkey—and I remember that Professor Stuart, who was my teacher, when some of his class quoted Adam Clarke's Commentary somewhat frequently, exclaimed, on one occasion, " *Come, come! let's have no more monkey commentaries here!*"

Professor Stuart is a laborious and distinguished Hebrew scholar and commentator on the scriptures; in his sphere a profound and prayerful man. I remember his prayers,

which were marked with simplicity and power, more clearly
even than his instructions. But it may not be improper to
mention of him, that like multitudes of college professors
and ministers in the free States, he has had, and probably still
has sons, sharing with slave-holders in the profits of the slave
system in the South. I will not undertake to say that such
a circumstance could bias the mind of an interpreter of the
scriptures, but it is difficult to say how far such a fact might
go to prepare a tender hearted father to fall in with established, and wide spread error. Certain it is, that some terribly blinding cause has darkened the intellect of this nation,
and paralyzed its heart upon the question of justice to our
enslaved population.

There is no want of distinguished names to quote against
the principles and measures of abolitionists, or indeed against
any other principles and measures which may lay upon
those who embrace them, the necessity of encountering difficulty or enduring reproach. I remember, when at Andover, some agitation arose on the question of slavery, and Dr.
Woods, the president professor, proposed to the students to
lay down both the colonization and anti-slavery organization, as a means of promoting harmony in the institution;
and that state of suspension continued until I left the institution. Thus the spot which was supposed to contain more
religious intelligence and means of correct judging, on moral
questions, than any other in the country, claimed the privilege of avoiding, so far as possible, all responsibility for,
and all connection with, any principles, and any measures,
of any kind whatever, on the subject of slavery. I determined, at that time, that if all prospect of reforming the
church should fail, it would become my duty to forsake the
church itself; and all that I have since witnessed, has but
confirmed me in the correctness of that judgment.

The most painful duty which has devolved on me during
this debate, and the one which I should have most gladly
have shunned, is that of saying something in reply to my
friend's triumphant reference to opinions put forth by the

members, at the late meeting of the American Board of Commissioners for Foreign Missions.

I know that the members of that Board are distinguished men, but I know, too, that whenever there is an evil, overbearing and polluting public sentiment, the high places of society are commonly poisoned first. The trade of slavery, centers in eastern cities. The watering places, the fashionable hotels, the factories, the coast-wise shipping, and ten thousand ramifications of interest and intercourse unknown, together with the direct personal influence of slave-holders themselves, who never suffer slavery to lose a point of advantage through any want of assiduity in themselves—all these, like so many invisible conductors, discharging at once their streams of paralyzing power from the heart of the slave system upon public men and public institutions meeting in our eastern cities; to stand exposed to such a battery without being more or less stupified and slackened in their consciences by the shock, would be a miracle.

I know that when I was in Andover, the same individual (such was the state of sentiment,) would receive more consideration from the fact of his holding slaves, then if he had none. And it must and will be so until the Christianity of the country is separated from, and ranged in opposition to slavery. That time, I trust in God, is near and hasteth greatly. I feel morally certain that no such document will ever be adopted by the American Board again, and no such speeches will be uttered at its meetings, as were had at its last, at least, by the same individuals.

Numbers of the New England clergy are openly and strenuously committed to the cause of delivering our poor slaves from their utter degradation, and our country from its direst curse, and I should not be at all taken by surprise if some of those members of the American Board who were instrumental in adopting their late Report, which, while it condemns slavery, tolerates slave-holding, temporarily, at least, in the church of Christ; should vote for different principles, in other ecclesiastical bodies, before the next meeting of the Board.

My brother is welcome to their authority while it lasts him, to sustain his doctrine that slave-holding is not sinful. I will remind you, however, that authorities quoted to support a controverted principle, of *men who are* THEMSELVES *engaged in the controversy, and while the controversy is depending,* is like owning birds on trees. The next time you need them, they may not be there. The American Board cannot and will not stand, before the American churches on the doctrines of their late Report; much less upon the sentiments uttered by some of its members in their speeches, which *Dr. Rice,* I deeply regret, has been able to quote here in support of his doctrine, that " slave-holding is not sin." The Board will recede from its ground. I now take up my argument to bring it to a close.

I was, when I sat down, upon the proposition that, *the constitution of Christianity is a repeal of the slave code ;* and its practice an abrogation of slavery, so that the two could not have existed in the Christian communities at their beginning.

I had reminded you that the constitution of Christianity, that is, the grand, controlling, and characterizing principles on which the Christian community was built, was nothing else than the Jewish constitution, revised, enlarged, and adapted to the whole world of mankind. I had shown you that the Jewish constitution, which is contained in the Pentateuch and illustrated by the prophets, was not a slave code; but that the Jewish church was both a *non-slaveholding ;* and, by its exertions to keep out the slave-holding customs of surrounding nations, which we see in Jer. xxxiv, chap., were creeping in among them ; and *especially,* by its harboring runaway slaves, (Deut. xxiii, 15,) the Jewish church was an anti-slave-holding body in the strongest sense possible. I had quoted the texts showing that the Jewish constitution was anti-slavery as to *stealing men; the holding of men stolen ;* and the rendering up of fugitives

(Ex. xxi, 16, *et al.*) and you can all see that the honest adoption and faithful carrying out of these three principles would make the United States a nation of abolitionists. Every town on the Ohio, which harbors fugitive slaves, is now regarded by the slave-holders as an abolition town of the worst stamp; and the admission of that single principle, with the abrogation of one other, which was not in the Jewish constitution, would make the *constitution* of the United States an immediate abolition document.

I had then showed that in this non slave-holding, anti-slave-holding Jewish church constitution, Christ and the apostles laid the foundation of Christianity. *i. e.* He founded the Christian constitution upon Moses and the prophets, with certain alterations and additions by Christ. That so Peter preached on the day of Pentecost, when he was founding the Christian Church. "*The promise is unto you and your children*," that is, Christianity is made out of the same promises which the Jews' religion was made of.

I was then showing what alterations Christianity made in the constitution of Judaism.

And first, That, *it abrogated the Jewish distinction of male and female.* Whereas the Jewish woman was bought by her husband, and was his menial, could be divorced at will for hatred; had no name in the rolls of the church, nor any part in the ceremonies of religion, or seat in the synagogue; that all this degrading serfdom of woman was abolished by Christianity out of the Jewish constitution, so that "*in Christ*," there was "*neither male nor female.*" Gal. iii, 28, and Col. iii, 11.

2. In the second place, I observe that, Christ's constitution destroyed the distinction between Jew and Greek, or generally, that between Jew and gentile or barbarian.

In the ancient tabernacle worship, there was an outer court for the gentiles, who were regarded as unclean. They were called "dogs," in comparison of Jews: and in the last times of the nation, all Jerusalem was set on uproar, because they said that Paul " *had brought Greeks into the temple and polluted that holy place.*"   Acts xxi, 28.

This distinction, Christianity swept away. It taught, that the " middle wall of partition was broken down," which shut off the gentiles from the congregation of the Lord— that the Jewish branches were broken from the olive tree, and Jew and gentile grafted in, as *Christians*, upon the same stock. In Christianity, every man held the same relation to every other man, and to God, as a Jew held to every other Jew, and to God. The promises made to Abraham were opened to all, in the whole world, who would embrace them ; and thus all came into the Christian community on the summit-level of Christian brotherhood and equality.— Even Dr. Rice, in this debate, admits that one Jew could not hold another Jew as a perpetual slave. And as "in Christ" men were exalted upon the Jewish platform of rights, it is plain, that, under the constitution of Christianity, one *man* could not hold another *man* as his slave.

3. The third alteration of Judaism by Christianity was this—that *it annihilated the distinction between* "BOND AND FREE."   There was a bond service in the Jewish code; but "In Christ there is neither bond nor free." (Gal. iii, 28, and Col. iii, 11.) Moses legislated for a peculiar people, who were on all sides pressed upon by a world of barbarism and idolatry, and he had, on the one side, to preserve a discipline so liberal that families should not be changed into slave-prisons, work-houses, and jails—and yet, on the other hand, the discipline must be stringent enough to prevent members of families running back and forth, to and from the pollution and filth of the worship and life of idolaters. This was the reason and principle, the object and end of the *bond service* which was a part of the Jewish constitution. The whole world was then both pagan and slave-holding.— *Now*, the world is learning to respect human rights, and many nations have fully abolished slavery; and hence all the reason on which Hebrew bond service was founded is expired.   Then, the strong man was the law—the whip and

the chain were the insignia of office, and force the only impulse to obedience to authority in the religions and governments of all but Jews. Yet now, when the era of truth and moral power is come, and the empire of force is passing away, the gentleman's doctrine carries us back to the pagan maxims of Moses' day, and to the pagan slavery which Moses abolished and legislated out of Judea. When we go, back to Moses, we find a world of absolute despotism, and Judea a free spot in its centre. And while Moses preserved as much freedom in her constitution as would be consistent with national preservation, he allowed a system of bond service—a service in which *life, property,* and *civil liberty* should be protected—while a wholesome restraint was thrown upon personal liberty for a term of years, in order to preserve the order and discipline necessary to the national preservation of the chosen people of God amidst the idolatrous and tyrannous and barbarous tribes around them.

That bond service was a system for drawing men out of heathen slavery into the freedom of the children of God. All the servants procured from the heathen had to become Jews, by circumcision, within one year, or they must be sent back. When circumcised, they were reckoned among the Hebrews, and of course the law of the Hebrews applied to them, which was, that they should serve their masters for six years, and then go free, except the ear-bored servants, who were free also at the jubilee. It was a missionary mill, to manufacture heathen into the children of God.

But, under the Christian constitution, *even this modified bond-service was done away,* and "there is neither bond nor free" in Christ Jesus! The constitution of Christianity entirely and forever annihilates slavery, wherever and as soon as it touches it. There is no need of a special denunciation of slavery, and a separate statute of abolition. In Massachusetts, the common law and constitution abolished it. In Ohio, the ordinance of 1787 excluded it, before there were white people here to hold slaves, and the Indians never did. In Massachusetts, in Vermont, here in Ohio, we have no

State statute forbidding to hold slaves. Nor would it do any good if there was; for those who will violate a constitution will break a statute. So, in Christianity, *whose constitution was, and, when enforced, will again be, an immediate abrogation of slavery.*

II. My second main proposition on the New Testament, is, that *the character of the first Christians was a complete guaranty against slave-holding in the church.*

Paul, (in 1 Cor. i, 26,) says, "For ye see your calling, brethren, how that not many wise men after the flesh, not many mighty, not many noble, are called." This shows what kind of people the first Christian churches were made of? They were a poor despised set of abolitionists who were everywhere accused of "uprooting society" to get rid of its evils, and "*turning the world upside down*" to correct its errors and reform its abuses; and the treatment experienced by Christ and the apostles has been, in a measure, dealt out to them. If we had been holier men, we should have suffered more.

Now we all know, without stopping to examine, how such a church must have treated slave-holding. Take only the fact of their condition in life, and the principles and reasonings inseparable from it. How would they look on some wealthy Virginia or Alabama slave-holder coming into the church with his fifty slaves, wishing to hold them as his property, while he recognized them as his equal brethren in Christ in a church where none of the members said that aught he possessed was his own, but they had all things in common!! If the Christian constitution was enforced, that, as we have seen, annihilated slavery; and if it was not enforced, human nature itself would shut *such* men as our slaveholding Presbyterians in the South from the churches founded by the apostles of Christ.

Why, I am told, that some of the aristocratic members in this city, tired of the democratic tendencies in the Methodist Episcopal church, are about to form here a "Methodist Episcopal Church South." If they do, when they erect their building I suggest that this scripture be cut in stone over the door, as containing the trinity of their worship: " *The lust of the flesh, the lust of the eyes, and the pride of life.*" 1 John ii, 16.

But, when we see the slave-holders, and those who have their spirit, separating themselves, to escape disturbance, from the free principles which are struggling for life in the Methodist Episcopal church, it is easy to see how a slave-holder would have fared if he had come into one of the apostolic churches, made up of a set of poor, pious Christians, and wishing to hold fifty or more of them as slaves, subject to his sole will. No, the character and condition of the members of the first Christian churches, was a sufficient guaranty against the admission of slave-holders.

III. But again. The history of the first church organization shows that it was an anti-slavery organization. Read the fourth chapter of Acts, vs. 31, 37. "And when they had prayed, the place was shaken where they were assembled together, and they were all filled with the Holy Ghost, and they spake the word of God with boldness. And the multitude of them that believed were of one heart and of one soul: *neither said any of them* THAT AUGHT OF THE THINGS WHICH HE POSSESSED WAS HIS OWN: *but they had all things in common.*"

This was at Pentecost, where three thousand souls were converted to Christianity, and the Christian institution set up. Now, what becomes of a man's slaves, in such a church? Would the slave-holder sell his slaves, and take the price and divide it among the Christians, his slaves among the number? Or, would he cut them up, as the man of Mount Ephraim did his concubine, and give each brother and sister a piece? Or, would he simply recognize his slaves as men and women, his equals in Christ. *There* WAS NO SLAVERY *in such a church as that!* But again, verse 33d, "and with great power gave the apostles witness of the resurrection of the Lord Jesus: and great grace was upon them all. Neither was there any among them that lacked: *for as many as were possessors of lands or houses sold them, and brought the prices of the the things that were sold, and laid them down at the apostle's feet ;* and distribution was made unto every man according as he had need." What, are we to say, "that they gave up their lands and houses, but kept their slaves?" What did they want with slaves, when their houses and lands were sold. Tender stomachs indeed ; must they have had to give up lands for religion, and keep *persons* as property! True, there were no slaves in Judea ; but the Pentecost converts were from all parts of the world, and there may have been slave-holders among them.

Now, remember, that this was the first founding of the Christian church, and, of course, a model for the rest. And the Holy Ghost which wrought these effects in the Pentecost converts, came afterwards on the gentiles, the *same as on the Jews at the beginning of the Christian community."—Acts.* xi, 15. Thus, the history of the first Christian organization perfectly and forever stultifies the idea, so gravely put forth by learned men, that chattelizing human beings found fellowship in the apostolic church!

IV. My last proposition is, *that the enforcement of* DISCIPLINE *in the first Christian church, always and everywhere, must have annihilated slavery.*

When Christianity was set up in free Judea, it was established in a non-slave-holding country, by anti-slavery Jews, converted to a freer system of religion than Judaism itself. Of course the world did not need to be told that theirs was not to be a slave-holding church. But when they went outside of Judea to found churches, they encountered slavery ; and "doulos," as our word "servant," doubtless, in slave States, and in the lips of slave-holders meant, slave. Though in the New Testament, it is not as my brother said, but it takes " *Doulos hupo zugon"* to make a slave. *Doulos* alone no more means slave, than " *bird,"* alone means *"owl."*

But admitting, as I do, that the gospel was planted amid slaves. The question is, when it went to Ephesus, *what did the Christian discipline do to slavery there?* Take a living case. Suppose a young free man had married a slave girl converted to Christianity, with her master, and the church. This case is not uncommon in our own country, where a free colored man has a slave wife, and they, with the master, profess religion. But such cases must have been still more frequent where there was no difference of complexion. . Now suppose this pious master wishes to remove to Colosse, or somewhere else; as Aquila went with Paul, and he wishes his slave girl, now married, to go with him. Her husband cannot pay for her. The master does not wish to sell her if he could ; and the husband refuses to let her go. The case comes before the church on complaint of the owner, the question being *which shall have the young woman—the slave-holder, or the husband?* The trial comes up before the brethren in the place of Christian worship in Ephesus. Now how would this work in Charleston, South Carolina ? The house of course would be thronged to suffocation, windows, doors and all, with slave-holders, and other people, anxious to hear the decision. The slave-holder rises, opens *Dr. Rice's lectures,* if not familiar with the Bible, and he finds quoted, Ephesians vi, 5. *'Servants be obedient to them that are your masters according to the flesh."* "Now brethren,' continues he, "I claim this girl as my servant— She is my slave: and our founder and apostle Paul, says, in his letter to this church, *'Servants be obedient to your masters.'* I therefore command her obedience to me who am her master. I am called of God to remove hence, and she must go with me."

After the slave-holder (who generally has the first hearing with our northern divines) has got through his argument; the young husband comes meekly forward with the Bible under his arm, which opens at Matth. xix, 5, 6, and reads the words of our Lord : "*For this cause shall a man leave father and mother and cleave unto his wife, and they twain shall become one flesh. Wherefore they are no more twain, but one flesh.* WHAT THEREFORE GOD HAS JOINED TOGETHER, LET NO MAN PUT ASUNDER." Brethren, this young woman is my wife: and having thus spoken, sits down incapable of uttering more.

Which now, by the law of the church, would get that

young woman? If you say the husband, and surely he will, unless you emancipàte the church from the law of Christ, every slave-holder in that audience would say:—"Let's clear out! This is an abolition concern: This is no place for us and our slaves: We can never keep them with such examples before them. Indeed the whole fraternity are a gang of incendaries." So, calling out their slaves, they would go home hatching schemes of persecution against the Christians.

Take another case, of parent and child. The slave-holder claims the child of a fellow Christian, as his property, and determines to take it away. The parent says that the law of God, "*Parents, bring up your children in the nurture and admonition of the Lord*," gives the parent control of the child: and the claims of parent and owner conflict. This case must follow the other, and the parent get his child. Take still another case, which shows how the discipline of the first churches applies to the mere business aspects and relations of slavery.

A man came to my house, who for years hired the mother of his children of her owner, he being a free man, and she a slave. The husband I think had paid fifty dollars per year, for the hire of his own wife, to the wife's master.

Now suppose these parties had joined the church at Colosse, and the husband had refused longer to pay his Christian brother fifty dollars per year, tor the privilege of having his own wife suckle and tend her own babes: and the case comes before the church upon this issue. Would the church command the husband still to pay for the use of his wife, fifty dollars per year, to his equal Christian brother? Or would they take up the epistle written them by Paul, and under the precept, "*masters give unto your servants that which is just and equal*" Col. iv, 1; require the master to pay back all the hire which he had received of the husband, with reasonable dues for the woman's service before she was married? And would not one such decision so *abolitionize* the church in public estimation, that not a slave-holder would join it till he was willing to give up his slaves?

I put all these cases to *Dr. Stowe*, who I regret on his account to say, has uttered sentiments which brother Rice can quote in support of his doctrine, that the apostolic churches fellowshipped slave-holding: and *Dr. Stowe* unhesitatingly declared, that in every such case, the claims of slave-holders were extinguished by the law of the church (which, was the law of Christ) in favor of husband and parent.

How then do he and others reach the conclusion, totally inconsistent with this admission, that slave-holding was admitted to fellowship in the apostolic churches?

Why, in this way:—They say that the *legal relation*, as created by the civil law, still vested in slave-owners, after they became members of the Christian churches; and that they were not required to abjure this relation before they were received into the church. Supposing this true, it does not alter the case. For, as the cases cited above show, they could not retain their slaves by the law of Christianity; and saying that the rights of slave-owners still remained in them by the *civil law; is subjecting the Christian church to the heathen State.* But if the law of Christ was superior to that civil law which gave them their slave-holding rights, then they ceased to be slave-holders when they joined the church.

More than this: The first Christian who should have gone to a civil court to prosecute his claim to the body of his brother or sister as his slave, would have had an excommunication launched after him, under the injunction of the apostle, as a most aggravated case of "brother going to law with brother, and that before unbelievers." Those civil courts were among the things which Christians came out of, when they left the world to follow Christ. They could not prosecute claims there without practising idolatry. Justice was administered by these in the name of Jupiter, and the emperor, and attended with pagan rites. The witness took a flint, and, jerking it from his hand, said—"*So let Jupiter thrust me from among the good, if I deceive in this case.*" Thus a Christian could not have established his claim to a slave, in the civil courts, without subjecting the church to the State—violating the apostle's injunction—and practising idolatry.

Thus, I have proved, that slave-holding was not allowed in the New Testament church:—1. By the constitution of Christianity; 2. The character of the members; 3. By the history of the foundation of the first Christian community; and, 4. By the discipline of the church.

And now—*Gentlemen and fellow-citizens*—with many and sincere thanks for your long and patient attention, during this debate, (having no time to recapitulate,) I bid you an affectionate farewell. And I pray God, that when you shall have well considered the arguments here presented, and when you shall read them in the book which is to be published, you may be led by His Spirit to "Remember them that are in bonds as bound with them"—so that when you shall appear before the final bar you may yourselves hear with joy the welcome of the judge: not (according to the shocking interpretation of my brother) of "well done, thou good and faithful *slave*,"—but that welcome, fit for Christ's lips to utter, and saved men to hear, "Well done, good and faithful SERVANT—enter thou into the joy of thy Lord."

For me, I know that when a few days are come, a thousand miles shall stretch between your dwellings and mine— and when, hereafter, this toil-worn frame shall be sinking to its last earthly rest, it shall please my failing memory to remember, that my last effort among you was in vindication of the oppressed. Happy, if, when my toils are over, I can raise my dying head, like Wolf upon the Heights of Abraham, and hear the gathering shout of my countrymen, that the enemies of freedom and God's truth are routed, and the slave is free; and when my weary head shall at last lie low amid the wild flowers of yonder prairie, my future home, it shall content me well, if they shed their dewey honors above the grave of one who, having humbly striven in all things to follow his Lord, like Him, also, has been faithful to His poor.   [*Time expired.*

[MR. RICE'S SIXTEENTH SPEECH.]

Gentlemen Moderators, and Fellow-Citizens:

I do not by any means call in question the sincerity of the gentleman in his abolition sentiments ; and 1 can sympathise with him in his zeal for a cause which he imagines to be the most important of all others. But whilst I give him due credit for his sincerity, I cannot forget, that his declamation and exhortation are not *argument.*

I called on my friend to prove the truth of his assertion, that bondmen purchased by the Jews from the heathen, could hold property. In reply he has not once quoted the Bible, but has referred me to the Roman Catholic professor Jahn— Yet Jahn does no where say, either that they went out of servitude at the end of six years, nor that they held property. He says only that they were numbered among the people of Israel. So they were, as to all church privileges. They were so *ecclesiastically.* But this they could be, and neither hold property nor be free. I have seen Jahn's book to which Mr. B. refers ; and he expressly says the Jews had a right to buy bond-servants from the heathen.

I cannot but remark here, that one of the most unpleasant features of modern abolitionism, is its utter recklessness in relation to the characters of even the most eminent, and honored, and useful servants of Jesus Christ. I cannot hear charges the most injurious, so frequently recurring, as we have heard them from the gentleman, without being constrained to think, that there must be something in abolitionism itself, which produces in its advocates a *self-sufficient, conceited spirit,* that leads them to regard themselves as wiser and better than all other men.

Dr. Adam Clarke has been lauded by the gentleman, and quoted as authority: but the moment I shew that he confirms my exposition of the Old Testament on the subject of slavery, he is ridiculed as a "monkey commentator." Such a man and such a scholar as Professor Stuart, of Andover, is not to be trusted in his exposition of the scriptures, we are told, because some of the young men whom he taught, are settled in the southern States !

[MR. BLANCHARD rose to explain. I said he had sons, (not students,) in slave-holding families.]

Very well: and because he has sons settled at the South in slave-holding families, he can be so influenced, so warped in judgment by that circumstance, that he has grossly perverted the Word of God, and on his responsibility as a biblical expositor, has said, that it is *"impossible to doubt"* that the Bible teaches a certain doctrine, which is most detestable! Is it not truly strange that a wise and good man, whose reputation is such as that of Prof. Stuart, is to be condemned, as blindly, or perversely teaching the most abominable and cruel doctrines, on grounds so trivial—and this too, by a professed minister of the gospel !

In the same manner, the American Board is to be treated. They sometimes sit at one of our watering places, where they see the face of a slave-holder; and behold! they never can see the truth again !

The eminent learning of many of them, their character for vital piety, and for wisdom and prudence, cannot shield them from the charge of sinister motives, of sacrificing the truth to the influence of slavery ! Slave-holders were seen by them at the watering-places ; and therefore they are blinded ! And the gentleman has even ventured to denounce one of those ministers as "an ecclesiastical Talleyrand!" I had learned from an inspired apostle, that the character of ministers of the gospel, was to be respected, and that no charge was to be received against them, unless sustained by at least two witnesses ; but abolitionism practices according to a different rule.

The Methodist church, even in the North, I have said, has never made slave-holding a bar to Christian fellowship. This statement is true. It is admitted, that the Methodists forbid *trafficking* in slaves ; and so do I condemn it.

The gentleman, by way of proving that the Jews had no slaves, refers us to the law of Moses against man-stealing. But who denies that stealing men was made a capital offence under the Jewish law? No man, surely, who reads his Bible; but that law never forbade the purchase of a bond-servant from a heathen master. On the contrary, as I have proved, the law gave express permission to do so; and the reason probably was, that it effected a favorable change in the man's condition, and brought him under the influence of that religion which might make him happy on earth and in heaven.

Mr. Blanchard attempts to prove, that there were no slaveholders in the Christian church, because in the constitution of Christianity "there is neither male nor female, neither barbarian, Scythian bond or free." And, strangely enough, the gentleman seems to understand this language literally! just as if it would not prove as conclusively, that there were no *females* in the early church, as that there were no *slaves* there! Who denies (what that text imports) that in the privileges of the Christian church and in the blessed hopes of the gospel, there are no distinctions—that at the table of the Lord the richest man takes his seat by the poorest of the poor? But a king is a king still, though his meanest subject is on a par with himself in the things of religion. The equality of all men on the great platform of Christian privilege and hope, does not prevent great inequalities in their civil condition. I go for both—for defending their equality in Christian privileges, whilst I would not interfere with the order of society in things touching this life. The equality of a Jew and his slave in their right to the passover, did in no wise destroy their relation to each other as master and slave.

The gentleman has repeatedly asserted the sinfulness of slave-holding in itself, on the ground, that the master takes the labor of the slave *without wages.* Now, on this subject, what says God's law? That law, as I have proved, expressly required that the wages of the *hired servant (sakir)* should be promptly paid; but it says not a word about the wages of the bond-servant (*eved*) bought from the heathen. How shall we account for this fact? The reason is obvious, if the doctrine for which I contend is true; but the thing is wholly unaccountable, if Mr. B.'s principles are correct. The law did not require wages to be paid to the bond-servant, because the master had already paid for his labor what, under the circumstances, it was worth, and because the master was bound to provide his slave food and raiment, and shelter, in sickness and health, until death. This support was the servant's wages—quite as much, by the way, as most men obtain for their labor.

Mr. B. proves, that the primitive Christians were not slave-holders, from the fact that they were generally poor people, in the lower walks of life. Admit the truth of the statement; does it follow that the apostles excluded slave-holders, as such, from their churches? Surely the premises are at a great distance from the conclusion.

But he tells us, that the first converts at Jerusalem sold their houses and lands, and had all things in common; and he asks, what became of their *slaves?* I answer—1. He has himself informed us, that the Jews, after the Babylonish captivity, had no slaves. If his statement is true, the question is answered. 2. But Paul and Peter teach us, as plainly as language can teach, that there were in many of the churches, as at Ephesus and Colosse, both masters and slaves; and they give such directions to both, as cannot apply to employers and hired-servants. They exhort the slaves to obey their own masters " with fear and trembling," not only the "good and gentle," but also the froward. 3. If there had been slave-holders amongst those converts, they certainly would not have sold their slaves for money for the church. Any Christian would have cheerfully given up his other possessions for the general interest, but not the servants of his family, whose happiness he is solemnly bound to regard, and whom God requires him to instruct in the things pertaining to their salvation. Doubtless every Christian master would, if he consistently could, liberate his slaves; but certain it is, that the servants of the family are amongst the last of a pious master's possessions with which, when in difficult circumstances, he would part. The silence of the inspired record concerning slaves, therefore, affords no evidence that slave-holders were not received into the churches organized by the apostles.

The gentleman asserts, that the word *doulos* does not mean slave. This is merely *assertion;* but we call for *evidence.* I called upon him to tell us what word in the Greek language does mean slave, if this word does not. He has not given us the information. A similar question was asked concerning the Hebrew *eved ;* but the gentleman could find no other word signifying *slave.* Indeed he told us, virtually, that there is no word either in the Hebrew or Greek language, which does definitely signify slave ! a statement contradicted by every Greek Lexicon, by classic usage, by Bible usage, and by all Greek and Hebrew scholars. Stuart, McNight, Barnes, and a host of others, commentators, critics and theologians, say unhesitatingly, that the literal and proper meaning of *doulos*, is slave.

But Mr. B. presents a supposed case which he regards as entirely conclusive. " Suppose," says he, " a church member had come to one of those churches and claimed as his servant a man who had run from him, and had become pious and had married in the place. Which relation would the church regard, the conjugal or the property relation ?" How this supposed case proves, that there were no slave-holders in the apostolic churches, I know not. It is not difficult, however, to answer the question. The church, so far as it had authority, would, of course, sacredly regard the marriage relation, and so would every pious master. It would not be difficult, however, if the master were not pious, to satisfy him, if he were a reasonable man, by paying him what his slave was worth. Precisely in this way did primitive Christians liberate the slaves of men, when they liberated them at all. Instead of combining to run them off from their masters, as do many modern abolitionists, they united to purchase them. Our abolitionists, however, are quite too *conscientious* to imitate their *example!*

Having now answered so much of the gentleman's speech as required notice, I proceed very briefly to recapitulate, that the audience may have distinctly before them the ground over which I have travelled.

The question before us, as I have repeatedly stated, is not, whether it is wrong to force a free man into slavery; nor whether all the particular laws by which, at different times and in different countries, it has been regulated, are just and righteous; nor whether it is right or wrong for a man to treat his slaves cruelly, to separate husbands and wives, &c.; nor whether a man may rightly regard and treat his slaves as mere chattels personal, not as rational, accountable, immortal beings; nor whether a great amount of sin is often actually committed in this relation; nor whether slavery, as a system, is an evil, the removal of which should be sought by all proper means; nor whether it is the true policy, and the duty of the several slave States to abolish slavery immediately or gradually; nor whether " the system of American slavery," or any other system, is right, *but simply whether the relation, divested of all abuses, is in itself sinful.*

To prove, that slave-holding is not in itself sinful, but that there have been, and may be circumstances justifying it, I have advanced the following arguments:

1. The great principles of the moral law are written on the human heart; and, when presented, they do commend themselves to the understandings and consciences of men. The truth of this proposition is universally admitted. Now it is a notorious fact, that the doctrine that slave-holding is in itself sinful, has not commended itself to the understandings and consciences of even the great body of the wise, and the good. Therefore it is not true. The feeble effort made by the gentleman to reply to this argument only proves it unanswerable.

2. The history of the church and of the world cannot furnish one instance of a man or a society of men heretical

on one fundamental principle of morality, or article of Christian faith, and yet sound on all others. But it is admitted, that the ministers and churches in the slave-holding States are as orthodox on all the principles of morality and doc trines of Christianity, as blameless in their lives, as benevolent, and in all respects, except the matter of slavery, as exemplary Christians as any in the world. If, then, the doctrine of abolitionism is true, we have presented before us two spectacles, such as the world never before saw, viz: 1. The great body of eminently wise and good men pronouncing one of the very grossest violations of the moral law, such as kidnapping, man stealing and robbery, not in itself sinful. 2. A large number of Christians and Christian churches rotten on one fundamental point of morality, and perfectly sound and conscientious on all others! The gentleman attempted to answer this argument by giving the Pharisees as an instance of men sound on all points of faith and morality, except one! But this he soon abandoned. Then he referred us to John Newton, just at the time when his mind was emerging from the midnight gloom of ignorance and deep depravity! Such are his only answers!

3. It is a fact, admitted even by the gentleman himself, that there are Christian slave-holders, and Christian churches, whose members are involved in slave-holding, accepted and blessed of God, often enjoying seasons of the outpouring of the Holy Spirit. And it is a fact, that many of the best ministers in the free States, if converted at all, were converted in those churches, in answer to the prayers of those Christians. Nay, it is a fact, that all, or nearly all, our older churches were organized in States where slavery then existed, and admitted slave-holders to their communion. Now one of two things is true, viz.: either God hears the prayers and blesses the labors of the most scandalous sinners, or abolitionism is not true. The gentleman attempted to evade the force of this argument, by saying—1. That those revivals are granted in answer to the prayers of those who are not actually slave-holders. But the reply is obvi-

ous—that those who countenance slave-holding Christians, and hold fellowship with them, are no better than they.— 2. But he told us, those revivals were granted in answer to the prayers of goodly men who were opposed to slavery, such as David Rice, of Kentucky. But the reply is no less obvious—that he was not an abolitionist; and if he had been, the Bible affords not an instance in which God has, for the sake of the pious dead, poured out spiritual blessings upon professors of religion who were gross sinners, and continued in their sin. All seasons of revival recorded in the Bible, were seasons of general reformation.

4. The faith of the abolitionists induces them to pursue a course widely different from that pursued by the apostles of Christ, in regard to prevailing sins, particularly in regard to slavery. Abolitionists stand at a distance, and denounce and villify all slave-holders; the apostles never did so. On the contrary, they preached the gospel both to masters and slaves, enjoining on each the faithful discharge of their respective duties. Abolitionists seek to render the slaves discontented, and to induce them to leave the service of their masters; the apostles pursued an opposite course. In a word—the apostles, though assailed with many odious charges, were never represented as abolitionists, or as seeking to interfere with the relation of master and slave. They, in their epistles and discourses, so far as they are recorded in the Bible, never denounced the relation itself as sinful. They sought to reform men, not by abusing and denouncing them in papers, pamphlets and public meetings, but by going amongst them, and kindly reasoning with them. The course of the abolitionists is precisely opposite to this. Now if it be true, as the apostle James teaches, that men show *their faith by their works*—it follows, that, since the works of abolitionists are widely different from those of the apostles, and opposed to them, their faith is equally different from the faith of the apostles.

5. The tendency and necessary effects of abolitionism prove it false. What are its tendency and its effects? They

are the following:—1. To irritate slave-holders to the highest degree, and thus to rivet the chains on the slave, and make his condition far worse than it would be; 2. To take from slave-holders the preached gospel, the only influence by which they ever will be induced to liberate their slaves. The abolitionists will not go and preach the gospel to them. If they hear it, therefore, they must hear it from the mouths of ministers who are denounced and calumniated by abolitionists. 3. The tendency of abolitionism is to take from the slaves, as well as their masters, the glorious gospel, which only can elevate their character, make them happy even in bondage, and make them eternally free and happy in heaven. The abolitionists will not go and preach the gospel to them. If they ever hear it, then, they must hear it from ministers denounced and villified by these pretended reformers. For whom, I again ask, will the millions of Christian slaves before the throne of God, thank the Judge on the great day—for the ministers who went and preached to them the word of life in their bonds; or for those who, at a safe distance, abused and calumniated their masters? If such is the tendency of abolitionism, (and facts already stated prove that it is,) and if we are to judge of the principles of men by their *fruits*, what shall we think of it?

6. The *golden rule*—"whatsoever ye would that men should do to you, do ye even so to them"—as I have said, requires us to improve the condition of all our fellow-men, so far as we can do so, without disregarding other paramount duties. But inasmuch as, in a multitude of instances, it is impossible for masters to liberate their slaves, without neglecting paramount duties—and in other instances the only way in which they can consistently improve the condition of a slave, is to buy him and hold him as a slave—it is clear that the golden rule does not prove slave-holding in itself sinful, does not require masters to liberate their slaves without regard to circumstances, but in some instances, makes men slave-holders.

7. The truth is self-evident, that God never did, and never

could give any man permission to do that which is in itself
sinful, or to form a sinful relation. But it is a fact, clearly
proved by the express language of the Old Testament, that
He not only recognized the relation of master and slave as
lawful amongst the patriarchs, but did give express permission to the Jews to buy bondmen and bondmaids from the
gentiles, and from strangers dwelling amongst them. Therefore, slave-holding is not in itself sinful. Amongst the Jews,
as I proved, there were several classes of servants—as hired
servants, whose wages were to be regularly paid; Jews who
had become poor, and sold themselves for six years, who
were to be treated as hired servants; the bondmen and bondmaids, owned by the patriarchs, or bought by the Jews, from
the heathen, who were slaves during life.

To this last class I directed your attention particularly.
That they were slaves, I proved by several arguments: 1. They
were *bought with money.* 2. They were the "possession"
of their masters. The word *possession,* is one of the strongest
words in the Hebrew language, to denote that which really
belongs to a man. 3. They descended as an *inheritance* to
the children of the master, just as did ordinary possessions.
4. The master claimed their labor, and could enforce their
obedience by chastisement; and the reason why, if a servant died, after a day or two, when he had been chastised,
the master was not to be punished, was—*that he was his money.*
5. The word *eved,* translated *bondman,* is the proper Hebrew
word to signify *slave,* and stands in contrast with *sakir,* the
hired servant. The gentleman himself has not been able
to find any other word in the Hebrew language, which does
signify *slave.* The conclusion is inevitable, that God did give
express permission to the Jews to buy and hold slaves; and so
is the language of the Bible understood by all respectable
commentators, critics and theologians. Consequently, one
of two things is true, viz: either God gave the Jews express permission to commit sin, or slave-holding is not in
itself sinful.

8. I have proved, as I think, the fact that the apostles

of Christ did receive slave-holders into the churches organized by them.   That they did so, I proved by several arguments, viz: 1. The word *kurios*, translated *master*, signifies
an *owner*, master,'or—and as applied to designate the relation between master and servant, signifies a slave-holder.
2. The word *despotès*, also translated *master*, is admitted to
mean properly a holder of slaves; and we read of believing
despotai, (masters,) "faithful and beloved, partakers of the
benefit," of "good and gentle" *despotai*.   3. The word *doulos*,
translated *servant*, means literally and properly, a slave.
This is proved—1st, by the lexicons, which uniformly so
define it; 2d, by classic usage—the Greek writers themselves
so used it; 3d, by Bible usage—the word *doulos* being there
constantly used in contrast with the word *eleutheros*—free.
4. Exhortations are addressed by the apostles to masters
and servants, which are not applicable to employers and
hired servants, but are precisely applicable to masters and
slaves.

5. I have not asked you to depend upon my assertions,
touching these important points, but have referred you to a
number of the best commentators, critics, and theologians,
such as Poole, Scott, Henry, Horne, Bush, Barnes, Stuart,
McNight, Doddridge, and others; and I have challenged the
gentleman to produce one respectable commentator, critic, or
theologian, who agrees with him in his views of the scriptures quoted, or who gives a different exposition of them, from
that which I have given.   He has not done it, because he
cannot.

You have heard his replies, so far as he has attempted to
reply to these arguments; and you have observed how carefully he, from the very commencement of this debate, shunned the Bible, as if deeply conscious that it would condemn
the principles he was advocating.   He felt that an apology
to the audience for pursuing such a course, was necessary;
and he tells you, he avoided the Bible, because he knew, if
he went into a scriptural argument, we should be troubled
with *eved* and *doulos*, lexicons, commentators and critics;

and he very much feared I would confuse the minds of the people in this way!!!

[Mr. BLANCHARD rose to explain. I said I did so because if you took the brother from the slaveholders' texts in the Bible, you put him out of his track.]

The gentleman is right. It is true, that I cannot discuss great moral and religious questions, without the Bible—the only infallible rule of right. On such subjects my "track" takes me directly to the "Blessed Book," the fountain of truth !

I repeat, I did not ask you to depend on my assertions concerning the meaning of that book, I gave the gentleman standard authorities in great abundance. Poole, Henry, Scott, Gill, and many other eminently, wise and good men, who, if they were here now, would be denounced and excommunicated, because they were not abolitionists ! But the gentleman, though bold in his assertions concerning the Bible, has not one sound scholar to agree with him.

If Poole, and Henry, and Scott, and Gill, and Horne, and Dick, and Chalmers, and Cunningham, and Woods, and Stuart, and Tyler, and Spring, and Wayland, and Bacon, and the whole Church of Scotland, are ignorant of the Bible, and all in error concerning the facts there recorded about slavery and slave-holders; I am quite content to be denounced in such company; and I am clearly of opinion, that if they, and such as they have failed to understand the Bible on this subject, we cannot expect much light from the gentleman and his coadjutors.

I repeat what I have said before, that I oppose abolitionism, not because it tends to abolish slavery, and improve the condition of the slave, but because it tends to perpetuate it, and aggravate all its evils. Never as I firmly believe, will slavery be abolished by your abolition lectures, your newspaper and pamphlet denunciations of slave-holders, without regard to the character or circumstances; or by attempting to exclude them from the Christian church. In New York, New Jersey, Pennsylvania, Connecticut, it has been abolished, but not by the principles of abolitionists. So long as the system continued, masters and slaves were members of the same churches, and sat at the same table of the Lord. Ministers of the Gospel, faithful to their high commission, such men as many who are now denounced by abolitionists as pro-slavery, proclaimed the Gospel both to masters and slaves; and through its elevating and purifying influence upon the public mind, slavery was gradually abolished. And thus it must be abolished, if abolished at all, in the present slave-holding States.

But my time has expired ; and now, in closing this dis-cussion, I cannot but express my gratification in view of the patient and respectful attention which has been paid to this discussion by so large a portion of my fellow citizens, who have heard it. I leave you to determine in view of your responsibility to God, on which side of this import-ant question the truth is found.

And to you, Gentlemen Moderators, my thanks are due, for the time you have been willing to spend in presiding over this discussion.